Jura Ecclesiastica

~~~~ courts are also subordinate
to the Controul of the Superior
Temporal Courts, where the
Matter and the Person or
Both, or one of them, are of
Ecclesiastical Nature.————

A.⁵ The Matter or Cause.——

B.⁵ The Person.————

C.⁵ Both.————

Jura Ecclesiastica:

OR, THE

PRESENT PRACTICE

IN 570. C

Ecclesiastical Courts.

SHEWING

Their Origin, Extent, Increase, Power, Authority and Operation, and in what Manner subject to, and restrained by, the Temporal Laws and Courts of Judicature; Ecclesiastical Courts what they are, how governed, and their Proceedings.

COLLECTED

From the Best AUTHORITIES, and Intersperfed with various NEW CASES, never before printed.

By a BARRISTER of the *Middle-Temple.*

VOL. II.

In the SAVOY. Printed by HENRY LINTOT (Affignee of *Edward Sayer*, Efq,) for T. Waller, oppofite *Fetter-Lane, Fleet-Street.* MDCCXLIX.

Jura Ecclesiastica.

VOL. II.

V. *The Ecclesiastical Courts are also subordinate and subject to the Control of the Superior Temporal Courts in many Cases, where both the Matter and the Person, or one of them, either are of Ecclesiastical Sort, or are so pretended by Ecclesiasticks to be.*

A. The Matter.
B. The Person.
C. Both.

Jura Ecclesiastica.

A. *The Matter.*

1. *Who are such.*
2. *Relief amongst them.*
3. *Whether Trustees for next of Kin.*
4. *Where the King is Executor.*
5. *The Executor's Assent to Legacies.*
6. *His Authority and Power over the Testator's Estate.*

   1. *Before* ⎱ *Probate.*
   2. *After* ⎰

7. *The Probate.*

   1. *General to*
   2. *To whom to be granted.*
   3. *The Necessity of the Will's being proved.*
   4. *Where to be proved.*

   1. *Where the Testator had no Assets in England.*
   2. *Bishops Wills.*
   3. *Where* Bona notabilia.
   4. *Where particular Custom.*
   5. *Peculiar Jurisdictions.*

   5. *How far good.*
   6. *Whether may be, and wherefore, and how, delayed*
   7. *Where Fraud or Practice.*

   1. *Where to be tried.*

8. *Revocations.*

   1. *Of Wills.*

   1. *General.*

2. *Whether*

2. *Whether good, and how far.*

1. *Where* pro toto. —————— } 82

2. ——— Pro tanto. —————— 83.

  2. *Of Probates.* ———————— }

  1. *Whether good Cause, or not, of Refusal.* } 84.

   9. *Renunciations of Executorships.* } 85.

  1. *Good, or not.* ——————— }

   10. *Assets.* }

  1. *What are.* } —————— 87.

~~1. General to.~~

2. *How to be marshalled.* ———— 88.

   11. *Accounts.* — — — — — }

  1. *Whether of Ecclesiastical Cognizance.* } 89.

   12. *Suits concerning these Matters.* }

1. *General to them.* ————

2. *How, where, and in what Cases, to be in the Temporal Courts.*

  13. *Appeals in.*

   III. *Administrator and Admini- tion.* } 90.

  1. *The Ordinary's Authority.*

1. *Follows him.* - - - -

2. *He is but a ministerial Officer of the Law.* 91

3. *If*

5. *Ac-*

2. *Where*

6. *What*

A. *The*

A. *The Matter.*

I. *Matters Matrimonial, or of Legitimation, or Bastardy.*

1. *General.*

I. MY next Endeavour shall be to shew the Inferiority and Subjection of these Spiritual Courts to the Superior Temporal Courts, even in Cases where both the Matter and Person, or one of them however, are Ecclesiastick, or of Ecclesiastical Cognizance, or at least contended by Ecclesiasticks so to be And first where the Matter is, or contended to be, of Ecclesiastical Jurisdiction And first of all of Matters Matrimonial. And tho' all Matrimonial Causes have long been determined in the Ecclesiastical Courts, and are now properly within the Cognizance and Jurisdiction of the Clergy; yet they were not always so; for both Matrimonial and Testamentary Causes, as indeed all other Causes whereof they have Cognizance, were originally Civil Causes, and belonged to the Jurisdiction of the Civil Magistrate, till Christian Emperors and Kings, to grace and honour Prelates, granted and allowed to them Cognizance and Jurisdiction in such Causes; and therefore the King of England, who is and always of Right was the Fountain of all Justice, and Jurisdiction in all Causes, as well Ecclesiastical as Civil, within his Dominions, though he allowed the Prelates of the Church to exercise their several Jurisdictions

Godolp. Reper.
489

in thefe Caufes, yet by the Rules of the Common Law, he hath a Superintendency over their Proceedings, with Power of Direction when and how they fhall proceed, and of Reftraint and Correction, if they do not proceed duly; as is clear from many Writs of different Natures, directed to Bifhops, where he commands them to certify Baftardy, Excommunication, Profeffion, *Accouplement en loyal matrimonie, De admittend' Cler', De cautione admittenda, &c.* as well as by the Writs of Prohibition, Confultation, and Attachment *fur* Prohibition, *&c. Dav* 51. *b.* 52. *a.*

2. Difpenfations for inceftuous Marriages brought great Profit to the Church *Gilb* 159.

3. *The Difference between general and fpecial Baftardy is, that general Baftardy is on Certificate from the Ordinary of the Diocefe to the King's Juftices, after fuch Inquiry made, that the Party inquired of is a Baftard, or not a Baftard,* upon fome Queftion of Inheritance, *&c. and this can only be after the fame hath been moved in the Temporal Courts, and the Ordinary demanded to certify, whether,* &c. *Whereof is a notable Cafe in* Davis, *of an arbitrary and corrupt Bifhop, who, without any fuch previous Demand, contrary to Law and Confcience, was pleafed to inquire and fentence a Strumpet a lawful Wife and Baftard Mulier, to the Defamation, Scandal and Difinherifon of a virtuous and lawful Wife, and her lawful Iffue, for no other or better Reafon, as I can find, than that the Whore, if not her Baftard, were of his Lordfhip's Kindred; as will appear from the Cafe at large in the Book, and mention'd hereafter in the prefent Work.* Special *Baftardy is a Suit commenced in the King's*

2   *Court*

Court of one who calls another so, and is sen-
tenced, for that Baftardy is the principal Thing
in Trial, and no Inheritance, &c. contended
for, from whence it appears, that in both these
Cases Baftardy is rather taken for an Examin-
ation or Trial whether a Man's Birth be legi-
timate or defective, than for Baftardy it self

4. If Baron and Feme are fued in the Ecclefiaftical Court for Polygamy, and it appears, that the Wife was married before to
J. S. within the Age of Confent, and after
Age of Confent difagreed, and married the
Defendant, whereupon the Court acquits
them; yet if they tax Cofts to the Plaintiff, no Prohibition fhall go; for that they
have Jurifdiction of the Caufe, and it is
their Ufage there to tax Cofts where the
Plaintiff hath *Caufam Litigandi* Mich 8 Ja.
Blackdone's *Cafe.* Rol Abridgment, Prohibition, 299 Cafe 9. *Q as to the Cofts.*

5. None may write to the Bifhop to certify Baftardy, Mulierty, Loyalty of Matrimony, and the like Ecclefiaftical Matters,
but the King's Courts of Record; but in
Cafes of Inferior Courts, as *London, &c.* the
Plea muft be removed into the Court of
Common Pleas, and that Court muft write
to the Bifhop, and then remand the Record *Co. Lit* 134 *a. And this, as I take it,*
in Honour to Prelates, who, as I conceive, in
thefe Cafes of Certificates, as in many others,
are but Minifterial Officers to the King and his
Superior Temporal Courts, that yet they might
not be fubject to the Command of thefe Infe-
rior Courts.

The Pope himfelf with all his Might cannot marry two People a-verfe to Mar-riage, it is true, he may celebrate the Sacrament of Marriage, but it is effential that the Con-fent of the Parties be firft had, elfe the Marriage, tho' his Holinefs's own Act, is void *Father* Paul's *Right of Sovereigns* 340

For

For more Matter on Rights of Matrimony, see 5 *Co. De Jure Regis Eccl* 9. *a.*
See also *Vaugh. Rep. Harison*'s Case, and
also *Hill*'s Case.

2. *Who may marry, and what necessary thereunto.*

1 BY *Stat.* 32 *H.* 8. *cap.* ~~19~~ ³⁸. If a Spiritual
Court proceeds to impeach, or diffolve,
a Marriage out of the *Levitical* Degrees,
then the Temporal Courts are to prohibit
them; for by that Statute all Marriages out
of those Degrees are declared to be good
and lawful; and therefore if the Spiritual
Court moleft People in doing what is declared lawful to be done by the Statutes of
the Realm, they are to be prohibited by the
Temporal Courts, because they exceed their
Jurisdiction thus bounded by the Temporal
Law. *Gilb.* 156.

2. All Marriages between Coufin Germans and other Collateral Coufins are made
lawful by the Statute 32 *H.* 8. *cap.* 38. and
if Marriages, *infra* these Degrees, should be
queftioned as inceftuous in the Spiritual
Court, a Prohibition lies *fur le ftat'.* Vaugh.
218, &c. Hale's Anal fo. 42.

3. Suit was in Court Chriftian for marrying his Wife's Sifter's Daughter; a Prohibition went; for that such Marriage was not
prohibited by the *Levitical* Law. *Moor* 907

4 Consent is neceffary to every Marriage;
for *Confenfus, non Concubitus, facit Matrimo-
nium, & confentire non poffunt ante annos nu-
biles.* 6 *Co* 22

3. *Who*

3. *Who a Baſtard, and how diſabled as ſuch.*

1. **B**Aſtardy ſignifies a Defect of Birth objected to one born out of Wedlock. *Bract. lib. 5 c 19*

2. As to Baſtardy, all the Biſhops inſtanced the Lords that they would conſent, that all ſuch as were born before Matrimony ſhould be legitimate as well as thoſe born within Matrimony; as to the Succeſſion of Inheritances; foraſmuch as the Church accepteth them for legitimate And all the Earls and Barons, with one Voice anſwered, that they would not change the Laws of the Realm, which hitherto had been uſed and approved. *Stat.* 20 *H* 3. *cap* 9.

3. He is not a Baſtard who is born within Eſpouſals. A Baſtard has no Father. *Fitz. Abr.* Tit. *Baſtard* 1.

4. Divorce *Cauſa Conſanguinitatis in parentela*, ſhall not make the Iſſue a Baſtard. *Fitz.* Tit. *Baſtard* 21.

5. *Cui Pater eſt Populus, pater eſt ſibi nullus*
                       [& omnis;
Cui Pater eſt Populus, non habet ipſe Patrem.

Such Baſtard cannot inherit, nor any inherit to him; but one of his own Body. *Lit ſect.* 401 Or if the Child be begotten by him, who marries her after the Birth of the Child; yet it is, in Judgment of Law, a Baſtard, tho' the Church holds it legitimate. *Stat* 20 *H.* 3 9. 1 *H.* 6 3 *Co Lit.* 244

4. *Where these Matters are to be tried.*

1 COusinage. Special Bastardy was tried *per Pais.* Bro. Abr. Trial, 34. Bastardy, 18. Trials, 81.

2. Bastardy antiently was tried *per Pais;* but now it is triable by the Ordinary. *Bro. Abr* 99. *Trial.*

3. *Per Norton:* Where Bastardy comes in Question of one dead, it shall be tried *per Pais,* and not by the Bishop. *Bro. Abr. Trial,* 26. *Bastardy,* 9. *Visne,* 61.

4 Bastardy was alledged in one by whom the Demandant conveyed in Formedon, and for that he was no Party to the Writ, and dead, it was tried *per Pais,* and not by the Bishop's Certificate *Bro Abr Trials,* 10, 70.

5. In Trespass, on Issue, whether *J. N.* was born within Espousals, or out, was tried *per Pais.* Bro. Abr. Trials, 32. Bro. Abr. Visne, 40, 48, 50

6. Assise. They were at Issue on Special Bastardy, if the Tenant was the Son by the first Wife, by whom the Land descended, or by the second Wife; and the Espousals and Birth were alledged in a foreign County, and it was awarded, that the *Visne* should be of both Counties *Bro. Abr* Tit. *Visne,* 97, 98, 12

7. Appeal by the Wife *de morte Viri.* The Defendant pleaded, *Que el ne fuit unques accouple in loyal Matrimonie,* and it was tried by the Bishop's Certificate. *Bro. Abr. Trials,* 74, 88, 90

8. *Per Belknap:* Feme Covert, or *Sole,*
born before Marriage, *& hujusmodi,* shall be
tried *per Pais;* but General Baftardy, *ou
ne unques accouple en loyal Motrimonie, & hujusmodi,* shall be tried by the Bifhop's Certificate. *Et hoc est de*-Baftardy of one who
is Party to the Writ   *Bro. Abr.* Tit. *Trial,*
16, 21, 22, 53.

9. Mr. Juft. *S Eyre:* There are many
Cafes which are properly and purely of Ecclefiaftical Cognizance; but if a Title of
Land comes to be tried in the Temporal
Court, into which thofe Matters accidentally
fall in, they are to be judged of and tried
by that Temporal Court. As in a Trial
upon Marriage, if Iffue be joined, Marriage,
or no Marriage, this is to be tried by Certificate from the Bifhop; but if there be a Queftion upon a Trial of a Title of Land, whether a Perfon under whom either of the Parties claim was married to another, or no, the
Temporal Court will judge of that Matter
without Certificate, as was done in a famous
Cafe in this Court, in my Lord *Hale's* Time,
The Cafe of the Lord *Danby's* Lady *and*
Mr. *Emerton.* If any one claims as Heir to
his Father, and the Queftion arifeth, whether his Mother was married to him or
not, this Court (*B. R*) will try the Matter.
Skin. 455.

10. Prohibition was moved for to the
Ecclefiaftical Court of *Coventry,* Suit being
there againft Plaintiff for Inceft, in marrying his firft Wife's Sifter, fuggefting that the
faid fecond Wife was dead, by whom he
had a Son, to whom an Eftate was defcend-
ed, as Heir of his Mother, and though he

had pleaded this Matter, they went on to annul the Marriage, and bastardize the Issue. *Et per Cur':* A Prohibition shall go as to annulling the Marriage, or bastardizing the Issue; but they may proceed to punish the Incest. *Salk.* 548 Vide *Must be first moved in the Temporal Courts.*

11. How Bastardy is to be proved or inquired into, if pleaded, see *Rast Ent. Bastardy, fo* 104 and *Stat* 9 *H.* 6 *c.* 11. *Kitch. fo.* 64. *Bro.* Tit *Bastardy.*

12 In *B R. Pasch.* 2 *Geo* 2. *Sampson & Ux' v Cooke. Per Cur': Uxor, aut Non uxor,* was proper for a Trial by the Country, as well as *Copulatus in Matrimonio.*

13 In Case of a Bishop's Certificate of Bastardy, any one may take Advantage of it. *Doct. & Stud lib.* 2 *cap.* 5 *fo.* 68. *a* But this must be understood of one who is Party to the Writ; for if Bastardy be imputed to one not a Party, but a Stranger to the Writ, there the Bastardy shall be tried by twelve Men, in which Case the Party in whom the Bastardy is laid shall not be concluded, because he is no Party to the Trial; and may have no Attaint, but he who is Party to the Issue may have Attaint, and therefore he shall be concluded. *Ibid.* 68. *b.*

5. *Must be first moved in the Temporal Courts.*

1 IT was said, the very Cause and Reason wherefore the Ecclesiastical Judge might not inquire of Legitimation, or Bastardy, before he had Direction or Command from the

the King's Temporal Courts was, because
the Court Christian had no Jurisdiction or
Power to intermeddle with Temporal Inheritances directly, or indirectly, for it was observed, that *Christ* himself refused to meddle
in such Case, when petitioned thereto. *Luc.*
12. *Magister, dic Fratri meo ut dividat me-
cum Hæreditatem;* he answered, *Quis me con-
stituit Judicem, aut Divisorem, super vos;*
and therefore *Tempore II* 3. when the usurped Jurisdiction of the Pope was elevated
higher than ever it was, either before or
since, in the King of *England*'s Dominions,
Pope *Alexander* the Third having granted a
Commission to the Bishops of *Winton* and
Exon, to inquire *de legitima Nativitate* of
Agathe the Mother of *Robert de Ardenna,*
and if she should be found legitimate, to restore him to the Possession of certain Lands,
whereof he was dispossessed, being informed
that the King of *England* was very much offended with this Commission, he revoked
and countermanded it in Point of Restitu-
tution of Possession, acknowledging and con-
fessing that the Establishment of Possession
belonged to the King, and not to the
Church; which Case is reported in the Canon Law. *Decretal, Antiquæ Collectiones* 1.
lib. 4. Tit *Qui filii sunt legitimi, cap* 4 &
cap 7. In the 4 *Cap* the Commission is set
forth, and in the 7 *Cap* the Revocation, or
Countermand, appears in this Form. *Cau-
sam quæ fuit inter Fr.* and *R de Ardenna super eo quod mater jam dicti R. dicitur non fu-
isse de legitimo matrimonio nata, experientiæ
nostræ commisimus terminandam verum, quia
in literis nostris inseri fecimus ut præfat R.*

posses-

possessionibus, quarum possessor extitit, facere-
tis restitui si eadem possessione spoliatus esset,
nos attendentes quod ad Regem, non ad Eccle-
siam, spectat de talibus possessionibus judicare,
ne videamur Juri & Dignitatibus charissimi in
Christo filii Henrici Regis Anglorum detrahere,
qui, sicut accepimus, motus & turbatus est,
quod de possessionibus scripsimus, cum ipsorum
Judicium ad se asserat pertinere, volumus
quod Regi possessionum Judicium relinquentes,
de Causa principali cognoscatis, &c. Dav.
54 a. b.

2 It was resolved, that the Question of
Bastardy or Legitimacy ought to be first
moved in the Temporal Court of the King,
and Issue there joined upon it, and then to
be transmitted to the Ecclesiastical Court
by the King's Writ, to be examined and
tried there, and thereupon the Bishop is to
certify to the King's Court; to which Certificate, being duly made, the Law gives
such Credit, that all the World shall be concluded and estopped by it; but, on the o-
ther Hand, if any Suit of Bastardy or Legitimacy be first stirred in the Ecclesiastical
Court, before any Question has been had
of it in the Temporal Court of the King,
Prohibition lies to restrain such Suit, and if
it be accompanied with Practice or Fraud,
as was in the principal Case, (*vide le Case*)
it is a Misdemeanor punishable in the Star-
Chamber To this Purpose the Case of
Corbet was put, 22 *E* 4 *Consultation,* 6. which
was, Sir *Robert Corbet* had Issue two Sons,
Robert and *Roger, Robert,* the Son, being
within the Age of fourteen, took to Wife
M. ild, and lived with her to his full Age,
&

& cognati & reputati ſunt pro viro & Uxore
palam (*publickly, or to all the World*) yet after *Robert*, the Son, put away *Matild*, who
ſtill living, he married *Letice*, and had Iſſue
by *Letice* a Son, and then *Robert*, the Son,
died , after whoſe Death *Letice* preached
(*or publiſhed*) and declared publickly, that
ſhe (*Letice*) was the lawful Wife of *Robert*,
and that her Son was Mulier and Legitimate. Whereupon *Roger*, the youngeſt Son
of Sir *Robert*, commenced his Suit in the Spiritual Court to reverſe the Eſpouſals between *Letice* and *Robert*, and to ſilence *Le-*
tice, &c. Whereupon *Letice* purchaſed a
Prohibition, and thereupon *Roger* ſhewed
this whole Matter, and prayed a Conſulta-
tion, which was denied, chiefly upon this
Reaſon, (*viz*) that the Intent of the Suit
in the Spiritual Court was to baſtardize the
Iſſue between *Robert* and *Letice*, and to
prove *Roger* Heir to *Robert* , and the Action
or Original to baſtardize a Man ſhall not be
firſt moved in the Spiritual Court, but in
the Temporal Court, *&c.* And for the making this Point more clear, two Caſes put
by *Bracton, lib.* 5 Tit. *De Exceptionibus, c.* 6.
were remembered. 1 *B* having Iſſue by
an Heireſs, which Iſſue was born before
Marriage, claimed to be Tenant *per le Cur-*
teſy ; but being for this Cauſe barred, in
Aſſiſe brought by him againſt *A* he obtained
the Pope's Bull, and by Authority of that
he commenced a Suit in the Eccleſiaſtical
Court to prove his Iſſue legitimate, *quod fa-*
cere non debuit, as *Bracton* there ſays , and
therefore a Prohibition went to ſtay this Suit,
ſhewing all the Matter, *& quod prædictus B.*

ad

ad deceptionem Curiæ nostræ, & ad infirmandum Judicium in Curia nostra factum, trahit ipsum A. in placitum coram vobis in Curia Christianitatis Authoritate Literarum Domini Papæ ad prædict' puerum legitimandum, &c. Et cum non possint Judices aliqui de legitimat' cognoscere, ni si fuerit loquela prius in Curia nostra incepta per Breve & ibi Bastardia objecta, & postea ad Curiam Christianitatis transmissa, vobis prohibemus quod in placito illo ulterius non procedatis, &c. In the same Chapter of *Bracton,* see the Form of another Prohibition, which made the Matter still more plain *Rex talibus Judicibus, &c. Ostensum est nobis ex parte A quod cum in Curia nostra coram Justiciariis nostris Itinerantibus in tali Comitatu arramavit quandam Assizam Mortis Antecessoris versus B. de quadam terra in N. idem B timens sibi posse opponi notam Bastardiæ in eadem Assiza, & ante prædictum adventum Justiciariorum & antequam ei Bastardia apponatur in Curia nostra in dicta Assiza, & antequam fuerit per nos ordinario loci Inquisitio de Legitimitate probanda, secundum Regni nostri consuetudinem demandata, Literas Domini Papæ ad vos directas impetravit, ut de Legitimitate sua cognoscatis, & ad probationem illius testes admittatis, ut per hoc remaneat Hæreditas & Successio contra Consuetudinem Regni quæ hucusque obtinuit, ut approbata, & sede Apostolica confirmata, quod in Causa Successionis, & Hæreditatis petitione, debet prius moveri Placitum in Curia nostra, & cum ibi objecta fuerit Bastardia tunc deinde transmitti debet Recordum loquelæ & cognitio Bastardiæ ad Curiam Christianitatis, ut ibi ad mandatum nostrum de legitimitate inquiratur, quod quidem in hac parte non est observatum, & cum hoc sit manifeste contra consuetudinem Regni nostri, quod habita vel habenda inter alios contentione de Jure Successionis, debeatis ad inquisitionem de legitimitate procedere antequam a nobis hoc fuerit vobis demandatum, vobis prohibemus, &c.* By which it is sufficiently manifest, that if the Ecclesiastical Court proceed to the Examination of Bastardy, or Legitimation, without Direction from the Temporal Courts, it shall be restrained by Prohibition, and if there be Fraud or Practice in such Proceeding, it is censurable in the Star-Chamber And *Babington* Chancellor of *Litchfield's* Case, *Trin* 3 *Jac.* is a direct Precedent in Point. *Dav* 51, 52, 53 *Dy.* 369. a

3 An Information was exhibited in the Castle-Chamber of *Dublin* against the Bishop of *K* and *C B.* and others, who by Practice and Combination between them, and by undue Course of Proceeding have endeavoured to prove that *C B.* who had all along before been reputed a Bastard, to be the legitimate Son and Heir of *G B* Esq, to the Disinherison and Defamation of *E B* who was the sole Son and Heir of the said *G. B* And upon Hearing this Cause the Case appeared to be thus: About 26 Years before the Bill exhibited, the said *G B* had Issue the said *C B.* on the Body of one *Jervis Damosel*, who, for so long as *G. B.* lived, was never reputed his Wife, but his Concubine, and the said *C B.* was only accepted for the natural Son of the said *G B.* and not for legitimate. After this, (viz) 16 Years after the Birth of *C B.* whose Mother was then alive, *G. B.*

took

Godolp: Reper: 488

took to Wife a Lady of good Estate and Reputation, with the Consent of Friends, and had Issue by her the said *E. B* and died; after whose Death *C. B.* his reputed Bastard Son, nor his Mother, who is still alive, said nothing for the Space of 9 Years; but now lately they have practised and combined with the said Bishop of *K.* being of their Consanguinity, and many other, to prove the Legitimacy of the said *C. B.* by an irregular and undue Course, with Intent to bastardize and disinherit the said *E. B* according to which Practice and Combination, without any Suit either commenced or being moved in any Temporal Court of the King, or any Writ directed to him to certify Bastardy or Legitimation in this Case, and what is more, without any Libel exhibited in his Ecclesiastical Court concerning this Matter, of his own Head secretly, and not *Convocatis convocandis,* some Years after the Death of the said *G. B* took the Depositions of many, or several, Witnesses to prove the said *G. B.* nine and twenty Years before had lawfully married and taken to Wife the said *Jervis Damosel,* Mother of the said *C B* and that the said *C B.* was legitimate Son and Heir of the said *G B* and these Depositions, thus taken, the said Bishop caused to be ingrossed and reduced into the Form of a solemn Act, and having signed and sealed the said Instrument, he delivered the same to *C B* who published it, and by Colour of such Instrument or Act declared himself to be the Son and lawful Heir of the said *G. B.* and for this Practice and Misdemeanor

meanot the said Bishop of *K.* and the Rest
were cenfured. *Dav 51. a &c.*

2. What the
Cenfure was,
fince the fame
very likely was purpofely omitted by the Reporter, out of Regard to the
Bifhop's Charader, and I am more inclined to think fo, as I obferve
he only ufes the initial Letters and no Name for the Bifhop, but the firft
Letter of his See, and no Name at all to the Caufe.

6. *They muft, on receiving the
King's Command, proceed incontinently, notwithftanding any Appeal or Inhibition.*

AS the Ecclefiaftical Judge may not inquire of Baftardy, or Legitimation,
without the King's fpecial Direcdion or Commandment, fo when he hath received the
King's Writ to make fuch Inquifition, he
ought not to furceafe for any Appeal or Inhibition; but ought incontinently to proceed till he hath certified the King's Court:
And this alfo appears in *Bracton, lib. 5 De
Exceptionibus,* 14 *Cum autem Judex Ecclefi-
afticus Inquifitionem fecerit, non erit ab eo ap-
pellandum, nec a Petente, nec a Tenente, a Petente non, quia talem Jurifdictionem & talem
Judicem elegi; a Tenente non, quia fic poffet
caufam in infinitum protrahere de Judice in
Judicem, ufque ad Papam, & fic poffet Papa
de Laico feodo indirecte cognofcere* But this
Point is ftill clearer from a notable Record
(comprifing a Cafe in *Ireland*). *In Archiv'
Turris clauf' 8 H. 3. memb' 29. in dorfo,* in
this Form : *Rex Dublin Archiepifcopo Jufti-
ciario Hyberniæ Salutem : Ad ea quæ vobis nuper dedimus in mandatis, ut nobis refcriberetis,*

quatenus

*Godolp —
Reper
491*

quatenus fuiſſet proceſſum in Cauſa Nicholai de
la Felda, qui contra Abbatem & Canonicos
Sancti Thomæ Dublinienſis in Curia noſtra, coram Juſticiariis noſtris, petiit duas Carucatas
terræ cum pertinentiis in Kilredbery, per Aſ-
ſiſam de Morte Anteceſſoris, cui etiam coram
eiſdem Juſticiariis objecta fuit Baſtardia, per
quod ab ipſis Juſticiariis noſtris ad vos fuit
tranſmiſſum ut in foro Eccleſiaſtico de Baſtardia ſive Legitimitate agnoſceretis : Nobis per
Literas veſtras ſignificaſtis, quod cum in foro
civili terram prædictam peteret per Literas
noſtras de morte Anteceſſoris, verſus memoratos
Abbatem & Canonicos, objecta fuit ei nota
Baſtardiæ, quare in foro eodem tunc non fuit
ulterius proceſſum : Memoratus etiam Nicholaus de Mandato Juſticiariorum noſtrorum, in
foro Eccleſiaſtico coram vobis volens probare ſe
eſſe legitimum, teſtes produxit, & publicatis at-
teſtationibus ſuis, poſt diutinos alterationes &
diſputationes, tam ex parte Abbatis, quam ip-
ſius Nicholai, cum ad calculum difinitivæ Sen-
tentiæ procedere velletis, comparuerunt duæ Pu-
ellæ minoris ætatis, filiæ Richardi de la Felda
Patris prædicti Nicholai, & appellaverunt ne ad
Sententiam ferendam procederetis, quia in hoc
manifeſtum earum verteretur præjudicium, eo
quod alias præcluderent eis via petendi hæreditatem petitam, nec poſſit eis ſubveniri per
reſtitutionem in integ. um. Unde de conſilio vi-
rorum prudentium (ut dicitis) appello deferentes,
cauſam ſecundum quod coram nobis agitata eſt,
Domino Papæ tranſmiſiſtis inſtructam, de quo
plurimum admirantes non immerito movemur,
cum de Legitimitate prædicti Nicholai per te-
ſtium productiones & atteſtationum publicationes
plene vobis conſtiterit, vos propter appellatio-

nem

*nem puellarum prædictarum, contra quas non
agebatur, vel etiam de quibus nulla fiebat men-
tio in Assisa memorata, nec fuerunt aliquæ
partes illarum in causa prædicta, Sententiam
diffinitivam, pro eo distulistis pronunciare, &
male, quia nostrum declinantes examen, id
quod per nostram determinandum esset Jurisdic-
tionem, ad alienam transferunt d'gnitatem
quod valde perniciosum esset exemplo Cum etiam
si adeptus esset prædictus Nicholaus possessionem
terræ prædictæ per Assisam prædictam, beneficium petitionis Hæreditatis prædictis puellis
plane suppetat in Curia nostra per breve de
recto maxime cum per Literas de morte Antecessoris agatur de possessione, & non de proprie-
tate, & ex Officio nostro in casu proposito ni-
hil aliud ad nos pertinebat, nisi tantum de ip-
sius Nicholai Legitimitate probationes admit-
tere, & ipsum cum Literis nostris testimonialibus ad Justiciarios nostros remittere. De Con-
silio igitur Magnatum & Fidelium nobis assisten-
tium vobis mandamus, quatenus non obstante
appellatione præmissa, non differatis pro eo sen-
tentiare, ipsum ad Justitiarios nostros remit-
tentes cum literis nostris testimonialibus, ut de
Loquela coram eis agitata postmodum possint
secundum Legem & Consuetudinem terræ nostræ
Hyberniæ Justitiæ Plenitudinem exhibere
Teste H apud Gloucester,* 19 *die Novembris.* See
also to the same Purpose 39 *E.* 3. 20. *a.*
where a Writ of Dower *Ne unques accouple
en loial Matrimony* was pleaded, and Issue
thereupon joined, whereupon Commandment was to the Bishop to certify, wherein
he said, he could not certify by Reason of
an Inhibition to him out of the Arches,
this Return was held insufficient; for there

I   Ie

Inhibitions not to be granted *sans* Subscription of it is said, that he ought not to surcease to obey the Commandment of the King for no Inhibition whatsoever. *Dav.* 53. *a. b.* 54. *a.*

Advocate practising in the Court, or if no Advocate, then of a Proctor. *Can.* 96 Not to be granted till Appeal exhibited. *Can* 97. Nor till Promise and Subscription *Can.* 98.

7. *Certificates of these Matters.*

1. *What previously necessary thereunto.*

WHAT previously necessary to the Ecclesiastical Judge's Certificate of Bastardy, *vide Stat.* 9 *H.* 6. *c.* 11. *Rast. pl. fo.* 29, 105, 161, 280, 577, 609 Also see before *The Pope an Usurper. The Opposition the same have met with.*

8. *What Evidence good in these Cases.*

THE Party's own sole Confession, however taken upon Oath, either within, or without, the Court shall not have Credit ; but the Truth, as far as possible, must be sifted out by Depositions of Witnesses and other lawful Proofs and Evictions. *Can.* 95. *Vide Comb.* 137.

I

9. *Sen-*

9. *Sentences of Separation and Divorce.*

1. *Where to be pronounced, and with what Solemnity.*

NO Sentence shall be given, either for Separation *a Thoro & Mensa*, or for annulling of pretended Matrimony, but in open Court and in the Seat of Justice, and that with the Knowledge and Consent either of the Archbishop within his Province, or of the Bishop within his Diocese, or of the Dean of the Arches, the Judge of the Audience of *Canterbury*, or of the Vicars General, or other Principal Officials, or *sede vacante*, of the Guardians of the Spiritualties, or other Ordinaries, to whom of Right it appertaineth in their several Jurisdictions and Courts, and concerning them only that are then dwelling under their Jurisdiction. *Can.* 106.

2. *The Cautions therein.*

In all Sentences for Divorce and Separation only *a Mensa & Thoro*, there shall be a Caution and Restraint inserted in the Sentence, that the Parties separated shall live chastly and continently, neither shall they during each other's Life, contract Matrimony with other Person ; and for the better Observation of this last Clause, the said

Yet the Ecclesiastical Court may not examine the Party on Oath, whether he, or she, hath contracted Matrimony, or not, &c for Nemo tenetur se ipsum prodere

See *Clifford* and *Huntley*'s Case, *Rol Abr Prohibition*, (T) Case 6.

said Sentence of Divorce shall not be pronounced until the Party or Parties requiring the same, having given good and sufficient Caution and Security into the Court, that they will not any Way break or trespass the said Restraint or Prohibition. *Can.* 107.

10. *The Judges in these Causes.*

1. *Their Neglect of, or exceeding in, their Duty, how punished.*

IF any Judge giving Sentence of Divorce or Separation shall not fully keep and observe the Premisses, he shall be, by the Archbishop of the Province, or the Bishop of the Diocese, suspended from the Exercise of his Office for the Space of a whole Year, and the Sentence of Separation so given, contrary to the Form aforesaid, shall be held void to all Intents and Purposes of the Law, as if it had not at all been given or pronounced. *Can* 108.

11. *Appeals in these Causes.*

1. *General to.*

In Cases Matrimonial. 4 *Inst.* 339.

II. *Mat-*

II. *Matters Testamentary and Legatary*, &c.

1 *The Authority of the Ecclesiastical Courts in these Matters, and from whence derived.*

1. IN all Countries, except *France*, the Probate of Wills was of Temporal Cognizance, which also may be in Court-Baron, where such Custom. *Gilb* 207. *Dr & Stud. lib* 2 *c* 28 *fo* 235.

2 Testamentary Matters were originally of Temporal Jurisdiction *Show. Rep* 158.

3. The Probates of Testaments belong to Ordinaries *de Consuetudine Angliæ, & non de communi Jure. Rex Angliæ olim erat Consiliorum Ecclesiasticorum Præses, Vindex temeritatis Romanæ, propugnator Religionis, nec ullam habebant Episcopi Authoritatem præter eam quam a Rege acceptam referebant, Jus Testamenta probandi non habebant, administrationis potestatem cuique delegare non poterant,* as Archbishop *Parker* says in his Book published *Anno Dom.* 1573. *Vide* 9 *Co* 38 *a.*

4 The Probate of Wills did not originally belong to Ordinaries, but to the King, who seised the Deceased's Effects to pay his Debts, and advance his Wife and Children, &c. But after the Power was derived down to Ordinaries; but they neither ever had, nor have, any Power to give or sell the Goods, neither to dispose them to their own or other's Use, though in Danger of perishing, neither could or can release Debts

due to the Deceased, neither have any Action, though liable thereto, &c. 9 Co. 37, &c.

5 Wills originally were merely Temporal. *Yelv.* 92. 2 R 3.

6. Probates of Wills did not belong to the Ecclesiastical Courts, but of late Time. *5 Co. De Jure Regis Eccl.* 16 *a. b.*

7. The Jurisdiction of the Ecclesiastical Courts, touching Testamentary Matters, is by the Custom of *England*, and not by the Ecclesiastical Law. Lord *Gilbert* says, he does not find that any of the Canonists themselves pretend that Wills are of Ecclesiastical Cognizance *sua natura*, but only such Wills as were made for pious Uses. *Gilb* 205

8. In 11 *H* 7. *Fineux* asserts, that the Probate of Wills did not belong to the Spiritual Courts by the Ecclesiastical Law, but came to them by Custom and Usage; and these are the Foundations on which my Lord *Coke* in *Henslow's* Case, 9 *Rep.* 38. concludes, that when the Will is proved in the Ecclesiastical Court, the Court has executed its Authority; but the Executors are to sue in the Temporal Courts to get in the Estate of the Deceased. *Gilb* 207.

9. Though *de Jure communi* the Cognizance of Wills and Testaments does not belong to the Ecclesiastical Courts, but to the Temporal or Civil Jurisdiction, yet *de Consuetudine Angliæ pertinet ad Judices Ecclesiasticos*, as *Linwood* himself agrees. *Exercit. de Testamentis*, *c* 4. *in Glossa.* So that it is the Custom or Law of *England* that gives the Extent and Limits of their external Jurisdiction

rifdiction *in foro Contentiofo. Hale's Hift.
Law* 31, 32.

2. *General to Wills and Tefta-ments.*

1. **U**Ltima *voluntas eft legitima difpofitio de eo quod quis poft mortem fieri velit.*
Swynb 18. Orph Leg fect. 2.

2. The Will hath Relation to the Teftator's Death, and not no the Making, for
till Death he is Mafter of his own Will.
See the Cafe *Burk* and *Morgan,* 28 *Jan.*
1717, before the Houfe of Lords.

3. *Whether good or not.*

1. **A** Will good, tho' no Executor named.
2 Reports in Ch 112

2. It is a good Will, tho' in the Form of
an Indenture. 1 *Ch. Ca.* 248. *Nelfon* 195.
le mefme Cafe.

3. A Will not good, *fine animo difponendi;*
nor a Teftament, *fine animo teftandi* Swynb
19.

4 A Will made in Writing, but not according to the Statute of Frauds, not good.
2 *Chan Ca.* 127.

5 A Devife to one on Condition, and the
Teftator dies after the Devife made, but be-
fore the Condition written, this is a void
Devife. *Comb* 28. *Gilb.* 45.

6. A Feoffment is made to the Ufe of
a Will, if the Will was declared, either be-

fore, or at the Time, such Will cannot be altered, because it is executed. *Fin Law* 33

7. A Will, wanting Witnesses, and so not good by the Statute of Frauds, will not operate as an Appointment to a Charity by the Statute 43 *Eliz.* Prec. in Chan. 270, 389.

8. A Testator, after having made his Will, makes a Feoffment, which he intends in Affirmance, this shall be taken as a Revocation. 1 *Reports in Ch.* 42, 43

9. A Will is made of Lands, before the Statute of Frauds, without the Number of Witnesses, or other Selemnity required by that Statute, though the Testator die after the Commencement of the Statute; yet this is a good Will, because it was so at first. 2 *Reports in Ch* 302. *Vide Prec. in Ch.* 77, 184, 270. 2 *Vern.* 429.

10. A Will in *Dutch*, or *Latin*, must be so framed as to operate according to the Rules of our Law. 1 *Vern* 85.

11 An Infant at Seventeen may make a Will 1 *Vern* 255. 1 *Chan. Ca* 157. *Nelf* 383 Lord *Gilbert* says, an Infant Male may make a Will at Fourteen, a Female at Twelve, as they may at those respective Ages, consent or marry *Gilb.* 74 *Vide Prec. Chan* 316 2 *Mod* 315. wherein they follow the Rule of the Civil Law of *Justinian.*

12. A Will obtained *in extremis,* and upon Importunity of the Testator's Wife, his Hand being guided in the Writing his Name, was set aside. See Case *Monypeny* versus

verſus Brown, before the Houſe of Lords, 15 *May* 1711.

13 A Will was ſet aſide after forty Years Poſſeſſion under it, on Account of the Inſanity of the Deviſor, and that, tho' a Purchaſer was in the Caſe. See Caſe *Squire* and *Perſhall*, before the Lords, 24 *Feb.* 1726.

14 A Will, obtained by Fraud, was proved in the Spiritual Court; decreed, as to ſo much of the Will as ſubjected the Lands to Payment of Debts, ſhould ſtand; but, as to the Reſt, the Executor to be Truſtee for the Deviſee of the former Will. By Lord Chancellor, *but, as I take it, reverſed before the Lords.* Kirrick *v.* Blanſby, 11 March 1727

15 Deviſe was of Lands to *A.* and after the Deviſor deviſes the ſame Lands to *B.* who was a Papiſt, both Deviſes void, for though the laſt is void as a Will, yet it is good as a Revocation. See Caſe before the Houſe of Lords. *Roper* and *Conſtable*, 11 *July* 1713.

16 *In Canc. Bennet* and *Bayly*, 15 *June* 1735, A Will obtained by Fraud, in taking Advantage of a Lunatick, decreed null. *Vide Gilb.* 181. *Haid.* 375. 3 *Rep. Chan.* 150, 155. 2 *Vern.* 612, 685, 293. *Prec. Cb.* 354, 459

17 Lands deviſed to Charitable Uſes, but the Will not publiſhed in the Preſence of three Witneſſes, as the Statute of Frauds requires, though not good, either as a Will or an Appointment, as to the Freehold; yet was good for ſo much as was Copyhold, they paſſing by Surrender, and not by the

D 3   Will;

Will; and though there were three Witnesses to the Codicil, that would not help the Will. 2 *Vern.* 597, 598. See 3 *Mod.* 262. *Hob.* 136. *Moor* 888

18. By Decree in Chancery, a Will of Lands attested by three Witnesses, who, at several Times, subscribed their Names at the Request of the Testator, but were not present together at once, is a good Will, within the Statute of Frauds. 2 *Chan. Ca.* 109. *Prec. in Chan* 184, 270 2 *Vern* 429.

19. A Devise to Issue *in Ventre sa mere* good. *Dy. Read sur le Statute of Wills,* fo 6. *Vide Nelson* 267, 268.

20 A Devise of 10000 *l.* to procure a Dukedom to the Head of the Family by all lawful Means, so it be within a Twelvemonth; Bill dismissed, as not being within the Year, but rather as Honour ought not to be purchased. 1 *Vern* 22.

21 Words of Recommendation and Desire in a Will are always construed a Devise. *Prec in Chan* 201. *Vide* 1 *Chan. Ca.* 310. *Gilb* 127, 128.

4. *Who may make a Will or Testament, and who not.*

1. The King.

1 *The King and Queen*

1. The King. 2. The Queen.

1. The King.

THE King of full Age may make a Will of Lands-Parcel of his Duchy of *Lancaster,* but of no other. *Dy. Readings on the Statute of Wills,* 1. 2. *The*

2. The Queen.

The Queen cannot make a Will, without the Confent of the King, neither can fhe devife to the King, though fhe may to a Stranger. *Dy. Readings upon the Statute of Wills,* 1.

2. Femes Covert

A Feme Covert has Power given by her Husband to make a Will ; the Probate thereof *per Teſtes* is fufficient, becaufe, as to that Purpoſe, the Husband has made her a Feme Sole. *Prec. Chan.* 84.

3. The Regular Clergy.

Regular Clergy cannot make Wills *Dy. Readings on the Statute of Wills,* 2. Vide ante *The Regular Clergy.*

4 Biſhops.

1 A Biſhop of his own Inheritance, or Purchaſe, may make a Will, as he alfo may of Arrearages of Rents of his Biſhoprick; the fame Law of a Dean or Parſon *Dy. Readings on the Statute of Wills,* 1, 2.

2. It appears by many Records in the Reign of *H.* 3. and *E.* 1. that by the Law and Cuftom of *England,* no Biſhop could make his Will of his Goods or Chattels coming of his Biſhoprick, &c. without the King's Licence. The Biſhops, that they might freely make their Wills, yielded to give to the King, after their Deceafes refpectively for ever, fix Things. 1ft, Their beft

Horfe

Horfe, or Palfry, with Saddle and Bridle. 2 A
Cloak, with a Cape. 3. One Cup, with a Co-
ver. 4. One Bafon and Ewer. 5. One Gold
Ring. 6. His Kennel of Hounds, and for thefe
a Writ iffueth out of the Exchequer after the
Deceafe of every Bifhop ; for Example: *Rex,
&c Vic' Ebor' Præcipimus tibi quod non omit'
propter aliquam libertatem quin etiam ingred' &
d'firing' omnes executores Teftamenti & ult' vo-
luntat' Reverendi in Chrifto Patris Mathæi nuper
Archiepifcopi Ebor' defunct', ac Adminiftrato-
res & Occupatores bonor' & cattallor' quæ fuer'
dicti nuper Archiepifcopi, nec non hared' & te-
nent' terrar' & tenementor', quæ nuper fua fuer',
per omnes terras & catalla fua in baliva tua, ita
quod nec ipfi nec aliquis ipfor' ad ea man' appon'
donec ad inde tibi præceperimus. Et quod de
exitibus earundem terrar' nobis refpond', &
quod habeas corpora eorum coram Baronibus de
Scacc' noftro apud Weftm' a die Pafchæ in tres
Septimanos ad refpondend' nobis de 'uno optimo
equo five Palfrido, Sella & Fræno, una Clami-
de five Cloca cum Capella, uno Cipho cum co-
opertorio uno Pelve cum Lavatorio five aquar',
& uno annulo Aureo, nec non Muta Canum quæ
nuper fuer' ejufdem nuper Archiepifcopi tempore
mortis fuæ, & quæ ad nos ratione prærogative
noftræ fpectant & pertinent, & de precio five
valore inde unde nobis nondum eft refpon'. Et
habeas ibi tunc nomina executor' & alior' præd'
& hoc breve.* 4 Inft. 338. Lord *Coke* fays,
the moft antient that we find and remember,
(but certainly fays his Lordfhip there were
fuch Writs before) is *Inter Memorand' de
Scacc' anno* 2 *E.* 2. The Bifhop of *Bath* and
Wells's Cafe, *Trin* 36 *E.* 3. *ibid. inter* ——
The Bifhop of *Chefter*'s Cafe, *Hill.* 5 *E* 4.
ibid.

ibid. adjudged upon Demurrer, That the Duty being to the King after the Deceafe of every Bifhop, it extendeth to an Archbifhop, *The Archbifhop of* York's *Cafe*; for every Archbifhop is a Bifhop : It is called *Mulctura de Epifcopis,* fometimes *Monutier,* &c. 4 Inft. 338.

5 *Citizens of* London.

A Citizen of London *could not make his Will in Derogation of the Cuftom of that City till the late Statute enabled him fo to do.*

6 *Infants.*

1 An Infant may make a Teftament at the Age of Seventeen. *Nelfon* 383. 1 *Chan. Ca.* 157.

2. An Infant Male at Fourteen, a Female at Twelve, may make their Teftaments. *Prec Ch* 316 *Vide Nelfon* 383. *Gilb.* 74. 2 *Mod.* 315. Herein they follow the Civil Law of *Juftinian.*

7. *Perfons outlawed and convict in* Premunire.

1. ~~Outlaws,~~

One outlawed cannot make a Teftament, unlefs only outlawed in a perfonal Action, and then he may of his Lands, but not of his Goods. *Dy Readings on the Statute of Wills,* fo 2. *Vide Fi. Ley* 27.

2. *Per-*

2. *Perfons attaint in* Premunire.

One attaint in *Premunire* cannot make his Will. *Lord* Bacon's *Readings on the Statute of Ufes, fo.* 2.

8. *Aliens.*

An Alien makes his Will and after is Denizen, it is good. *Dy. Readings on the Statute of Wills, fo.* 3.

9. *Jointenants.*

A Jointenant cannot bar Survivorfhip by Will. *Doct & Stud. lib.* 2. *c.* 25. *Vide Prec. Ch.* 120, 121, 124, 163.

10. *Perfons excommunicate.*

An Excommunicate cannot make a Will. *Cafes in Law and Eq* 2 *Part, fo.* 113.

5. *Of a Donation,* Caufa mortis.

1. *What, and it Operation.*

1. **D**Onatio, *Caufa mortis*, is where a Man lies in Extremity, or being furprifed with Sicknefs, and not having an Opportunity of making his Will, left he fhould die before he can make it, gives his Goods, with his own Hands, to his Friends about him; this, if he dies, fhall operate as a Legacy;

gacy; but if he recovers, the Property re-
verts. *Prec Chan* 269.

2 A Donation, *Caufa mortis*, is in the Na-
ture of a Legacy waiting on the Death of the
Teftator, and is ambulatory, and open, till
that Time; and by a Revocation of all former
Wills it is revoked; and a fubfequent De-
vife is to be taken in Satisfaction of fuch a
Donation; it is a Gift *in præfenti*, to take
in futuro, &c. Prec. Ch. 300. *See* Cafes in
Law and Eq. 2 Part, *The Cafe of* Mitford *c.*
Lord Herbert & al'.

2. *Not favoured in Law.*

Thefe Donations are not to be countenanced, or favoured, as it would open a
Way to Fraud and Perjury; and therefore
ought to be fully proved in all its Circum-
ftances. *Prec. Chan.* 300.

6. *How, and by whom, Wills and Teftaments are to be conftrued.*

1 IT is a Rule, that a general Claufe in a
Will is not to prejudice a particular
Devife. 1 *Rep. Ch.* 145.

2. *In Teftamentis, ratio tacita non debet
confiderari, fed verba folum fpectari debent.
Multa poffunt movere mentem Teftatoris quæ
nobis latent, ideo per divinationem mentis
durum eft a verbis recedere* 2 Chan Ca 155.

3. A Man devifes feveral fpecifick Legacies, and (*inter al'*) to his Grandchildren,
to be paid at Twenty-one, or Marriage, and
after devifes, that all his Legacies fhall be
paid

paid in a Year after his Deceafe *Cur²:* The fubfequent Claufe, which feems to contradict the Payment of the Legacies to the Grandchildren, in Point of Time, muft be fo conftrued that it be not repugnant to the former Claufe; and therefore the later Claufe muft relate only to the other fpecifick Legacies given to the other Legatees, and not to the Grandchildren's Legacies *Cafes in Law and Eq.* 2 *Part,* *Adams c. Clerk's* Cafe, *fo.* 154. *Vue le mefme Livre, fo* 57, 58

4 The Will is to be taken together as one intire Scheme. *Acherley* and *Vernon's* Cafe, *Cafes in Law and Eq* 2 *Part,* *fo* 68 to 80. *Vide ibid fo* 77. *Nelfon* 27.

5. No Words are to be rejected that are capable of Signification. *Barker Ar.* v *Ayres* and *Smith,* *Cafes in Law and Eq* 2 *Pt fo.* 157, *&c.* 1 *Chan. Ca.* 178. *Poph.* 131. *Gilb.* 11, 118, 133, 136, 209.

6. The Teftator's Intent is to govern, and artificial Reafon not to be admitted. *Ibid.* 1 *Chan. Ca* 79, 80, 178

7. The Intent of the Teftator is to be collected out of the written Words, and nothing is to be admitted in the Conftruction which is in any wife contrary to the Words; neither are Words to be rejected which may be reduced to any legal Conftruction; but if any Words are contrary to the Law, or infenfible, fuch Words muft be rejected *Ibid. Vide And.* 29. 3 *Lev.* 180, 181, 373. 3 *Mod.* 290. 2 *Lev.* 56, 156. 3 *Cro.* 52. 1 *Cro* 356 *Latch* 40.

8. The Words in a Will, being ambiguous and capable of a Conftruction in Favour

vour of the Heir, is to be fo conftrued.
See *Sparrow* and *Shaw's* Cafe, before the
Houfe of Lords, 15 *April* 1729

9. The Intention of the Teftator is to be
purfued in the Conftruction of Wills, as far
as may be confiftent with the Rules of Law.
Sparrrow and *Shaw, fupra.*

10 The Devifor fuppofing he had Power
to difpofe the Inheritance, devifeth the
fame, and orders Incumbrauces to ue difcharged thereout ; if afterwards turning
out that this Eftate could not pafs according
to his Intention, it fhall not (though in Favour of the Heir) be conftrued he intended
to faddle his other Eftate with thefe In-
cumbrances See the Earl of *Tankervile* c.
Gray & al', before the Houfe of Lords,
14 *March* 1728.

11. The Ecclefiaftical Court may not tranf-
late a Will, but Equity will. 1 *Peer Will.* 527.

7. *Executors.*

1 *Who are fuch.*

UPON an *Englifh* Bill in the Exchequer, the Cafe was, Several Executors were, and one proved the Will, the
Reft refufing, and then he who proved it
dies, and another took out Letters of Adminiftration, and brought the prefent Bill.
Held clearly by the Court, that by proving
of the Will by one of the Executors, all
are Executors, and tho' he who folely proved it be dead, yet none other Perfon can
adminifter fo long as any of the other Executors

cutors are living ; though they joined not in
the Probate, neither ever acted in the Execution of the Will; and in the principal
Cafe, it did not appear, that they who
refufed were dead ; fo Bill difmiffed. *Hard.*
111. *Vide* 9 *Co. Henflow's* Cafe. 21 *E* 4. 1.
Ven 77. 1 *Sid* 266. 1 *Mod.* 213. 21 *E.* 4.
23. *Office of Executors* 6. *Dy* 160. 9 *Co.*
37. *a. Salk.* 3, 307, *&c.*

2. *Relief amongft them.*

1. *A.* and *B.* being appointed Executors,
they both proved the Will, but only *A* acts
as Executor, and then dies, leaving his
Wife his Executrix; a Legatee fues *B.* in the
Spiritual Court; he is liable there, having
joined in proving the Will; yet *per Lord
Keeper,* the Judgments of the Ecclefiaftical
Courts are as well fubject to the Equity of
this Court, as to Judgments at Law, and
he inclined to give Relief in the particular
Cafe, the Party being without Remedy; for
that the Delegates muft judge according to
the Ecclefiaftical Laws. 1 *Ch Ca.* 200. See
Prec. Chan 83. 8 *Co.* 136. *Cro. Car.* 373.
Plow. Com. 184. *Co. Lit.* 264. *Toth* 150.
2 *Vern. Ca.* 532.

2. Where one Executor, releafed alone
without his Companions, he is accountable,
whether he received the Duty or not. *Elf
Obf.* 104, 105, 107, 108. See 176, 177. *Salk*
153, 154. *Yelv* 160.

3 An Executor not joining in the Probate, yet may come in before the Mafter to
prove his Right. *Gilb.* 76 See *Gilb.* 80.
8 *Co.* 136. *Cro. Car.* 373. *Orph. Leg* 71, 113.

Plow. Com. 184. *Swinb.* 5 Part, *fo.* 7. *Salk.*
153. 5 *Co.* 29. *Tot.* 158. *Nelson* 171, 410.

3. *Whether Trustee for next of Kin.*

1. The Residue undisposed of is to be distributed according to the Statute; there being Legacies to the Executors: And though
the Will was not finished, yet the Presumption is, the Testator intended them no more.
Gilb 74, 75, 126, 184. *Vide* 200, 208, 209.
1 *Vern* 473. 2 *Vern.* 648. *Prec. Chan.* 92.
Nelson 351, 177, 178, 352.

2. The Residue belongs to the Executors
where the same is expresly so given, notwithstanding other express Legacies. *Prec.
Chan.* 94.

3. Devise of Lands to be sold to pay
Debts, the Rest to go to his Executors, as
Part of his personal Estate, and gives the
Executors 100 *l.* Decreed, The Executors
Trustees; for the Residue is to be distribu-
ted *Prec. Chan.* 82.

4 One devises all his Books to another,
except ten Books, such as his Wife should
chuse, as Plays, Romances, Sermons, but not
Law-Books, this is no Devise of Books
to her, but an Exception out of the Devise
of his Library, or Study; and it is not to be
thought he intended to bar his Wife of the
Benefit of the Executorship by so inconsidera-
ble a Devise *Prec. Chan* 231 *Vide* 263, 264.

5. There are two Executors, and one has
a beneficial Legacy, the other brings his Bill
for Account of the personal Estate, and to
have the Surplus; but decreed to take equally, notwithstanding the Legacy to one, for
his

his Lordſhip ſaid, the Queſtion would rather be, Whether a beneficial Legacy to
one ſhould not exclude both Executors, becauſe both but repreſent the Teſtator, and
come in as one Perſon, and cited the Caſe of
Foſter and *Munt*, which he ſaid had been
ſomewhat ſhaken by the Caſe of the
Ducheſs of *Beauford* and *Littlebury*'s Caſe
in the Houſe of Lords; yet thoſe were becauſe the Legacies to the Executors were
not beneficial, and ſo *Atkinſon*'s Caſe, at the
Rolls, where 10 *l.* for Mourning was but a
Decency required on ſuch Occaſion; but in
the principal Caſe, the Legacy was beneficial; but that not being the Caſe, he made
no Decree concerning it, but that the Executors ſhould come in equally, notwithſtanding the ſpecifical Legacy to one. *Prec Chan*
324 *The Reporter notes, if the Law be as
hath been lately held, this ſeems no Contradiction to* Foſter *and* Munt's *Caſe, which was decreed only on the Fraud in the Executor*

6. Giving a Legacy to one Executor
where are two, neither are thereby exclu-
ded; and Mourning is not to be deemed a
Legacy to ſuch Intent   *Vide* Caſe *Maſon*
and *Hawkins*, before the Houſe of Lords,
4 *March* 1729.

7. *Upton* deviſed 50 *l* each to his two Si-
ſters, and 50 *l* to his Neices, and makes
them Executrixes, without diſpoſing of the
Reſidue, it ſhall be diſtributed amongſt
the next of Kin, and not go to the Execu-
trixces; for Executors in theſe Caſes are but
Truſtees. If he had intended them the Surplus, he could eaſily have ſaid ſo   Since the
Statute of Diſtributions Succeſſion to perſo-
2   nal

hal Eftates was fettled, &c. See Cafes cited
in this Cafe Prec. Chan. 566.

8 A Man, having a Daughter and two
Brothers, made his Will, and thereby gave
5 l a-piece to his Brothers, appointing them
Executors, but made no Difpofition of the
Surplus, on the Teftator's Death, the Daughter, as next of Kin, libelled in the Spiritual
Court for the Refidue of the perfonal E-
ftate, and as there was, (as was fuggefted)
exprefs Legacies given to the Executors, they
ought to have nothing further; and in the
Spiritual Court the Daughter obtained a
Sentence for the *Refiduum*; and from this
Sentence the Executors appealed to the Delegates, and now moved *in Banco Regis* for
a Prohibition to the Delegates. Lord Chief
Juftice *Holt* faid, the Daughter not being
refiduary Legatee had no Pretence to fue
for this Surplus in the Spiritual Court; and
afterwards, on Debate, a Prohibition was
granted; and yet on Bill in Chancery by the
Daughter againft the Executors, for an Account of the Surplus, fhe obtained a Decree,
and that though there were Proof, that the
Teftator intended his Executors fhould have
the Surplus, in regard that the Daughter had
incurred his Difpleafure, by having married
againft his Confent; yet there being fome-
what doubtful, it was decreed firft by Sir
John Trevor, Mafter of the Rolls, and after
by Lord Cahncellor *Sommers*, on Appeal,
That the Executors fhould be but Truftees
as to the Surplus, after their Legacies paid;
and that fuch Surplus fhould go according
to the Statute of Diftributions, and that it

was dangerous to admit parol Proof, &c. 1 *Peer Will.* 7, 8, 9.

9. *Selwin* and *Browne* in the House of Lords, 21 *Mar.* 1734. *John Brown* seised in Fee of a real Estate, and possessed of a considerable personal Estate, devised thereout several Annuities and Money Legacies to several Persons in the Will named, and gave a particalar Legacy of 500 *l.* to one *Brown*, the Testator's Nephew, as also his Manor of *Hubbard*'s Hall in *Essex* in Tail Male, Remainder to *William Selwin* in Fee, another of the Testator's Nephews, to whom he also devised his Leasehold House in *Bow-street*. *And as for the Rest, Residue and Remainder of my Estate, whether real or personal, whereof I am seised or possessed, or which I am any Ways intitled unto, and which I have not herein and hereby before devised, given, bequeathed, or disposed of, I give, devise and bequeath the same, and every Part thereof, and all my Right, Title, Claim, and Interest therein and thereto, unto such my Executor or Executors hereinafter named as shall duly take on him or them the Execution of this my Will according to the true Intent and Meaning thereof, his and their Heirs, Executors, Administrators and Assigns, as Tenants in Common, and not as Jointenants ;* and made the said *Brown* and *Selwin* Executors, who accordingly took upon them the Executorship, and paid the Testator's Debts, Funeral Charges and Legacies, and divided equally between them great Part of the Residue of the Estate, but there being a Bond-Debt of 3000 *l* due from *Selwin* to the Testator, which he refused

fused to account for to *Browne*, as Part of
the Residue of the personal Estate of the
Testator, insisting, that the same was extinguished for his sole Benefit, by his being
made an Executor, *Brown* exhibited his Bill
against him for Relief, and particularly that
he might be paid Half the Money due for
Principal and Interest on the said Bond. On
hearing this Cause before his Honour the
Master of the Rolls, he was pleased to *admit the Evidence of one* Vinar *(tho' objected
to) to be read, who drew the Will, and who
fully proved, that the Testator's Intention was,
that* Selwin *should have the sole Benefit of the
Bond, without being any Ways accountable for
the same to the other Executor; that his In-
structions were to draw the Will accordingly,
but that he told the Testator, there was no Occasion to say any Thing about it in the Will;
for that, by making him Executor, he had extinguished the Debt; and that he had advised
with Counsel on this Point, who told him, it
was a clear Case, and had been so adjudged in
Law , at which the Testator was well satisfied;
it was also admitted by* Brown *in his Answer
to a Cross-Bill, that both* Selwin *and* Vinar
*had, in the Testator's Life-time, told him that
this was the Testator's Intention, and particularly that* Selwin *told him, that if he was not
satisfied herewith, in Order to prevent Disputes
hereafter, he might then ask the Testator about
it, but that he acquiesced in what they told
him, and said, he would pay great Regard to
the Testator's Intention.* Upon this Evidence
and the Nature of the Case, the Master of
the Rolls decreed, that *Selwin* should have
an equal Moiety of the Residue of the Te-

ſtator's Eſtate, after Debts, &c. excluſive of
the Bond, and that the ſame ſhould be delivered up and cancelled. From this Decree
Brown appealed to the Lord Chancellor,
who alſo admitted the Proof, &c. (*ut ſupra*)
to be read; but reverſed the Decree, not
thinking the Teſtimony of a ſingle Witneſs,
according to the Circumſtances of the Caſe,
ſufficient to control what appeared on the
Face of the Will. From this Decree *Selwin*
appealed to the Houſe of Lords, where the
firſt Thing objected to by the Reſpondent
was, the admitting *Vinar's* Evidence to be
read, it was inſiſted upon by the Appellant's
Counſel, that there were many Inſtances in
the Courts of Equity, where parol Evidence
had been allowed to be read, in Order to
ſupport the Conſtruction of the Law, and
rebut an Equity that might otherwiſe ariſe
againſt the legal Operation of a Deed or
Will; and for this were cited 2 *Vern.* 252.
Counteſs and *Earl of Gainsborough,* and ſeveral other Caſes On the other Side it was
inſiſted upon, as a ſettled Rule of Law, to
reject all Proof brought to ſupply the Words
of a Will, or to explain the Intent of the
Teſtator, that this was the expreſs Doctrine
laid down and reſolved in Lord *Cheyney's* Caſe,
5 *Co* 68 and was the Opinion of my Lord
Chief Juſtice *Holt,* in the Caſe of *Cole* and
Rawlinſon, 1 *Salk* 234 where he ſays, that
the Teſtator's Intent muſt be collected from
the Words of the Will, and not from Circumſtances, or any Matters *debors* , and
that to ravel into the Affairs of the Teſta-
ſtor would render Property precarious, and
introduce Incertainty and Confuſion into
the

the Law it felf, that this was not like admitting *Evidence to afcertain* the Perfon or Thing, as where the Teftator had two Sons named *John,* and he devifed Lands to his Son *John ,* for in fuch Cafe, without admitting parol Evidence to fhew which of his Sons he meant, the Devife muft be void; but in the principal Cafe there is a Devife of the Refidue of the Eftate to the Refpondant by plain Words in the Will And the Queftion is, whether the Appellant fhall be allowed by parol Evidence to prove a contrary Intention in the Teftator? Which to permit would, they conceived, be contrary to the Rule of Law, and the exprefs Words of the Statute of Frauds and Perjuries, which enacts, *that no Will in Writing fhall be repealed, nor fhall any Claufe, Devife, or Bequeft therein, be altered or changed by any Words, or Will, by Word of Month only.* Upon the Counfel's withdrawing, Lord *Hardwick* for reading the Evidence, and decreeing on the Strength of it, faid, that he thought the Evidence offered in the prefent Cafe was extreamly proper, and what in like Cafes was every Day admitted , that if, by making the Appellant Coexecutor, the Teftator has effectually extinguifhed the Debt by Operation of Law, as if he had difcharged it by exprefs Words , and if it only fubfifted by the Notions of a Court of Equity, which arife from a Prefumption, that the Teftator did not intend by any Act in Law to extinguifh the Debt, furely the Executor may rebut this Equity, by giving parol Evidence, that the Teftator's Intent was agreeable to Law. So where the Teftator gives several Legacies, and, amongst the Rest, gives a Legacy to his Executor, without making any Disposition of the Surplus of the Estate, though in this Case the Law gives the Executor the Surplus; yet in Equity he shall be considered as a Trustee for the next of Kin; but, as this is by Implication and Construction only, the Executor has been allowed to encounter it by parol Evidence, and he thought the said Cases, on this Head, had gone as far, if not farther than the present one. Lord *Carteret*, against admitting the Evidence, said, there was no Case in which the Courts of Justice ought to be so careful in sticking to the Letter of the Law, as in the present; that Admitting this Evidence was going directly contrary to the Statute of Frauds, which bounds the Courts of Equity as well as the Common Law Courts, and would introduce that Perjury, Contrariety of Evidence, and other Inconveniences, which that Statute was made to prevent; that by giving Way to this Kind of Evidence their Lordships would constantly be troubled with reading the Depositions of unskilful Lawyers, who, to excuse and varnish over their own Blunders, would swear hard; that Nurses, Tenders and Apothecaries, and others, who may have bad Memories, and worse Consciences, would be affirming that for Fact, which was only a loose and unguarded Expression, or perhaps made use' of by the Testator to controul and disguise what he was doing, or to keep the Family quiet, or for some other secret Motives and Inducements, which could not, after his Death, be found out. Upon

a Dia Divifion it was carried by a great Majority, that the Evidence fhould not be read. The Day following the Caufe came on to be further heard, when upon reading the Refpondent's Anfwer, it was objected to that Part of it that related to what *Vinar* and *Selwin* told him, as to the Teftator's Intention, and the Lords conceiving, that it was an Attempt, by a Side-Wind, to have that Evidence made ufe of, which they rejected the Day before, it was held to be contrary to that Refolution, and upon this Occafion the Lord Chancellor expreffed an intire Satisfaction at the Refolution their Lordfhips came to in this Cafe. It was then infifted upon, that taking it upon what appeared upon the Face of the Will, the Decree ought to be reverfed: That the Obligee, by making the Obligor one of the Executors, this Act of the Teftator extinguifhes the Debt; for the Debt confifting only of a Right to recover it by Way of Action, which one Executor cannot maintain againft another, the Teftator, by making the Debtor one of his Executors, does thereby difcharge the Action, and confequently difcharges the Debt, there is no Foundation to make a different Conftruction in this Cafe in Equity, where there are no Creditors, nor any Perfons who are difappointed of their Legacies, and though it may be faid, that the Teftator has devifed over the Refidue of his Eftate to both his Executors; yet this 3000 *l.* cannot be deemed Part of the Refidue, being before extinguifhed On the other Side it was faid, that the admitting one Executor could not fue another at Law,

or

or that an Executor could not sue himself, which is the Reason why in some Books it is said, that the Obligee's making the Obligor Executor is an Extinguishment, yet it was never doubted, but that such a Debt remained Assets to satisfy Creditors; and in *Yelv* 160 it is resolved, that it shall be Assets to satisfy Legacies, and in *Salk* 306 my Lord *Holt* says, that tho' the Action be discharged, yet the Debt is Assets, and the making the Obligor Executor does not amount to a Legacy As therefore this Debt remains Part of the Testator's Assets, and as he has devised the same by the Name of the Residue of his Estate, such Residuary Legatee may sue for and recover the same in the Ecclesiastical Court, in the same Manner that a particular Legatee may recover his Legacy. And as the Courts of Equity have a concurrent Jurisdiction with Ecclesiastical Courts in Matters of this Nature, it is but fitting the Subject should have the same Measure of Justice, in which soever of those Courts he pleases to sue; And for these Reasons the Decree was affirmed.

N B I have been informed, That Lord Chancellor, at the Hearing before him, said the Evidence ought not to be read, being *dehors*, and against the Statute of Frauds. To whom Surplus, *Gilb.* 74, 81, 125, 184, 200, 208, 209, 280. *Nelson* 350. 1 *Vern.* 736, 473. 2 *Vern* 571, 601, 602, 648, 736, 737. *Prec. Chan* 82, 92, 94, 184, 231, 263, 324, 566 *Abr Eq.* 246, 247. 1 *Vern.* 462. Lord and *Lady Gainsborough's* Case, *Littlebury's* Case, *Ball* and *Smith's* Case; *The Duchess of Beauford's* Case, *Gilb.* 127. *Comb.* 378. 1 *Peer Will.* S C. 4. *When*

4. *Where the King is Executor.*

When the King is made an Executor to another, he doth appoint certain Persons to take the Execution of the Will upon them, (against whom such as have Cause of Suit may bring Actions,) and appointeth others to take the Account. See *Parl Roll*, 15 *H.* 6. *Catherine*, Queen Dowager of *England*, Mother of *H* 6. made her laft Will and Testament, and thereof appointed that K ng her fole Executor, and thereupon the King appointed *Robert Rawlinfon, Cl* Keeper of the Wardrobe, *John Maifden* and *Richard Alfeed*, Efquires, to execute the faid Will under the Overfight of the Cardinal, the Duke of *Gloucester*, and the Bifhop of *Lincoln*, or two of them, to whom they fhould account. 4 *Inft.* 335

5. *The Executor's Affent to Legacies.*

1. Where Debts are unpaid at the **Time**, Affent to Legacies not good 1 *Chan. Ca.* 257. See *Nelfon* 461. *Orph Leg.* 144. *Co. Litt* 292. *b.* Perk. *fect.* 481. 4 *Co.* 28. *March* 137.

2 If the Spiritual Court attempt to compel the Executor to pay a Legacy, without Security to refund, a Prohibion fhall go; for though this Court will compel a Legatee to refund at the Suit of a Creditor, or even of other Legatees, where there is a Deficiency of Affets; yet the Executor having once affented to a Legacy may be concluded. 1 *Vern.* 27, 93, 127, 162, 453, 455. 1 *Chan. Ca.*

Ca. 136, 137, 149, 271. 2 *Chan. Ca.* 119, 171, 132. *Nelson* 136, 381, 411, 422. *Gilb.* 87. *Prec. Chan.* 392.

6. *His Authority and Power over the Testa-tor's Estate.*

1. *Before* ⎱
2. *After* ⎰ *Probate.*

1. *Before.*

1. An Executor may meddle with and dispose of the Goods of his Testator before Probate. *Bacon's Use of the Law* 67. *Vide Orph. Leg.* 144. *Co. Litt.* 292. *Perk. sect* 481. 4 *Co.* 28. *Mar.* 137 1 *Chan. Ca* 257. *Nelson* 461.

2. Executors by the Will and Death of the Testator have all the Property of the Testator's Goods and Chattels, Leases for Years, Wardships, Extents, and all Rights concerning them, and the Executors may meddle with the Goods and dispose them before any Probate, but not bring any Ac-tions. *Aliter* of an Administrator. *Use of the Law* 67. 5 *Co.* 28. *Nelson* 176.

2. *After.*

1. He may take his Testator's Effects, sell them, bring Actions, release, &c. may prefer himself to other Creditors, &c.

2. The Executors have their Title by the Testator, and the Testament, and not by the Probate , and the Probate of one Exe-cutor, where there are several, by the Com-

i

mon

mon Law shall enable all the Executors, tho'
never so many, to sue; so that it is not
the Probate, *the Act of the Ordinary*, which
gives them any Interest, or Title, either to
Chose en Action, or Possession; for they have
their Titles and Interest by the Testament,
and not by the Probate; so the Ecclesiastical
Judge has no Power to take a Renunciation
or Refusal of an Executorship. The Probate is nothing but a Confirmation or Allowance of what the Testator hath done.
9 *Co* 37. *b.* 38, 40, 41. *Moor* 273. *Go.* 311.
Ow. 44. 2 *Bro. & Go.* 58. 1 *Leon.* 206.
Hard 111. *Tho. Jo* 72 *Plow. Com.* 280.
5 *Co.* 28. 2 *And.* 150. *Hett.* 77, 105. *Hutt.*
30. *Trials per Pa.* 13, 331, *&c.* 309, 326.
2 *Keb* 610, 337. *Ray* 405 *Sty.* 228, 346.
2 *Show* 293. *Comb.* 46, 170, 185. *Dy.* 160,
367, 372. *Fitz. Abr* 3, 148 *a.* 3 *Keb* 344.
2 *Mod. Ca.* 90 2 *Rol* 263. 1 *Keb.* 567.

3 Upon an *English* Bill in *Scacc.* the Case
was, Several Executors were, and but one
proved the Will, the rest refusing, and then
he who proved it dies, and another took out
Letters of Administration and brought a
Bill here; and held that, by proving the
Will by one, all are Executors. 9 *Co. Henflow's* Case 21 *E* 4. *Hard.* 111. 1 *Ven.*
77 1 *Sid* 266. 1 *Mod* 213. *Dyer* 160.
Salk. 3, 307. 9 *Co.* 37. *Office of Exec.* 6.

7. *The*

7. *The Probate.*

1. *General to.*

1. THE Probate of Wills did not origi-nally belong to Ordinaries, but to the King, who seised the Intestate's Effects to pay his Debts and advance his Wife and Issue, *&c.* but afterwards the Power was de-rived to Ordinaries, but they neither had nor now have any Power to give or sell the Goods, neither to dispose them to their own or another's Use, tho' in Danger of perishing, neither could, nor can, release Debts due to the Deceased's Estate ; neither have any Action, tho' Actions lay against the Ordi-nary and his Committee, by Name of Exe-cutors, if they meddled with the Effects and did not pay Debts. *Stat.* 31 *E.* 3 *c.* 11. 9 *Co.* 37

2 When the Will is proved in the Eccle-siastical Court, that Court hath executed its Authority ; but-the Executors are to sue in the Temporal Courts to get in the Estate of the Deceased *Gilb.* 207. *Vide* 9 *Co* 38

3 A Will cannot be proved in the Eccle-siastical Court further than respects Goods, for in Regard to Lands, such a Probate will not avail, but the High Court of Chan-cery will prohibit their proceeding any far-ther than concerns the Chattels, as a Court of Law will prohibit their Proceed-ings in the Ecclesiastical Courts, in Matters cognizable at Law. *Practical Register.*

4. The

4. The Probate of a Will is no Evidence in a Litigation for Lands either *pro* or *con.* in any Court at Law, but a Proceeding *coram non judice*, yet is it good as to Goods. *Salk.* 552, 553

5. Every Bishop's Will is to be proved with the Provincial.

Vide 5 Co De Jure Regis Eccl 9 a. 3 *Bulst.* 315 *Latch* 64. *Palm.* 416, 422.

2 *To whom to be granted.*

1. The Ordinary cannot refuse Probate to him, who is appointed Executor, though a Bankrupt, the Testator thinking him proper, and intrusting him, neither can the Ordinary insist upon Security, for as the Testator has thought him a fit Person, the Ordinary shall not adjudge him otherwise; he has a Temporal Right, though he cannot sue before Probate, and he is in by the Testator, and not by the Ordinary *Salk.* 36, 299 See *Show.* 293, 294 1 *Vern.* 200, 335

2 In the Case of Death of the Testator before Probate, Administration must be *cum testamento annexo* 2 Rep Ch 300

3. If an Executor die before Probate, his Executor cannot prove it; but Administration *cum testamento annexo* must be granted to the Residuary Legatee, if any, or to the next of Kin. 1 *Vern* 200

4 The Plaintiff, as Executor or Administrator, out of an Inferior Court sought Relief for a Debt; the Defendant pleaded that there were *bona notabilia*, so that the Plaintiff

could

could not difcharge. Allowed *ex parte.* 3 *Rep.*
Ch. 71.

5. *Mich.* 9 *Geo.* 2. B R. *Tucker* and *Towel.*
My Lord Chief Juftice declared, that where
a Will was made, and an Executor appointed, who after dies Inteftate, his Adminiftrator cannot be reprefentative of the firft
Teftator, and that in fuch Cafe Adminiftration *de bonis non* of the firft Teftator muft
be committed. *But an Executor of an Executor is a good Reprefentative of the firft Teftator, the firft having proved the Will.*

3. *The Neceffity of the Will's being proved.*

By the Court of Exchequer, no Relief
here for a Legacy before the Codicil proved,
(for in that Cafe the Will was proved, but
not the Codicil, wherein 100 *l.* which the
Plaintiff owed the Teftator, was given, and
the Bill was to compel Probate, to ftay the
Suit on the Bond, and for Relief,) this is no
proper Court to prove it in, but it belongeth
to Court Chriftian ; and Common Law hath
nothing to do with it, but where the Ecclefiaftical Law cannot determine, which in
the prefent Cafe they may ; but when the
Codicil is proved, and made Part of the
Will, then it will be proper for this Court
to relieve on Account of the Legacy ; but
not till then ; but becaufe the Matter was
not determined in the Ecclefiaftical Court,
this Court continued the Injunction till the
Hearing there. And Lady *Swynnerton*'s Cafe
in Chancery was cited. *Hard.* 96, 97.

2

4. *Where*

4. *Where to be proved.*

1. *Where the Testator had no Assets in* England.

One dying abroad and leaving no Effects in *England*, it was not necessary that his Will should be proved in *England*, no more than if a Man died and left an Estate in *Scotland*. 1 Vern. 297.

2. *Bishops Wills.*

The Probate of every Bishop's Testament, or granting of Administration of his Goods, though he had none, but within his own Jurisdiction, belongeth to the Archbishop. 4 *Inst.* 335. *Vide* Case *Justice* and *Jones, posiea, & quære.*

3. *Where* Bona notabilia.

Vide post, *Administrator and Administration.* Vide etiam 1 *Peer Will.* 43, 44. 1 *Sid.* 179. *Cro. Eliz.* 718, 719. 5 *Co.* 29, 30. 8 *Co* 135. *For the Ordinary's Duty in such Case,* see *Can.* 92, 93.

4 *Where particular Custom.*

1. The Probate of Wills may be in Court-Baron, where there is such a Custom. *Gilb.* 207. 5 *Co.* 2 *Pt.* 73. *b.*

2. Cer-

2. Certain Lordships or Seigniories have the Probate of Wills by Prescription. *Doct. & Stud lib 2 cap 28*

3. The Courts of divers Manors of the King and other Lords have anciently had the Probate of last Wills and Testaments, and it appears by 11 *H*. 7 that Probates did not appertain to the Ecclesiastical Courts, but of late Time. *5 Co. De Jure Reg Eccl.* 16 *a b.*

4 If the Lord of a Manor hath Probate of Testaments within his Manor, if any such Will be proved in the Ecclesiastical Court, a Prohibition lieth; because that the Jurisdiction of it belongs to another. *5 Co Orph of Lond Case, fo* 73. *b*. *Rol. Abr. Prohibition, fo* 313. *Case* 1.

Dr *Gibson*, in his *Codex*, seems to me to slur Custom, when it thwarts Canon, as he thinks such Custom in its Beginning was an Incroachment; whereas I think every reasonable Custom is considered as Part of the Law; whilst Canon, if not received and used by Consent of King and People, is certainly Incroachment And I apprehend, to maintain any immemorial Custom allowed by the Common Law to be an Incroachment, is an Impeachment of the Common Law it self, which allows such Custom.

5. Peculiars, ~~Jurisdictions~~

1. So called from the *French*, *Peculier*, that is private, proper, one's own It is a Peculiar Parish, or Church, which hath Jurisdiction within it self for the Probate of Wills, &*c.* exempt from the Ordinary and Bishop's Courts. The King's Chapel is a Royal Peculiar, exempt from all Spiritual Jurisdiction, and reserved to the Visitation and immediate Government of the King himself; who is Supreme Ordinary. In the Province of *Canterbury* there are reckoned to be 57 Peculiars. It is an antient Privilege of the See of

Can-

Canterbury, that wherefoever any Manors or Advowfons do belong to it, they forthwith become exempt from the Ordinary, and are reputed Peculiars, and of the Diocefe of *Canterbury*. Blount's Law Dict *Peculiars*

2 Where the Teftator dies within any Peculiar Jurifdiction, the Probation of the Teftament belongs to the Judge of the Peculiar *Orph. Leg 58* See *The Bifhop of Norwich* and *The Mayor of Thetford's Cafe* Vide *Court of Peculiars*, &c.

5. How far the Probate is good.

1. Where a Will doth contain in it Lands and Goods, a Prohibition fhall not go for the whole in general; but if in fuch Cafe it be alledged that the Party who made the Will was *de non fane Memorie*, a Prohibition fhall there be granted for the whole; but fuch Prohibition is not to be granted in all Cafes where a Will contains in it a Difpofing of both Lands and Goods; for then it would tend to hinder all Proceedings in the Ecclefiaftical Court, which is not to be granted but in fpecial Cafes only; for the Law allows of a Probate, therefore before the Will proved an Executor cannot bring an Action. *Cro. Jac. 346. Vide 6 Co 23.*

2. A Prohibition was prayed to ftay the Suit in the Spiritual Court concerning the Probate of a Will of Goods and Lands, which was alledged to be revoked, (and fo proved.) On Suit at Law for the Land, on Iffue *Non devifavit*, it was proved revoked *in toto*, and a *Non devaftavit* found; and now Suit is in the Spiritual Court to find it a good

Will and not revoked; on this Suggestion
the Court gave Day, if Cause were not
shewn to the contrary, that a Prohibition
should be granted; for the Court held, that
if the Question had been in the Spiritual
Court for a Probate of a Will of Goods and
Lands, and making an Executor, that they
should not proceed to prove the Will *quoad*
the Land, but that a special Prohibition as
to the Lands should be granted. *Cro Car.*
94, 115, 166, 391, 396. 2 *Cro* 279, 346.
3 *Cro* 274. *Sid.* 246, 279. 1 *Ven* 207.
1 *Mod* 90, 211. 2 *Mod.* 315 *Salk* 36, 552.
1 *Vern.* 256, 397. 2 *Vern.* 76. *Skin.* 174.
2 *Sid* 143

3 If a Man devises Lands and Goods,
upon Suggestion that the Devisor *Non fuit
compos mentis* at the Time of the Devise, a
Prohibition shall be granted *quoad* the Lands
only, and not *quoad* the Goods; because if it
should be granted to the Goods, the Executor might not have an Action in the mean
Time, *quod esset inconveniens.* Pasch. 14 Ja.
B. R. Rol. Abr. Prohibition, fo. 315. (F)
Case 1

4 If a Man makes his Will of Lands only, and makes no Executor of his Goods by
the same Will, but it is a distinct Will of it
self, and is endeavoured to be proved in the
Spiritual Court, a Prohibition lieth; because
it is made devisable by the Statute 32 & 34
H. 8 and concerns real Things, whereof the
Spiritual Court have not to do. *Hill* 10
Car. B. R. Bret and *Netter, per totam Curiam* agreed. *Rol. Abr. Prohibition,* fo. 316.
Case 5.

5. One

5. One deviseth, that his House, Lands and Goods should be equally divided by his Executors between his four Daughters, who were married; the Legatees sued for their Legacies in Court Christian, and the Executors prayed a Prohibition, the Lands and Houses not being testamentary, and the Court Christian not having Jurisdiction to compel the Executors to pay these Legacies; and the Will of the Testator was, that the Legatees should have the Lands and Goods in Hotchpot; so that the Execution of the Will being a Temporal Concernment, the Ecclesiastical Court might not meddle with the Execution of such Will, so a Prohibition should go for all All the Justices agreed, that it would be mischievous to prohibit the Ecclesiastical Court for the personal Estate, because, as to that, the Execution belonged to them. And if we award a Prohibition as to them, we do not do Right to the Parties, and so the Executors ought to retain. But they unanimously agreed, that for the Lands and Houses wherein the Testator had a Freehold, the Court Ecclesiastical might not meddle with them, nor with the Money arising from the Sale thereof; because they are not testamentaty; and therefore a Prohibition lies for so much, and the Legatees shall have Remedy in Chancery, wherefore they awarded a Prohibition for the Houses and Lands not testamentary, and not for the Goods, and *Hoghton* commanded, that a Clause should be put in the Prohibition, that they might proceed for the Goods *Palm* 120. *Vide Dy.* 191, 264. *b.* 6 *Co.* 23. *b.*

6 By

*

6. By Lord Chancellor *Talbot*, a Will cannot be proved in the Spiritual Court, further than respects Goods ; for in Regard to Lands, such Probate will not avail , but the High Court of Chancery will prohibit their Proceeding any further than concerns the Chattels ; and yet the Ecclesiastical Court is the proper Place to discover and establish a Testament in, as well as to demand an Account of the personal Estate or Assets. *At* Lincoln's Inn Hall, 7 *April* 1736.

6. *Whether may be, and wherefore, and how, delayed.*

1 A Prohibition was prayed *Banco Regis* to the Prerogative Court to restrain their Proceedings there, in proving the Will of Sir *John Egerton,* who thereby had disposed of all his Personal and Real Estate, and disinherited his right Heir, and given nothing to any of his Grandchildren. The Ground whereupon this Motion was made to have a Prohibition to the whole Will, was in Regard it was intended to have a Trial at Law, whether a Will or not ; and if they should be suffered to proceed and prove the Will there, and it be allowed there for his Personal Estate, it would then be a very great Evidence to induce the Jury upon the Trial to pass for the Will ; therefore to prevent the Prejudice to the Trial, which afterwards was to be had in this Court, a Prohibition was prayed for the Whole , it was also further shewed, that Sir *John's* Daughters (during
ring

ring the Suit for the Probate of the Will) had taken Letters of Adminiſtration out of the Prerogative Court for the Perſonal Eſtate, by which Act they had there in a Manner diſallowed of the Will; and this the Court conceived to be very Strange, and granted a Prohibition for the Whole, both Lands and Goods, and that after the Trial here had, the ſame to be remanded to them as to the Goods. And this Difference was then taken and agreed for Law, by the whole Court, that where a Will doth contain in it Lands and Goods, the Court ſhall not grant a Prohibition for the Whole in the Generalty, but if in ſuch a ſpecial Caſe it be alledged, that the Party who made the Will was then *De non ſane Memorie*, a Prohibition ſhall there be granted for the Whole, but ſuch a Prohibition is not to be granted in all Caſes where a *Will* contains in it a Diſpoſing both of Lands and Goods; for then it would tend to hinder all the Proceedings in the Eccleſiaſtical Court, which is not to be granted but in ſpecial Caſes only; for the Law allows of a Probate there, becauſe before the Will be proved an Executor cannot bring an Action. *Cro. Jac.* 346. *Vide* 6 *Co.* 23.

So is Ro Abr. 315 Caſe 6.

2 Upon a Suggeſtion for a Prohibition, from the Exchequer to the Spiritual Court, to ſtay the *Probate of a Will* for Lands and Goods, becauſe the Teſtator was *Non compos*, *Atkins* argued, that upon ſuch Suggeſtion as this, which goes to the whole Will, a general Prohibition ought to go, ſo upon Suggeſtion of a Revocation; otherwiſe where the Suggeſtion is particular and con-

cerns

cerns the Land only; he cited 6 *Co.* 23. The Marquis of *Winchester*'s Case, *Hob* 290 *Serles* and *Williams*'s Case, *Pasch* 10 *Jac.* *Banco Regis, Semaine*'s Case, 2 *Cro Egerton*'s Case. *Cro* 1 *Part* 94, 114, 115, 165, 391. *Vide Dy.* 201 *Stephens* against the Prohibition, as to the Goods, and the Court declared, that unless the Plaintiff would go to Issue this Term, *Compos,* or *Non compos,* they would not grant a Prohibition. *Hard.* 131. *Mich.* 1658. Sir *Richard Minshal* and *Spicer.*

3 The Surmise was, on Motion for a Prohibition, that it concerned Lands; the Case was this: Will was proved in usual Form, and after the Plaintiff suggesting that the Testator had made another Will, and on Dispute thereupon, the Second was sentenced to be his Will; from which Sentence there was an Appeal to the Delegates, and now a Prohibition was prayed to them, for that the Testator had disposed of Lands by this Will, which *prima facie* is a good Ground of a Prohibition. 6 *Co. Mountagu*'s Case, *Cro. Car Bret* and *Netter*'s Case, *&c.* *Hale* Ch. Baron, at first the Course was to grant a Prohibition upon all such Suggestions; and if on Trial it appeared that nothing was disposed of but Lands, then the Prohibition was perpetual, and in Case there was a personal Estate, and Executor in the Case, then a Consultation was awarded *quoad, &c* Afterwards on Suggestion, that the Will concerned Lands and Goods, a Prohibition was used to be granted *quoad* the Lands; but of later Times, upon Suggestion, that the Will disposed of Lands, if
the

the perfonal Eftate were concerned likewife, they have ufed to deny a Prohibition; for that the Party is at no Prejudice by it, with Refpect to the Lands; the Probate in the Ecclefiaftical Court being no Evidence againft him at Law for the Lands, whereas the Executor would be at Prejudice, if a Prohibition fhould iffue; becaufe then the Executor would be hindred from proving the Will, before which he cannot fue for any Debt due to his Teftator's Eftate, which might be a Means to diminifh the Eftate; *fed adjournatur*; but coming on another Day, many Precedents were cited for granting Prohibitions *quoad* the Lands; *fed per Hale* Ch. Baron, there ought to be no Prohibition on this Suggeftion; becaufe in this Caufe before the Delegates the Suit is only to put the Party into a Condition of doing the fame Thing the Plaintiff himfelf hath done already; (*Viz*) to prove his Will, and is grounded upon an Act done by the Plaintiff himfelf; and if it were not profecuted, the Defendant would have no Means of Proving his Will, being tied up by a Prohibition, which is unreafonable: But becaufe the Plaintiff had brought his Action here to try his Title to the Land, and the Validity of the Defendant's Will, and offered to proceed in it with Effect, the Court ordered a Prohibition *quoad* the Lands, unlefs the Parties would confent to be concluded by the Probate. *Hard* 313. Vide *Hard* 131. *al mefne Purpofe.* Vide *Nelfon*, fo 403, 433

4 A Prohibition was prayed to the Spiritual Court to ftay the Probate of a Will,

which contained a Devise of Lands, and several Legacies, suggesting this Matter, and that the Testator was *Non compos*, the Marquis of *Winchester*'s Case, 6 *Co.* 23. was relied on; but the Court denied that Case, and said, that the Statute of *H.* 8. never intended to lessen the Jurisdiction of the Ecclesiastical Court as to the Probate of Wills, and to grant a Prohibition might be inconvenient, for without Probate, the Executor cannot sue for Debts, which by this Means may be lost and the Will unperformed, as for granting it *quoad* the Lands, it would be vain, because it is no Evidence, either *pro* or *con.* in any Court at Law, but a Proceeding *coram non Judice*; yet it is good as to the Goods. 2 *Salk* 552, 553.

Banco Regis, *Hill.* 3 *Geo.* 2. *Justice* and *Jones*.

* 5. Mr *Reeve* and Mr. *Lee* moved for a *Mandamus* to be directed to Dr. *Betsworth*, Judge of the Prerogative Court of *Canterbury*, to prove the Will of the late Lord *Londonderry*; and this Motion was founded upon an Affidavit, that this Judge had refused till a Commission of Appraisement executed, and cited a Case in *Raym.* 235. where the like Motion was granted; so the Court granted the present Motion without making any Rule to shew Cause, by Reason of the Inconvenience of a Delay in a Matter of this Nature; afterwards Mr. *Reeve* moved for a Rule upon the Doctor to return his Writ of *Mandamus*, the Return being out the Day before, to which Mr. *Strange* said, the constant Practice in these Cases is, only to grant four Days Rule,

but

but the Court said, they knew of no such Practice, and accordingly ordered the Writ to be returned in two Days, and the Dr. now returned to the *Mandamus*, That the Law and Practice of the Ecclesiastical Courts was constantly to grant these Commissions, at the Request of any Creditor, upon his entering a Caveat against the Probate of the Will. Mr *Willes* and Mr. *Strange* argued, that this Return was good. They said, that Commissions of this Sort were for the Benefit of Creditors, by which Means they have a sure Account of the Effects, to their Satisfaction; whereas otherwise they have only the Executor's own Oath, as to the Truth of the Inventory; but the Court declared they would not suffer Commissions of this Sort to delay the Probate of Wills; and that because till Probate, the Executor has not legal Power and Authority over the Effects, and in the mean Time the Effects of the Testator may be all wasted; and *Page* Just. observed, That *Mandamus's* have been allowed to enforce the Probate of Wills where the Ecclesiastical Courts insisted upon Caution; for that the Executor was a Bankrupt. Commissions of this Sort are at the Expence of the Assets and not of the Creditors, and the Court thought them of dangerous Consequence to delay a Probate. *Reynolds* Just. said, that where a Will is under Litigation, Commissions of this Sort are reasonable to protect the Estate, but here they put a Stop to a Man's enjoying the Benefit of a Right, which the Testator himself hath given him. Mr *Strange* then excepted to the *Mandamus*, that it on-

ly

ly recited, that my Lord *Londonderry* died at *St. Christophers*, having *Bona & Catalla* in *Westminster*, and several other Places, and upon that commanded the Archbishop of *Canterbury* to grant the Probate of the Will, but did not set out that these Places are within the Province of *Canterbury*, and *Westminster* he said was a distinct Jurisdiction, and not Part of the Diocese of *London*, and the Court could not take Notice that it was Part of the Province of *Canterbury*, but besides he observed, that the Probate of the Testaments of all Persons dying in the foreign Plantations belongs to the Bishop of *London*, but the Court said, that it was resolved in the Case of *Adams* against the Tertenants of *Savage*, that they are bound to take Notice under what Ecclesiastical Jurisdiction they sit. And they said, that it is true indeed, that where a Person dies beyond Sea, having no Goods, here the Bishop of *London* grants the Probate of the Will, but where there are Goods in one Diocese, the Archbishop has a Right of Probate, and accordingly the Court granted a peremptory *Mandamus*. 6 *Mod.* 154. The Court, by Way of a second Answer to this Exception, said, That the Judge by his Return had admitted his Exercising a Jurisdiction in the Probate of the present Will, and therefore they could not suffer him to except against having Authority to prove it. Vide 3 *Cro* 106.

Vide post *Administration*, wherefore may be stayed.

7. *Where Fraud or Practice.*

1. *Where to be tried.*

1. Where a Will of a Perfonal Matter was obtained by Fraud, and by getting the Party to fwear fhe would not revoke it, yet after Probate it is not to be drawn in Queftion in Equity; yet if the Party claiming under fuch fraudulent Will come into Equity for Relief, he fhall not have it. *2 Vern.* 76.

2 Adminiftration is granted, where is a Will and Executor, though the Will was concealed, yet the Adminiftration was abfolutely void, and it is all one, though the Executor, when the Will appeared, refufed to intermeddle, or if feveral Executors, and all dead before any Notice of the Will. See Cafe *Wangford* and *Wangford,* *Term Mich.* 11 *W* 3.

3. A Covenant and Bond was upon it to pay three of the Daughters of a Stranger 10*l* each at their feveral Ages of twenty-four Years, and the Obligor lying fick made his Will, and in Performance of the faid Covenant devifed to each of the faid Daughters 10*l* to be paid at their feveral Ages of twenty-one Years; one of the Daughters, (to wit) *Margery Davis,* fued the Executor in Court Chriftian for her Legacy, and the Executor brought a Prohibition, fuggefting that he is bound by the Covenant and Bond to pay it at Twenty-four; and if he fhould pay it now at Twenty-one; he is not difcharged

charged of the Covenant, and shews further, that it was the Intent of the Devisor, that he should not be twice charged, but was an Election to the Executor, and if the Covenantees would release the Covenant, he would pay them according to the Will; and all the Court was of Opinion, that this was a good Suggestion to have a Prohibition, and took the Case to be in every Point as the Plaintiff had alledged. *Mo.* 246.

4. A Testator was got away by false Surmises, and a new Will tendred to him, which he was prevailed with by fraudulent Practices to execute; yet the Court would not set it aside. 3 *Chan. Cases* 61. See 87, 94.

5. *A* the Plaintiff's Uncle had made his Will, and given the Plaintiff the greatest Part of his Personal Estate; but in his last Sickness his Maid-Servant had prevailed with him, being *Non compos*, to make another Will, and to marry her about a Week before his Death, at Six o'Clock at Night, though it was really proved by two Ministers, she was actually married before to the Defendant, and that he procured the Licence for the Marriage of *Archer* to the other Defendant, and that the Defendants suppressed the first Will, and that the Testator in his Health and Sound Mind knew the Defendants to be married; yet this fraudulent Will being proved, and the Matter merely of a personal Estate, his Lordship was of Opinion, that whilst that Probate stood, the Matter was not examinable in Chancery, and though the Fraud was fully
proved

proved and read to him, yet he would not hear the same read, but dismissed the Bill. 2 *Vern.* 8, 9

6. A Will of the Personal Estate was   * proved in the Spiritual Court; the Respondent having a former Will in his Favour, brings his Bill in Equity to discover by what Means the latter Will was obtained and for an Account of the Personal Estate, and to discover whether the Testator was not incapable and imposed upon, the Defendant demurred, because it belonged to the Spiritual Court only to prove the Validity of Wills, and the former Will was not proved in the Spiritual Court, as the Will in his Favour; but the Demurrer was over-ruled. See *Andrews* and *Powis's* Case before the House of Lords, 6 *Feb.* 1723.

7. A Will obtained *in Extremis*, and up-   * on Importunity of the Testator's Wife, his Hand being guided in Writing his Name, was set aside. See *Moneypenny* and *Browne's* Case before the House of Lords. 15 *March* 1711.

8 An Executor of a Will obtained by   * Fraud, though proved in the Spiritual Court, was decreed Trustee for the Devisee of a former Will. See the Case of *Skirrick* and *Bransby* before the House of Lords, 15 *May* 1711

9. A Will was obtained by Fraud in ta-   * king Advantage of a Lunatick, decreed *nul* in Chancery, 31 *Jan* 1735 *Qu. if not after affirmed by the House of Lords, as I think it was.* Vide *Gilb.* 181. *Hard* 375. 3 *Rep. Ch.* 155 2 *Vern.* 293. *Pre. Ch* 459.

10 *Much.*

*

10. *Mich. 9 Geo 2. B. R. Tucker* and *Towel.*
Mr. *Agar* moved for a Prohibition to the
Archdeacon of *N* to ftay a Suit there, for
a Legacy, where the Cafe was, One *Eleanor
Tucker* by Will gave the Legacy, which is
the Ground of the prefent Queftion, and
made *John Tucker* therein, for that Purpofe
named, her Executor of her faid laft Will,
John proved the Will, and died; and thereupon Adminiftration was granted to the Defendant below, who pleaded this Matter in
Bar, which Plea the Ecclefiaftical Court rejected; he faid, he agreed, if Adminiftration *de bonis non* had been granted to the
Defendant, then the Suit againft him had
been regular; but as that was not the Cafe,
but only a general Adminiftration granted,
he fubmitted it, that the Suit was improper,
and my Lord Ch Juft. faid, that undoubtedly the Law was fo; yet his Lordfhip faid,
had the Court before admitted the Plea, he
fhould have inclined to think that the Matter
would have been more properly remedial by
an Appeal than by Prohibition; however as
the Ecclefiaftical Court had rejected the
Plea, a Rule was made to fhew Caufe, and
Mr. *Fortefcue* now coming to fhew Caufe,
he fubmitted it, that whatever the Law
might be in the Temporal Court; yet in
the Ecclefiaftical Court a Suit might well be
inftituted againft the Adminiftrator of an
Executor, for a Legacy; to which Purpofe
he cited *Godolp* 258 and *Swinb Part* 6.
Page   the laft Edition, and if this was
fo, he contended, the Court, at leaft, might
leave the Party to his Remedy by Appeal,
and not interpofe their Prohibition, and to
this

this Purpose cited *Rol. Rep.* 10. *Mar.* 92. *pl*˙ 2. and further he obferved, that in the prefent Cafe the Libel fet forth, that the Executors had Affets of *Eleanor Tucker's* in his Hand, fufficient to fatisfy her Debts and Legacies, and that *John* and *Thomas*, the Sons of the Executor, had Adminiftration committed to them of all the Goods belonging to the faid Executor, at the Time of his Death, fo that, as he faid, the Defendant below appeared to be charged as Executor *de fon Tort*; and if that was the Cafe, he fubmitted it, they were well liable; for which Purpofe he cited 1 *Rol. Abr.* 919. Letter A. My Lord Ch. Juft. declared, that it was certain that where a Will was made and an Executor appointed, who after dies Inteftate, his Adminiftrator can be no Reprefentative of the firft Teftator, and in that Cafe that Adminiftration *de bonis non* of the firft Teftator muft be committed; and as to the Objection which has been made, that the Defendants appear to have been charged as Executors *de fon Tort*, his Lordfhip obferved, in the firft Place, that in Fact this was not fo, for though the Executor had fufficient in his Hands to fatisfy the Debt of *Eleanor*; yet it doth not appear that ever any of thofe came into the Hands of the Defendants, and as to charging one as Executor *de fon Tort* in the Courts of Common Law, he faid, the Manner is not to charge them, that they were Executors of their own Wrong, (for that was held once to be bad on Demurrer) but they muft be charged as Executors *Teftamenti & Ult. Voluntatis*; neither is there any Way to charge Executors

de

ſee p. 62.

de son Tort in the Ecclesiastical Court, but
the Remedy is for the Administrator *de bonis non* to commence a Suit in a Court of
Equity upon the Foot of a Breach of Trust
and Fraud ; and as to the Objection that has
been made, that an Appeal is the proper
Remedy, he said, in my Lord *Holt*'s Time,
an Executor was sued in the Ecclesiastical
Court for an Account by a Person who was
neither Creditor, nor Legatee ; and it was
objected thereunto, that an Appeal was the
proper Remedy, but in that Case the Court
said, he had been called into a Jurisdiction
which had no proper Cognizance of the
Matter, for which Reason they granted a
Prohibition; the rest of the Court were of
the same Opinion with my Lord in the particular Case, and accordingly the Rule was
made absolute.

8. *Of Revocations.*

1. *Of Wills.*

1. *General.*

THE Revocation of a Will is a Matter
meerly Temporal, and discharges the
Court Christian from having any Thing to
do with it, it is in no Sort dependent upon
the Will; for those Things are called dependent which go in Affirmance of the Will,
and not which disannul and disaffirm it, as
the Revocation doth , and a Revocation by
our Law is sufficient before one Witness:
And though the Court Christian hath

4   Power

Power of the Will, and of what is demand-ed thereby, namely, the Legacy, *yet, it is to be noted, that,* in its original Nature, the Will it self was Temporal, as appears by 2 *R* 3. Testament, and Things which go in Abridgment and Restraint of the Common Law shall be taken strictly, and shall not be favoured in Construction; so that the Revocation being a Thing meerly colla-teral to the Will remains at Common Law, as to the Proof, as is 1 *R.* 3 *Yelv* 92, 93 See 9 *Co* 37, 38.

2 Wills are ambulatory, and always changeable. *Hob.* 349.

3. Revocations are favoured for the Be-nefit of the Heir *Mod. Cases,* 2 *Part* 71, 77.

4. Yet the Revocation of a Will is not to be intended no more than the Disinheri-son of the Heir, but must be by the express Words. *Idem* 73

5 As a Will is to be construed as one in-tire Act, though the Heir is to be favoured where the Case is doubtful; yet if a Man devise to one, and then by the same Will devise to another the same Estate, this is not to be taken as a Revocation, but that they are Jointenants, which shews that the Will is to be construed as one intire Clause, and not as different; and by this means Contradictions will be avoided in Construc-tion thereof *Idem* 77.

6 If a Testament be made of Lands and Goods, and a Suit is in the Ecclesiastical Court for the Goods, and the Question be, whether the Testator revoked the Will in his Life-time, or not, a Prohibition shall be granted *quoad* the Land, and not as to the

Goods. *Mich* 13 *Jac Rol Abr.* 315. (E).
Cases 3, 4 *Qu. As the Question is a Revocation, or not.*

* 7. A Will may be revoked by a subsequent one, tho' such subsequent one be a void one it self, yet it is good as a Revocation. See *Constable* and *Roper*'s Case before the House of Lords *July* 11. 1713 *Pre. Ch* 459 *Gilb* 18. *Hard.* 375. 2 *Vern.* 293 3 *Rep Ch* 155

8 Privacy in making of a Will, or loose Words to hide the Testator's Intent, or to keep the Family quiet, &c. are not to be regarded, much less to be taken to amount to a Revocation. 3 *Chan. Cases* 81, 82, 87, 88, 117, 127.

2. *Whether good, and how far.*

1. *Where* pro toto

1 *A.* makes his Brother his Executor, and gives him all his Real and Personal Estate, after the Testator marries, and by Codicil made his Wife Executrix, she shall have the Personal Estate, and not the Brother, for the Devise was not to him by Name, neither as his Brother, but to his Executor. 1 *Vern.* 23

2 If one having made a Will, and Duplicate, revoke either, this is a Revocation of both; for they making but both one Will, must stand or fall together. 2 *Vern* 742.

2. *Where*

2. *Where* pro tanto.

1 Lands devifed to one firft, and after to another, in the fame Will, the laft Claufe fhall not revoke the firft, but they fhall be joint Devifes   1 Vern. 30   *So it is a Revocation only* pro tanto.

2 One devifes in Fee, and then leafes for Years to a third Perfon, this is only a Revocation *pro tanto*, but if the Devifor leafes the Land to the Devifee, to commence after Teftator's Death, this is a Revocation *pro toto*, as being inconfiftent with the Devife.   1 *Vern* 97.

3 A fubfequent Mortgage is a Revocation in Law, but not a total Revocation in Equity   1 *Vern* 329, 342.

4 Devife was of Lands in *S* to his Son *A* for ninety-nine Years, determinable upon three Lives, and by the faid Will charges thefe Lands with an Annuity of 40 *l.* a Year to his Daughter, and after demifes the fame Lands to —— for ninety-nine Years, determinable upon three other Lives, referving 50 *l* a Year Rent, this is, during the Continuance of the Leafe, a Revocation, but it is no Revocation as to the 40 *l* a Year, there being Rent enough referved to fatisfy that   See *Packer* and *Lambe*'s Cafe before the Houfe of Lords, 14 *April* 1706.

2 *Of Probates.*

1 *Whether good Caufe, or not, of Refufal.*

Upon a Motion for a Prohibition the Cafe
was, *Hill* made *Mills* h s Executor, who after became a Bankrupt, and being thereupon cited in the Prerogative Court, and
there *ure tenus* examined if a Commiffion of
Bankruptcy was awarded againft him,
whereto he anfwering Yea, the Court revoked the Probate, and committed Adminiftration, as it was agreed they might in the
Cafe of Lunacy, or other natural Difability, but this Court was clear of Opinion
that this Revocation is void, and that the
Teftator having trufted him, Bankruptcy is
not fuch a Difability, but that he may continue Executor, *non obftante*; for the Teftator's Eftate is not liable to be affigned by
the Commiffioners, but remains fubject to
the Trufts in the Will, and a Man dying,
having made his Executor, fhall never be
faid to die inteftate, fo long as he has an
Executor alive, who will intermeddle and
has proved the Will, and therefore, though
after a Sentence and Appeal brought, the
Court granted a Prohibition. *Skin.* 299 *As
the Ordinary had granted Probate to the Executor, I take it he had executed his Authority,
and his pretending to revoke the fome was a
nude and void Act, as being* extra *his Jurifdiction, and as having nothing more to do in
the Matter; he had performed his Duty in
granting Probate to the Executor appointed by
the*

the *Testator*, *whereto he had been compellable,
had he refused or even delayed it,* by Mandamus *from the* King's *Temporal Court*, *and as
he had done this Act which he was bound to
as a Ministerial Officer to the Temporal Law,
he had nothing more that he could do,
for I take it he has no Power to judge of
the Fitness of an Executor, for he comes in
by Appointment of the Testator, and not by the
Act of the Ordinary, the Ordinary indeed is
the Conduit-Pipe, Instrument, or Mesne, to
convey or derive down the Authority to the Executor, but he comes in by his Testator, for
the Ordinary cannot possibly make an Executor
to another Person.*

9. *Of Renunciations of Executor-ships.*

1 *Good, or not.*

1. THE Probate of Wills did not originally belong to Ordinaries, but to
the King, who seised the Intestate's Effects
to pay his Debts and advance his Wife and
Issue, &c but afterwards the Power was
derived to Ordinaries; but they had, *nor
have*, no Power to give, or sell, the Goods,
neither to dispose them, either to their own
or another's Use, though in Danger of Perishing, neither could, nor can, release
Debts, nor have any Action, tho' Actions lay
against them or their Committees, by Name
of Executors, if they meddled with the Effects, and did not pay Debts. Now this
Power being given to Ordinaries, is the

Reason

Reason that when some Executors refuse to
act, and one or more of the Executors named prove the Will, still they who refused
to act, may act notwithstanding, because
the Power of the Ordinary is executed when
the Will is proved, and the Ordinary hath
not Power to take the Refusal of any one or
more of the Executors to prove the Will
Stat 31 *E* 3 *c* 11   9 *Co* 37, *&c.*   •

2 But Renunciation of an Executorship
before the Ordinary is void, when he has
proved the Will his Authority is executed,
• and the Ordinary has no Power to take the
Refusal of any of the Executors who proved the same, but the same is an absolute
rude and void Act   The Executors have
their Title by the Testament, and not by
the Probate   And the Probate of one Executor, where several, by the Allowance of
the Common Law, shall enable all the Executors, though never so many, to sue, so
that it is not the Probate which gives them
any Interest or Title either to *Chose in Ac-*
tion, or Possession, for they have their Title and Interest by the Testament, and not
by the Probate, so the Ecclesiastical Judge
has no Power to take a Renunciation, or
Refusal, in such Case.   The Probate is nothing but a Confirmation and Allowance of
what the Testator hath done   9 *Co* 38, 40,
41   *Mo* 273.   *Go* 311   *Ow.* 44.   2 *Bro.*
and   *Go* 58   *Plow Com* 280   5 *Co* 28.
Dy   2 *Mod* 150.   *Het* 77, 105   *Hut*
30. 326.   2 *Keb* 33ᵗ.   *Raym.* 405.   *Sty*
228, 346   2 *Show* 293.   *Comb.* 46, 170,
185.   3 *Kel* 344   2 *Mod Cases* 90.   2 *Ro*
Rep 263.   1 *Keb* 567.   2 *Keb.* 610   1 *Leon.*
206.

206. *Hard.* 111 *Tho Jo* 72. *Trials per Pais* 13, 331, *&c.* 309, 326.

10. *Assets.*

1 *What are.*

1. LAnds, purchafed in Truft, decreed Affets to fatisfy Judgment Creditors 2 *Rep Chan.* 143, 62, 137   3 *Vol* 3   26, 88, 217 to 222. *Eq Abr* 242, 275.   1 *Ch Cases* 24, 128.

2 Lands devifed to pay Debts are Affets in Equity. 3 *Rep Ch.* 222, 23, 56, 78, 83, 85. 1 *Vol.* 222, 223. *Gilb* 2, 3, 106, 122. *Eq Abr.* 310

3. But Lands devifed to be fold are not to be any Part of the Goods or Chattels of the Deceafed, by the Stat. 21 *H.* 8 *c* 5. *So not cognifable in Court Chriftian.*

4. For Affets, by Defcent, in the Hands of the Heir, fee 1 *Vern* 172, 410, 411.

5 Upon a Bill *in Scac* the Court held clearly, That if Lands were devifed to be fold by the Executors for the Payment of the Teftator's Debts, the Money arifing therefrom fhould be Affets in the Executor's Hands. *Hard.* 405. *Paf.* 17 *Car* 2 *Burwel* ver. *Currant.* Vide 1 *Chan Caf.* 14. *Nelfon* 313. 1 *Chan Caf* 128. *Pre. Ch.* 39, 52, 58, 127, 136, 232, 286

6 An Advowfon real Affets in Equity to pay Judgment, Bond, and Simple-Contract Creditors   See Cafes *Tonge* and *Beckets* con *Robinfon*, before Houfe of Lords. 23 *March* 1730.

Vide plus 1 *Vern.* 45, 482, 453, 460, 469.
2 *Vol* 104, 341, 357, 188, 189. 2 *Rep Ch.*
152, 160   3 *Mod.* 45   1 *Vern.* 234, 282,
172, 419, 471, 28, 29, 63, 69, 99, 100,
101, 104, 432. 2 *Vern.* 134, 764, 188, 189,
341.

2 *How to be marshalled.*

1. Upon a special Report the Question
was, in what Place a Debt decreed should
take Place, in Relation to other Debts, in
Point of *Priority*, and ordered a Decree
should precede Bonds, and take Place next
to Judgments, and the Case of *Parker* and
            was cited, where this was resolved
It was objected, that on Debt upon Bond,
at Law, the Executor could not defend
himself by pleading he had no Assets *ultra*
what would satisfy the Decree, it was answered he might defend himself by Bill here
in this Court, which would take Care to
protect him therein. 1 *Vern* 143.

2 After a Suit commenced here, an Executor shall not be allowed any Payment
made voluntarily without Suit, and a Judgment confessed by an Executor, pending a Suit
here, shall not be allowed. 1 *Vern* 369.
Vide 457

11 *Accounts.*

11. *Accounts.*

1. *Whether of Ecclesiastical Cognizance.*

1. **P**AS 3 *Geo* 2 *B. R. Hatton* and *Hatton.*
The Court said, that they would in
no Case suffer the Ecclesiastical Court to call
an Executor to account for the *Residuum,*
and before the Statute of Distributions they
would not have suffered it, even in the Case
of an Administrator, and they said, that
that was one chief Occasion of the Statute,
as appears by a very long Case at the End
of *Raymond's Rep.* See 5 *Co de Jure Regis
Ecclesiastico.* 9 *a.*

12. *Suits concerning these Matters.*

1. *General.* to them

1. **I**N some Cases, Executors may sue one
another, and in others not, in *some,*
they must sue in the Ecclesiastical Courts,
and in others, they have Remedy in the
Temporal Courts. *Vide antea* Matters cog-
nisable in the Temporal Courts, &c. *Orph.
Leg* 156 *Bro Tit. Executor,* N° 98, 99,
104, 32. Tit *Prohibition.* 36 *H* 6 *c.* 7.
8 *Co* 135 *Stat* 2 *R.* 3. *c.* 17. *Stat.* 32
H. 8. *c* 37.

2. *How,*

2. *How, where, and in what Cases, to be in the Temporal Courts.*

Mich. 9 *Geo.* 2. B R. *Tucker* and *Towel*
At Law one muſt not be charged as Exe-
cutor *de ſon Tort,* but as *Executor Teſtamenti
& Ult Voluntatis,* neither is there any Way
to charge Executors *de ſon Tort* in the Eccle-
ſiaſtical Court; but the Remedy is, for the
Adminiſtrator *de bonis non,* to commence his
Suit in Equity on the Foot of a Breach of
Truſt and Fraud. *Vide antea* where Fraud
or Practice. See this Diviſion *ſupra.*

3. *Appeals in.*

In what Caſes Appeals are to be made in
Matters teſtamentary, ſee *Appeals,* &c.
alſo 4 *Inſt* 339.

III. *Adminiſtrator and Admini-ſtration.*

1. *The Ordinary's Authority.*

1. *Follows him.*

A Biſhop of *Ireland,* being in *England,*
committed Adminiſtration of the Goods
of one who died Inteſtate within his Dioceſe in *Ireland;* and adjudged good. *Cro.
Car.* 214

2. *Ho*

2 *He is but a ministerial Officer of the Law.*

1. In Matters of Administration, the Ordinary is but a ministerial Officer of the Law, appointed by Statute, to execute the same *sub modo* the Directions thereby given to him, and is not at Liberty to grant Administration at his Will and Pleasure, and to whom he pleaseth, &c. 9 Co 37, &c.

2 The Law could never intend to give Labour and Pain to the next of Kin to the Intestate in getting in and defending the Intestate's Estate, and for the Ordinary to have the Disposal of the Surplus, as was contended by Sir *John Bennet*, Judge of the Prerogative Court, who finding a Surplusage, would have compelled the Widow and Administratrix to have distributed to the next of Kin of her Intestate, not his Children, &c. *Hob* 83.

3 *If he refuse Administration to whom the same is due, how to be punished.*

The Ordinary refusing Administration to whom due, lies liable to a Penalty. *Cro. Car Wilson* and *Packman's* Case *Dy* 339. *Orph* Leg. 177. *Lau Tett* 477. *it done by the first Administrator (the Stranger to the Deceased) doe &c &c —*

it the ordinary should not grant admon to a stranger before the next of Kin unless intimated be it in parliament

4. *Where*

4. *Where he hath the Deceased's Effects in his Hands.*

1 Ordinaries bound to pay the Debts of Inteſtates, as far as Aſſets will extend, as Executors ſhould where are Executors appointed. *Stat.* 13 *E.* 1 *cap.* 19. *Reg fo.* 141 *Fitz. Brief* 822. *Executor* 77. *Vet. N. B. fo.* 61

2. If the Ordinary hath Goods in his Hands by Sequeſtration of one who dies Inteſtate, Debt is brought againſt him *ſur in Obligation* made by the Inteſtate, the Ordinary may not diſpoſe of any Parcel thereof to other Creditors at his Pleaſure, but is obliged to ſatisfy the firſt Debt on which the Action is. *Et hoc per Opinionem Juſtic in Hoſpitio Servient.* and this Queſtion was moved for the Biſhop of *Lincoln. Dyer* 232 *a.*

3 If a Man be indebted and die Inteſtate, or the Executor refuſe to be Executor, ſo that the Goods come to the Ordinary's Hands, the Creditors may have Debt againſt the Ordinary by Stat. *W. 2 cap.* 19 *Fitzb. N B.* 120. D. This Statute *cum poſt mortem alicujus* was made in Affirmance of the Common Law. 5 *Co.* 83.

4 The Biſhop cannot give Inteſtate's Goods, or releaſe, or give expreſs Authority ſo to do 8 *Co.* 135.

2. *Who to grant Administration.*

1. Sede vacante.

TEmpore *Vacationis* of an Archbishoprick or Bishoprick, the Dean and Chapter shall commit Administration. *Bro Ab.* Tit. *Administrator and Administration, Case* 46. Q. *Vide post,* whether good, void or voidable

2. *Where* Bona notabilia; *and here what so deemed*

1. One having Goods in several Counties at the Time of his Death, the Administration belongs to the Archbishop, &c *Quære* if this Word *County* should not be *Diocese. Bro. Ab Administrator and Administration. Ca* 31

2 By *Keble, Finneux* and *Bryan,* where a Man dies intestate having Goods in divers Dioceses, the Administration shall be committed by the Metropolitan, and if the Bishop of the Diocese where the Party died commit Administration, this is void, and that, though the Metropolitan never committed Administration. *Bro Ab.* Tit *Administrator and Administration, Case* 48

3. If a Man dies Intestate having *Bona notabilia* in *England* and *Ireland,* several Administrations shall be granted by the proper Archbishops, for the respective Goods in their several Dioceses.

4 If

4 If the Party dead had at the Time of his Death *Bona notabilia* in divers Dioceses, then the Archbishop of the Province where he died is to have the Probate of the Will, and to grant the Administration of his Goods as the Case falleth out , otherwise the Bishop of the Diocese where he died is to do it. Lord *Bacon's Use of the Law* 68. But if *Bona notabilia* be in both Provinces , then the Archbishop of *Canterbury* shall prove the Will, or grant Administration, as the Case may require. 8 *Co* 135 *Cro Eliz.* 472. *Hugh's Abr Administrator Lit. Sect.* 69. *Plow. Com.* 281 *Bro.* Tit. *Executor* 129, &c. Orph. *Leg* 144, 145.

5 Where the Personal Estate lies in both Provinces, Administration must be granted by the Archbishop of *Canterbury.* Cro. Eliz. 472 Dy. 305

6 If a Man dies on a Journey, Goods with him shall not make *Bona notabilia.*

7. If a Man leaves *Bona notabilia* in several Dioceses of the same Province, there must be a Prerogative Administration If one leaves *Bona notabilia* in two Dioceses of the Province of *Canterbury*, and in two Dioceses of the Province of *York*, there must be two Prerogative Administrations , but if he leaves *Bona notabilia* in one Diocese of *Canterbury* and in one Diocese of *York*, then the Administration must be in both Dioceses. *Salk. Administrator, Quere* and *vide antea Case* 4 *etiam* 8 *Co* 135, &c.

8 Upon a Bill in Equity the Case was, that Sir *Edward Wittington* died possessed of a Personal Estate in both Provinces, and his Will was proved in the Prerogative Court

I of

of *Canterbury*, and upon a Suit there for a Legacy, there was an Appeal after Sentence, and after that, Administration was granted of his Goods within the Province of *York*, from which there was an Appeal, and pending these Appeals, the present Bill was brought in the Exchequer Equity, to discover the Personal Estate of the Intestate, and an Agreement to have Administration; to which the Defendant pleaded the Administration granted of the Goods within the Province of *York*, and concluded generally, whether he ought to make Answer to any the Matters contained in the Bill, in any other Manner *Et per Curiam* clearly, where there are *Bona notabilia* in both Provinces, there must be several Administrations, so is 33 *H* 6 and Administration granted in one Province is void as to the Goods in another; because there are distinct supreme Jurisdictions, and they held the Plea good, as to those Goods. And that the Appeal, if brought within fifteen Days, suspended the former Sentences, and they were clearly of Opinion, that the Conclusion extended to make it a Plea to the whole Bill, though the Matter of the Plea was special; and therefore, that as to what was not contained in the Plea, the Defendants ought to answer; and so it was awarded. *Hard* 216

Appeal, it's Effect

What to be deemed *Bona notabilia, &c.* Vide *Orp Leg.* 69, 71, *&c.* 4 *Inst* 74. *Dy* 58, 305. *Perkins* 489. *Ro. Ab* 909 4 *Leon.* 211 1 *Sid.* 179. *Cro. Eliz* 718, 719. 5 *Co.* 29, 30. 8 *Co.* 135. *a.* 3 *Rep. Chan* 71. 1 *Pe. Will.* 43.

3. *Where Cuftom or Prefcription.*

Certain Lordfhips or Seigniories have, by Prefcription, the Probate of Teftaments within their peculiar Limits. *Doct. & Stud Lib 2. cap.* 28.

4 *Whether it may be, and wherefore, and how delayed.*

1. Whilft an Executorfhip is under Litigation the Ordinary cannot commit Adminiftration. *Orph Leg.* 64.

2 *Mich.* 7 *Geo* 2 *Banco Regis. Anonymus.* Mr *Strange* moved for a *Mandamus* to be directed to the Judge of the Ecclefiaftical Court, requiring him to grant Adminiftration to the Refiduary Legatee, the Executor having renounced, the Will, he faid, was of one Mr *Kinafton*, who left two Sons, one of which he had made Refiduary Legatee, and the Judge of the Ecclefiaftical Court has refufed granting Adminiftration, till he has had a Return made to a Commiffion of Appraifement, which he has iffued forth: In the Cafe of Lord *Londonderry's* Will. *Hill* 3 of the prefent Reign, the Ecclefiaftical Court refufed to grant Probate, till fuch Commiffion returned, and there the Court ruled fuch Commiffion to be illegal, and granted the *Mandamus fans* Rule to fhew Caufe, he faid, he remembered lately, before the Court of Delegates, the Civilians on all Hands agreed, that the

1   Courfe

Course of their Courts is constantly to grant Administration to the Residuary Legatee, where the Executors renounce, and he submitted it, that the *Mandamus* was equally reasonable in the present Case. But the Court thought that the present Case much differed from that cited, in the Case cited the Party had a Right by the Common Law, to have the Probate, and therefore it was proper for the Court to grant their *Mandamus*, that the Common Law Right should be executed: But in the present Case, at most, has only a Right to Administration, by the Rules of the Ecclesiastical Court, and therefore it was not proper that this Court should interfere, by granting a *Mandamus*, however a Rule was made to shew Cause; and Dr. *Straughan*, coming now to shew Cause, said, that the granting Commissions of Appraisement, in these Cases, is agreable to the Course of the Ecclesiastical Courts, but as soon as the Commission was returned, Administration with the Will annexed would be undoubtedly granted. The Commission, he said, in the present Case, was a Commission of Inspection, as well as Appraisement, in order to inspect the Papers of the Deceased, and likewise that the Personal Estate may be appraised and inventoried. My Lord Chief Justice said, in these Cases of Administration, the Court would not interfere by granting their *Mandamus*, but where the Party applying for Administration is intitled to it by some Act of Parliament, or where the Ecclesiastical Judge is unreasonably dilatory in his Proceedings; which his

Lordship did not think was any Ways the present Case, and accordingly the Rule was discharged *Mich* 7 *Geo* 2. *Banco Regis*, The Earl of *Suffolk*'s Case.

3 This was upon a Rule to shew Cause, why a *Mandamus* should not be directed to Dr. *Betsworth*, Judge of the Prerogative Court, requiring him to grant Administration of the Goods of the late Earl of *Suffolk*, to the present Earl, the Countess Dowager having renounced, Dr *Henchman* said, the State of the Fact was, That 17 *Oct.* last, being soon after the Death of the late Earl, a *Caveat* was entered by his Creditors, on the second of *November* last the Countess Dowager executed a Deed, thereby renouncing all Right and Title to the Administration. Her Proctor produced this Renunciation before the Officer, and he admitted it, whereupon the Creditors withdrew their *Caveat*. On the 13 *Novemb* Complaint was made to Dr *Betsworth*, that the Renunciation ought to have been on Oath ; and that the *Caveat* therefore was withdrawn upon Surprize Whereupon the Doctor ordered, that the Countess either exhibit an Inventory, or declare upon Oath, that she had not intermeddled with the Effects, before the Renunciation should be admitted, and that when she had so done, and not before, Administration should be granted to the now Earl Upon this State of the Case the Doctor submitted it, that the Proceedings below, were very regular, and therefore the Rule ought to be discharged To which my Lord Chief Justice said, he did agree that the Ecclesiastical Judge had a Power to object

ject to the Security which any Person shall offer who prays Administration, and therefore his Lordship said, a *Caveat* was very proper for that Purpose, however he said further, he did not know, in the present Case, the Judge of the Ecclesiastical Court had any Method of compelling the Countess Dowager to deliver in such an Inventory, or to make such an Oath, and therefore his Lordship said it was, that he could not think that the Administration could be delayed to be granted till that Time, for which Reason his Lordship declared, he thought the *Mandamus* ought to go. The rest of the Judges concurring with his Lordship, Rule was *per tout le Cure* for the *Mandamus* to go. *Page* Just said, in Case where there is a Will, he agreed that a Renunciation of the Executor is necessary, because he hath something in him before Probate, but the Widow or next Kin have nothing in them before Letters of Administration granted, and therefore in such Case he could not think a Renunciation was reasonable *Probyn* Just (now Chief Baron) said, that Dr. *Betsworth* himself has ordered, that in Case the Countess renounces, the Administration shall be granted to the present Earl, therefore he said, now the *Mandamus* is proper to direct that the Administration shall be granted to the present Earl by Name; otherwise it might properly have been excepted to the *Mandamus*, that it ought to have been general *Lee* Just (now Lord Ch. Just) said, that he thought it very proper that Dr *Betsworth* should make a Return to this Writ, accordingly the Rule was made absolute.

H 2   5. *Whe-*

5. Whether Administration be good, void, or only voidable

1. Administration granted by the Archbishop, or the Guardian of the Spiritualties *sede Vacante*, tho' there are not *Bona notabilia*, is only voidable, and if the inferior Ordinary grant Administration before the former by the Archbishop, *&c* are revoked, such second Administration is void; for to allow of such second Administration, before the former revoked, would breed Confusion, nay, though the former Administration is revoked, yet is not the second made better, *Quia quod in initio non valet, tractu Temporis non convalescit.* 8 Co. 135.

2 As the Ordinary cannot himself give the Intestate's Goods, neither release Debts due thereto, *&c.* so it is he cannot give express Authority to another so to do. 8 Co. 135. *For this would be to allow the Ordinary by himself or his Agent, to do a tortious Act, whereas all Wrong and Injury is odious in Law.*

3. It was adjudged between *Vere* and *Jeffeses*, if the Metropolitan grant Administration where the Intestate hath not *Bona notabilia* in divers Dioceses, this is voidable but not void; but it was held clearly, that if the Bishop of a Diocese grant Administration which belongeth to the Metropolitan, it is absolutely void. *Mo* 145. *pl.* 228.

4 Metropolitan, upon Suppofal of *Bona notabilia*, where in Reality there is none, grants Letters of Administration; yet such Admi-

Adminiſtration is not void, but voidable only, becauſe he hath Juriſdiction over all the Dioceſes in his Province, but if the Ordinary of an *Inferior* Dioceſe commit Adminiſtration, where are *Bona notabilia*, becauſe he hath no Juriſdiction, in ſuch Caſe, it is abſolutely null and void. *5 Co* 29 *b.* *Cro Eliz* ſays Adminiſtration is abſolutely void in both Caſes; *tamen Quere, for I conceive the Law to be with Lord* Coke *and Serjeant* Moore.

6 *Adminiſtration Bonds.*

1 *Muſt be as the Statute directs.*

1. In the Prerogative Court, Sir *John Bennet*, the Judge, according to the Cuſtom, had taken Bond of one *Slawney*, on granting Adminiſtration, on the Conditions uſual there, one whereof is, That the Adminiſtrator ſhall diſpoſe the Surpluſage of the Goods, after the Debts and Legacies paid, according to the Direction of that Court, whereupon the Inteſtate having left a Wife, to whom Adminiſtration was committed, this Judge now found a Surpluſage in her Hands, and ſentenced ſhe ſhould give certain Portions to certain of the Kindred of her Husband, being not his Children, whereupon ſhe prayed a Prohibition, and the Court was clear of Opinion, That whereas the Statute 21 *H.* 8 appoints the Adminiſtration to be granted, *&c* and that the Ordinary ſhall take Sureties for the Adminiſtration of the Goods of the dead, that

H 3 he

he may not impose any other or further Condition upon the Bond, and though he will pretend that the true Administration mentioned in the Statute is to be extended, as well to the Disposition of the Surplusages, as to Debts and Legacies, yet that is not under their Judgment, for they must take their Bonds according to the Law, and when it is sued, the Meaning and Exposition of the Statute, and the Obligation and Condition are to be judged by the Courts of Common Law. And if a Man observe well the Statute, he shall perceive that by preferring the Wife and Children to the Administration, the Statute imitates the Mind of the Intestate to prefer them, that it is likely he would have preferred, if he had made a Will, which must be by giving the Profit of the Estate to them, and not Labour and Dolour, in suing and being sued, to bring in and defend the Estate, and then, after all, to give this vast Power to the Ordinary to give the Surplusage where he will. To which Opinion and Reason the rest of the Judges did incline, but yet the Cause, with the Consent of Sir *John Bennet* himself, was referred to the Order of Serjeant *Harris* and *Hutton*, who were of Counsel for the Prohibition. *Hub* 83. *vide* 250. also *Thorpe's Readings* in *Gray's Inn*, in *August Anno* 1641. *sur le Statute* 31 *E* 3. *vide Pcl* 527

7 *To whom Administration to be granted, and with what Caution*

It is provided by the Statute 31. *E*.3 That when one dies Intestate, the Ordinary shall

shall make Deputies of the next of Kin, and trueft Friend to the Inteſtate, to Adminiſter his Goods and Effects, who ſhall bring Actions, *&c* and his Refuſal thus to grant Adminiſtration, is a Contempt to the King, and Injury to the Party, ſo that he is not at Liberty to grant Adminiſtration at his Will and Pleaſure, and to whom he pleaſes, for he is but, *as I take it, a Miniſterial Officer of the Law, created thereby,* quo d hoc, *and appointed to execute the ſame* ſub modo *the directions thereby given him* 9 Co. 37, *&c.*

2. By the Statute 21 *H.* 8 *cap* 5 Biſhops are impowered to grant Adminiſtration to the Wife, or next of Blood to the Inteſtate, and by the ſame Statute where divers demand Adminiſtration, being of equal Degree, there indeed the Ordinary hath his Election to accept any one or more of them ſo equally intitled 9 *Co.* 37, *&c But I conceive he may not, under any Notion or Pretence of his own, by Colour of the Words, Trueſt friend of the Inteſtate, mentioned in the Statute, wave the next of Kin in Favour of any other, for theſe Words being general and uncertain, and the next of Kin certain, who is the trueſt Friend, muſt be by Conſtruction on the Statute, and what was the Meaning of the Makers of the Statute, and that is not a Matter within their Province to determine, the Conſtruction of Acts of Parliament, tho' concerning Eccleſiaſtical Matters, nay, Eccleſiaſtical Perſons and their Juriſdiction itſelf, belonging to Temporal Authority to ſettle, and not to theſe Leſſer and Subordinate Judges.*

H 4 3. If

3. If an Administration be granted to a Cousin of the half Blood, and hereupon a Suit is by another, who pretends himself a Cousin of the intire Blood, where his Father was a Bastard by our Law, and an Appeal is to the Audience, and there they intend to repeal the first Administration, and to grant it to the Son of the Bastard according to the Ecclesiastical Law, a Prohibition lies, because the Statute is to be interpreted according to our Law *Hil* 22 *Ja Banco Regis,* Prohibition granted. *R. Abr.* Prohibition 303 *Case* 28

4 If an Administration be granted to the next of Blood, and thereupon an Appeal is sued to the Delegates, and there they intend to revoke the Sentence, and to grant it to another, not so near of Blood by our Law, but is by the Ecclesiastical Law, a Prohibition lies, because it being ordained by Statute ought to be interpreted according to our Law, *Mich.* 21 *Jac B R Wingate* and *Fitch,* and a Prohibition, because Administration was granted to a Brother of the Half Blood, and on Appeal to the Delegates they were inclined to repeal it, and to grant it to the Brother of the Whole Blood, and the Prohibition was granted to try their Law upon it, by our Law. *Ro. Abr* Prohibition 303 *Case* 27

5 *Carolus,* Duke of *Suffolk,* had Issue a Son by one Venter, and a Daughter by another, and devised Goods to the Son and died, and after the Son died Intestate without Wife or Issue, and the Mother of the Son, who was of the second Venter (for the

the Daughter was of the first Venter) adminiftred by the Statute 21 *H* 8. which is,
that Adminiftration fhall be committed to
the next of Kin of the Inteftate ; and upon
Grand Argument in the Spiritual Court,
*tam per Legis peritos Regni, quam peritos
Legis Civilis*, the Adminiftration was revoked, *& fic Vide*, That Adminiftration might
be revoked, *& fic fuit fimiliter in Cafu inter
Brown* and *Shelton, de bonis Willi Rawlins
Clerici*, which was committed to Sir *Humphry
Brown*, who had married the Sifter of *Rawlins*, and after came to *W. Shelton* and *J.
Shelton*, the Sons of Sir *Humphry's* Lady by
a former Husband, and reverfed the firft
Adminiftration, and obtained Adminiftration to be granted to them. *Quod nota, & in
Cafu fupra*, the faid Duke had Iffue *Frances*, by the *French* Queen, and after the
Death of that Queen, he married Lord *Wil-
loughby's* Daughter, and had Iffue by her
Henry, and died, and then *Henry* died,
without either Wife, or Iffue, and his Mother Adminiftred, and after the faid *Frances*,
Lady to the Marquis of *Dorfet*, fued and
reverfed the Adminiftration, and obtained
Adminiftration to be granted to herfelf;
though fhe was but Sifter of the half Blood
to the faid *Henry*; for that fhe is the next
of Kin to the faid *Henry*, he having no
Children; for the Mother is not next of
Kin to her own Son in refpect to this Point,
as the Law then ftood ; for it ought to de-
fcend, and not afcend by the Law of *England*, or by the Civil Law, and the Children
are *de fanguine Patris & Matris, fed pater*

&

& *mater non funt de fanguine puerorum*, and by *Ifidore, Pater & Mater, & puer funt una Caro*, and therefore no Degree is between them, otherwise it is between Brother and Sifter, and the half Blood is no Impediment as to Goods. *Bro. Abr* Administrator *C* 47 and *Vide Cafum De Propinquioribus Heredibus de fanguine puerorum* 30 *E* 3. *Lib Aff p* 47. *Fitz Devife* 14. *plus de Admi nifiratoribus,* Title *Adminifiration* in *Fitzher bert & in ftatut.* Tit *Adminifirators.*

6. *In Canc.* 1. *May* 1740. *Havers* and *Havers.*

The Cafe was, one *Matthew Havers* died, having firft made his laft Will and Tefta- ment, and thereby bequeathed to *Anne* his Wife, the Refidue of his perfonal Eftate making his faid Wife his Executrix. Some- time after the Wife died, leaving behind her her Infant Daughter and only child of that Marriage, hereupon the Grandmother of the Infant, as her next of Kin, was ap pointed her Guardian, and the Surrogate granted Adminiftration *durante minoritate* the Infant to the Grandmother, who was but in very neceffitous Circumftances· *Anne,* the Infant, was intitled to a Perfonal Eftate of 600 *l.* Value, befides the Arrears or Rent of a real Eftate. The Grandmo- ther found Security, who entered into an Adminiftration Bond in the Penalty of 200 *l* conditioned for duly Adminiftering the Eftate of her Inteftate Sometime after this Adminiftration was compleated, fhe found Means to give a further Security of 600 *l.* to the fame Purpofe, and fometime after

ter this, she also took out Letters of Administration *de bonis non* of the Father, and having these several Administrations committed to her, she brought several Actions at Law, in order to get in what was owing to the Estate of the Father and Mother; whereupon a Bill was brought by the *Prochein amy* of the Infant, and several of the Defendants in the Actions at Law, against the Grandmother, praying an Injunction to stay her Proceedings on those Actions, and that he might be compelled to bring into Court for safe Custody all Money of the Infant's, which she had got into her Hands. To this Bill was an Affidavit annexed of the Truth of the Allegation. The Defendant put in her Answer, and the Attorney General now moved for a Receiver of the Infant's Real and Personal Estate, and shewed Cause why the Injunction should not be dissolved. Lord Chancellor said, That he neither liked the Manner of the Bill, nor the Defence which had been made against it. 'Tis an odd thing for Debtors to make themselves Plaintiffs in a Cause under Pretence of taking Care of the Estate, and to pray an Injunction to stay the Proceedings in Actions commenced against themselves, nor did he like the Defence which had been made to this Bill, That a Woman, who was under necessitous Circumstances, should insist upon keeping the Possession of an Infant's Estate. She appears to be very poor, and on that Account, was very unfit to have been trusted by the Ecclesiastical Court with the Administration during the Minority of the Infant, it is therefore incumbent on this Court

to

to take Care of the Infant's Intereſt. It has
been ſaid, that the preſent Bill is not proper; becauſe the Eccleſiaſtical Court has the
ſole Right of determining concerning the
Fitneſs, to whom Adminiſtration is to be
granted; but it by no Means follows from
thence, that the Nature of the preſent Bill
is not a proper one for this Court to relieve in; and where it ſees Reaſon to think
that there will be a Miſapplication of the
Effects of the Inteſtate, and an Abuſe and
Waſting, to the Prejudice of an Infant, by
a limited Adminiſtrator who is only a Truſtee
for the Infant; it is incumbent on this Court
to take Care that the Infant be not prejudiced, and in ſuch Caſe, if they ſee the
Exerciſe of a Juriſdiction by the Surrogate
to the Infant's Prejudice, this Court will interfere. The Adminiſtration during the
Minority of the Infant, in the preſent Caſe,
his Lordſhip ſaid, had been granted in the
moſt careleſs, ſlovenly, and ſcandalous Manner that he ever ſaw, this is an Adminiſtration which the Grandmother had not any
Right to, and that was a Circumſtance,
which his Lordſhip ſaid he thought was of
conſiderable Weight in the preſent Caſe;
it was therefore incumbent upon the Surrogate to have taken Care, that this Adminiſtration ſhould have been granted to a re-
ſponſible Perſon; at the Time of granting
this Adminiſtration Security is only taken in
the Sum of 200*l* and under this Adminiſtration, the Grandmother was in Hopes of
poſſeſſing herſelf of the whole Eſtate of the
Infant; and as to what is ſaid of her being
Adminiſtratrix *de bonis non* to the Father,
and

nd under that Pretence juſtifying the Actions ſhe has brought, in order to get in the
Eſtate of the Father, his Lordſhip ſaid, the
obtaining that Adminiſtration was only an
After-thought, in order to ſubſtantiate the
Proceedings in thoſe Actions. The Infant
is intitled to a Perſonal Eſtate of the Value
of 600 *l*. beſides the Arrears of Rent of a
Real Eſtate; and yet ſo little Care has been
taken of her Intereſt, as to grant Adminiſtration, during her Minority, to an Alms-
Woman, with the Security only of 200 *l*.
This Negligence of taking ſo ſmall a Security
has been endeavoured however to be ſup-
plyed by taking of another Bond in a larger
Sum; but by the taking of the firſt Bond,
and the granting Adminiſtration upon it,
the Surrogate had done his Office; and
therefore his Lordſhip ſaid, he did not ſee
what Authority he had to take this ſecond
Security, for theſe Reaſons his Lordſhip
ſaid, he would direct that a Receiver ſhould
be appointed, both of the Real and Perſonal
Eſtate of the Infant; his Lordſhip ſaid, he
would direct further, that the Maſter ſhould
ſee what Securities were proper to be called
in, and that the Receiver ſhould put ſuch
Securities in Suit, and ſaid, he would direct
further, that the Receiver ſhould carry on,
in the Name of the Adminiſtratrix, the Suits
which are already begun, and ſhould commence any other Suits in her Name, indem-
nifying her, and that Coſts ſhould be taxed
the Adminiſtratrix as far as ſhe has proceeded
in theſe Suits However, his Lordſhip ſaid,
That the Cauſe for the continuance of the
Injunction ſhould be diſallowed, and ordered
accord-

* accordingly. *Vide etiam* Case *Devals* a[n]
Peacock in *Conc* 8. of the same Month wh[ere]
the present Case to like effect.

7. *Per Holt* Ch. J In the Vacation Tim[e]
one may resort to the Chancery, and upo[n]
a Suggestion, That the Spiritual Court h[a]
proceeded to grant Administration to [a]
wrong Person, may have a Prohibition ou[t]
of that Court returnable *B. R* or *C B* [in]
Peere Will. 42. *Vide* 476.

3. *Administrator.*

1. *Who, and what, he is.*

1. A Dministrator is he who hath the Good[s]
of one dying Intestate committed t[o]
him by the Ordinary, and is accountable fo[r]
the same; and for and against him Actio[ns]
lie, as for and against an Executor; and he [is]
liable to the Value of the Assets come i[n]
his Hands, but not further, unless in Cas[e]
of false Plea, and Devastation. Administratrix is she, who hath such Goods committe[d]
to her as aforesaid

Selden p 29.

2 Letters *ad Colligendum Bona Defun[ti]
ad Usum Episcopi* is not Administration
Bro. Abr Administrator 49. *So he to who[m]
granted, no Administrator*

2. *General to.*

Granting Administration was Originally
Temporal, and came to Church-Men by the
Indulgence of Princes, &c. 1 *Ven* 307. *Da[v]
&c.* 3. *Wen[s]*

3 *When the Goods of the Intestate are said to be in the Administrator.*

1 After the Ordinary hath granted Administration, the Goods are in the Administrator, and the Ordinary hath nothing more to do therewith. *Cro. Car.* 29, 202. *Jo* 228. *Hob* 83, 191. *Mo* 864.

2 By the Statute 31 *E.* 3. Administrators have as absolute a Property as Executors, They shall recover Debts, shall bring Actions, of Debt, Covenant, Case, and all other Actions as Executors may; they shall Answer to Actions in the same Manner as Executors, and shall be charged by the Name of Administrator. 9 *Co.* 37, *&c.*

4 *He is not compellable in the Spiritual Court to distribute, or account.*

1. Tho' Granting Administration is in the Ecclesiastical Court, yet Distribution does more properly belong to Chancery. *Pre Ch* 112. 1 *Lev* 233.

2. Distributions are, according to the Statute of Distributions of Intestates Estates, made in Chancery as well as in the Ecclesiastical Courts, 2 *Rep. Chan.* 373. and the same *Rep fo.* 371, *&c.* See the Statute of Distributions explained

3. Upon long and solemn Arguments and Hearing the Civilians at large, it was resolved that the Ecclesiastical Court could not oblige an Administrator to distribute, and that

that Bonds or Obligations taken for such Purposes were void *per tout le Cur.* 1 *Lev.* 233.

4. *Wood* died Inteftate, and the Ordinary committed Adminiftration, &c. and took a Bond from the Adminiftratrix to account, and to diftribute, &c. the Brethren of the Inteftate fued the Adminiftratrix, being the Inteftate's Widow, for an Account and Diftribution, the Inteftate dying without Iffue. Prohibition granted. *Palm* 527. *Vide Hob.* 83.

5. This Bill is againft an Adminiftrator and others to have Diftribution of the Inteftate's Eftate according to the late Statute of Diftributions, which Statute the Defendant pleaded, and that by the Statute the Ordinary is made Judge, and is appointed to take Security; and therefore the Plaintiff ought to fue there. The Lord Chancellor over-ruled the Plea, and ordered the Defendants fhould anfwer. 2 *Ch. Ca.* 95. 2 *Ven.* 362.

6. By Lord Ch. Juft. If the Spiritual Court, fince the Statute of Diftributions, fhall attempt a Diftribution contrary to the Rules of the Common Law, we will Prohibit them; for by the Statute, they are reftrained to the Rules allowed amongft us. 1 *P. Will* 49.

7. The Spiritual Court cannot compel Diftributions, becaufe they cannot enforce the Execution of a Truft. 1 *P. Will.* 549.

3. In what Order he is to pay Debts.

1 If Executors, or Administrators, or the Ordinary, pay Simple-Contract Debts before Specialties, they are chargeable *de bonis propris. Bro. Ab. Administrator. Case 50, 51, 52. Nelson* 336, 397. 1 *Ch. Cas* 249. *Gilb.* 96, 97.

2. Debts are to be paid before Legacies. *Nelson* 381. *Pre. Ch.* 521. 1 *Ch. Cas.* 248, 257, 275. *Dr. and Stud. lib.* 2. *c.* 10.

3. In Equity all Debts are equal. *Pre. Ch.* 181, 190.

4. If a Man gives a Note on borrowing Money to make a Mortgage, it is to be accordingly preferred. *Pre. Ch.* 190.

5. Debts are not to be paid, pending Suit in Chancery. 2 *Ch. Cas.* 200, 201. *Pre. Ch.* 188, 189.

4. *Distribution.*

1. How to be made.

1. *Must be according to the Rules of the Common Law.*

1. **P**Rohibition upon a Suit in the Spiritual Court to compel an Administrator to distribute, and on long and solemn Argument, and Hearing all the Civilians could say, it was determined the Ecclesiastical Court might not compel him to distribute; and further that the Bond taken for

that Purpose, was void, *per tot Curiam.* 1 *Lev.* 233.

2 By Lord Ch. Juft. If the Spiritual Court, fince the Statute *Ch.* 2. of Diftribution, fhall attempt a Diftribution, contrary to the Rule of the Common Law, we will prohibit them; for by the Statute they are reftrained to the Rules allowed amongft us. 1 *P. Will.* 49.

5. *Accounts.*

1. *Fraud in paffing.*

1. *To be relieved in Equity.*

THE Widow in the Spiritual Court fet up a Procurator for her Children, the Infants, and got her Accounts paffed there, and each Child's Proportion afcertained, and Diftribution decreed, and on giving new Security, got the old Security difcharged; the Court, without Regard had to the Proceedings of the Spiritual Court, decreed an Account of the whole Eftate. 2 *Vern.* 47. *Vide ante* Cafe *Havers* and *Havers*, and alfo where cognizable in Equity, *&c.*

6. *Where Matter of Adminiftration is to be tried.*

DOddet idge Juft. Courts Chriftian have Cognifance of a Legacy, and therefore may well try Fully adminiftered *per Teftes*, they have the Cognizance of the Legacy; and therefore of the Plea concerning
plem-

pleinment Adm. 3 *Bulst.* 319. *Pal.* 416, 422. *Lat.* 67.

7. *Appeals in.*

1. *Their Effects.*

PER *Cur.* In Cases of Administration where the Appeal is brought in 15 Days, it suspends the former Sentence. *Hard.* 216. *Vide Appeals, and also the several Courts Appeals from, &c.*

IV. *Matter of Tithes.*

1. *General.*

1. TITHES, a Lay Fee Stat. 32 *H* 8. *Fitzh. N. Br.* 49. 20 *H.* 6. 11. 22 *H.* 6. 23. *Cro. Car.* 201.

2. *Fitzherbert* in his *Natura Brevium fo.* 50. holdeth, that before Stat. 18 *E.* 3. *c.* 7. Right of Tithes were determinable in the Temporal Courts at the Election of the Party. 5 *Co De Ju. R. Eccl.* 16. *a.*

3 Tithes are more collateral to Lands than any Warren which the Owner of the Land hath in the Land; for by Feoffment of the Land, without a Saving of the Warren, the Warren is extinct, as it is held 5 *H.* 6. 56. But if a Prior who hath a Parsonage impropriate infeoff one of Part of the Glebe, yet he shall have Tithes against his own Feoffment, as is held in 42 *E.* 3. 13. *a* and it is like to a Leet, and

yet if the Lord of a Leet purchase Lands within it, his Leet is not suspended ; but if he make a Feoffment of his Land, his Leet in it is extinct, as is holden 7 *E.* 2. *Tit. Avowry* 211. and 8 *E.* 2. *ibid* 212. But he hath an Inheritance, by the Common Law, in the Leet, which is descendible, and which he might grant over to whom he pleased. 11 *Co.* 13. *b.* 14. *a.*

4. *In Cases of Tithes.* 4 *Inst.* 339.

2. *The Sorts.*

TITHES are of three Sorts, Predial, Personal, and Mixt, Predial are such as come of the Ground only, as Corn, Hay, Fruits of Trees, &c. Personal are such as come by the Labour, and Industry of Man, as Buying and Selling, Gain of Merchandize, and Handicraft Labours, and such as work for Hire, as Carpenters, Masons, &c. Mixt, as of Calves, Lambs, Pigs, &c. which increase, partly of the Ground they are fed upon, and partly of the Keeping, Diligence, and Industry of the Owner. *Vide Terms de l' Ley, sub Tit. Dismes.* 2 *Inst.* 649. 1 *Roll.* 653.

3. *What, how, and to whom due.*

1. TITHE naturally is but the Tenth of the Revenue of the Ground, and not of Man's Labour, where it may be divided, as in Grass, tho' not in Corn *Hob.* 250.   2. Tithe

2. Tithe is an Ecclesiastical Inheritance, collateral to an Estate of Land, and of its own Nature due only to Ecclesiasticks by the Ecclesiastical Law. 11 *Co.* 13. *b.*

3. Tithes are due by the Law of God, *ex Debito*, into whose soever Hands the Land come, unless in the Hands of the Parson. *Dy.* 43. *a.* Q.

4 Before the Council of *Lateran* there were no Parishes, nor Parish Priests to claim Tithes (tho' it is true they are Things of common Right, and do of Right, belong to the Church) but a Man might give them to what Spiritual Person he pleased, yet he must give them to the Church. And now, since Parishes are erected, they are due to the Parson, so that what comes in Discharge of Tithes must be considered as a Plea in Bar against common Right; and if you will discharge a just Demand, you must shew the Court of your Discharge, &c. *Hob.* 296. *Poph.* 156.

4. *What great and what small.*

1. BRidgman, *Minutæ Decimæ* do not include Tithes of Lands, but only of Gardens, and Hemp and Hops, &c. *Palm.* 222.

2 Saffron is small Tithes, for it is a Flower. 38 *Eliz.* The Dean of *Norwich* was Parson, and had great Tithes, and the Vicar had the small Tithes, and arable Lands were converted to Saffron Ground, and the Vicar had the Tithes. *Palm.* 222.

　　3. Tithe

3. Tithe-Lambs and Wool included within small Tithes. *Poph.* 144. *Palm.* 220. Saffron, small Tithes. *Palm.* 220. Garlick, Wool, Pot-herbs, *Ova, Lacticinia, Casia & Agni,* Hemp, Flax, *&c.* are small Tithes; so that it is the Nature of the Thing, and not the Value, which makes Tithes great or small. *Palm.* 220. Wood is *Minuta Decimæ.* Cro. Car.

5. *Who capable of.*

1. OF common Right all Tithes are due to the Parson, and the Vicarage is derived out of the Parsonage, and no Tithes, *de Jure,* belong to the Vicar, but only upon Endowment or Prescription, which ought to be shewed *ex parte* the Vicar, and the Court may not intend it, for the Vicarage is a Diminution and impairing to the Parsonage, whereof the Court may not take Notice *sans* shewing. *Telv.* 86, 87.

2. A Layman could not, at Common Law, have an Inheritance in Tithes, and Tithes would not pass by such Words as would pass Temporal Possessions; and therefore *Mich.* 31 *&* 32 *Eliz* in a Prohibition between *John Perkins* and *Thomas Hynde,* Parson of *Babington* in *Somersetshire,* the Case was, That the said Parson by Deed indented leased his Glebe *cum proficuis & Commoditatibus eidem spectantibus* for ninety-five Years, rendring Rent *pro omnibus exactionibus & demandis quibuscunque dictæ Rectoriæ pro clauso prædicto spectan',* and the Question

ſtion was, if the Leſſee ſhould have the ſaid
Cloſe diſcharged of Tithes, during the
Time; and it was reſolved *per totam Curiam*,
That the Tithes did not paſs by ſuch general
Words; and as they are Tithes not ſevered
they are meerly, and but, Eccleſiaſtical,
for Subſtraction whereof there is no Remedy
at Common Law. 11 *Co.* 14. *a.*

3. If a Parſon purchaſe Lands within his
Rectory, and leaſe the Rectory, the Leſſee
ſhall have Tithes of theſe Lands purchaſed;
and with this agrees 30 *H.* 8. *Dy.* 43.
Vide 32 *H.* 8. *Bro.* Tit. *Diſmes.* 11 *Co.*
14 *a.*

6. *Who, and how, diſcharged from.*

1. T Ithes before the Severance are meerly
Eccleſiaſtical, and ſo collateral to
the Eſtate of the Land, that no Unity may
extinguiſh or ſuſpend them; but notwithſtanding any Unity, they remain *in Eſſe*,
where the Words of the Act are to be
conſidered, that as well the King, his Heirs
and Succeſſors, as all and every ſuch Perſon
and Perſons, their Heirs and Aſſigns, which
have, or hereafter ſhall have any Monaſteries, Parſonages appropriate, *&c.* Meſes,
Lands, *&c.* diſcharged and acquitted of
Payment of Tithes, as freely, and in as
large and ample Manner, as the ſaid late
Abbots, Priors, *&c.* had held, *&c.* the ſame,
at the Days of their Diſſolution, and upon
theſe Words, for as much as the Unity doth
not diſcharge or ſuſpend the Tithes, but
that they were *in Eſſe* at the Time of the

Diffolution, and forafmuch as these Words, *difcharged* and *acquitted*, imply actual Immunity and Freedom, and that the King and his Patentees fhould not have them difcharged and acquitted, but *fub modo*, that is to fay, in as large and ample Manner, *&c.* as the faid late Abbots, *&c.* and the faid Abbots might not hold the faid Lands, in Cafe of Unity, difcharged but charged with the Payment of Tithes; therefore on the Queftion, whether the faid Act fhould extend to the Cafe of perpetual Unity, and upon great Confideration it was refolved and adjudged, that perpetual Unity, Time whereof, *&c* till the Diffolution fhall be *prima facie* a Difcharge of the Land from the Payment of Tithes, by Force of the faid Branch of 31 *H.* 8. 11 *Co.* 14. *b.*

2. Unity within the Act 31 *H.* 8. ought to have four Qualities 1ft, *Talis Unitas,* that is, it ought to be juft, rightful, and not tortious. 2dly, It ought to be *æqualis, fc.* Fee in one or other; for if that Abbots, Priors, *&c.* have held by Leafe, Time whereof, *&c.* it is no Unity within the Statute. 3dly, It ought to be perpetual, Time whereof, *&c.* 4thly, It ought to be *libera,* free from the Payment of any Tithes, for if their Farmers at Will, for Years, *&c.* have paid any Tithes to them, the perpetual Unity will not ferve. 11 *Co.* 14.

3. It was refolved that a general Allegation of Unity at the Time of the Diffolution, *&c. fans Averment,* that it was perpetual, was not good. 11 *Co.* 14 *b.*

4. If the Abbey, or Priory, was founded within Time of Memory, then he might not
prefcribe

prefcribe to be difcharged of Tithes *omnino.* 11 Co. 15. a.

5. Of common Right all Lands ought to pay Tithes. 11 *Co.* 15. *a.*

6. If the Parfon of a Church purchafe a Manor within his Parifh, now by this Purchafe and Unity of Poffeffion, the Manor which was tithable before is now become *Non decimabilis,* for as much as he cannot pay Tithes to himfelf; but if the Parfon make a Leafe of his Parfonage and Rectory to a Stranger, now the Parfon himfelf fhall pay Tithes *de fon Manor* to the Leffee of the Rectory; and if the Parfon make a Feoffment of the Manor, the Feoffee fhall pay Tithes to the Feoffor Parfon; fo that Tithes may not be extinct by any Unity of Poffeffion. *Dy.* 43. *a.*

7 Many Things are by our Law privileged from Tithes, which by the Common Law are tithable, as Timber, Oar, Coals, *&c.* without a fpecial Cuftom fubjecting them thereunto. *Ha. Hift. Law* 32.

7. Modus.

1. *What a good one.*

1. PEter Baker, Vicar of *S P.* libelled in the Spiritual Court for Tithe Lambs againft *Coaker,* and laid that Cuftom was, that all Lambs engendred, fallen and bred upon any one Tenement or Living in that Parifh, tho' they belonged to feveral Owners, had been reckoned together, as tho' but one Man's, and the Tenths, or Tithe-Lambs

Lambs of them, fo counted together, have been paid for Tithes; whereupon _Hender_ prayed a Prohibition; for that all Cuftoms againft common Right are triable at Law, which was granted; and the Court was further of Opinion that the pretended Cuftom was unreafonable and againft Law; for by this Means it might fall out that fome one might have but one Lamb, and that might be taken for Tithe, and he who had more fhall pay nothing at all. _Hob._ 329.

* 2. See Cafe _Mafon_ and _Mapleton_ in _Banco Regis_, _Mich._ 8 _Geo._ 2. Under Divifion of what not to be paid, Of Agiftment.

2. _Whether deftroyed._

1. _By Variation._

* Tho' the _Modus_ had been varied by fubfequent Compofition for fixty-fix Years, and had been once paid in Kind, yet that did not deftroy it. _Clifton_ con. _Orchard in Canc._ after _Mich. Term_ 10 _Geo._ 2. _Vide_ where to be tried _Cafe_ 1.

3. _How to be pleaded._

* _Hill._ 4 _Geo._ 2. _in Banco Regis._ _Stephenfon_ and _Hale._

This was on a Rule to fhew Caufe why a Prohibition fhould not go to the Spiritual Court in a Suit there for Tithes. Mr. _Fazakerly_ faid, the Defendant below had pleaded a _Modus_; but then he had by another

other Part of his Plea destroyed the Whole
of it, by Pleading further, that the Lands
were in the Hands of the Monastery of
and so were discharged; and he
said it had never been determined, but that
where the Plea of a *Modus* had been mispleaded,
the Ecclesiastical Court might reject the
Plea; and the Court declared that, according
to the Common Law, such Pleas were
not allowed; but said, they did not see
why they should not, in the Spiritual Courts,
as they thought they would in Chancery,
and the Exchequer; and therefore there was
no Reason to intend that this Plea was rejected
there, for Want of Form; and accordingly
the Rule was made absolute. See
the Case, *Sharpe* and *Lowther*. *Term. Trin.* *
10. of his present Majesty.

4 *Where to be tried.*

1 A Prohibition for Tithes against the
Defendant, being a Farmer of a Rectory in
Essex, on Surmise, that from Time whereof,
&c. he hath used to pay four Shillings *per
Annum* in Discharge of all Tithes, and his
Proof was, that he used to pay four Shillings
and six Pence *per Ann.* and on this Variance
a Consultation was prayed; and because it
appeared there were not any Tithes due in
Kind to the Parson, as he hath sued, but it
is a *Modus decimandi*, tho' not in such Manner
as the Plaintiff surmiseth, the Court
would not grant Consultation; for that he
had not any Cause to sue for Tithes of that
Land; and so ruled. *Cro. Eliz.* 819.

2. If

2. If a Prohibition be granted upon *Sug-* gestion, and the Parties go to Issue upon this Suggestion, and it is found against the Plaintiff in the Prohibition; yet if it appears to the Court, upon the finding of the Jury, that there is a good Discharge of Tithes upon a *Modus decimandi,* tho' the Plaintiff hath mistaken his Issue, no Consultation shall be granted; for that it appears that they had not Jurisdiction of it in the Spiritual Court. *Hob. Berrie's* Case. *Ro. Abr. Prohibition, fo.* 320. *Case* 1.

3. If Issue be joined in Prohibition, whether all the Lands ought to be discharged of Tithes, by a certain *Modus decimandi,* and the Jury find that all the Lands, *præter* certain Acres, ought to be discharged, *&c.* but not those Acres; tho' the Issue be found against the Plaintiff in the Prohibition, yet no Consultation shall be granted for any of the Lands, but for these Acres; forasmuch as it appears that there is a real Discharge, and good Composition for it *Mich.* 15 *Jac. Perry* con. *Bawtrey. Hob. Ro. Abr. Prohibition, fo.* 320. *Case* 2. Vide *Case* 3.

4. If there be a Suit in the Ecclesiastical Court concerning the Manner of Tithing, *&c.* for a Custom for the Owner to have fifty-four Sheaves of Corn, and the Parson five as Tithes, if this Custom be denied, a Prohibition lies; for they are not to try the *Modus;* because it is to charge the Inheritance. *Hob. fo.* 247. *Scot* con. *Wall.* Prohibition granted. *Ro. Abr. Prohibition, fo* 307. *Case* 20.

5. They may not try a Custom in the Ecclesiastical Court by which the Inheritance

rance is to be perpetually charged, and yet it is but, in Effect, a Denial of the Prescription. *Ro. Abr. Prohibition, fo.* 308. *Case* 20.

6. If where a Prescription is general for all the Inhabitants and a Prohibition is granted for one who is sued, if the Parson sue another upon the same Title, the first not being determined, an Attachment lies. *Mo. fo.* 599.

7. *Hill.* 9 *Geo.* 2. *Banco Regis. Anonymus.* On Rule to shew Cause why a Prohibition should not be granted to the Ecclesiastical Court, Mr. *Filmer* observed this was a Suit for Tithes of the Agistment of unprofitable Cattle, brought by the Vicar, whereto the Defendant had pleaded a *Modus* for to pay fifteen Shillings to the Impropriator in Lieu of all Tithes from those Lands, and he submitted it, that this Matter the Ecclesiastical Court might well proceed in to try, and cited to the Purpose *Taylor* and *Draken's* Case, *Pas.* 4 *Geo* 1. which was a Suit by a Vicar against the Lessee of the Rector for Tithes of Turnips; the Defendant pleaded they belonged to the Rector, and not to the Plaintiff, as Vicar; whereupon was a Rule to shew Cause why a Prohibition should not go; but on Argument the Rule was discharged; he also cited 2 *Ro Abr.* 313. 2 *Bulstr* 157. Mr. *Denison*, on the other Side, denied the Case in *Bulst.* to be Law, and insisted, that as this was a Plea of a *Modus*, the Ecclesiastical Court had no Jurisdiction, and the Court being of the same Opinion, the Rule was made absolute. *Vide post,*

post, what a good Evidence of a Custom or Prescription.

8. *Of what Tithes not to be paid.*

5. *What good Evidence of.*

❧ Vide ante, *where Custom or Prescription comes in Question, what good Evidence of.*

1. A Man shall pay Tithes but once for the Produce of the same Land in the same Year *Yelv.* 86, 87. *Vide Hob.* 250, 296. *Pop.* 156. *Palm.* 219.

2. Lands are not tithable by Law, that is, Things of the Substance of the Earth and not Annual, as Quarries of Stone, Turf, *&c.* No Tithe of Timber-Trees, because they are of Parcel of the Inheritance, nor of Lops, Tops, nor Bark, *&c.* 2 *E.* 6. No Tithe to be paid of Coals or Quarries, *&c. Fitzh. N. Br.* 53 G.

3 If one be sued in the Spiritual Court for Tithes of seasonable Wood, the Party aggrieved may suggest, either in Chancery, or in *B. R.* that he is sued *in Curia Spirituali* for Tithes of gross Trees, which are past the Age of twenty Years by the Name of *Silva Cædua, &c.* and pray a Prohibition, and have it *Lit. Bro.* 37. *Case* 193.

4. Suits were in Court Christian for Tithes of Cherry-Trees, and Aspe and Beech-Trees in *Buckinghamshire*, but a Prohibition was granted; for in this Country Timber is so scarce, that these Kinds of Woods served
for

r Timber, and Afpe ferves for Arrows,
hich are for the Defence of the Realm.
Ro Rep. 83, 355.

5. No Tithes due of Slate or Stone; for
e hath it of the Grafs or Corn, which
rows on the Surface. *Cro Eliz.* 277, 8.

6. Tithes not due of Things which come
f the Labour of a Man, but of Things
enovant, &c. *Cro. Ja.* 524.

7. Tithes fhall not be paid for Cattle fed
o be eat in the Family, neither of Cattle
eared for the Pale, or the Plough *Cro. Ca.*
37. Tithes not payable for Fifh, unlefs
y Cuftom. *Cro. Ca.* 339, 264. Tithes not
o be paid of Mines of Coals, or Stone, nor
or Wood fpent in Hedging or Fuel in the
Houfe where, &c. *Cro. Car* 526.

8. In Prohibition the Plaintiff prefcribed,
hat all Tenants and Occupiers of the Mea-
low had ufed to cut the Grafs and to ftrew
t abroad, called Tedding, and then to ga-
her it into Winrowes, and then to put it
nto Grafs-Cocks in equal Parts, without
Fraud; and then to fet out every tenth
Cock, great or fmall, to the Parfon, in full
Satisfaction as well of the firft as the latter
Making; upon Traverfe of the Cuftom it
was found for the Plaintiff, and Exception
was that the Cuftom was void, becaufe it
contained no more than every Owner ought
to do, and fo no Recompence for the fecond
Making; but the Court gave Judgment for
the Plaintiff; for Tithe naturally is but the
Tenth of the Revenue of my Ground, not
of my Labour and Induftry, where it may
be divided, as in Grafs it may, tho' not in
Corn; and in diverfe Places they left out
the

the Tenth Acre of Wood standing, and so of Grass, and so here the Jury having found this Form of Tithing to be the Custom there, it is well. *Hob.* 250.

9. For Tithes of After-mowth, that there is a Custom, in Consideration that he should make the first Tonsure in good and sufficient Hay, and set it out in Cocks sufficiently dried and ready to carry away, that he should be discharged from the Tithes of the After-mowths; and that was held a good Suggestion; because of the Expence he was at in making it perfect Hay. And upon a Surmise that he was sued for Tithe of Bees, in Consideration that he paid it of Honey and Wax, and was at the Charge of Maintenance of them in the Winter, he was discharged of the Tithes of the Bees. *Cro. Ca.* 404.

10. *Austen*, Vicar of *A.* in *Essex*, libelled in Court Christian against *Green* for Tithes of Herbage and Agistment of Cattle upon the Grounds there, after Harvest, and lays the Custom there, *quod quælibet Persona habens & possidens aliquod Pratum sive Fundum in aliquo uno Anno infra Paroch. præd. unde Fœnum eodem Anno nactum fuit sive provent. a tempore cujus, &c. usus fuit & consuevit aptis temporibus anni illius gramen super hujusmodi Pratis sive Fund. crescens, ad expensas suas proprias, metere & defalcare, & gramen sic messum postea ad similia Custagia, &c in Cumulos, vocat.* Cocks, *congerere, & quemlibet decimum Cumulum sic inde congest. a cæteris novem Cumulis, &c. ad usum Rectoris Ecclesiæ Parochial. prædict. sive ejus Firmar', & dividere & exponere, in plenam & integram*

content.

*content. folutionem, fatisfactionem & exonera-
tionem, ac nomine & loco omnium & fingularum
Decimarum quarumcunque de, in, vel fuper, ali-
quibus hujufmodi pratis five Fundis, unde Fœnum in hujufmodi Anno nactum fuit, eodem
Anno furgens, renovans, &c. quem quidem decimum Cumulum, &c. in forma, &c. congeft', &c.
omnes & finguli Rectores, &c in plenam & integram content', &c. ac nomine & loco, &c.
acceptaverunt, &c.* and alledges in Fact Performance of the Cuftom that very Year, in
which the Vicar libelled, *&c.* Upon this the
Defandant the Vicar demurred, and Judgment was for the Plaintiff, and two Points
were refolved; Firft, that a Payment of
Tithes to the Parfon is a good and fufficient
Difcharge againft the Vicar; becaufe of
common Right all Tithes are Due to the
Parfon, and the Vicarage is derived out of
the Parfonage; fo that no Tithes, *de Jure,*
belong to the Vicar, but only upon Endowment, or Prefcription, which ought to be
fhewed *ex parte* the Vicar, and the Court
might not intend it; for the Vicarage is a
Diminution and Impairing to the Parfonage,
whereof the Court may not take Notice
fans the fhewing of the Party.   2. That the
Cuftom *fupra* is good; for as the Owner of
the Ground pays Tithes of Hay; he is
therefore difcharged, of Common Right,
from Tithes for Agiftment of the fame
Lands in the fame Year; becaufe the fame
Land fhall anfwer but one Tithe for one
Year; and the Agiftment is nothing but the
Profit by the Beafts feeding there upon the
fame Land, whereof the Parfon before had
Tithes of Hay.   And Juftice *Tanfield* faid,

That it was adjudged in *Edolph's* Case in *Com Oxon* that paying Tithes of Rye or Wheat in the Sheaf, he need not after pay Tithes of the Straw of the same Land; for this Straw is nothing but Part of the Stalk, upon which the Tithe Sheaf grew according to *Fitzh Nat. Brev.* 53. G. *Yelverton pro Quer. Yel.* 86, 87

11. Tithes for Malt-Mills are only Personal; for it is not natural Increase, being only a Profit arising from an Invention of a Machine, and the Labour of a Man and Horse, and if only Personal, can only be for the Tithes of the neat Profits, deducting all Charges, and Personal Tithes can only be due by Customs, and not of Common Right. *Vide* Case *Chamberlain* and *Plimpton* in the House of Lords, 20 *Jan.* 1706.

12 Of Milch Cows no Tithes for Depasturage. *Mich.* 10 *Geo.* 2. *in Canc. Clifton* and *Orchard.*

13. *Mich* 7 *Geo.* 2. *in Banco Regis,* *Donalt* and *Lowther.*

The Defendant had libelled in the Spiritual Court for the Tithe of a Corn-Mill, as Predial Tithes; the Plaintiff set forth in his Answer, that he conceived the Tithe of a Corn-Mill to be Personal Tithe, and therefore prayed to be allowed all his necessary Charges in attending the Mill before the Tithes should be paid, and the Spiritual Judge thought fit to over-rule this Plea and Sentenced the Plaintiff to pay Tithes *sans* Deduction; whereupon Mr. *Denison* moved for a Prohibition, and cited the Case of *Chamberlaine* and *Plimpton* determined in the House

House of Lords 20 *June Anno* 1706, wherein he said it was resolved, that the Tithe of a Corn-Mill was Personal Tithe; accordingly Rule was to shew the Cause.

14. *Mich.* 8 *Geo.* 2. *Banco Regis. Mason* and *Mapleton* ✻

This was upon a Rule to shew Cause why a Prohibition should not be directed to the Ecclesiastical Court. Mr. *Wynne now Serjeant* said, that the Suit below was for Tithes of the Agistment of Pasture Lands, and on Lands which had been mowed, and the Sentence of the Judge below was, that the Defendant should pay the Plaintiff Seven Pounds on this Account; he said, he did agree that the Lands which had been mowed were possibly not subject to pay Tithes for the Agistment; but he submitted it, that it did not necessarily appear that the Sentence of the Judge below was for the Tithes of the Agistment of these Lands, but it might be for the other, at least he submitted it, that the Prohibition should only go as to the Tithes of the Agistment of the mowed Lands. My Lord Ch Just. said, that it could not be intended but that the Sentence was for the Agistment, as well of the one as the other, and that in this Case the Sentence was intire; for which Reason the Rule was made absolute, that the Prohibition should go generally. Mr *Wilbraham* came *Term. Paschæ* following, and moved in Arrest of Judgment; he said this was a Declaration in Prohibition, wherein two *Modus's* were set out in Discharge of Tithes, each of which he conceived was void. The first *Modus* was to be discharged of all Tithes of Grass in the Land in Queſtion, in Conſideration of making the Graſs into Cocks; but that he conceived was no more than the Occupier of the Land is bound to do; he ſaid, it has been doubted whether the Occupier is not bound even to make the Graſs into Hay, but that he agreed the Law did not require; but to make the Graſs into Cocks has always been underſtood the Occupier is bound to do, and if this were ſo, then the doing of it could not be in Diſcharge of all Tithes of Graſs of this Land, for it is known that there is an After-mowth and a Tithe due of that, tho' of the after Paſture a Tithe is not due, for which Purpoſe he cited *R. Abr.* 640. 2 *Inſt.* 652 *Yelv* 86. *Mo.* 910 *Hob.* 250. *R. Abr.* 644. The 2d *Modus* was to pay a Penny for every Cow, in Lieu of the Agiſtment of all Cows, and to pay a Halfpenny for every Calf, in Lieu of the Agiſtment of all Calves; but he ſaid, he conceived this *Modus* likewiſe void; for from Milch Cows no Tithes of Agiſtment is due, neither from the Agiſtment of Calves the firſt Year, and accordingly Judgment was ordered to ſtay till the Court ſhould be further moved, and now Mr. *Ager* came and moved for Judgment, and with Regard to the firſt *Modus*, he ſubmitted it to be clearly good, he ſaid it was, that in Conſideration that he, and all thoſe whoſe Eſtate he had, had Time out of Mind at their own Coſts and Charges mowed the Graſs, made it into Graſs-Cocks, and ſet out the Tenth Graſs-Cock for the Parſon, they had Time out of Mind been diſcharged from all Tithes of Agiſtment due from the Land the Year it

was

was so mown. This, he submitted, was doing more than by Law the Occupier was bound to do; and therefore was a good *Modus*; and for this Purpose he relied upon *Hob* 250 cited on the other Side. *Yelv.* 86. 2 *Cro.* 116. 2 *Lutw.* 1071. Besides he said the Conclusion of setting forth the *Modus* was, which said Tenth Cock of Hay the Parson has accepted; but that he thought there was no Occasion to rely upon. With Regard to the second *Modus*, he submitted it, that was good also; and he conceived that as the *Modus* is only pleaded to be in Discharge of the Agistment of Cattle, the Construction of that Part of it which alledges the Penny to be paid for every Cow, and a Halfpenny for every Calf, must be, that this Money was to be paid only for such Cows and Calves as were agistable Cattle, for which Purpose he cited 2 *Salk.* 662. But even supposing these *Modus's* not to be good, yet still he said the Plaintiff could not have a Consultation; for he has libelled for nothing else save the Tithes for the Agistment of Cattle after the Grass is mown, and of such Agistment no Tithes are due. The Court was of Opinion that these *Modus's* were both good, and if they were not, that yet the Plaintiff could not have a Consultation for Reasons mentioned by Mr. *Ager*; and Judgment was given accordingly.

9. *Who*

9. Who may have any, and what Remedy against a Demand of Tithes.

IF Leſſee for Years be ſued in Court Chriſtian for Tithes, he in Reverſion may have a Prohibition. *Cro. Eliz.* 55.

10. *Suits.*

1. *General.*

1. IF a Parſon ſue for not ſetting out of Tithes, according to the Statute 2 *E.* 6. and the Defendant ſays he ſet them out, which Plea is refuſed, becauſe it is not a ſufficient ſetting out, if the Parſon be not preſent, yet a Prohibition ſhall be granted, for that it is ſufficient by the Common Law, tho' the Parſon be not preſent. *Mich.* 15 *Jac. R. Abr. Prohibition* 302. *Caſe* 19. 3 *Mod.* 286. *Vide where the Eccleſiaſtical Courts refuſe ſuch Plea as would be good in the Temporal Courts, per tout.*

2. If a Right of Tithes comes in Queſtion, the Spiritual Court has Juriſdiction, if a Diſcharge, the Common Law has. *Mod.* 42. Cardinal *Poole's Caſe, Cro. Car.* 395. *Hard.* 480, 481.

3. A Vicar libelled againſt the Parſon for Tithes of the Glebe; the Parſon brought a Prohibition, and it was adjudged maintainable. *Mod* 457.

4. Suit was by the Vicar for Tithes of the Glebe Lands againſt the Leſſee of the impropriate

propriate Rector; the Defendant pleaded that Tithes were never paid of thefe Lands to the Vicar or his Predeceffors; to fhew which Plea fufficient were cited. *Lutw.* 1062. 3 *Cro* 479, 578. 2 *Ro Abr* 335. My Lord Ch Juft. agreed that if this Demand had been by the Rector, the Plea had been good, (*as Tithes are, as I conceive, due to every Rector of common Right*) but as it was by the Vicar, who can only claim by Endowment, or by Prefcription, his Lordfhip was of Opinion it was not good. *Barecroft* and *Price,* *Trin.* 8 *Geo.* 2 *B. R.*

5. If a Prohibition be granted upon a Difcharge of Tithes *fur le Stat.* 31 *H.* 8. in the Hands of an Abbot, and it be tried at Law, and the Plaintiff nonfuited, and a Confultation granted, and the Plaintiff in the Prohibition pleads the fame plea in Difcharge of the Payment of Tithes, which was alledged in the Prohibition, which the Ecclefiaftical Judge accepts and proceeds to Trial, a Prohibition lies, for the Trial at Law is final upon this Libel, and it fhall not be tried in the Ecclefiaftical Court again, it being proper for (*and having receiv'd*) a Trial at Law. *R. Abr. Prohibition, fo.* 319. O

6. By Lord Chancellor, when a Suit for Tithes is inftituted below, the Party has his Election to apply for a Prohibition, or file a Bill of this Sort; and his Lordfhip further faid, if the Party had applied for a Prohibition, it had gone in Courfe, in Order to have tried the *Modus*; and he thought it reafonable in the prefent Cafe to direct an Iffue to try the three *Modus's* in the Principal

K 4   Cafe.

Cafe. *Clifton* and *Orchard*, after *Mich.*
Term 10 *Geo.* 2. in Chancery.

2. *Where to be tried.*

1. *General.*

1. If the Farmer of the King fue in the
Exchequer againft a Parfon for retaining of
Tithes, Parcel of the Poffeffion leafed to
him by the Crown; tho' the Right of Tithes
come in Debate between them, yet the
Court fhall not be oufted of its Jurifdiction.
Ro. Abr. Prohibition, C.

2. In Trefpafs if the Right of Tithes
come in Debate between a Parfon and a
Layman, the Court fhall not be oufted of its
Jurifdiction. 29 *E* 3. 39 *b. Ro. Abr Probibition,* B. 2.

3. In Trefpafs if the Right of Tithes
come in Queftion between a Parfon and a
Layman, being Farmer of another Parfon,
the Court fhall not be oufted of Jurifdiction.
20 *H.* 6. 17. *b. Ro. Abr. Prohibition, D.*
Cafe 1.

4. If one, not a Parfon, bring Trefpafs
de fon blees taken againft another, who
claims as Tithes being a Parfon, the Court
fhall not be oufted of Jurifdiction, becaufe
they are not two Parfons; and therefore the
Plea is but a Traverfe of the Writ, *fcil.*
that it is not the Plaintiff's Corn. 38. *E.* 3. *b.*
Ro. Abr. Prohibition, X. 3.

5. If a Prior bring Trefpafs againft an
Abbot *de fes blees emports,* if the Defendant
fay that the Plaintiff is Parfon, and that the
Lands

Lands of the Defendant ought to be free of Tithes, by Compofition, and that the Action is brought for Tithes, there the Court fhall not be oufted of Jurifdiction, becaufe that the Plaintiff hath not fuppofed himfelf Parfon, nor that the Action is brought for Tithes. 38 *E* 3 8. *Ro. Abr. Prohibition,* X. 4.

6. A Bill in *Canc.* to eftablifh a *Modus* was difmifs'd as Matter proper for Common Law. 1 *Rep Chan.* 25, 27. *Note the Time, fuch Bills being frequent both before and fince. 1 think this Difmiffion was when Bifhop* Wilhams *was Chancellor.*

7. Prohibition was granted upon a Difcharge of Tithes *fur le Stat* 31 *H* 8 in the Hands of an Abbot, and on Trial at Law, the Plaintiff was nonfuited, and a Confultation was awarded, and the Plaintiff in this Court pleads the fame Plea in Difcharge of the Payment of Tithes, which was alledged in the Prohibition, which Plea the Spiritual Judge accepts and proceeds to Trial, there a Prohibition lies; for the Trial at Law is final upon this Libel, and it fhall not be tried in the Ecclefiaftical Court again, it being proper for a Trial at Law, and had been there tried and properly belonged to the Judges at Law. *Hob.* 286.

2. *Where Compofition.*

1. In Trefpafs againft a Prior of his Corn taken, the Defendant fays, that he is Parfon, *&c* and thefe were fevered for Tithes from the nine Parts and fo he took them; if

if the Plaintiff plead an ancient Privilege to be quit of Tithes, and a Composition made between the Plaintiff and the Defendant, rendring a certain Sum to the Defendant yearly, yet the Court shall not be ousted of their Jurisdiction; for that the Right of Tithes came in Question. 38 *E.* 3. 6 *b.* *Ro. Abr. Prohibition,* X. *Case* 5.

2. In Trespass against a Parson, the Defendant justifies, as of Tithes severed from the nine Parts, and the Plaintiff pleads the Grant of the Defendant of the Tithes of these Lands for one or two Years, the Court shall not be ousted of Jurisdiction. 38 *E.* 3. 6. *b.* *Ro. Abr. Prohibition,* X. *Case* 6.

3 *Lapthorne* sued for Tithe Wood in the Spiritual Court of *Gloucester,* and *Bridgeman* moved for a Prohibition, for that the Suit was for Beech, which are of great Age, *scilicet,* 80 Years of Age, at least, and also the Parson hath had a Consultation for Tithe Wood, *viz.* certain Wood in the Woods of the Lord for Time immemorial, and never had Tithe Wood; *Ergo Cooke,* Buck is a Beech, and the County of *Buckingham* hath its Name from the Beeches there, and this is good Timber in that Country; and therefore it was adjudged in Sir *Edward Carey's* Case, that Waste lies for Beech in this Country, and in the Parish where I live Tithe Wood has never been paid, but the Parson hath Wood that is called Tithe Wood, and he pays for it four Pence a Year to the Lord of whom held; and therefore it shall be intended, that it was given for a Composition for all Tithe Wood within the Parish; in as much as no Tithe hath ever been

been paid for Wood; and a Prohibition was granted 1 *Ro. Rep.* 355.

4 *Pringe*, Vicar of *Easton* in *Com Oxon.* libelled in Court Christian for small Tithes upon Composition between him and the Parson appropriate against *Childe*, who pleaded the Prescription against the Composition. *Pringe* had a Prohibition in the King's Bench against his own Suit in the Ecclesiastical Court, and upon many Arguments the Prohibition stood, *hoc Term. Pas.* 4to *Jacobi Reg.* And also it was decreed in Chancery for *Pringe*, that the Prescription was not lawful against the Composition, and an Injunction was awarded for the Vicar to stay the Suit of the Parson for the Tithes limited to the Vicar upon the Composition. *Mo* 780, 781. *Vide* 5 *Co. de Ju. Reg. Eccl.* 9 *a. Ha. Hist. Law.* 3 *Mo* 907, 908, *&c.*

5 It shall be tried *per Pais*, if the Suit in Court Spiritual be for Tithes or for Debt upon it, *&c.* which is a Lay Chattel, and not by the Rolls of Ecclesiastical Court, so their Proceedings are not of Record. *Bro. Abr. Trials* 12.

6 Prohibition on Issue, whether for Tithes or Debt reserved thereupon which is a Lay Chattle, it is to be tryed *per Pais*, and not by the Rolls of the Commissary, *& sic Vide* that they are not of Record. *Bro. Abr. Tit. Visne* 17.

7 *Small* sued for Tithes, and the Plaintiff suggested an Accord and Agreement, he being a Parishoner, for 40 Shillings a Year to retain his own Tithes, and did not prove it within six Months *Et per Cur.* he need not; for such Proof goes only to a *Modus Decimandi*,

mandi, and not to other Suggeftion on Leafe or Contract, and fo it is in the King's Bench. *Telv.* 102.

8. Where a Man grants Parcel of his Manor to another to be quit of Tithes by Deed, and the Parfon with the Affent of the Ordinary grants he fhall be quit for that Parifh, if he or his Affignee be after impleaded in the Spiritual Court for Tithes, they may have a Prohibition on the Deed, and if the Deed were before Memory, and fo had continued to be quit of Tithes, he fhould have a Prohibition on the Matter fhewed. *Fitz N. B.* 41. G.

9. Prohibition for Tithes. *Fitz. N. B.* 40. N. (See there the Form of the Writ.) 41 *H.*

10. Prohibition by the Plaintiff in the Spiritual Court to ftay his own Suit, for that he fuing for Tithes in the County of *Norwich*, by Virtue of a Leafe made by the Vicar of *Toftes* for three Years, the Defendant claimed to be difcharged of the Tithes by a former Leafe and Compofition by Deed; and the Court held, that the Plaintiff himfelf might have a Prohibition to ftay the Suit; for they are not to meddle with the Trial of Leafes or real Contracts, tho' they have Jurifdiction of the original Caufe, (*viz.* Tithes) for the Leafe is in the Realty, and it is not merely incidental. *Et non refert*, although the Plaintiff in the Spiritual Court brings this Prohibition to ftay his own Suit; for if this Court hath Knowledge by any Means that the Spiritual Court meddleth with Temporal Trials, they ought to grant a Prohibition. *Cro. Ja. fo.* 350, 351.

Vide

Vide 1 R 3 4. 2 *Show.* 406. *See hereafter*
Parifh Clerks, Jervis and *Auftin's* Cafe,
B. R.

3. *Where Bounds of Parifhes, &c. come in*
    Queftion.

1. If the Iffue be, whether the Place
where the Tithes are be within the Parifh
of one Parfon or another, the Court fhall
not be oufted of its Jurifdiction.   50 E. 3.
20. 20 H 6. 17. *b.*   22 E 4. 22   38 E. 3.
5 *b.* 39 E 3 23. *b.*   Rol. *Abr Prohibition*,
E. 1.

✱ The Bounds of a Parifh, whether Tithes
grew in one Parifh or another, were tri'ed
per Pais   Bro. Abr Trial, 16.

3. A Parfon fues for Tithes in the Spiritual Court, and the Defendant fays, that
the Place where is in another Parifh, a Prohibition lies. *Rol. Abr. Prohibition*, E. 3.

4. If in a Parifh there be a Chapel of
Eafe, and a Vicar of it diftinct from the
Parifh-Church, and the Vicar is indowed of
Tithes of Parifhioners who are inhabitant
within the Chapelry, and the Vicar fue one
of the Parifhioners not within the Chapelry,
and he fays he is of the Parifh, and not of
the Chapelry, a Prohibition fhall be granted;
for now the Bounds of the Chapel come in
Queftion.   *Hill.* 15 *Ja.* B. R. *enter le Vicar*
del Chapel de Bofton in Cornubia & un auter
de Parifh de ————, Rol. *Abr.* Tit. *Prohibi-*
tion, 291. L. 4.

4. *Where*

4. *Where severed from the nine Parts.*

1. Trespass lieth against him who carries away Tithes severed from the nine Parts, *aliter* where he will not sever his Tithes, but carries them all away; in such Case there lies a Suit in the Spiritual Court. *Bro. Abr. Trespass,* 108.

2. If one be put out of his Tithes by a Severance of nine Parts from the ten, and after carries away the Ten, the Parson may not sue in Court Christian; for that by the Severance it was become a Chattel, for which he might have Trespass. *Rol. Abr. Prohibition,* fo 41. *Cro. Eliz.* fo. 607 *Leigh* and *Wood*'s Case, and also *Blackwell*'s Case, *Cro. Eliz.* 843, 844.

3. At Common Law Notice to the Parson, in Case of Tithes, of a Severance from the nine Parts is not necessary; though by the Ecclesiastical it is. 3 *Mod.* 268 *Rol. Abr.* 300. Case 9.

5. *Where the Validity of a Deed comes in Question.*

1. If a Man sue for Tithes *versus* J. S in the Ecclesiastical Court and make Title by a Lease from the Parson to him made thereof, and *J. S.* also makes Title to them by Force of a former Lease made to him by the same Parson, so that the Question there is, which of those Leases shall be preferred, a Prohibition shall be granted; for they may not try which of the said Leases shall

4

shall be preferred, though they had Cognizance of the original Suit; for the Leases are Temporal *Mich* 12 *Ja. Wrots* and *Clifton, Rol. Abr. Prohibition,* U. Case 4.

6. *Where the Suit is improper, how the Party to be punished.*

1. By all the Judges, if a Parson libel for Tithes, and a Prohibition is brought, and he libel for Tithes of another Year, the first not being determined, an Attachment shall be awarded. *Mo* 599.

2 If a Man lease his Vicarage for Life or Years, rendring Rent, and sue *in Curia Ecclesiastica* for the Rents, a *Præmunire* lies; for the Rent is a Lay Fee. *Bro. Abr. Præmunire,* 5.

3. 17 *H.* 7. *Spelman* reporteth, that one *Turbervile,* as well for the King as himself, sued a *Præmunire* against a Parson for suing for Tithes in the Ecclesiastical Court, alledging the same to be severed from the nine Parts; and Judgment was given against the Defendant 3 *Inst.* 121. *So that, as I apprehend the Matter, the* Præmunire *is incurred by suing in the Ecclesiastical Court for a Matter notoriously remedial at Law, this being a Drawing the Matter* ad aliud examen.

V. *Cha-*

V. *Charities.*

The Introduction, or Author's Apology.

I *had not, save for the following Cause, here introduced any Thing of Charities and other Exemptions from Ordinary Jurisdiction, notwithstanding their Relation to my present Purpose, and that principally for two Reasons, namely, first ; For that I hold the particular Learning on these Heads deservedly challenge a separate and distinct Treatise and Consideration. Secondly , For that I have now got by me ready prepared, and disposed, the Materials necessary to such a Work, which I find, to take no more than what is essentially necessary to the thorough Understanding of that Doctrine, would swell the present Work to too great a Bulk; therefore I shall satisfy myself, at the present, with such general Notions on these Heads as may serve the Lay Founder, Donator and Impropriator, &c. to prevent Ecclesiastical Incroachments on their Temporal Properties, and to right themselves where these Abuses have already began. But I am aware, if I have, as I confess I have, an Intention of publishing a particular Treatise on these several Heads, this Question will be objected to me, wherefore do I at all meddle with them now? To this I have given sufficient Answer already, namely, to prevent and correct such Abuses as have or may be offered to the Property of Lay Founders, Donators, &c. in the mean Time.* But

4

But to thofe, to whom fuch Reafons may not be conclufive, I further Anfwer, that I had his further Reafon inducing me to meddle with thefe Matters at this Time, and in this Place, (to wit) that as I have, from my own Experience, of which in thefe Matters I have not had the leaft of all Men, as well as from the Obfervation of others, difcovered (I had like to have faid a general and) an infatiable Thirft, not only in fome Church Lawyers and Creatures of Ecclefiaftical Tyranny and Power; but alfo in fome Ecclefiafticks themfelves, and thofe not of the very meaneft and moft inferior Sort, but in fome of more exalted Degree and Station, notwithftanding their fpecious Pretences to Spiritualization after the Vifitatorial Power, &c over thefe Things; and that maugre all the wife Provifions and Care of our Common and Statute Laws againft fuch Incroachments, and even exprefs Admonition and Advice what the Superior Temporal Laws, in fuch Cafes, had determined and enacted, and what Penalties were annexed to the Tranfgreffion of fuch Temporal Laws, I fay, notwithftanding thefe Things, ftill finding Provifions, Premunires, &c through Want of Ufe, to have loft their due Weight, and Advice ineffectual, with fome at leaft of thefe Gentlemen, I could not have excufed myfelf to my own Mind, had I paffed by thefe Matters totally without Obfervation, or with lefs Notice than I have here taken of them: And having thus given the Reafons of my own Conduct, I crave Leave to add what I take to be one of the greateft Supports, if not the principal Bulwark to the Reformation; namely, that thefe Authorities were given to Founders, &c. particularly in the Cafe of Charities. *This Power, as I conceive, is allowed to incourage Donations thereto, as the same were always to be visited either by the Founders and their Heirs, or to be ruled and governed by Laws of their own framing and constituting, and as to Lay Impropriations, I conceive it, their being in Lay Hands, and particularly in the Hands of the Nobility and prime Gentry, as they generally are, and as they all at first were, is of the greatest Security to the Reformation; for to argue from the Practice of the Clergy themselves; has it not heretofore been found, and I have some Apprehension that it might, even now, and will hereafter be found, that they, the Clergy, have been carried further, and have battled with more Warmth and Zeal, however their Religion stood affected, where Interest and Religion have been coupled together, and gone Hand in Hand, than when Religion has stood singly by herself, and on her own Legs, and Interest has had no Concern with her. And if this be so, to suppose the Laity to have no more Religion than any of those who have stronger worldly Reasons for being so, yet Interest to keep the Benefits and Authorities annexed to these Impropriations must needs be supposed to bind them to that Reformation, which alone can maintain and keep them in the Possession and Enjoyment of them, so that these very Livings being impropriate is, in my Apprehension (supposing the Laity to act upon the same Motives with Men of Holy Church) of the greatest Security to Religion, as she now stands reformed and purged from the Idolatry, Superstition, Tyranny, and Fopperies of what she held before that Reformation brought about: To say nothing of their being a Counter-balance*

alance to Church Power it felf, which, from
me Authorities in the Books, a Man would
e inclined to think has been fometimes not a
ttle abufed, it muft be allowed, that by this
Means, the Honour, Strength, Wealth, and
earning of the Nation, are ingaged in the
Maintenance of our moft pure Religion. There
another Thing, whereof fome, perhaps the
fs knowing of the Clergy, have moft loudly
ied out and complained of, that putting thefe
things into the Hands of the Laity was rob-
ing the Church, and what not ; but alas!
thefe ignorant Objectors do not give themfelves
leave to confider what People, better acquainted with thefe Matters, as having taken
pains in the Search of them, very well know,
namely, that thefe Appropriations were given to
the Support and Maintenance of idle, lazy, vicious Monks and Friars, &c who with the
Priefts of thofe Times were the firft Corruptors
Religion, and not for the Support of true
Religion pure and undefiled ; and therefore
when the Profeffors of our Holy Religion take
us with them, it is imagined that they will
t fo readily calumniate Lay Impropriators, as
Sacrilegious and Church-Robbers, &c. but on
the contrary, confidering thefe were Eftates appropriated to Regulars, and by them proftituted
the very wickedeft of Purpofes, and therefore,
we find from the Example of the Children of
Ifrael, not fit or lawful to be applied to Holy Ufe,
but where any fuch have been given to the
Support of Men of Holy Church, or other godly
, they will be furrendered to the Crown, to be
pofed to Ufes lefs Holy ; but if thefe Gentle-
n fhall ftill think fit to continue Things
s profaned to Holy Ufe, they will not wonder

it

it is to be hoped, that Lay Impropriators shall use the same prophaned Things to honest Uses, and defend themselves in such Use against all Ecclesiastical Encroachments, though they think them not fit for the most Sacred ; but to consider this Matter thought so great and just a Cause of Complaint a little further , from whom were these Estates taken ? Why, from the religious or regular Clergy, when they were a Scandal to Religion, and sober Society, when their Bodies were dissolved, vanished and gone, and there were none such left to enjoy them But then they should, says the Clerical Objector, have been given to the Church, or rather to Churchmen, which is much better, and indeed is what they always mean when they speak of the Benefits and Advantages of the Church. A Bishoprick is the Support of a Bishop, a Deanery of a Dean, and so down to the Country Vicar, whose Maintenance is his Vicaridge ; but I am sorry again to have Occasion to tell these Church-Worthies, they err not knowing the Law, nor History, in this particular These Benefices were appropriated to Regular Clergy, and never either given, or their Donation intended for the Secular Clergy, and our present Claimants happen only to be secular , as well, if not with more Reason, might the Lord Chancellor and Judges claim the Bishopricks and other Ecclesiastical Benefices, where their Predecessors were Bishops, or other Dignitaries, for that they exercise the same Temporal Jurisdiction , but our Claimants are nothing the same with the other, save that they both fall under the general Denomination of Clergy, with these unlucky Differences, that one happens to be Regular, the other meerly and simply Secular Clergy, the one has

owed wilful Poverty, too many of the others
have refolved if not Sworn to be as rich as
Jews; one has vowed Chaftity, the other is
only bound to it in Common with other Chrifti-
ans, (except their Ordination and other religious Vows) whilft too many of them practice
it the leaft, one has vow'd Obedience, the
other, it is to be fear'd, troubles not his Head
about it farther than ferves his own Ends;
but however this Matter may be, I fhould be
content, for my Part, could it be with Confcience, the Clergy, tho' not fo regular, fhould
have thefe additional Benefices, on thefe Conditions, namely, that as they become refpectively
worfe than the Laity generally are, they feverally fhould for ever, irrecoverably for themfelves and their Succeffors, forfeit thefe Temporal Additions together with all other their
Temporal Eftates, for them their Heirs, Executors and Adminiftrators to go to fome laudable and general Temporal Ufe.　Before I can
leave thefe Gentlemen I muft crave Leave to
ask them, what is their Opinion of fuch, who
by Fraud or Art refufe to pay, or retain and
keep back their Tithes, Oblations, Obventions,
Mortuaries, Penfions, Proxies, Procurations,
Synodals, and other Dues? Are fuch honeft, or
not, in the Opinion of thefe Gentlemen? I can
make no Doubt but they will anfwer, una
voce, that fuch are Wrong-doers, injurious,
Invaders of other Men's Rights, Church-Robbers, Contemners of Temporal Laws, which
have in their great Bounty given, or allowed
and indulged to the Clergy thefe Benefits, and
here I will venture to tell thefe Gentleman that
their beft and moft fubftantial, if not only,
Right to thefe Advantages is by the Indulgence

of

of our *Princes*, and the *Common* and *Statute-Laws* : And if *Laymen* by like *Royal Favour*, and by *Laws*, as *strong* and as *binding* as *these* the others hold by, are *lawfully* and *rightfully* in of *Lay Fees*, &c exempt from all *Ordinary Jurisdiction*, &c and are *sole* (*under the Supreme*) tho' *Lay*, *Visitors*, &c. *themselves of* their own *Charities*, &c. what shall be said of those *Clergymen*, who shall be found not *only injuriously invading* their *Neighbours Property*, *weakening* the *Security* of the *Reformation*, and *acting* in *Defiance* to known *Laws*, (for if any of them *know* them not, it is their *Crime* that they do not *seek Information* from those who do, and *learn* the *Laws necessary* to their *Functions*,) but also most *ungratefully* to their *Benefactor* and *traitorously* to their *Sovereign acting* to the *Disinherison* of the *Crown itself*, to whom often, if not always, these *Men* have the *highest Personal Obligations*, and so owe the greatest *Returns* of *Gratitude* as well as *Duty* and *Allegiance?* I *say*, what shall be said to, or of such *Men?* But that their *Crime* is too big for a *Name*; and that their *holy Character* is no small *Aggravation* of their *Sin*, if they are, not only, as all *Christians* are, but also by their *solemn Oaths* and *Promises* made and taken at their *entring into* their *several Orders*, still further *bound* to be *Examples* of *Virtue* and *Piety?* They are *surely*, a *fortiori*, to be *just* and *honest*, and ought to *leave others* in the quiet *Enjoyment* of their *Temporal Inheritances*, and of all *Immunities* and *Authorities incident thereto*, as well as their *Sovereign Lord* and *Benefactor* to the *Exercise* of his *rightful Jurisdiction*, whether *Temporal* or *Ecclesiastical*.

1 *Ge-*

1. *General.*

1 CHarity is not barred by length of Time, or any Statute of Limitations. 2 *Vern* 399

2 There's no Statute of Limitations againſt God and Religion, what was once given to Charity ought to be ſo applied, and what had been imbeziled ought to be reſtored 2 *Vern.* 389.

3 A Gift to Charity muſt be for Relief of Neceſſity only, and not for Ornament, or Superfluity, it muſt be according to, not againſt, Law. *Du. Ch Uſes,* 132.

2. *Rules.*

1. PANIS *Egentium Vita Pauperum,* & *Qui defraudat eos homo Sanguinis eſt.* 8 Co. 131.

2 *Summa eſt Ratio quæ pro Religione facit.* 2 Ch. Ca. 18 Jenk. 233

3 *Favendum eſt Eccleſiæ quam Parſonæ.* 1 Ro Rep 452.

4. Truſtees for a Charity may improve for the Benefit of the Charity, but can do no Act to prejudice it, in Breach of the Founders Rules 2 *Vern.* 412

5 If one will receive a Charity with the Yoke tied to it by the Founder, he muſt bear it· The Charity cannot be ſevered from the Yoke; if they will have the one, they muſt ſubmit to the other. *Skin.* 491. *Vide ante General.*

L 4

3. *Colleges, and Hospitals.*

1. *The Difference.*

THE Difference between an Hospital and a College is only in Degree; an Hospital is for those who are poor, and mean, and low, and sickly, a College is of another Sort of indigent Persons, but it hath another Intent, to Study in, and breed up Persons in the World, who have not otherwise wherewith to do it; but still is as much with n the Reason of an Hospital: And if in an Hospital the Master and Poor are incorporated, it is a College; having a Common Seal to act by, though it hath not the Name of a College (which always supposeth a Corporation) because it is of an inferior Degree: And in the one Case and the other there must be a Visitor; either the Founder and his Heirs, or one appointed by them; and both are Eleemosynary. *Skin* 484

2. All Colleges in the Universities are Lay Corporations, and though the Members of the College may be all Spiritual Persons, yet the Corporation is a Lay and Temporal, because the Institution and End is Temporal, *viz* to advance Learning. *Salk.* 672.

4. *Charity must not hurt another's Right.*

A Copyholder surrendred to the Use of a Grammar School; the Lord is compellable to admit the Tenant, because it is not pre-

prejudicial to him as he has but one Tenant, after whofe Death his Fine is due, as it was before, and the Ufe of the Land is only in the Corporation. *Ranfhaw* and *Robottoms* Cafe at *St. Albans*, *aliter* had the Surrender been to a Corporation; for then the Lord would have been hurt in his Services; the fame if the Cuftom of the Manor be to devife to one only, and to have a Harriot after his Death, the Tenant may not furrender to two to a Charitable Ufe, becaufe the Lord is delayed of his Harriot. *Du. Ch. Ufes* 140

5. *What may be given thereto, or out of what, and when.*

1. NO Charity can arife out of Ufury. *Du Ch. Ufes* 136.

2. A Copyhold may be charged with a Charitable Ufe. *Tot.* 92. *Hern's Ch. Ufes* 97

3 A Debt owing by Statute, Judgment, Recognizance, or Bond, which is but a *chofe en action*, was given for the Creation of a School, and decreed a good Appointment within the Statute to maintain a Charitable Ufe. *Herne of Ch Ufes* 94.

4. A Debt in Action given for the Erection of a School good. *Tot.* 91, 92.

5. The Statute 9 *Geo* 2. of *Mortmaine* recites, That whereas fuch Gifts are prohibited and reftrained by *Magna Charta*, and divers other wholefome Laws, as prejudicial to and againft the Common Utility, and to the Difinheriting of lawful Heirs, for Remedy whereof

whereof it is enacted, That from and after 24 *June* 1736. No Manors, Lands, Tenements, Rents, Advowsons, or other Hereditaments, Corporeal or Incorporeal whatsoever, nor any Sum or Sums of Money, Goods, Chattels, Stocks in the Publick Funds, Securities for Money, or any other Personal Estate whatever, to be laid out or disposed of in the Purchase of any Lands, Tenements, or Hereditaments, shall be given, granted, aliened, &c. or any ways conveyed or settled, to or upon any Person or Persons, Bodies Politick or Corporate or otherwise, for any Estate or Interest whatsoever, or any ways charged or incumbred, by any Person or Persons whatsoever, In Trust or for the Benefit of any Charitable Use whatsoever, unless such Gift, Conveyance, &c. of any such Lands, &c. Sum or Sums of Money or Personal Estate, (other than Stock in the Publick Funds) be and be made by Deed indented, sealed and delivered in the Presence of two or more Credible Witnesses, twelve Kalendar Months at least, before the Death of such Donor or Grantor, (including the Days of Execution and Death) and be Inrolled in the High Court of Chancery, within six Kalendar Months next after the Execution thereof; and unless such Stock be transferred in the Publick Books usually kept for the Transfer of such Stocks, six Kalendar Months at least before the Death of such Donor or Grantor (including the Days of the Transfer and Death) and unless the same be made to take Effect in Possession, for the Charitable Use intended immediately from the making thereof, and be without any
Power

Power of Revocation, Refervation, Truft, Condition, *Limitation*, Claufe or Agreement whatfoever; for the Benefit of the Donor or Grantor, or of any Perfon or Perfons claiming under him; provided that nothing in the faid Statute before mentioned relating to the Sealing and Delivery of any Deed or Deeds, twelve Kalendar Months at leaft before the Death of the Grantor, or the Transfer of any Stock fix Kalendar Months before the Death of the Grantor or Perfons making fuch Transfer, fhall extend, or be conftrued to extend to any Purchafe of any Eftate or Intereft in Lands, *&c.* or any Transfer of Stock, to be made really and *bona fide*, for a full and valuable Confideration actually paid, at or before the making fuch conveyance or Transfer, without Fraud or Collufion. And it is thereby further enacted, That all Gifts, Grants, *&c.* Transfers, and Settlements whatfoever, of any Lands, *&c* or of any Eftate or Intereft therein, or of any Charge or Incumbrance affecting or to affect the fame, or of any Stock, Money, Goods, Chattels, or other Perfonal Eftate or Securities for Money, to be laid out or difpofed of in the Purchafe of any Lands, *&c.* or of any Eftate or Intereft therein, or of any Charge or Incumbrance affecting or to affect the fame, to or in Truft for any Charitable Ufes whatfoever, which fhould at any time after the faid 24th of *June* be made in any other Manner or Form, than by the faid Act is directed and appointed, fhould be abfolutely, and to all Intents and Purpofes, null and void; fave to the Univerfities in *Great Britain*, or Colleges, or

Houfes

Houses therein, or the Colleges of *Eaton, Winchester* and *Westminster*; provided that no such Colleges or Houses which hold so many Advowsons of such Benefices, as is equal to Half the Numbers of their Fellows, or Students be capable of Purchasing, &c. any other Advowsons by any Means whatsoever; the Advowsons, as are annexed or given for the better Support of the Headships, not to be computed therein, and provided the said Act extend not to *Scotland.*

6. In *Canc.* 26.

April 1740   *Ashburnham* and *Bradshaw.*

The Case was this; One made his Last Will and Testament before the Commencement of the above Act, and died after the Commencement; on this Case the Lord Chancellor directed, that the Opinions of all the Judges should be taken, on the Question a good Will or not, and all the rest of the Judges (*Denton J. Sick*) were of Opinion that the Will was good, notwithstanding the Intervening of the Statute, and so his Lordship was pleased to decree, and that the Trust of the Charity be carried into Execution.

* See Case in *Canc.* 28 *July* 1740. *Adlington* and *Cann.*

6. *To pursue the Intent of the Founder.*

1. THE Intention and Will of Founders or Donors shall bind the King, tho' not named in the Statute, as appears *in Statuto*

tuto Templariorum, Anno 17 *E.* 2 where it is said, *Ita semper quod pia & celeberima Voluntas Donatorum in omnibus teneatur & expleatur, & perpetuo sanctissime perseveret, &c.* 11 *Co* 73. *a.*

2 A Decree of Commissioners of Charitable Uses was reversed for varying from the Intent of the Founder or Donor. *Cases in Law and Equity,* 2 *Part, Wright* and *Hobart's Case,* 64, 65.

3. *Pas* 10 *Geo.* 2 *The Attorney Gen.* and *Stephens*

The Case was, Dr. *Radcliffe,* the late Physician, by Will devised 300 *l per Annum* to two Persons to be chosen by the Archbishop of *Canterbury* and certain other Trustees out of University College in *Oxon,* which Sum he directed to be paid them for ten Years for their Maintenance, five Years whereof they were to spend in *England,* in the Study of Physick, and the other five abroad, the Defendant was one so chosen and studied here according to the Directions of the Will, and for that Time he received his five Years Salary; but after did not go abroad on account of his ill State of Health, and thereupon *Anno* 1730 resigned to the Trustees, who accepted his Resignation, and chose another in his Room, and *Anno* 1735 the present Information was exhibited against the Defendant, that he might account for the five Years Salary, by him thus received. Mr *Fazakerley* for the Defendant argued, that in a late Case which came before the House of Lords, upon an Appeal, their Lordships were of Opinion that the Word, *Maintenance,* included Education, and therefore,

fore, though that Word was used in the present Will, *Education* must be intended by it, as implied. He argued, that when the Defendant had spent Half his Time in his Education here in *England*, and was prevented by ill Health from going abroad, and thereupon had resigned, and his Resignation accepted, and another chosen in his Stead, he submitted it, that the present Bill must be thought an unreasonable one. My Lord Chancellor was of that Opinion, and said, that the Name of the Case cited was *Gandy* and *Anstis*, so dismissed the Information.

7. *How favoured.*

1. *General*

1. IF a Daughter being Heir gives the Lands descended upon her to Charity, and then a Son is born, he shall avoid the Gift; but if the Father had been Feoffee, *sur* Condition that he and his Heirs should give the same Lands to Charitable Uses, and the Daughter had given, *ut supra*, before the Son born, the Son had been bound, for this clear Reason, because the Daughter in this Case had done no more than the Son himself should have performed by Reason of the Condition. *D. Char. Uses* 138, 139

2 A Copyholder surrenders to the Use of his last Will, and thereby devises that the Parson, Church-wardens, and four honest Men of the Parish of *Allhallows*, should sell his

his Copyhold for a charitable Use, the Copyholder dies, and his Heir is admitted, the Parson, &c. sell the Land to *J. S.* the Heir was compelled to surrender accordingly. *Guiddye's* Case, decreed 4 *Ja.* in *Canc'.* D. *Char Uses* 140.

3. It was urged in this Case, that in Cases of Charity, where the most speedy and least expensive Methods ought to be chosen, an Issue ought not to be directed, but that the Court ought to decree upon the Proofs. *Bishop of Rochester* and *Attorn. Gen',* March 1721.

2 *By Construction.*

1. Upon a Will of a Lease of the Rectory of *Hains* in *Com' Wilts,* resolved by *Egerton* and *Popham,* that a Devise of Money to be distributed to twenty of the poorest of his Kindred, shall be a good Devise, although it doth not appear that he had any poor Kindred. *Tot.* 92. Vide *Charities, favoured in general.*

2. In the Case of *Kerry* and *Dethick,* adjudged a Devise to one and his Heirs, of the Rents and Profits of his Land, this is a Devise of the Land it self: Also resolved, when one deviseth the rest of his Land to a Charitable Use, it shall be taken largely for a Devise of the Rent then reserved, or after to be reserved upon an improved Value. *Herne of Charitable Uses* 77.

3. Money was given for the Good of the Church of *Dalk,* and resolved good, notwithstanding these general Words. *Herne of Char Uses* 97.

4. When

4. When no Use is mentioned or directed in a Deed, it shall be decreed to the Use of the Poor, tho' the Feoffees be Gentlemen living out of the Town, and no Inhabitants within the Town. *Herne of Char. Uses* 100.

3. *Where not good, as a Will, whether good as an Appointment.*

1. *Collison* seised of Lands in Fee in *Papa Street* of *Eltham*, 25 *H.* 8. devised the Rents of his Lands to his Executors for Reparation of Highways within the Parish for ever, and upon a Reference to *Mountague* and *Hobart* Ch. Just. out of Chancery, they certified it good. If one demise the Rents and Profits of his Lands to another and his Heirs, this is good of the Land it self, and secondly, though it were void in Law, because made 25 *H* 8 so long before *Stat* 32 & 34 *H.* 8. before which no Lands were devisable, but customary Lands; yet by the Statute 43 *Eliz* it is made good, and shall be taken within that Statute for a good Limitation and Appointment to a Charitable Use; and it was decreed according to their Certificate. *Herne of Char Uses* 81, 82

2. *Stoddard* devised a Rent of 10 *l* a Year out of his House called the *Swan with two Necks*, in the *Old Jury, London*, for Maintenance of two Scholars at *Oxon* and *Cambridge*, and willed that one *Hugh*, the Scrivener, should put it into Writing, which was accordingly done; this being found by Inquisition was decreed, and that confirmed on Appeal, for though by Law Rent cannot be created or granted without Deed or Will

Will in Writing, yet this nuncupative Will was good to create the Rent to a Charitable Use, by the Words of the Statute of Limitation or Appointment, for though not a good Gift, yet it is a good Limitation or Appointment. *Herne of Char Ufes* 98, 99. Note; *This before Statute of Frauds, the Law being now otherwise under that Statute.*

3. Money was given to maintain a preaching Minister; this is not a Charitable Use named in the Statute, yet by the Lord Keeper and two Judges, it was decreed to be good, and the Use a Charitable Use within the Equity of that Statute, and the Executor accordingly was ordered to pay the Money for the Maintenance of it. *Herne of Char Ufes,* 101, 102

4. Lands were given to the Churchwardens of a Parish, to a Charitable Use; tho' the Devise was void in Law, yet decreed good in Chancery, by the Words *limited and appointed within the Statute.* Herne of Char. Ufes 101.

5. Information was, that *Stephen Newman* feifed of Lands, devised them to *Trinity College* in *Cambridge*, for the Maintenance of a Scholar there, and in the Will was this Claufe *If any Cavil shall hinder this Devise, or that the fame cannot go to the College, by Reason of the Statute of Mortmain, then I devise them to* Robert Newman *and his Heirs*, and under Pretence that by the Statute of Mortmain the College could not have them, *Robert Newman* entered and held the Poffeffion, whereupon Attorney General brought this Information to have the Lands eftablished with the College, and this all appeared upon the Bill and Anfwer; and

it being a Charity, it was held by Lord Keeper *Bridgman,* that it ought to be efta-blifhed with the College by Statute 43 *Eliz.* notwithftanding the Statute of Mortmain, and notwithftanding the Claufe in the Will, and fo it was decreed; and Lord Keeper faid, that this Cafe differed not from *Lloyd's* Cafe in *Hob.* 136 1 *Lev.* 284.

6. *Prat* devifes his Houfe in St. *Sepucher's* Parifh to St. *John's* College, he being Tenant *in Capite,* and the Corporation mif-named, which was a void Devife to pafs the Lands, and fo on former Proceedings certified by the Opinion of the Judges Lord Keeper notwithftanding decreed it a good Appointment within the Statute 43 *El.* but then it was objected, if fo, that then the Procefs and Method appointed by the Statute ought to be held, (*viz.*) a Commiffion, and Inquifition, and Decree by Commiffio-ners, and fo to come at laft to a final De-cree by Lord Chancellor, or Lord Keeper, but not to fue by original Bill, as in this Cafe; but the Lord Keeper decreed the Charity, though before the Statute no fuch Decree could have been made. 1 *Chan. Ca.* 267.

7. Tenant in Tail of the Manor of *Mid-hill* in *Berks* made a nuncupative Will, which being after reduced into Writing, was proved as fuch by three Witneffes, and by this he devifed, that his Executors fhould purchafe a Parcel of Ground in *Cricklade* in *Wilts* for the Erecting of a Free-School there, and gave to the faid School 20*l* per *Annum* Rent, to be paid out of his faid Ma-nor of *Midhill,* and died: This Will and the
Death

Death of the Testator were both before the Statute of Frauds, and also the Probate therefore in the Spiritual Court, as a nuncupative Will, and in Pursuance of this Will the Executors bought the Ground in *Cricklade*, and built the School, and the Commissioners for Charitable Uses decreed the Issue in Tail of the Manor of *Midhill* to pay the Arrears of the 20 *l.* a Year Rent to the School, the Issue in Tail excepted to the Decree, and the Exception coming on before Lord Chancellor *Harcourt*, it was insisted for the Decree, that though this was void as a Will, yet it was good as an Appointment by *Stat.* 43 *Eliz. of Char Uses.* As if Tenant in Tail had devised Lands without levying a Fine, or suffering a Recovery, or a Copyholder had devised to Charity, without Surrender to the Use of his Will, such Devises would be made effectual His Lordship allowed the Exception and reversed the Commissioners Decree; for that at Law, Land, or a real Estate, were not devisable, and by *Stat* 32 *H.* 8 it is as much required that a Will of Land should be in Writing, as that by Statute of Frauds it is required that there should be three Witnesses, and as in *Johnson*'s Case decreed by Lord Chancellor *Cowper,* a Devise of Lands in Writing to a Charity, since the Statute of Frauds, but not attested by three Witnesses, was held to be void, so a Devise of Land without Writing should be void also, especially it being by Tenant in Tail, and of a Rent too, which cannot pass but by Deed, and it would be very dangerous to allow of Nuncupative Wills of Lands

Sed quære, says the Reporter, and *vide Du.
Char Uses* 81. *Stoddard's* Cafe, where one
fore the Statute of Frauds devifed a Rent
of ten Pounds *per Annum* out of Lands to
a Charitable Ufe, and willed that one *Hugh,*
the Scrivener, fhould put it into Writing,
which was accordingly done; and decreed
that this Nuncupative Will was good, for
though a Rent cannot be created, without
Deed, yet by the Words of 43 *Eliz* it may
be appointed without Deed, and though the
Nuncupative Will be void, as a Will, it is
good as an Appointment, (*thus far the Cafe*)
and it feems (*continues the Reporter*) that
the Statute 43 *Eliz.* which makes thefe Appointments to Charities good, being fubfequent to the Statute 32 *H* 8 of Wills, fu
perfedes and repeals that Statute, but it is
true, that the Statute of Frauds and Perjuries, being fubfequent to the Statute 43 *El*
does repeal that Statute, and therefore fince
the Statute of Frauds, *&c* an Appointment
of Lands to a Charity by a Will, not at
tefted by three Witneffes, is void   2 *Pet
Will fo* 247. *Jenner* con *Harper.* P*rec.* Ch
389, 390, 391   S. C   and *Gilb.* 44, 45. S C

8 If a Will be defective it fhall not operate as an Appointment to fupport a Charity. *Prec Chon* 390.

9. A Will wanting Witneffes will not o-
perate as an Appointment to a Charity by
the Statute 43 *Eliz*   P*rec Chan fo* 270 &
389   See and note 3 *Rep Ch.* 150, *&c*

10. Parol Devife to a Charity out of Lands,
being defective as a Will, cannot be fupported
as an Appointment; becaufe being defective
as a Will, which was the Manner of Conveyance

ance he intended to pass it by, it can have no Effect as an Appointment, which he did not intend, and of this Opinion my Lord Chancellor seemed to be, and decreed accordingly in the principal Case *Prec Chan* 391.

11 Lands devised to Charities, and the Will not published in the Presence of three Witnesses, as the Statute of Frauds requires, not good either as a Will or an Appointment, but was good for so much as was Copyhold, they passing by the Surrender, and not by the Will. And tho' there were three Witnesses to a subsequent Codicil, that cannot help the Will. 2 *Vern* 597, 598 Ca 536 *Attorn Gen.* con *Barnes & ux* See and note 3 *Mod* 262. *Hob* 136 *Mo.* 888. It was insisted in the above Case, that the Statute of Frauds and Perjuries makes Wills of Lands absolutely void, if not three subscribing Witnesses thereto, and the Statute is to be strictly taken to prevent Frauds in the Time when People are easiest to be imposed on. *Vide Gilb Rep* 5 where Lord Chancellor seemed of this Opinion

4. *Where have been long dormant.*

Money long since given to a Charitable Use decreed with Interest. *Tot. Rep* 91. Vide antea *General.*

5. *Defects supplied for.*

1 *Where it would be void in any other Case as being against the Rules of Law*

1. If a Feoffment be made to Dean and Chapter, on Condition to perform a Charitable Use, it is good, tho' they cannot be seised to another's Man's Use A Bankrupt, an Accountant, a Recusant, may be Feoffees, or Donees to Charitable Uses *Du Char Uses* 138.

2. A Lease for Years is made, rendring Rent to a common Midwife for poor Women, good, though a Reservation of Rent cannot, at Common Law, be to a Stranger. *Du Ch. Uses* 140.

3. If there be two Jointenants, and one release to the other to a Charitable Use, good; *aliter*, if one grant to the other for such Use, for Jointenants cannot grant one to another. *Du Char Uses* 140.

4. A Man makes a Feoffment with Power of Revocation, and then sells the Lands to a Charitable Use, good, and he cannot revoke. *Du Char. Uses* 140.

5. A Man devises a Term of Years to a Woman during her Life, the Remainder to another to a Charitable Use, tho' the Remainder limited be void, yet the Executors of the Woman, who shall have the Residue of the Term, shall be charged with the Use. *Du. Char Uses* 140

6. A Man devised by his Will Monies to a Charitable Use to be bestowed for poor People, and the Residue of his Goods to be imployed to such Uses as his Feoffees shall think meet, Devise is good, tho' to a Corporation *Tot* 95.

2. *Where the Poor, either are not a Corporation, or not one capable.*

1 A Devise to the poor People maintained in the Hospital in the Parish of St. *Laurence* in *Reading* for ever. Exception was taken, that the Poor were not capable by that Name, for no Corporation, yet because the Plaintiffs (the Mayor and Burgesses)

geffes) were capable to take Lands in Mortmain, and did govern the Hofpital, It was decreed the Defendant fhould affure the Lands to the Mayor and Burgeffes for the Maintenance of the faid Hofpital. *Tot.* 93.

2 *Ridley* feifed of Copyhold Lands in *Barking* in *Com' Effex* devifed, that the Parfon and Church-wardens in *Thames-Street London*, and four honeft Men of that Parifh, fhould fell the Land, and imploy the Money for the Poor and Charitable Ufes in that Parifh, and it was objected, that the Devife was void, becaufe the Parfon and Church-wardens were not a Corporation to take Land out of *London*, nor to fell it for fuch Ufes; but it was decreed, that the Devife was good, and that they had a good Authority to fell the fame. *Toth.* 93.

3 *Where given by Tenant* in Capite.

1 An Annuity devifed out of Lands holden *in Capite* to Charitable Ufes judged good *Du Char Ufes* 94

2 This Cafe, by the King's Command, was referred to the Juftices of the King's Bench, and was thus. *Afcough* feifed in Fee of the Manor of *D* holden by Knight-Service *in Capite*, devifeth the faid Manor to be fold by his Executors, Part of the Money to be paid to his Wife, and Part in feveral other Legacies, and the Refidue thereof he gave to Charitable Ufes, (*viz.*) for the marrying of poor Maidens and Relief of Prifoners, *&c.* The firft Queftion was, whether this was a good Devife to

bind the King and to bar him of his primer Seisins by the Stat. 43 Eliz of Charitable Uses; and all the Justices held clearly that this should not bar the King for his Interest of Wardship, Livery, or primer Seisin, because general Words where the King is not named shall never bind or bar him The second Question was, whether such a Devise by the said Statute be good against him for the whole, and shall bar the Heir to claim a third Part; and they also resolved, admitting it to be a Conveyance within the Statute, yet it is void against the Heir for the third Part; for by the 32 & 34 H 8 he hath no Power to dispose but of two Parts, so for the third Part it is clearly void. The third Question was whether this were a Conveyance within Stat. 43 Eliz because here is not any Disposition of the Lands to Charitable Uses, but an Appointment, that the Land shall be sold and the Money divided, Part to his Wife (who is clearly out of the Statute) another Part to satisfy divers Legacies, and the Residue, which, in truth, was the greatest Part, to the said Charitable Uses; but as to this, they all resolved not. *Cro. Car.* 525, 526. See and note 3 *Rep* Ch. 68, 69 2 *Vernon* 454.

4. *Where given by Tenant in Tail*

1. Tenant in Tail settles Lands for a Charity, and *Anno* 1652 a Decree was by the Commissioners of Charitable Uses for applying these Lands to the Charity, then the Estate-Tail is spent, and *Tay*, the now Plaintiff, being Remainder-Man in Fee and an Infant,

fant, put in Exceptions to the Decree, that he ought not to be bound by it, not coming in under Tenant in Tail. This came on before the Lords Commiſſioners, who were all of Opinion, that all Appointments of Tenant in Tail to a Charity, are by the Statute good and binding againſt the Remainder-Man, as well as againſt the Iſſue in Tail, and therefore confirmed the Decree with Coſts. *Prec. Ch* 16, 271. *Gilb* 44.

2 The Queſtion was, whether a Deviſe by Tenant in Tail, who levied no Fine, nor ſuffered any Recovery, be a good Appointment, within the Statute of Charitable Uſes, againſt the Defendants who claimed under the Intail, the Commiſſioners below had decreed for the Charity, and now on Exceptions it was confirmed by Lord Keeper, who ſaid, he was of Opinion, that the Intent of the Act of the Queen for Charitable Uſes, was to make the Diſpoſition of the Party as free and eaſy as his Mind, and not to oblige him to the Obſervance of any Form or Ceremony either of Leaſe or Releaſe, or Common Recovery, or Fine, *&c.* and cited the Caſe of *Colliſon* in *Hob* where before the Statute of Wills, a Will of Land made 15 *H* 8 deviſing the ſame for Repair of Highways adjudged good within the Statute of the ſaid Queen; tho' made long after, *Mo.* 888 the ſame Caſe, but there called *Rolle's* Caſe, *Griffith Lloyd's* Caſe in *Hob.* A Deviſe to *Jeſus* College being in Mortmain and void at Law, yet allowed good within the Statute of the Queen *Damus's* Caſe, *Mo.* 822 A Feme Covert, Adminiſtratrix, deviſes to Charity, and held good. *Rivet's* Caſe,

Case, *Mo.* 890. Devise of a Copyhold
without a Surrender to the Use of the Will
held good, and so in *Reppington* and *Rep
pington,* and the Town of *Chaid* and *Opie* and
Higgins against the Town of *Southampton*, on
the Will of one *Mill*, 26 *June* 1671. A Devise out of a Manor held *in Capite* decreed
good, being to a Charity, tho' otherwise the
Will void, as to a third Part. *Wild* and
Windham, who assisted in that Case, say
ing, that the Statute of the Queen was
an enabling Statute, giving Power in any
Manner to dispose to Charitable Uses. In
the Case of Sir *John Platt* and St *John's*
College, 27 *Car.* 2 a Misnomer supplied 1 *Ch*
Rep. 267 *Prec Ch* 16, 271

3. The Reason why a Devise by Tenant
in Tail to a Charitable Use shall be good
against the Issue in Tail is; because the Te
stator had it in his Power by Fine to have
barred the Issue, and tho' he did not live to
perform the Ceremony, yet as a Will being
perfect and compleat by the Aid 43 *Eliz* it
might work as an Appointment, for that at
Common Law there were no Fines, nor Re-
coveries, nor Estates-Tail, and therefore that
Statute was a restoring of the Common Law
So of a Deed of Bargain and Sale, tho' not
inrolled, by Statute 27 *H* 8. *Prec. Ch* 391

5. *Where given by Copyholder.*

A Copyhold Inheritance not surrendered
to the Use of the Will to a Charity, supplied.
3 *Ch Rep* 220 *Mo* 890. 2 *Vern.* 454

6. *Where*

6. *Where given by Feme Covert*

The Feme having Power to difpofe of her
Perfonal Eftate, which only comprehended
fuch Perfonal Eftate as fhe had before Coverture, having (after being married) in a fe-
cret Manner gotten into Poffeffion of a large
Perfonal Eftate by her Father's Death, which
fhe concealed from her Husband, difpofes of
her Perfonal Eftate to Charity, yet decreed
that what was fo concealed fhould not be difcovered and taken from the Charity and
given to the Husband, fo as to difappoint
the Charity. See Cafe, *Pilkington* and *Cuth-
bertfon* in Houfe of Lords. 11 *March* 1711.

7 *Whether may lay the whole Burden on any
one or more, or muft feek feveral Remedies
in Proportion.*

1 A Decree upon the Statute of Charitable Ufes being made for the Town of
Raifen, and the Defendant poffeffing fome
Part of the Land liable to the Money decreed, infifted on paying but his Proportion,
there being feveral others who had Lands
chargeable with the fame Ufe, as well as the
Defendant; the Court declared, that a Decree being made for the Town, they may
lay the Whole on any one liable, and he to
pay the Whole, but he may compel the
others to contribute **1** *Ch. Rep* 91, 92.

2 Where Money to Charity is iffuing out
of Lands in Poffeffion of feveral, they may
levy all upon one, or otherwife at their
Pleafure, but the reft fhall contribute, on
the

the Application of the other Parties 1 *Rep.* *Ch* 91, 92. 3 *Vol* 22 *Eq. Abr* 98, 99. *Salk.* *Attorney Gen.* and *Shelley.* *Vide Salk.* Cha- rity, or Charitable Ufes.

8. *To take Improvements*

1 *Davis* erected an Almshoufe in *Henning-* *ton Haftings* for Eight poor Men, and being feifed of Lands in *T. M* and *B.* then let at 10 *l.* a Year, devifed his Rents for the Main- tenance of the faid poor in the faid Alms- houfe, and dies, and his Heirs pays the 10*l* yearly at the Almshoufe, and at the End of the Term demifes again at 40 *l* a Year, the Commiffioners decree the whole Lands and Profits to the Charity, and the Arrears of the improved Rent, taken by the Heir from the Expiration of the old Leafe, till the De- cree, and that the new Leafe fhould be void and yielded up; and upon Appeal in Chan- cery brought by the Heir, and Exceptions taken to the Decree, the Lord Keeper refer- red the Cafe to the Judges, principally, whether if one devifes the Rent of his Lands to a Charitable Ufe, if by this Devife the Land paffed; and they certified their Opi- nion, that by Devife of the Rents of the Lands to a Charitable Ufe the Land it felf paffed, *&c.* and the Commiffioners Decree was affirmed. *Herne of Char. Ufes* 76, 77.

2. There was a Difpofition in 1579 (which was before the *Stat.* 43 *Eliz.* for Charitable Ufes) to a Charity, Part of the Lands were of a defective Title, and the whole Difpo- fition void, being before the Statute, yet an
Agree-

Agreement was had between the Parties interested and Trustee for settling the Use designed, so much as was proportionable in Value to what the Donor had to give; and this
was all done before the Statute, and long
Leases made of the Ground to several Tenants at small Rents to build, who had
thereby improved the Ground that was but
20 *l* a Year to 150 *l* a Year. The Commissioners by Decree avoided the Tenants
Leases, they not being, in Strictness of Law,
good. On Exceptions to this Decree, the
Court declared, tho' the Charity was precedent to the Statute, yet the Statute subsequent had a Retrospect, and would make it
a good Appointment that was not so before,
but void. And it was declared, that so as
the Terretenants be no Losers, they ought
not to be Gainers in the Case of Charity,
and so ordered, that during the Terretenants Leases there should be an Augmentation of 50 *l. per* Annum allowed by them in
Proportion to the poor. 1 *Ch. Case* 195.

3 The Reversion in Fee of divers Lands,
on which 70 *l per* Annum Rent was reserved, was given to the Corporation of *Coventry*, and the whole 70 *l.* reserved Rent
was appointed to particular Charities; after
the Leases expired, the Rents were consi-
derably increased, the Overplus to be applied to the Augmentation of the Charities,
and not to be for the Benefit of the Corporation See the Case of the Mayor of *Coventry* and the *Attorn. Gen.* 8 *May* 1720
before the House of Lords. *Vide* 2 *Vern*
397. and 2 *Ch. Cases* 53.

9. *Arrears*

the Charity

9. *Arrears to go in Augmentation of*

*   *Paſ.* 10 *Geo.* 2. *in Canc Cleik* and others
againſt *Brabant* and others.

This Bill was brought for the Poſſeſſion of
Lands ſubject to a Charity decreed to the
Plaintiff; the Fact appeared to be thus The
Charity conſiſted of three Lectureſhips (*viz*)
Hempſted, Barkhempſted, and *St Albans,* and
there had been reported from 1660 to 1678
an Arrear amounting to 540 *l.* which was directed to carry Intereſt at 6 *l per Cent.* and
to be laid out in Augmentation of the Charity, and there being a former Arrear due to
the Lecturers *Anno* 6 *Will.* 3. a Decree was
pronounced for putting them into Poſſeſſion
of the Premiſſes in Order ,that they might
receive what was ſo due to them, together
with the growing Charity, and pay over the
reſt of the Money, for the Benefit of the
Augmentation, under this Decree as well as
under a Letter of Attorney from one of the
Lecturers   Dr *Brabant,* who had the other
two Lectureſhips, took Poſſeſſion of the Premiſſes, and kept the ſame to the Time of his
Death , after which his Son continued ſuch
Poſſeſſion, and they (the Father and Son)
received all the Arrears, ſave 23 *l* 17 *s.* 6 *d,*
and whether, on Payment of this Sum, the
Plaintiffs, who were Purchaſers, ſhould not
be let into Poſſeſſion, was the Queſtion, for
which my Lord Chancellor decreed

10. *Whether to contribute.*

1 A Man by Will gave several Legacies, and particularly 40*l* to Charity, the Spiritual Court would pay the Charity first, and not in Average or Proportion with the other Legacies, Plaintiff brought the Bill setting forth the Matter, that there was a Deficiency of Assets, and moved for an Injunction, but Motion refused; for that the Civil Law, was the Law by which Legatory Matters were to be determined, and the Spiritual Court had undoubtedly the Jurisdiction thereof, and if by their Law a Preference was given to Charities, he could not alter that in that Point, neither would direct Security to be given for Refunding, in Case of Deficiency of Assets. 1 *Vern.* 230, 231. *Case* 226. *Fielding* and *Bond*

2 By the Civil Law, if a Man devises out of his Personal Estate to a Charity, and gives also a Legacy thereout to others, and the Personal Estate fall short to pay all, the Charity should be preferred; but here that Rule will not hold; but the Charity must abate in Proportion. *Prec. Ch* 390.

3 It was resolved in the Cause *Masters* and *Masters*, that the Charity, tho' preferred by the Civil Law, yet ought to abate in Proportion, for they were but Legacies. 1 *P. Will.* 422, 423

4 One *Penning* of *Saffron Walden* in *Essex* and others subscribed to the Charity School there of twelve Boys and twelve Girls, which Subscription was only during the Pleasure of the Benefactors. *Penning* took Delight in

seeing these Charity Children, and declared
he would leave them something at his Death.
There was also a Free-School in the same
Town, and *Penning* by his Will gave 500*l*
to the Charity School, and several Money
Legacies, and died. The Executors insisted
on Want of Assets. Lord Chancellor, tho'
the Free-School be a Charity School, yet
the Charity School for Boys and Girls went
more commonly by that Name, and as the
Testator was fond of the latter, and had de
clared he would leave them something,
therefore that, and not the Free-School, is
intitled ; so let the Legacy be brought into
Court with Interest from the End of the
Year after the Testator's Death, and in Case
of Deficiency of Assets, let all the Pecuniary
Legacies, as well that to the Charity, as
the rest abate in Proportion , for tho' the
Romans preferred a pious or Charitable Legacy to others, yet our Law does not, they
being all but Legacies, and equally intended
by the Testator to be paid, it would be hard
that one of them by being preferred should
frustrate all the rest, besides the other Legacies being given to several of the Testator's poor Relations, they are Charities also.
And because it is objected, that on the fail-
ing of the Charity School, the Charity ought
to revert to the Founder ; therefore in such
Case, I give Liberty to the Parties to apply
again to the Court. 1 P *Will* 674, 675.

5. Charity Legacies, being but Legacies,
must on a Deficiency abate in Proportion
2 P *Will* 25 But Charities of three Pound
each Parish, to the poor of three several Pa
rishes, the Court looked upon as Part of the
Funeral

Funerals, and as Doles thereout, and therefore held that no Abatement ought to be made out of them. *2 P Will. 25.*

11. *Out of what to be paid and secured, where no particular Estate or Fund appointed for that Purpose.*

1 *A.* deviseth Twenty Pounds *per Annum* to a preaching Minister, and dies, leaving Lands and Assets; Defendant refuseth to pay; but charged out of the Assets to buy Lands to perpetuate it. *Tot.* 96.

2. A Devise of Twenty Pounds a Year to a preaching Minister, and the Devisor makes his Wife Executrix, and dies, leaving Lands and Assets in Goods. The Executrix refuseth to buy Lands, or a Rent of that Value, the Lord Keeper and two Judges decree the Executrix to buy Lands to that Value, and to assure it for the Charitable Use. *Herne of Charit. Uses* 102.

12 *Trustees to execute the Trust, or transfer.*

1 If Lands or Goods are given to one by Will, or a Remainder limited to one by Deed, to perform a Charitable Use, if the Devisee will refuse the Legacy, or the Grantee wave his Remainder, and that by Fraud or Covin (*or that they do not care for the Charge or Trouble of the Trust, or otherwise, as I conceive it*) they are compellable to take the Land and to perform the Use. *Du. Ch. Uses,* 139 — *or to assign to others who will*

2 In Case of Misbehaviour, or Misapplication by Trustees of a Charity, Chancery

will oblige them to affign. See Cafe Coventry and *Attorney Gen.* in the Houfe of
Lords, 8 *May* 1720.

13. *Exempt from all Ordinary Jurifdiction,
and here of the Vifitatorial Power.*

1. *Vifitation.*

1. *Who may, and who may not.*

1. *The Ordinary may not.*

1 A Prohibition lies where the Vifitatorial Right is invaded *Gilb.* 181. *Show.
Parl. Ca.* 51. 4 *Mod.* 112. *Stillingfleet's
Cafes* 413.
2 Vifitation is a Sacred Truft in the
Crown to fuperintend thofe Orders and
Rules as have been given by the King, or
any of his Royal Predeceffors, touching their
Charities, as appears by the *Regifter* 40, 41.
And if this Right be invaded, a Prohibition lies, and this is the Privilege of every
common Founder, upon the general Rule
of Reafon, *Cujus eft dare ejus eft difponere,*
and this is mentioned in the Cafe of *Phillips* and *Bury, Show. Parl. Ca.* 51. 4 *Mod.*
112. and *Stillingfleet's Cafe* 413. and therefore the Vifitatorial Power is that Jurifdiction there is no Appeal to the Law
from. *Gilb* 182. The principal Cafe was
concerning the Vifitation of *Birmingham*
School, which was founded by King *Edward* the Sixth, and twenty Governors
were appointed for the Government of this
Charity, and they were to do fuch and fuch
Acts,

Acts, by the Advice and Consent of the Bishop of the Diocese. It was indeed contended, but without Foundation, that the
Governors had the Visitatorial Power, but
ruled, that it was in the Crown, as Founder, and Conservator of their one Charity;
and this was said to be the Case of every
Charity by private Persons, by the Rule,
Cujus est dare, &c but it was never pretended the Bishop had any Visitatorial
Power The Precedents were said to be
the same with the principal Case in *Win-
bourne* School, *Basingstoke* School, *Plymouth*
School and *Bethlem* Hospital, &c. *Gilb.* 178
to 183

3 *Un Visitor,* that is, when the King, or
any of his Progenitors, is Founder of the
House, there the Ordinary regularly shall
not visit them , but the Chancellor of *England* is appointed by the Law to be Visitor
of them, or where a special Visitor is appointed upon the Foundation, the Complaint
must be made to that Visitor. *Co Lit.* 96.

4. Whether an Hospital or College, &c.
to Charities there must be a Visitor, either
the Founder and his Heirs, or one appointed
by them   *Skin.* 484

5. Colleges are Lay Corporations, and
were so holden in *Appleford's* Case, and not
within the Jurisdiction of the Ecclesiastical
Courts, their Members have no Admission
or Institution from the Ordinary, and their *Note ,* Col-
Visitors, *quatenus* Visitors, are Lay Offic ers, leges in the
and have their Authority derived to them Universities
by the Common Law, and not by any are here
Commission, or Constitutions Ecclesiastical meant.
Skin. 494, 495.

6 *Mich.*

6 *Mich.* 3 & 4 *Eliz. Coveney Prefident del novel Coll' en Oxon deprive per le Evefque de Winton, Vifitor del dit Coll' & exempt de tout Jurifdiction Ordinary, fuit Appeal al Roy en fon Chancery, & Comiffion illonq, grant a A Brown & Wefton, Juftices que fur Conference ove auter Juftices & Civilians refolve que le Appeal ne gift, ne afcun auter remedie pur le Appellant, pur ceo cefte Cafe fuit hors del dit Stat' de 24 & 25 H. 8. car cef Deprivation eft mere temporal, & come pur le Ley prov. Ex quo fequitur que un Affize gift, &c* 4 Inft.

7 A common Perfon is Founder of an Hofpital which is Donative by Letters Patent, and is Temporal; if the Ordinary will vifit, the Patron fhall have a Prohibition, or if the Ordinary will cite any of the poor Men, or remove them, &c. the Founder, or his Heir, fhall have a Prohibition. *Fitz N B.* 42. B

8. Hofpitals not vifitable *per le Ordinar*. Palm. 451.

9. The Bifhop of *Winchefter*, Vifitor of the School of *Winchefter* of the Foundation of *Wickham*, late Bifhop of *Winchefter*, the Archbifhop of *Canterbury* and others his Colleagues, *anno 5 Car* cited the Ufher of the faid School by Force of their Commiffion to appear before them, and they proceeded there againft him, for which they incurred the Danger of a *Præmunire*, and fo did the Archbifhop of *Conterbury* and his Colleagues, by Force of an High Commiffion to them directed, cite one *Humphry Fronke A M.* and School-mafter of *Sevenock*, of the Foundation of Sir *William Sevenock*,

nock, in temqore H. 6. to appear before the High Commiſſioners at *Lambeth,* which Citation was ſubſcribed by Sir *John Bennet, L L.D.* Dr. *James* and Dr. *Hickman,* three of the High Commiſſioners, and Sir *Chriſtopher Perking* procured the ſaid Citation to be made, and when *Franke* appeared, the Archbiſhop being aſſociated with Sir *Chriſtopher Perkins* and Dr *Abbot,* Dean of *Wincheſter,* made an Order concerning the ſaid School, (to wit) that the ſaid *Franke* ſhould continue in the ſaid School until the Annunciation, and that he ſhould have 20 *l* paid him by Sir *Ralph Boſvile,* Knight. 13 *Co* 11.

2. *The Crown.*

1. *The Crown, or the Lord High Chancellor, as Viſitor for the Crown.*

1. Where the Preſentation belongs to the Crown, the Lord Chancellor is to preſent, and he is alſo to viſit for the Crown, as he is to adviſe the King, according to Equity and good Conſcience. *Elſin Obſ* 26. His Lordſhip is called the Mouth, the Ear, and the very Heart of the King. *Elſin Obſ.* 21 He is called *Pater Patriæ,* the King is only his Superior. *Elſ Obſ.* 3, 45, 6.

2 The King may have a Prohibition to the Ordinary, that he viſit not the Hoſpitals of Royal Foundation, becauſe the Chancellor of *England* ought to viſit them, and no Body elſe, and ſo it is of the King's or his Progenitors Free Chapels, no Ordinary ſhall viſit them, but the Lord High Chancellor *F N. B.* 42. A.

N 3　　　　　　3. Where

3. Where the King is Founder, his Majesty and his Succeffors are Vifitors, but where a private Perfon is Founder, there fuch private Perfon and his Heirs are, by Implication of Law, Vifitors. *Peer Will.* 326

3. *The Founder.*

1. *General.*

1. There are many Peculiars in the Hands of the Laity, where neither the Archbifhop, or Bifhop, have any Thing to do, or Power to vifit. 3 *Lev* 212

2 Founders, as they are Benefactors to the Publick, have the Power of forming and difpofing of their Charities, and may fafhion them as fuits beft with their Defigns, fo they give them legal Shape *Skin* 502

3. It is to be prefumed that a Founder, who has given largely to Charity, will keep the fame to Rule and Order. *Gul* 181

4. Where a private Perfon is Founder, fuch private Perfon and his Heirs are, by Implication of Law, Vifitors. 1 *Peer Will* 326.

※　5 *Trin* 2 *Geo* 2 Dr *Bentley* and *The Bifhop of Ely.* Where the Founder has not given Rules to the College of his own Foundation, his Heir has that Right devolving upon him, on the Death of his Anceftor, and this Right differs from that of a Vifitor by Appointment, in which Cafe the Law is the fame whether the College was of Royal or private Foundation.

6. *Heb*

6. *Holt* C J. It is not at the 'Pleasure of the Founder, whether there shall be a Visitor or not, for if he is silent during his own Time, and make no Appointment of a Visitor, the Right will descend to his Heir; and so it appears in the Case in *Telv.* 65. and *Cro Jac* 40. where it is admitted on all Hands, that the Founder is Visitor, and so is 8 *E* 3. 70. and 8 *Aff.* 29. so that Patronage and Visitation are necessary Consequents upon one another; for this Visitatorial Power was not introduced by any Canons or Constitutions Ecclesiastical; it is an Appointment of Law, it ariseth from the Property which the Founder had in the Lands; and as he is Author of the Charity, the Law gives him and his Heirs a Visitatorial Power, that is, an Authority to inspect their Actions and regulate their Behaviour, as he pleaseth; for it is not fit that Members that are endowed, and have the Charity bestowed upon them, should be left to themselves, but pursue the Intent and Design of him who bestowed it upon them. And as the Founder and his Heirs are Patrons, they are not to be guided by the common known Laws and Rules of the Kingdom, but by the particular Laws and Constitutions assigned them by the Founder or Patron *Skin* 483, 484

7 Where a common Person is Founder of an Hospital, which is Donative by his Letters Patent, *&c* if the Ordinary will visit, the Patron shall have a Prohibition against him, or if the Ordinary will cite any of the poor Men to appear before him for an Hospital Cause, or to remove him,

the

the Founder, or his Heirs, shall have a Prohibition. *F. N. B.* 42. B. *And* quære, *if
the Patron may not, as I conceive he may,
prosecute the Ordinary on the Statute of Provi-
sors, as I conceive appears from many Authorities.*

2. *His Authority.*

1. Citation, Monition, Visitation, and
administring the Oath, are Acts not to be
done as a private Person, but only as Visitor. *Skin* 474.

2. Visitor may adjourn the Visitation.
Skin. 474

3. Where there is a Visitor, the Court intends that the Visitor will do Right. *Skin* 454

4. *Lord Keeper:* Where once a Visitor
hath given Judgment, no Court can meddle
in it. *Skin.* 646, 647. *in Canc'*

5. *Holt* Lord C. J. I take it to be clear,
that where any one is Visitor of a College,
he has full and ample Power to deprive
and amove any Member of the College,
quatenus Visitor *Skin* 479

6. *Holt* Lord C J. The Question is not,
what was reasonable or fit for the Founder
to do, but what he has done ; it is not in our
Power to control for our imagined Unrea-
sonableness , for he had such an Authority
and Interest himself in what was of his
own Creation, as that he might invest the
Person he appoints Visitor with any Power
he pleased to give him ; and it is to be supposed that what he hath done, he had Reason for doing, though if he had not, it is
not material, his Will is his Reason in dis-
posing

poſing and ordering his own; and it is not in our Power to take away this Authority from him, becauſe we think it unreaſonable. Who knows what Reaſon a Man may have? Every Man is Maſter of his own Charity to appoint and qualify it as he pleaſes. *Skin.* 481.

7 *Holt* Lord Ch. J. In our old Books, deprived by Patron, and deprived by Viſitor, are all one; for it is a Benefit which naturally ſprings out of the Foundation, and it is in his, the Founder's, or Patron's, Power to transfer it, if he ſo pleaſe, to another; and when he hath ſo done, the other will have the ſame Right and Authority as the Founder himſelf had *Skin.* 484.

8 *Holt* Lord C. J The Sufficiency of the Sentence of a Viſitor (*and in the principal Caſe, it was a Viſitor by Appointment only*) is never to be called in Queſtion, nor any Inquiry to be made here (*in B. R*) into the Reaſons or Cauſes of the Deprivations, if the Sentences be given by him who is the proper Viſitor created ſo by the Founder or by the Law, you ſhall never inquire into the Validity or Ground of the Sentence; and this will appear if we conſider the Reaſon of a Viſitor, how he comes to be ſupported by Authority in that Office. *Skin.* 482.

9. A Viſitor (*by Appointment*) is to judge according to the Statutes and Rules *of the College, &c.* he may expel, and, as it is in 8 *Aſſ* 29, 30. he may deprive. The only Queſtion there was, who was Viſitor; for it was agreed on all Hands, that, *quatenus* Viſitor, he might deprive If he be a Viſitor,

Note the Dif-
ference.
tor, as Ordinary, there lieth an Appeal
from his Deprivation, but if, as Patron,
there is none · · That Deprivation, whether
by Right, or by Wrong, was to stand good
Skin 484, 485.

10. *Holt* C J. Where there is a Visitor,
and he hath Power to proceed to a Deprivation, you (*the King's Bench*) shall not examine his Proceedings more than those of
any Judge , and his Lordship said, he remembered, that my Lord *Hale* mentioned
and took it for clear Law, that it was as
binding as a Judgment in an Assise to bind
the Plaintiff, he is made Judge, and his
Person particularly designed by the Founder; but he hath his Authority from the
Law, and he is to judge by the Statute, &c
The Founder hath trusted this particular
Matter to his Discretion, and why should
we suspect him that he will not do right,
&c. *Skin* 489, 492, 493.

11. Visitors are not tied up to any particular Forms, are not to be prohibited for
Irregularity or Informalities in their Proceedings, or Acts, but only for want of
Jurisdiction See *Bishop of Ely* and *Dr*
Bentley's Case in the House of Lords, 6 *May*
1732. See 1 *Mod* 12, 84 3 *Lev* 211 *Gilb*
181, 178, 182. *Skin.* 474, 498, 646. 3 *Mod*
295. 4 *Mod* 106, 112, 236, 238, 240, 241,
5 *Mod.* 404, 452. 1 *Show.* 74.

12 A Visitor in his Citation, &c need
not call himself so, as the Parties to be visited are presumed to know their Visitor.
See the *Bishop of Ely* and *Dr. Bentley's* Case,
before the House of Lords, 6 *May* 1732.
Vue tout le Case, excellent Matter.

13 He

13. He who may vifit, may deprive, as well as cenfure; thefe being but feveral Degrees of Punifhment; for allowing his Power to vifit, all is admitted *Watfon*, Bifhop of *St David*'s Cafe in *Salk*

14 Allowing one Power to vifit, all is admitted, for he who may vifit, may deprive, as well as cenfure; thefe being but feveral Degrees of Punifhment By the 26 *H*. 8. and 1 *Eliz c* 1. the only Power given to the Ecclefiaftical Commiffioners was to vifit, without one Word of Deprivation, yet they were always allowed a Power to deprive. *Watfon*, Bifhop of *St. David*'s Cafe in *Salk*.

4 *Vifitor by Defignation, or Appointment.*

1 *General.*

1. Though this Vifitatorial Power refults to the Founder and his Heirs, yet the Founder may veft or fubftitute fuch Vifitatorial Right in any other Perfon or his Heirs. *Peer Will.* 326.

2. The Founder hath his Authority not by the Canons Ecclefiaftical, but by the Common Law, and this Law it is that allows him to delegate his Authority, and conftitute another Vifitor, as the Bifhop of *Exeter* is in the principal Cafe; but ftill the Authority of fuch Vifitor is wholly Temporal and not Ecclefiaftical, and the Power of conftituting him is allowed the Founder by the Common Law, and arifeth from a Temporal Right, and the Vifitor is a Temporal and not an Ecclefiaftical Judge. *Skin.* 495 *And as he owes no Obedience to the Ordinary,*

dinary or other inferior Jurisdictions, so he knows no other to govern and guide him in his Visitation than the Law of his own Conscience, ruled by the Law of holy Scripture and the superior Temporal Laws.

3. The Authority of the Founder to visit is an Authority by the Common Law, like that of an Escheator, or the like, whereof the Courts of Law will judicially take Notice; but the Authority of the Visitor constituted by the Founder is not so, it is a derivative Authority and limited, and therefore not general. *Skin.* 497.

4 Ju. *S Eyre.* The Visitor hath no greater Authority or Power than the Founder hath given him; he is the Founder's Creature, *quatenus* Visitor, and receiveth his Being, Power, and Authority from him, and if the Founder giveth him Authority in some Things and Cases, and not in others, and qualifies and limits that Power, which he gives him, the Visitor cannot exceed that Power and Authority which is given him, *qui potest dare potest disponere.* Skin. 454

5. *B. R. Hil 2 Geo.* 2. Dr. *Snape* and the Bishop of *Lincoln.* On Demurrer in Prohibition the Case was, that one *Dale*, a Fellow of King's College in *Cambridge* had made a Speech, upon a Publick Occasion, in the Hall of the College, wherein he reflected upon the Provost and Fellows; for which they put him out of Commons, and ordered him to retire to his Chamber; whereupon he sent them Word that he would appeal to the Visitor, and to that End, ask'd Leave to go out of the College, but not obtaining it, went without, and app aled to the B.shop of *Lincoln*,

colt; whereupon the College expelled him; from which Sentence he appealed again; and the Bishop came into the College, and visited them upon this Appeal, and whether he had a Right so to do was the present Question? Mr. *Reeves*, for the Plaintiff, laid it down, that in all Temporal Foundations, the Founder and his Heirs are Visitors by Law, unless another Person is particularly thereunto appointed: He said too, that either this Visitatorial Authority might be distributed into different Hands, or one Person may be appointed partial Visitor, and the remaining Part of this Power may continue in the Hands of the Founder and his Heirs, and this, he said, was the present Case, for King *Henry* 6 who founded this College, thought proper to intrust the Bishop with the Exercise of this Authority only in particular Instances, but the remaining Part of it he either kept to himself, or would not have exercised at all for the Sake of the Repose and Quiet of the Body; and this, he said, appeared from the Statute appointing the Visitor which gives them such and such particular Powers, and said, that the giving the Bishop some particular Powers in the last Clause was a Circumscribing the general Jurisdiction, which he might have seemed to have given him before, else this Clause would be without any Effect. But what, he said, fully determined this Matter was, that there comes afterwards a Clause which has negative Words in it, and says expressly, that this Visitor shall have no further Power than has been particularly given him, however he said, if he should admit that the Bishop

shop had a general Authority of examining into all Matters relating to the State of the College, when he came in his Triennial Visitation; yet there was no Pretence to say, he could come in upon a particular Appeal of a private Fellow, and that for that the Statute restrains him from coming at any other Time than his general Visitation, unless called in by the Provost and Bursers Besides, he said, the Statutes appoint that every Fellow and Scholar shall take an Oath not to appeal in any Case; for the Words are, that they shall obey the Orders of the Provost and Fellows, *absque Appellatione aut Querelæ obstaculo quocunque*, but the Attorney General, on the other Side, said, that as to the Extent of the Bishop's Authority, he thought it clear, that it was general and universal, for the instancing in some particular principal Part of the Authority could never take away the rest of it, which was given by the general Words; he said it was a common Way of penning almost all Statutes of this Nature, and he said this Point is settled in the Case of *Phillips* and *Burry* 4. *Mod.* As to the Negative Clause, that did confine the Bishop to the Place in which he should exercise his Jurisdiction, and to the Time in which he should make his general Visitation; but was far from tying him up to the Instances particularly mentioned Then as to the Bishop's coming in upon a particular Appeal of a private Fellow, he said, it was determined in the Case just before cited, that tho' a Time is stated by the Statute for the Visitor's Exercising his general Jurisdiction; yet as incident to his Office, he

he may *de jure*, at any Time, make a particular Visitation, on a private Appeal, and
examine into the Matters he was requested
to inquire into, unless there is an express
prohibitory Clause to the contrary; but that,
he said, was not in the present Case; for
at the most, the Clause which the other Side
relied on is but doubtful and obscure, the
Words being no ways proper to signify a
restraining of an Authority at that Time
given; but to take away an Authority that
was given, or might be thought to be given
before. Now as to that, the Attorney said,
it appears by another of these Statutes, that
King *Henry* 6 had obtained a Bull from the
Pope to take away the Ordinary Jurisdiction
from the Bishop of *Ely* over the Members
of this College, and to give it to the Bishop
of *Lincoln*, by which Act it was something
doubtful, at the Time of making these Statutes, whether the Bishop of *Lincoln* had not
a Power of visiting this College, as Ordinary, and said, there are several Opinions
scattered in the old Books which favour this
Notion; tho' now the Law is settled to the
contrary. Then the Design of this Clause
possibly might be to take away from the Bishop all Colour of Visiting upon that Account. Upon which, Mr. *Attorney* said, he
would now consider the Force of the Oath,
the Form whereof is not in general Terms,
as stated on the other Side; but only the
Party swears he will not appeal when he
shall be punished *propter sua delicta secundum
Exigentiam Statutorum*: Now who is the
proper Person to judge of the Deservedness
of this Punishment, but the Visitor? and as

2   to

to the Word, *Appeal,* which was relied on by Mr. *Reeves,* the Attorney General said, it might be understood of the foreign Appeals to Courts Temporal or Ecclesiastical, and not to this Statutable Visitor, who was appointed to redress all Grievances of this Nature; and to this Purpose cited Dr *Terbury's Case,* 1 *Keb.* 166. and *Appleford's Case, Mod* 82. Whereupon he moved for a Consultation, but the Court said, this was a Case of a good deal of Consequence and Difficulty; so they would not deliver their Opinions that present *Mich. Term,* 2 *Geo* 2. but that the same should stand over for the Opinion of the Court till next Term, when (to wit) *Hil.* 2 *Geo* 2. the Lord Ch. Just. delivered the Opinion and Resolution of the Court, and said, the principal Matter they relied upon was the same with that in *Phillips* and *Berry,* 1 *Mod.* That wherever a general Visitor is appointed, and his Time for visiting is prescribed to particular stated Times, the Court will always construe that to be understood of his visiting *ex Officio,* and not to hinder his coming in at other Times upon a private Appeal, unless there are direct negative Words to that Effect, for if it was not for such a Construction, the Body would be left without any Redress in the mean Time His Lordship also said, that the Reason of that Resolution warranted them in another they also made, that wherever a Visitor is appointed only to particular Purposes, and his Time of Visiting confined in this Manner, they will always construe it with the Distinction mentioned. His Lordship also observed, that here in the

2   present

prefent Cafe, the Bifhop is general Vifitor ; for the Words in the Recital in the Statute of Vifitation make him fuch, and the Conclufion reckons up all the Inftances which it can be fuppofed there may be Occafion of for exercifing this Authority; but tho' it had not, his Lordfhip faid, they were of Opinion, a certain Number of particular Inftances would not have circumfcribed the general Jurifdiction before given , and his Lordfhip alfo faid, he thought a proper Rule might be applied, that where particular Words are in the fame Sentence which the general Words are in, they may be conftrued to abridge the Senfe of them ; but where they are in diftant and other Claufes, the fecond fhall only be conftrued as a loofe Enumeration, and more efpecially fo in antient Writings, where perhaps fo much Accuracy was not obferved as now. Then as to the negative Words fo much infifted on, they were of Opinion they did not at all refer to this Right, which is now claimed as Vifitor ; for the Words are, *quoad alia,* than what is mentioned as Vifitor ; but they thought they might well refer to the general Notion which was at that Time received of his vifiting as Ordinary. Then his Lordfhip was pleafed to anfwer fome of the main Objections, and the firft he took Notice of was, the Provoft being Vifitor himfelf as to fome particular Matters ; but that, his Lordfhip obferved, could not be, for the Bifhop has undoubtedly a Right of controuling what the Provoft has done when he comes in upon a general Vifitation, and all Vifitors are neceffarily in the very Notion of the Words *final Judges.*

Then to the Objection about the Oath, his Lordship said, that it was determined that would not bind the Party in *Appleford's* Case, and in *Coleworth's* Case cited in the Case of *Philips* and *Bury*; but besides, in the present Case, the Oath is far from being general; for it is, that he will not appeal when he shall be punished *secundum exigentiam statutorum*; however this is one good Effect that this Oath may have, that if the Appeal be found unjust, it will be good Cause of Expulsion; for these Reasons his Lordship said, they were resolved, that a Consultation should be awarded. Upon which Mr. *Harding*, Counsel for the Bishop, said, he did not know but it might be proper to move for Costs; but the Court inclined, that they could not give Costs but where some Act of Parliament has allowed them; whereupon Mr. *Strange* said, that the Statute of King *William* does give Costs on Demurrer in Prohibition; upon which the Court held, that if so, they had a Right to them, without making this Application.

2. *How appointed.*

Trin. 2 *Geo.* 2. B. R. Dr. *Bently* and Lord Bishop of *Ely.* The Court said, they were very clear of Opinion, that the Words *Episcopus Eliensis Visitator sit*, extended to the Bishop's Successors for ever, and therefore they would not consider that Point any further.

5. The

5. *The Acts of the Visitors.*

1. *Whether may be enforced by the Authority of the Temporal Courts.*

1. *In B R. Trin.* 2 *Geo* 2. *The Archbishop of Canterbury* and *The Master, Fellows and Scholars of Trinity College Cambridge.* ✱

Mr. *Lee, now Lord C. J.* moved for Time till next Term, to shew Cause on a Rule which had been made for a *Mandamus* to be directed to this College, to admit a Librarian upon the Appointment of the Archbishop, he having this Power given him by the Statutes of the College; he said, there would be a good deal of Time necessary to the looking into several of these Statutes to see whether the Archbishop had such a Power or not; and that the College was not served with the Rule till *Friday* last. The Court said, if this had been a Motion for Time to make a Return to a *Mandamus*, the Suggestion of Difficulty might have been very proper, but five Days Time was enough to shew Cause, whether the *Mandamus* should not go; they also said, there can be no Prejudice to you by the going of the *Mandamus*; for if the Archbishop has not this Right, you will not be in Contempt by refusing to obey it; but there may be a Prejudice to the other Side; for if the Archbishop has this Right, the Librarian ought to be admitted immediately, and receive the Profit of his Office, which, if he is not admitted to now, he will have no Remedy for.

2. *Pas.*

2. *Paf.* 8 *Geo* 2. *B. R. The King* and *Walker.*

Mr. Serjeant *Eyre* moved for a *Mandamus* to be directed to Dr. *Walker,* Vice-Master of *Trinity* College in *Cambridge,* to put in Execution a Sentence of Deprivation against the Master, which the Bishop of *Ely,* as Vifitor over the Master, had pronounced My Lord Chief Justice, on this first Application, said, that he thought the proper Application would be to the general Vifitor ; however a Rule was made to shew Caufe. The Return of this *Mandamus* coming now to be argued, (*Hill.* 9 *Geo.* 2) Mr. *Wynn now Serjeant* said, that the Writ set forth, that King *Henry* 8. by his Letters Patent in the 19th Year of his Reign founded this College, and that King *E* 6. *anno* 7 gave certain Statutes to this College, by which it was provided, that the Bishop of *Ely,* for the Time being, fhould be general Vifitor over the Master and the Reft of the College, that Queen *Elizabeth* by her Letters Patent *anno* 2. gave them other Statutes, by which it was provided, that in Cafe the Master fhould be convicted of Dilapidations, he fhould be deprived by the Bishop, and that the Vice-Master, for the Time being, fhould execute the Bishop's Sentence upon him. The Writ fuggefted, that the Bishop of *Ely* vifited the Master, and deprived him for Dilapidations ; that this Sentence had been certified to the Vice-Master; that he had been required to execute it, and had refufed fo to do, whereupon the Writ was commanding the Vice-Master, that he fhould execute the Sentence ; whereto he returned, that the Statutes of *E.* 6. were cancelled

cancelled by the College accepting thofe from Queen *Elizabeth*; that by the Statutes of *Eliz.* the Bifhop of *Ely* was appointed Vifitor over the Mafter only, and that the Right of Vifitation was in the prefent King only. Upon this State of the Cafe, Mr. *Wynn* faid, that he fhould not offer any Thing to the Court, whether the Bifhop of *Ely* was general Vifitor over the College or not; but fubmitted it, that notwithftanding it fhould be allowed, that the Bifhop was Vifitor over the Mafter only, that ftill the *Mandamus* ought to go; for which Purpofe, he faid, he fhould confider two Queftions. 1. Whether this Court had no Power to compel the Vice-Mafter to execute his Duty, though the King might compel him likewife. And 2dly, As this Cafe really is, whether the King hath any Power to compel him at all. With Regard to the firft, he fubmitted it, that it was the Bufinefs of this Court to correct and affift all inferior ones. *Term. Hill.* of the late King, a *Mandamus* was granted to the Quarter-Seffions to give Judgment to abate a Nufance; the like was done *Mich* 11 of the fame Reign, to the Court of *Sandwich*, in the Cafe of *Bayly* and *Born*. *Mich.* 7. fame King, a *Mandamus* went to the Sheriffs of *London*, to command them to give Judgment on a Writ of Inquiry: The like in the Cafe of *The King* and *The Bailiffs of Andover*, *Term Trin. anno* 2. of the prefent King; and the *Mich.* following a *Mandamus* went to the Mayor of *Leverpoole*, to require him to hold a corporated Affembly to renew Leafes, and in *Style* 9 it appears, that an Adjudgment removed from the Cinque Ports

O 3 into

into this Court by *Certiorari*, a *Sci. fa.* if. fued from this Court to execute it; fo in the Cafe *Powis* and *Andrews*, *Feb.* 1723. before Lord Chancellor. (*before the Houfe of Lords*, 11 March 1727.) On Suit in the Ecclefiaftical Court, the Judge had ordered an Executor to bring Money into Court, that Sentence, on Appeal to the Delegates, was reverfed ; for that the Ecclefiaftical Court had no fuch Authority ; but on Demurrer to a Bill in Chancery, for that Purpofe brought, my Lord Chancellor ordered the Executor to bring the Money into Court. By thefe Cafes he fubmitted it, that it fufficiently appeared that this Court, as well as others, do often aid and affift one another ; and for that Purpofe he cited *Palm.* 50. 2 *Rol. Ab.* 106. *Lev.* 119 *Fitz. N. B* 34, 538. *Vent.* 32. and *Rol. Abr.* 530 *pl.* 12. And he further faid, that the Court had granted *Mandamus*'s even in the Cafe of this very Univerfity, as a *Mandamus* went hence to this Univerfity to elect a *Regius Profeffor* ; and another, in the late Reign, to reftore Dr. *Bentley* to his Degrees; yet the King is confidered as Vifitor of both Univerfities; and he faid, to come nearer to the prefent Cafe, *Term. Trin. anno* 12 of the late Queen, a Rule to fhew Caufe was obtained on (late Judge) *Page's* Motion, why a *Mandamus* fhould not be directed to the late Bifhop of *Ely*, requiring him to proceed to Judgment on the like Articles with the prefent ; the Rule indeed, he faid, was not made abfolute, becaufe the Bifhop did proceed ; and in the prefent Cafe he fubmitted it, there were the ftrongeft Reafons for granting this *Mandamus*; becaufe it is at the Requeft

Requeſt of the Judge himſelf. With Regard to the ſecond Queſtion, he ſubmitted it, that the King himſelf, had no Power of ſentencing the Vice-Maſter for not executing the preſent Sentence: He ſaid, it is agreed on all Hands, that the Biſhop is Viſitor of the Maſter, the King has delegated his whole Power of viſiting him to the Biſhop, and therefore the King can have nothing to do with the Execution or Examination of the Sentence. If this had been in the Caſe of a private Founder, he ſubmitted it, the Law would have been clear in this Reſpect, and this being the Caſe of a Royal one, he apprehended, made no Difference; and for Authority cited *Fitz.* 93. *Skin.* 484. and *Hob.* 105. Mr. *Strange* argued on the other Side, and ſaid, that with Regard to the Merits of the Queſtion, he ſubmitted it, that no *Mandamus* ought to be granted. In the Caſe *Wilkins* and *Mitchel, Trin.* 10 King *Will* in Debt for Rent in the Mayor's Court of *Cambridge* the Plaintiff was nonſuited, and the Mayor refuſed to grant Execution for the Coſts, having taking Security for his Indemnity; whereupon a *Mandamus* was moved for; but the Court refuſed to grant it, becauſe a Writ *De executione judicii* lay out of Chancery; and further for Authority cited *Show.* 74 *Car.* 92, 168. And he ſaid, he did not know that in any Caſe one Court aſſiſted another in executing its Proceſs; but in the preſent Caſe, he ſaid, was leſs Reaſon for doing it than in any other, becauſe the Vice-Maſter may be viſited either by my Lord Chancellor, or certain Commiſſioners, as was determined in the Caſe of *Birming-*

O 4 *ham*

ham School, *Hill* 5 of the late King; and
besides, in the present Case, he said, there
was a flat Exception to the *Mandamus*, in
Point of Form, for the very *Mandamus* sets
forth that the Bishop is general Visitor by
the Statute of *E* 6. and if that be so, there
can be no Colour that the Court should
interpose. My Lord Chief Justice said,
the general Question was, whether upon
this Writ and Return there was a Foundation to grant a peremptory *Mandamus*; the
general, his Lordship said, must be admitted
on all Hands, that where there is a Lay
Foundation, and the Visitatorial Power either in the Heir of the Founder, or of a
Visitor by his Appointment, the Court cannot, by any Means, interpose. These Powers
of Visiting, his Lordship said, were not so
properly Jurisdictions as Decisions of the
Founder himself in his own Charity; and
of this Opinion his Lordship observed my
Lord *Holt* seemed to be, in the Case *Phillips*
and *Bury*; his Lordship further thought this
might properly be called *Forum Domesticum*,
and he said, he did not know that the Court
had ever gone so far as to grant a *Mandamus* to make the Visitor execute his Sentence; tho' he would not say it would not
lay And as to the Case of *Regius Professor*,
he said, it was not shewn there that the
King was Visitor of the Universities; and
his Lordship agreed, that in the present
Case there was no Difference between this,
being a Royal Foundation, from what it
would have been in the Case of a private
one, but he said, these Rights were nothing
like Rights founded by Charter or Act of
Parlia-

Parliament; but this his Lordſhip clearly agreed, that when the Viſitor deprives a Man, he is immediately out, and the Party nominated in his Room may bring a collateral Action for the mean Profits or an Ejectment; and his Lordſhip alſo ſaid, he did not know, there was any Inſtance in the Law, of this Court granting a *Mandamus* to an Officer of another Court to put in Execution their Sentences, and by this Means to act as Miniſterial to them; and beſides, in the preſent Caſe, his Lordſhip ſaid, the *Mandamus* in itſelf was clearly bad; becauſe it admits the Biſhop to be general Viſitor. The Reſt of the Court were of the ſame Opinion; and accordingly agreed to conſider, whether they would quaſh or diſcharge the Writ, or allow the Return.

3 *Mich* 9 *Geo.* 2. *B. R* ✻

Mr. *Abney* moved now for a *Mandamus* to the Collegiate Church of the Bleſſed Virgin *Mary* in *Southwel*, to reſtore one ——— to his Stall of Vicar in the ſaid Church; he obſerved this was an antient Endowment from the Crown, and confirmed by a private Act of Parliament *anno* 25 *H* 8 by which Act they had a new Name given them, and the other Parts of it he owned were little more than Confirmation; however he ſaid, as there was an Act of Parliament in the Caſe, the King's Court were the proper Judges of its Conſtruction; for which Reaſon it was not neceſſary to apply to the King, as Viſitor, but this Court may properly interfere, and to this Purpoſe he cited one *Dowgate's* Caſe, where a *Mandamus* was to the Dean and Chapter of *Dublin*, to reſtore

store him *ad Staulum in Choro & Vocem in Capitulo.* So in Dr *Sherlock's* Case, who was Master of *Catherine Hall* in *Cambridge*, in that Case was a *Mandamus* to admit him to a Prebend in *Norwich*, which was annexed to his Headship; and *Hil.* 1. of the present King, there was a *Mandamus* for the Master of *Oriel College* directed to the Dean of *Rochester.* My Lord Ch. Just said, in the Case of Dr. *Sherlock* he well remembered, that the Foundation of that was, that the Prebend was annexed to the Office of Master by Act of Parliament; but yet he thought if this Act was meerly to be considered as an Act of Confirmation, this Court would hardly interfere; however a Rule was made to shew Cause, and after the Rule was made absolute *So that, as I conceive it, the Court was after satisfied that the said Act of Parliament was more than meerly an Act of Confirmation, and so gave this Court a Jurisdiction; else, as I apprehend, according to his Lordship's Opinion above, and the constant and uniform Opinion of the Courts, in almost innumerable Instances, this Matter must have received its Decision from the Crown, as Visitor, in Right of the Foundation's being a Royal one.*

*   4. *Trin.* 2 *Geo* 2. *in* B. R. Dr. *Bentley* and Bishop of *Ely.*

Per *Cur':* Wherever a Visitor (*by Appointment, as the Bishop was*) proceeds contrary to his Citation, or inflicts different Penalties from what the Statute prescribes, this Court always grants their Prohibition

*   5. *Mandamus's* have been frequent to admit Fellows of Colleges. Dr. *Bentley's Case.*

6. *What*

6 *What a good Evidence of the Visitatorial Power.*

B.R. *Paf.* 1726 *Cockman* con. *Mather & al'*
This was a Trial at Bar concerning the Right of Visitation of *University College Oxon* One of the Issues in this Case was, whether King *Alfred* was Founder, and the Counsel for the Plaintiff would have given in Evidence several Historians, as to this Point: But Lord Ch. Just declared, that such Evidence is never admitted, unless in Proof of some Point concerning the Government, the rest of the Court did not deny it, so it was waived. *Vide Skin.* 15.

7. *Whether the Visitatorial Power may be, and how, extinguished, or suspended, and the Remedy in such Cases.*

B R *Paf.* 1 *Geo.* 2. The King and the Bishop of *Chester.*
This was a *Mandamus* to the Bishop of *Chester*, as Warden of *Manchester College*, to swear in *Ashton*, Chaplain of the College The Bishop, as *Warden* return'd, that this College is of Royal Foundation, and that King *Charles* the first constituted the Bishops of *Chester*, for the Time being, Visitors, and so concludes that no *Mandamus* ought to go to him, and this was the only material Part of the Return. The Court admitted, that in all these Eleemosynary Foundations, where is a Visitor by Appointment, either by the Act of Law, or Act of the Party, the Court cannot interpose, unless in those Cases where the Visitatorial

tatorial Power is either extinguished or suspended; and that this Authority was sometimes so, they said, was evident from the common Question that is always asked in these Applications in *Mandamus*, whether there is any Body that can visit. Now they said, that this Question can only be applied to Extinguishment or Suspension of this Authority; for every one of these Eleemosynary Bodies must necessarily have one who is vested with a general Power of visiting them in general Cases. And the Court said, they would then consider, whether any one had a Right of Visiting in the particular Case. The Bishop, it is clear, cannot; for he is Party, and therefore cannot be Judge; the King cannot, for he has transferred his whole Right of visiting, to the Bishop, therefore this Case must fall into the general Current of Redress, in which all other Cases do. Mr. *Lee* cited a Case out of a Collection of Cases in Relation to the Privileges of the Universities, which was, that by the Statutes of *All Souls College* in *Oxon*, the Arch-Bishop of *Canterbury* is the Visitor by Appointment; and these Statutes say, if the Fellows cannot agree to chuse a Master within the prescribed Time, the Right of Nomination shall devolve upon the Archbishop; the Fellows did not agree in the prescribed Time, whereupon the Archbishop nominated one to them whom they refused to admit; whereupon the Archbishop visited them, and compelled them to it, and they rested under it, which Mr. *Lee* (*now Chief Justice*) said, was with him an Argument that they were advised that they could have no Redress elsewhere.

where. The Court faid, they were not obliged to confider how that Cafe was, but Lord Ch. Juft. and Judge *Reynolds* faid, that they did not know but there might be a Difference, upon which the Court made a Rule upon the Bifhop *nifi* on *Monday* next, which at the Time they made abfolute.

8 *Whether Offences againft the eftablifhed Statutes of a College, &c may be, and by whom, and how pardoned.*

Trin 2 *Geo in* B. R. Dr. *Bentley* and the Bifhop of *Ely*.

An Act of Grace is only a general Pardon of all fuch Crimes, not particularly excepted, as the King might pardon by exprefs Words, and therefore fuch Crimes to be forgiven as might be punifhed by Indictment, and were Crimes againft the State ; but Statutes of Colleges are only the Rules for the Government of a private Family ; and therefore Offences againft thofe Statutes cannot be fuppofed to be taken into the Confideration of the Legiflature in the paffing the Act, and fo the Court delivered their Opinions that the Act of Grace, pleaded by the Dr. could be no Bar to the Bifhop's Vifitation.

VI. *Railing.*

1. SMITH & *al* Church-Wardens of *Ridgewell* in *Effex*, prefented to the Archdeacon that one *Pannel* was a Railer, and a Sower of Difcord between Neighbours ;

bours; whereupon the Archdeacon injoined him Purgation, and the Court awarded Prohibition; for the Cauſe belongs to the Leet and not to them, except it were in the Church and the like. *Hob.* 246, 267.

2. If a Preſentment be made by the Church-Wardens of a Pariſh in the Eccleſiaſtical Court, that *J. S* a Pariſhioner is a Railer and a Sower of Diſcord in the Neighbourhood, a Prohibition lies, unleſs it was in the Church. *Rol. Abr.* Tit. *Prohib. Caſe* 45.

3 *Mich.* 9 *Geo.* 2. *B. R. Wilſon & al'* v *Reynolds.*

Mr. *Denniſon* moved for a Prohibition to the Defendant, as Judge of an Eccleſiaſtical Court in a Suit inſtituted by the Plaintiffs, as Church-Wardens of the Pariſh of *St.*   in the Town of *Northampton*, againſt one *Wright* for Brawling and Striking in the Church-Yard.   Proceedings had been to excommunicate, but he ſubmitted it, there ought to have been in this Caſe a precedent Conviction at Common Law, for which Purpoſe he cited *Vent* 146. and accordingly a Rule was to ſhew Cauſe; and then came Serjeant *Eyre* to ſhew Cauſe, and ſaid, that the Caſe cited out of *Vent* was a very looſe one, and one Part of it was plainly miſtaken, for it is ſaid, that becauſe the Words of the Statute are, that the Party ſhall be excommunicated *ipſo facto*, there is no Occaſion for Sentence of Excommunication *Lee* Ju ſaid, that the Law moſt certainly was miſtaken in that Reſpect, and my Lord Ch. Juſt ſaid, that the Note in *Vent.* was a very looſe one, and accordingly the Rule was enlarged to the next

next Term And now *Hil.* 9 *Geo.* 2 this
Matter coming on again, Mr. Serjeant *Eyre,*
in shewing Caufe againft the Prohibition,
faid, he apprehended that the Ecclefiaftical
Court had an Original Jurifdiction in Matters of this Nature, for which Purpofe he
cited *Lat.* 116; and if this was fo, he rea-
foned it could not be faid to be taken away
by *Stat.* 5 & 6 *E* 6. *c.* 4 and for this he
cited the Cafe of *Skreen* and *Cotteral,* *Trin*
3 *Geo.* 2. *in Com. B.* there it appeared, a
Suit had been inftituted in the Ecclefiaftical
Court againft a Quaker under fuch a Value
as the Juftice of Peace may relieve in by the
Stat W 3 but on Demurrer to a Prohibition the Court held, that notwithftanding
that, the Jurifdiction of the Ecclefiaftical
Court was not taken away, and to the fame
Purpofe, he faid, was 5 *Co. Cawdrey's* Cafe;
and by this he faid, it fufficiently appeared
that a Sentence of the Ecclefiaftical Court
was neceffary, and for Authority in this
Point he cited *Dy.* 255 *b* 3 *Cro.* 659 & *Het.*
86, fo that one Part of the Cafe in *Vent.*
146. cited before, which fays fuch Sentence
is not neceffary, cannot be Law, and the
other Part of it, which fays, if it is neceffary, it can only be founded on a previous
Conviction in the Temporal Courts, he fubmitted it, likewife was not Law: Alfo if the
prefent Sentence had been founded upon the
3d *Sect* in the *Stat. E.* 6. he owned the previous Conviction at Common Law might be
neceffary, but faid, the prefent Sentence
was founded meerly upon the 2d *Sect* for it
adjudges the Party to be guilty of Striking,
or laying violent Hands in the Church-Yard

4 on

on one *Wright* a Taylor; and such Act is only an Offence within the second Branch of that Statute, and tho' the Libel is for more, yet the Sentence, he said, was the only Thing to be regarded: And upon this Branch of the Statute, he said, he conceived, that a previous Conviction at Common Law would not be necessary, and for Authority on that Side, the Cases cited were *Noy* 104. 1 *Cro* 464. 3 *Cro.* 919 2 *L* 188. and *Register* 40 *B.* Serjeant *Chapple* on the other Side, submitted it, that before the *Stat E.* 6 the Ecclesiastical Court had no Jurisdiction in Matters of this Sort, unless where the Violence was committed upon a Person in holy Orders, and that by the Statute of *Circumspecte agatis*, and if this Case was so, he submitted it, that the Ecclesiastical Courts had no Authority to declare any Sentence in the present Case; the Case in *Vent* before cited, he insisted, was a full Authority for this Purpose; he further relied upon 6 *Co* 29, at least, he submitted it, the Sentence could only be founded upon a previous Conviction at Common Law, and this, he said likewise was warranted by the Case in *Vent* which hath been mentioned, and further, on that Side was cited *Salk* 555 *Godb* 218 2 *Cro.* 462. *Hob.* 121, 84, 246 & *Lit.* 142. My Lord Ch. Just. declared his Opinion, that the Ecclesiastical Court had no Jurisdiction in these Matters before the *Stat E* 6. which had been cited; but by that Statute he thought it clear, and compared this to Clauses in Acts of Parliament, which declare that in Cases of particular Offences the Party shall incur the Penalty of Felony, yet there

4

there muft be a Judgment, therefore this Part of the Cafe in *Vent.* could certainly not be maintained; and as to the other Part of it, he faid, the Word, which was made Ufe of in this Cafe was, Striking, by which the Reporter, perhaps, might mean Striking with a Weapon; and if fo, by the 3d Branch a previous Conviction at Common Law is neceffary, but the prefent Cafe muft be taken to be founded upon the 2d Branch of the Statute, where a previous Conviction, he thought, was not neceffary: The reft of the Court were of the fame Opinion, and accordingly the Rule was difcharged. *Vide Cafe Sloughton* and Dr. *Reynolds. Term. Trin.* 10 *Geo.* 2. *B. R.*

VII. *Scandal, Slander or Defamation.*

1. *General to.*

VIDE 5 *Co. De Ju. Reg Eccl.* 9. *a.* Bro. *Abr.* 170. 5.

2. *Incidents to.*

TOuching Defamations determinable in the Ecclefiaftical Courts, it was refolved, that they ought to have thefe Incidents 1ft, That it concern a Matter meerly Spiritual and determinable in the Ecclefiaftical Court. 2dly, That it concern Matter Spiritual only; for if fuch Defamation touch or concern any Thing determinable at Common Law, the Ecclesiastical Judge shall not have Cognizance of it 3dly, Tho' such Defamation be merely and only Spiritual, yet he who is defamed may not sue there for Amends or Damages, but the Suit ought only to be for the Punish-ment of Sin, *pro Salute Animæ.* 4 Co 20 a, *Fitzh. N. Br.* 53 (F.)

3. *Who may sue for.*

IF Baron and Feme are divorced in the Ec-clesiastical Court for Adultery, *a Mensi & Thoro & mutua Cohabitatione,* and after the Wife sues sole in the Ecclesiastical Cour' against a Stranger for Slander and Defama tion, and Sentence there given for her, and Penance injoined to the Defendant, *& ex pensæ Litis* assessed to the Plaintiff, and after the Husband releases all Actions, and this Suit and all belonging to it, and the Defen-dant pleads this Release in the Ecclesiastical Court where it is disallowed ; yet no Prohi bition shall be granted ; for tho' the Divorce does not dissolve the Marriage, but they re-main Baron and Feme ; yet forasmuch as by the Course of the Ecclesiastical Law, such Wife may sue sole, without her hus band, and this Suit is but to restore her to her Credit again, which was impeached by the Defendant, and the Costs of Suit are not for any Damages, but merely for the Charge of the Suit, and dependent upon it, therefore neither the Suit, nor the Costs so dependent upon it, shall be released by the Husband. *Mich.* 14 *Jac. Mottam & Mittam Res.*

Rol. Abr. Prohibition. fo 300, 301. *Cafe* 10. but if fuch Feme, after fuch Divorce, fue in the Ecclefiaftical Court for a Legacy given to her, and the Releafe of the Husband is pleaded, and difallowed, a Prohibition fhall be granted, for there the Legacy is origi- nally due to the Baron and Feme, and the Suit there is for a real Intereft, and there- fore the Releafe of the Husband will dif- charge it. 44 *Eliz. Stephens* and *Tott, Rol Abr Prohibititon* 301. *Cafe* 11 *Vide ante* in Courts of Law 7. Where the Party is fued in Ecclefiaftical Court for Acts done in the Temporal Courts, *per tout.*

4. *Where the Words are not intel- ligible.*

IF one Woman fue another for calling her Quean, a Prohibition lies, for that it is not well known what is meant by the Word, and it is but a Word of Anger. *Tr.* 3 *Car. B R Blackfhaw* and *Stevens, per Cur.* Pro- hibition granted. *Mich.* 8 *Car Yates* and *Glover.* Prohibition granted. *Rol. Abr. Prohibition,* 296. *Cafe* 14.

5. *Where are only Words of Heat.*

1. IF one Man fay to another, *thou art a Son of a Whore, and thy Mother was a Bitch,* for which he fues in the Ecclefiaftical Court, a Prohibition lies; for they are but Words of Anger. *Mich.* 3 *Car Lowns* and Sir *Ar-*

nold Herbert. Prohibition granted. *Rol. Abr. Prohibition,* 296. *Case* 15.

2. If one Man say to another, *Thou art a Knave, a paultry Knave, and a pocky-fac'd Knave,* for which a Suit is in the Ecclesiastical Court, a Prohibition lieth. *Pasch* 11 *Car. B. R. Packer* and *Moon.* Prohibition granted. *Rol. Abr. Prohibition, fo.* 296 *Case* 19.

3. If a Man say of another, *Thou art a Drunkard,* or *a drunken Fellow,* or *an idle Drunken Fellow,* if a Suit be in the Spiritual Court for it, a Prohibition lieth; for this is no Spiritual Slander. *Mich* 8 *Car. B R Star* and *Cuckow,* a Prohibition granted, for they are Words of Heat and Passion, and not any Spiritual Defamation 15 *Car. B. R. Haynes* and *Poynter.* The Words were, *Thou art a Drunkard, and art drunk three Times a Week.* Prohibition granted against the Opinion of *Berkley,* but after *Mich* 15 *Car* it was moved again, and *per Cur'* Prohibition granted; for the Court said, they might not hold Plea of a Defamation, where they had not original and direct Cognizance of the Fact of which he is accused, as they have not of Drunkenness, unless as an Offence against the Ten Commandments, as all Sins are. *Rol. Ab Prohibition, fo.* 296 *Case* 17.

6. *What*

6. *Where of Ecclesiastical Cognizance.*

1 IF a Man say to a Woman, *Thou art a Whore, and thy Children Bastards,* for which she sues in the Spiritual Court, no Prohibition lies; for the Statute of *Eliz* of Bastards saves the Ecclesiastical Jurisdiction. *Mich* 2 *Car. B. R. Wollis* and *Prater.* Prohibition denied. *Rol Abr Prohibition,* 296. *Case* 16.

2. Consultation refused where the Defamation was not merely and only Spiritual, or the Party sued for Amends. 4 *Co.* 20 *a. b.*

3. If there be a Suit in the Spiritual Court for calling a Man *Knave,* a Prohibition shall be granted ; because a Knave in the antient *Saxon* Language is a Male Child. 1 *Rol. Rep* 217.

4. *H.* libelled in the Spiritual Court for calling him a *Knave, a Knave and a Knave indeed,* and Prohibition was granted ; because nothing was said that could make him liable to Ecclesiastical Censure. *Salk* 548.

5 If one say of *J. S. He is a Railer and Sower of Sedition among his Neighbours,* he may not sue in the Ecclesiastical Court for these Words , for that they are in no Respect Spiritual, neither tend to any Spiritual Defamation, but are merely Temporal. *Mich.* 16 *Jac. Pannel* and *Smith,* a Prohibition granted accordingly. *Rol Abr. Prohibition,* N. *Case* 7

6. If a Parson call *A a Drunkard,* whereupon *A.* answereth *thou liest*; if the Parson

sue *A* in the Ecclesiastical Court for giving
him the Lie, a Prohibition lieth , for that
the Cause for which he gave him the Lie
was not Spiritual, but depended upon a precedent Temporal Matter. *Mich* 7 *Ja. Simpson* and *Water*, *Rol Abr.* 295 *Case* 5

7. *In B R. Hill.* 2 *Geo.* 2 *Anonymus.*

A Prohibition was prayed to be directed
to Commissary's Court of *Ely*, for holding
Plea of these Words, *You are a Jilt, and a
Strumpet* , but the Court said, it has been
determined, that they may hold Plea for
Words of calling a Man a *Cuckold*, for giving a Man that Name is by Implication
calling his Wife a *Whore*; and in the present
Case they said, the Word *Strumpet* signifies
a *Whore* and more, so refused the Motion
Vide 2 *Lev* 66. 1 *Co* 111. *Salk.* 207, 552,
692.

8 What shall be said to be a Defamation Spiritual to maintain a Suit in the Ecclesiastical Court. *Vide Rol. Abr. Prohibition,* N

7. *Where Words of Ecclesiastical Cognizance, are mixed with Words actionable at Law.*

1. THO' the Scandal be determinable in
the Spiritual Court , yet if mixed
with Matter determinable at Law, no Consultation granted. 4 *Co* 20 *a b.*

2. If one libels in the Ecclesiastical Court
for Words proper for the Jurisdiction of
that Court, and which will not, of themselves, maintain an Action at Law, yet upon

on Suggestion to the Temporal Court, on the Rest of the Words, that they will maintain an Action at Law, a Prohibition lies. *Mich* 38 & 39 *Eliz Butler* and *Butler, Rol. Abr Prohibition*, N. 4.

3. If a Man say of another, *that he keeps a Bawdy-house*, and he is sued for it in the Spiritual Court, though he might have an Action at Law, yet (as Mr. Serjeant *Rolle* saith) as the Spiritual Law hath a concurrent Jurisdiction, and the Words are mixed, no Prohibition lieth. *Rol Abr Prohibition*, N. *Case* 11, 13. tamen qu. *for, as I think, as the Words are actionable at Law, Remedy is there only to be sought, if the Party will pray a Prohibition*.

4. *Hill.* 10 *Geo* 2. *Legate* and *Wright*. Serjeant *Wright* moved for a Prohibition to the Spiritual Court of *Norwich*, in a Suit pending there for Defamation; the Words were, *You are on old Rogue and a Thief, and I will prove you so, and on old whoring Rogue, and a Bastard-getting old Rogue* , he agreed, the latter Words were of Spiritual Cognizance; but as the first were Temporal, a Prohibition will lie for the whole; for which Purpose he cited 2 *Inst* 493. Rule to shew Cause *Easter* Term following, Serj. *Eyre*, coming to shew Cause, submitted it, that these Words were not of a Temporal Nature sufficient to ground a Prohibition But the Court held the contrary, and accordingly the Rule was made absolute.

8. *Where the Words are actionable at Law.*

1. IF one libels in the Ecclesiastical Court for Words actionable at Law *sur le Case,* a Prohibition lieth. *Hill* 14 *Jac.* B R *Turnain* and *Thorne. Mich.* 38, 39 *Eliz Butler* and *Bartlet,* Rol *Abr. Prohibition,* N. *Case* 3.

2. If one having Lands by Descent sue in the Ecclesiastical Court against another for calling him *Bastard,* a Prohibition lieth, for it tendeth to a Temporal Disinheritance. *Mich* 31 *Ja.* B. R. *per Curiam.* Rol *Abr Prohibition,* 292 L. 7.

3 If *A.* sue *B* in the Spiritual Court for saying, *that he was false* or *forsworn before the Judges, in that he swore that* J S *was* a Prohibition lies, for that an Action lies at Common Law for these Words. 8 *Car* B R. *Robinson* and *Taylor,* Rol. *Abr. Prohibition,* fo. 297 *Case* 21.

4. A Prohibition was granted to Court Christian for holding Plea for calling him *Thief, and a Breaker of Coffers;* for this is a Matter which belongs to the King's Courts. *Hill.* 14 *E.* 2. *fo* 416.

9. *Whe*

9. *Where the Words are spoken in a Place where, by Custom, or Prescription, an Action lieth for them.*

1 A Prohibition was prayed to the Ecclesiastical Court, where the Libel was for these Words, *You are a Whore and ply in Moor-Fields*, and the Suggestion was, that the Words were spoken in *London*, where an Action lies for such Words, and therefore Prohibition granted; otherwise Suits might have been in the Court Christian for such Words, though not singly for the Word *Whore*, being a common Word of Brabling; otherwise, where joined with Words which shew the Intent to defame in that Kind. 1 *Vent.* 343.

2 *Finch*, Recorder of *London*, moved for a Prohibition to the Ecclesiastical Court, upon a Suit there for Defamation, in which *Skipwith* libelled there against his Client for these Words, *Thou art a Bawd, and there were two Couple upon one Bed in thy House.* Per Cur'. *Thou keepest a Bawdy-house*, are actionable here, for the Party might be indicted for it, but, *thou art a Bawd*, is a Matter Spiritual; and thereupon no Prohibition shall be granted. But he moved further, that the Party was indicted in *London* by the same Party, and this Indictment was removed to this Court (*King's Bench*); also he had brought an Action *sur le Case* now depending in this Court for the same Slander,

der, and thereupon prayed a Prohibition, *& habuit.* Palm. 379

3 *In B. R. Hill* 1726. *Bayley & ux' v. Robins.*

A Prohibition was moved for to ſtay Proceedings in the Conſiſtory Court of *London*; for that, as Counſel urged, it appeared, upon the Face of the Libel, that they had not any Juriſdiction; this being a Libel which charges the Defendant with calling the Plaintiff's Wife *Whore* in *London.* But as this was after Sentence, *Forteſcue* Ju ſaid, a Prohibition did not lie upon the Face of the Libel, without Affidavit of the Cuſtom of the City of *London,* in this Caſe, namely, that an Action lies there by Cuſtom; for, as the Judge ſaid, we are not obliged to take Notice of their Cuſtoms, and ſaid, he remembered two or three Caſes to this Purpoſe, the reſt of the Court ſaid nothing as to this Point; but did not grant the Prohibition, becauſe moved for the laſt Day of Term *Vide Salk* 547, 548.

4. *Mich.* 8 Geo. 2. *Holmes & ux' v. Haſt & ux'.*

This was upon a Rule to ſhew Cauſe why a Prohibition ſhould not be granted to the Conſiſtory Court of the Biſhop of *London* Mr *Strange* ſaid, that the Foundation on which the Rule was obtained was, that the Suit was for calling a Woman *Whore,* and that the Words appeared by the Libel to be ſpoke in *London;* but he ſubmitted it, that the Words did not appear to be ſpoke there; for they are laid to be ſpoke *in the Pariſh of St* Giles's Cripplegate, London, *or in ſome other Place in the Neighbourhood*

bourhood thereof, or near thereto adjoining; and in these Cases, where there is not a sufficient Certainty appearing upon the Libel, it is usual for the Party to make an Affidavit that the Words were spoke in *London*, and not elsewhere, and further he observed, that the Charge was only upon the Party for saying that the other had a *Bastard*, without directly calling her a *Whore*; and in these Cases the Court expects that the Word *Whore* should be particularly expressd, for which Purpose he cited 2 *Rol. Abr* 296. and *Lutw.* 1042. My Lord Chief Justice said, he thought there was a sufficient Reason for the Court's believing that the Words were spoken in *London*; and further his Lordship said, he thought the Words were sufficient of themselves, and his Lordship further said, this Court has allowed the Ecclesiastical Courts to proceed in Suits instituted by the Wife for calling her Husband *Cuckold*, and many Cases, he said, were contrary to those which have been cited, and accordingly the Rule was made absolute for so much of the Words as were spoke in *London*.

10. *Where the Words are not actionable at Law.*

A Prohibition lies to the Ecclesiastical Court for holding Plea for Words where is no Action at Law. *Mo. fo.* 607. Vide *For beating a Clerk*.

11. *Where*

11. *Where spoken by Men of Profession, as Judges, Counsel, &c.*

1 IF a Man be accused to be the Father of a Bastard before Justices of Peace, and the Justices in examining of the Matter say, *that it is his Bastard*, if they are after sued for these Words in the Spiritual Court, a Prohibition lieth, because that they said it in the Administration of their Office *Hill. 14 Ja. Cade* and *Windham,* and *Mich 14 Ja* it was affirmed again *Rol. Abr. Prohibition, fo.* 303 *Case* 1 But otherwise it had been, if the Justices said the Words at another Time, after the Examination. *Mich 14 Ja.* in the same Case of *Cade* and *Windham*, *Rol. Abr Prohibition, fo.* 303 *Case* 2.

1 Sir *Thomas Hughes* of *Gray's Inn* prayed a Prohibition by *Hendon* Serjeant, because he being of Counsel with the Defendant in an Action *sur le Case*, for saying *the Plaintiff had murdered three Children*, whereto the Defendant pleaded Not guilty; and at the Trial *Hughes*, to extenuate the Damages for his Client, urged and pressed the Fact to make the Matter probable, so far as might tend to the Defamation of the Plaintiff, and because it was his Profession, and pertinent to the Good and Safety of his Client, though not directly to the Issue, a Prohibition was granted. *Hob.* 328 *Vide* 2 *Rol Rep.* 59, 293 *Mo* 915. *Godb.* 215. *Reg* 49, 51 *Fi. Ley* 142. 2 *Sid* 152. 6 *Mod* 26, 287 *Dy.* 79 *Vide antea, at Law,* where

12. *Justification.*

1 COOKE sued *A.* in Court Christian, for calling him *Bastard-maker*, the Defendant justified, because he was proved to be such before two Justices of Peace, according to the Statute 18 *Eliz.* which Plea the Judges in Court Christian refused; wherefore a Prohibition was awarded. *2 Rol. Rep* 82.

2. Prohibition to stay a Suit in Ecclesiastical Court at *Norwich* for Defamation, and calling him *Whore-master*, and saying *that he had a Bastard*, and shews, that the Defendant who sues in the Spiritual Court was sentenced for this Cause of having a Bastard, and ordered to keep the Bastard at the Sessions at *Norwich*, and notwithstanding they would examine this again in the Spiritual Court: And upon this Suggestion the Defendant demurred. And it was adjudged that the Prohibition should stand; for being sentenced to be the reputed Father by the Justices of Peace at the Sessions, which is by the Authority of the Statute Law, it cannot be now impeached in the Spiritual Court, nor elsewhere, and all are concluded to say to the contrary, until it be reversed. *Cro. Jac.* 625. Vide post, *Where scandalous Words spoken of a Clerk.*

13. *Who*

13. *Who to hold Plea of.*

THE High Commiffioners may not hold Plea for fcandalous Words againft a Clerk, *fed de violenta manuum injeE' in Clericum.* Per Articulos Cleri, cap. 3. Mo Rep. fo. 607.

VIII. *Penfions and Annuities.*

1. BEcaufe he was fued for a Penfion be- fore the High Commiffioners, who had not Jurifdiction of the Matter, though the Ecclefiaftical Court had. Prohibition grant- ed. *Mo. pl* 1306

2. On Annuity between Spiritual Perfons by Reafon of certain Churches chargeable, grounded upon the Deed of Gift of the Pre- deceffor of one of them, though the Perfons and Things out of which it iffues are Spi- ritual ; yet, becaufe of the Deed, the Court fhall not be oufted of its Jurifdiction. *Rol. Abr. Prohibition,* D. 2.

3. Prohibition by *Collier,* Vicar of *Bram- ble* to ftay a Suit in the Spiritual Court, where the Cafe was, that the Church of *B* in the Time of *H.* 3 was appropriated by the Bifhop of *Sarum,* and the Vicar was then indowed, and upon that Endowment, the Bifhop made an Ordinance in thefe Words, *Statuimus & ordinamus,* that the Vicar fhall pay annually twenty Pounds *de fructibus Vi- cariæ* to the Precentor, in the Church of *Sarum,* to the Ufe of the Vicars Choral within the fame Church And for this Pen- fion

fion a Suit being depending in the Spiritual Court, and a Prohibition thereupon brought, Confultation was now prayed; becaufe a meer Penfion fueable in the Spiritual Court. *Vide* 11 *H.* 4. 85 *Fitz.* —— *Bro* 51. *Tanfield econtra,* That it is an Annuity, and that Annuity lies properly for it in the King's Courts, and in Proof thereof was cited 19 *E* 3 *Jurifdiction* 28. That Annuity lies for a Penfion, by Prefcription; and that the *Stat de circumfpecte agatis,* Prohibition third, is but an Ordinance, as there is faid. So *E* 4 12 of an Annuity granted for Compofition for Tithes, and 20 *E.* 3. *Annuity* 32 A Writ of Annuity was brought for fuch a Penfion as ours is; wherefore, *&c* But all the Court refolved, that the Suit was well brought in the Spiritual Court; for *Popham* and *Fenner* faid, that there would be a Difference where the Ordinary ordains fuch a Payment, as Judge; there the Suit fhall be in Court Chriftian: And where the Patron and Ordinary make a Grant in Time of Vacation; for there they charge as an Intereft; and *Gaudy* faid, that for fuch a Penfion Suit might be either in this, or the Spiritual Court; and that is not denied by the 20 *E.* 3. and fo is *N Br.* Whereupon Confultation was granted. *Cro. Eliz.* 675.

4. This was upon a Bill *in Scac* for a Penfion of Fifty-three Shillings and four Pence iffuing yearly out of the Vicarage of *St. Stephen* in *Norwich,* whereof the Plaintiffs are Patrons, and the Defendants confirmed therein by the Act of Minifters, tho' there was no Vicarage Houfe nor Glebe, nor Tithes, nor

I   other

other Profits, but only *Easter* Offerings, Burials and Christenings; yet *per Cur.* the Vicar is liable tho' he have only casual Profits, and that a Pension by Prescription, as this is, may be sued for here, as well as in the Spiritual Court, or at the Common Law by Writ of Annuity. *Hard.* 230, 231 *Trin.* 14 *Car.* 2. The Dean and Chapter of *Norwich* and Sir *John Collins.*

5. This was upon a Bill in the Exchequer for Recovery and Payment of One hundred Pounds a Year, agreed to be paid the Plaintiff by an Order of Vestry, which Order was made by the Defendants and other Parishioners of *St. Botolph's Bishopsgate* for a yearly Lecturer in that Parish, because it appeared to the Court that all the Parties to the Order were not made Defendants, and those who were had paid their Proportions of the Salary The Court were of Opinion, that the Plaintiff could not have a Decree in the Cause, but advised the Defendant to propound at their next Vestry the Payment of the Arrears, which the Court conceived justly due, and which it was a Disreputation to the Parish to refuse the Payment of *Hard* 333.

6. This was upon a Bill in the Exchequer Equity for an Annual Pension of Two Pounds ten Shillings issuing out of an Hospital granted to the Defendants, and now for divers Years in Arrear It was held *per Cur.* that all Pensions reserved by the King, or granted to him out of Lands, are in the Nature of Rents, and triable here and liable to be extinguished by Unity of Possession, but that such as are reserved to the King, or

2　　　　　　　　　　　　vested

vested in him by the Act 26 H. 8 cap. 3.
are of another Nature and collateral to the
Land, and not lost by Unity, no more than
Proxies *Vide* Sir *John Davy's* Case of
Proxies. *Hard.* 388 *Mich.* 16 *Ca.* 2 The
Bishop of *Ely* v. *Clare-Hall* in *Cambridge.*

7 If a Person have a Pension by Prescription, he may either bring his Action at
Law, or institute a Suit in Court Christian,
but if he bring his Writ of Annuity at Law,
he can never after sue in the Spiritual
Court, because his Election is determined.
1 *Mod.* 218

See 1 *Syd.* 146. 1 *Keb.* 523 *Co Lit.*
146 *a* 2 *Inst* 491 2 *Cro.* 666.

8 A Suit for a Pension may be in the Ecclesiastical Court, tho' by Prescription; but
if it be denied to be Time out of Mind,
then a Prohibition is to go; so that the Prescription may be tried at Law, as a *Modus
decimandi, mutatis mutandis.* But if a Writ
of Annuity is brought at Common Law,
he can never after sue in the Spiritual Court;
for his Election is determined. 1 *Vent* 265.
1 *Mod* 218. *Case Berry* and *Trobeswicke.*
1 *Sid.* 146 *On Twisden* and *Windham* Justices *dicunt, que fuit adjudge temps Reg. Jac.
que par Pension par Prescription Remedy serra
solement al Common Ley, ideo quære if the
Books may not be thus reconciled, that the
Party, before any Remedy sought, may take
his Choice, either to seek Relief at Law, or in
the Spiritual Court; but if he elects Redress
in the Ecclesiastical Court, they may determine
in the Matter, admitting the Prescription,
aliter non, as I conceive, has been determined*

For Pensions *Vide* 5 *Co. de Ju. Reg. Eccl.*
9. *a.*

IX. *Oblations or Offerings,* &c.

1. OBlations are Things offered to God
and his Church, by pious and faithful Christians. *Terms del Ley, Oblations.*

2 Oblations (*Oblationes*) in the Common
Law are thus defined, *dicuntur quæcunque
piis, fidelibus, Christianis offerantur Deo &
Ecclesiæ, five res folidæ, five mobiles funt.*
See *Spel. de Concil To.* 1. *fo.* 393. *Anno*
12 *Car.* 2. *cap.* 11. 5 *Co. de Ju. Reg.
Eccl* 9 *a.*

3. Offerings are defined by the Canonists
to be, *quæcunque a piis, fidelibus Christianis
offeruntur Deo & fanctæ Ecclesiæ, &c* Degg's
Par Coun 352.

4. *Nemo tenetur ad illas Oblationes, nifi vel
neceffariæ fint ad Suftentationem Ministrorum,
vel Confuetudo ad eas alicubi obliget.* Degg
353

5. These Offerings belong properly to the
Priest, or Minister of the Church, or Place
where they are made *Degg* 353.

6. There were two feveral Sorts of Offerings, one free and voluntary, and *ad Libitum,*
the other certain and obligatory, as those
for Marriages, Chriftenings, Churching of
Women, Burials, &c. these were, *fays our
Author,* due to the Priest or Minister
Degg 355. *Tho' my Thoughts are, that these
had their Beginning by the Incroachment of
impofing Priests,* &c.

Hard 230,
231.

7 The

7. The *Stat* 2 *E.* 6 hath enacted, that all and every Person and Persons, which by the Laws and Customs of this Realm ought to make or pay their Offerings, &c. shall from thenceforth pay them yearly to the Parson, &c of the Parish, &c where they dwell Those Offerings which were voluntary are now vanished, and not comprehended within this Law, but the customary Dues, which were certain, are thereby confirmed to the Parish Priest, &c and are only recoverable, either in the Spiritual Court, or by Action on the Statute. *Degg* 355.

X. *Obventions.*

OBventions, (*Obventiones*) Offerings. 2 *Inst. fo* 661. also Rents, Revenues, properly of Spiritual Livings *Anno* 12 *Ca.* 2 *cap.* 11. 5 *Co. de Ju.* *Reg. Eccl.* 9. *a.*

XI. *Mortuaries.*

1 MOrtuary (*Mortuarium*) is a Gift left by a Man at his Death to his Parish Church in Recompence of his Personal Tithes and Offerings, not duly paid in his Life-Time It is not properly and originally due to any Ecclesiastical Incumbent from any but those only of his own Parish, to whom he ministers Spiritual Instruction, and hath Right to their Tithe. *Blo. Law Dict.* Tit. *Mortuaries* *Vide* 5 *Co. de Ju. Reg Eccl.*

2. Mortuary is that Beast, or other moveable Chattel, which after the Death of the

Owner, by Cuſtom in ſome Places, become due to the Parſon, Vicar, or other Prieſt of the Pariſh, in Lieu or Satisfaction of Tithes or Offerings forgot, or which were not well and truly paid by the deceaſed. *Terms del Ley,* 'Tit *Mortuaries. I ſuppoſe where a Prieſt of good Conſcience has been ſatisfied that the deceaſed has acted uprightly with him, and not defrauded him in his Dues, ſuch Prieſt has honeſtly refuſed the Mortuary, becauſe, in ſuch Caſe, there is no Reaſon why he ſhould have it, but on the contrary common Honeſty forbids it.*

3 Mortuaries are in ſome Places called Coarſe-Preſents, becauſe, as Dr. *Cowell* holds, as they were due, they were uſed to be paid before the Coarſe was buried, when it was brought to be buried *Degg* 360

4 Lord *Coke* holds Mortuaries before the *Stat.* 21 *H* 8 were only due by Cuſtom, and not by any other Law, by Reaſon of the Statute *de circumſpecte agatis, ubi Mortuarium dare conſuevit, &c.* 2 Inſt 491

5. This Duty was only ſueable in Court Chriſtian, but now Debt lies *ſur le Stat* for tho' the Statute is only negative, that they ſhall not take above ſuch Rates, and where have been accuſtomed; yet it implies an Affirmative, as the *Stat.* 2 *E.* 6. But if a Suit be inſtituted for a Mortuary in the Spiritual Court, Sir *Simon Degg* is of Opinion, no Prohibition ſhall go, unleſs they proceed contrary to the Statute *Degg* 359 *Yet I conceive the Parſon may have Difficulty to prevail in the Eccleſiaſtical Court, for if they Sentence upon the Canon, it binds not the Laity, if on the Cuſtom, they may not try a Cuſtom*

Custom, *if on the Statute, they may not inter-*
pret a Statute, and if a Statute gives the Be-
nefit and no Remedy given in the Statute in
the Ecclesiastical Court or elsewhere, Remedy
must be in the King's own Courts of Law, as
I understand the Matter, ideo quære.

6 Since *Stat* 21 *H.* 8   If Suit be in the
Spiritual Court for Mortuaries, a Prohibition
lieth   *Dr. & Stud fo* 175 *b*   for the Statute hath fixed what shall be paid for Mortuaries   *Cro Car.* 238.   *Where, I conceive,*
is a very unconscionable Mortuary demanded by
a Bishop of Chester, *on the Death of a poor*
Country Priest from the poor Parson's poorer
Widow, being of his best Horse or Mare, his
Saddle, Bridle, Spurs, his best Gown or Cloak,
his best Hat, his best upper Garment, under
his Gown, his Tippet, his best Signet, or Ring,
as to the Bishop de Debito confuet' fore fup-
pon tur.

XII. *Proxies, Procurations, Syno-*
     dals.

1 PRocurations, as the Canonists define it,
     est Exhibitio Sumptuum necessar or' facta
Prælatis, qui Dioceses peragrando Ecclesias sub-
jectas visitant   Dav, 1 b

2. Proxies, or Procurations, are resembled
or likened to an Annuity *pro Confilio* or *pro*
Servitio impendendo, if the Counsel or the
Service be withdrawn, the Annuity is deter-
mined. So where a Corody is granted for
certain Service to be done, Omission of the
Service determines the Corody, as is 20 *E* 4 .
Dav 1. *a.*

3 By the Canon Law, *Procuratio exhibenda eft fecundum qualitatem Perfonæ vifi-
tantis.* Dav 2 a

4 It was obferved that Proxies had not
their Original or Foundation in the primitive
Church, for *St Paul* in his Vifitation of all
the Churches which he had planted in *Afia*
and *Europe* demanded no Proxies; but laboured with his own Hands *pur fon Suftenance,
ne ferrout* burthenfome *al Eglifes;* yet long
after the Canon Law, which declares that
Proxies are due to Bifhops in their Vifita-
tions, fays, that it is agreeable to the Doctrine of *St Paul, ut a quibus Spiritualia reci-
pimus eifdem Temporalia communicemus.* Inft.
Juris Canon Lib. 2 c. de Senfib. Dav. 2. b,
3. a.

5. Plaintiff, as Arch-Deacon of *London,*
exhibited his Bill in the *Englifh* Exchequer
againft the Defendants, as Parfons and Vicars of *London,* for certain Sums of Money
due for their Proxies by Prefcription, and
for which now there is no Remedy by the
Ecclefiaftical Law; whereto the Defendants
demurred, as the Thing in Demand was
meerly of Ecclefiaftical Cognizance and determinable in the Spiritual Court, *& non
alibi;* and if the Tithe by Prefcription alters
the Cafe, then the Plaintiff ought to have
his Remedy at Law, and not in Equity, but
of this the Court doubted; *& adjournatur
Vide* Sir *John Davies's* Reports, the Cafe of
Proxies; and the Ch. Baron quoted out of
Linw. Lib. 3 Decret. de Procuratzonibus, that
there are three Sorts of Proxies. 1. *Ratione
Vifitationis.* 2. *Ratione confuetudinis* 3. *Ratione Pacti,* and his Lordfhip faid, that
Proxies

Proxies of the second and third Sort were recoverable at Law; but becaufe the Matter in Queftion was doubtful, Defendants were ordered to anfwer, and that this Matter fhould be faved to them at the Hearing. *Vide Stat.* 34 *H.* 8. concerning the Saving of Proxies, and that they be recoverable as formerly *Hard* 180, 181. *Paf* 13 *Car* 2. Dr. *Thomas Parker Quer'* v. *John Seabrooke & al' Def'*.

6. In Prohibition to ftay an Excommunication for Non-payment of Proxies and Procurations, the Ground of the Prohibition was, becaufe by *Stat* 34 *H.* 8 19. all fuch Archbifhops, Bifhops, Arch-deacons, *&c.* as have Right or Title to claim any Penfions, Portions, Corodies, Indempnities, Synodals, or Proxies, againft any Perfons to whom the King had, or fhould grant the Lands, Tenements, *&c.* charged therewith, with a Claufe of Difcharge, *&c* fhould fue for their Remedy and Recovery thereof in the Court of Augmentations now annexed to the Court of Exchequer, and not elfewhere, and the Lands in this Cafe were granted by Patent difcharged, *&c. Sed non allocatur per Cur'*, Becaufe the Act extends only where particular Eftates are granted, as appears by the Words of the Act, *any Sale, Gift, Grant, or Leafe for Term of Life, or Lives, or Years,* and not where the Fee is granted, as was in this Cafe. *Hard.* 388.

See after *Impropriation,* 5 *Co. De Jure Regis Eccl.* 9. *a.*

XIII. *Simony.*

1. SImony determinable in the Spiritual Court. 4 *Co* 49 *b.* 3 *Inft.* 204.

2. The Spiritual Court may punifh for Simony *Watfon*, Bifhop of St. *David's* Cafe, *Salk Rep. Vue le livre, where that Bifhop was deprived for that Offence.*

3. To avoid the deteftable Sin of Simony, becaufe buying and felling of Spiritual and Ecclefiaftical Functions, Offices, Promotions, Dignities, and Livings, is execrable before God; therefore the Archbifhop, and all and every Bifhop or Bifhops, or any other Perfon or Perfons having Authority to admit, inftitute, collate, inftall, or to confirm the Election of any Archbifhop, Bifhop, or other Perfon or Perfons to any Spiritual or Ecclefiaftical Function, Dignity, Promotion, Title, Office, Jurifdiction, Place, or Benefice, with Cure, or without Cure, or to any Ecclefiaftical Living whatfoever, fhall, before every fuch Admiffion, Inftitution, Collation, Inftallation, or Confirmation of Election, refpectively adminifter to every Perfon hereafter to be admitted, inftituted, collated, inftalled, or confirmed, in or to any Archbifhoprick, Bifhoprick, or other Spiritual or Ecclefiaftical Function, Dignity, or Promotion, Title, Office, Jurifdiction, Place or Benefice, with Cure, or without Cure, or in or to any Ecclefiaftical Living whatfoever, the Oath in the faid Canon. *Can* 40.

4. Ac-

4. According to *Linwood*, It is Simony to take any Thing for burying, unless it be due by Custom, and a Custom to christen a Child, when he does not do it, is not good ; like the Case in *Hob.* where one dies in one, and is buried in another Parish, the Parson where he died, *notwithstanding any pretended Custom,* shall not have a burial Fee. The Parson ought not to have Money for Christening when he does not do it. *Salk.* 322.

Simony *5 Co. De Jure Regis Eccl.* 9. *a.* Vide *May punish their own Members.*

XIV. *Solicitation of Chastity.*

THE Indictment was for Assaulting, Beating, Wounding, and Endeavouring to ravish the Wife of *B* upon which the Party was convicted, and afterwards the Husband brought an Action of Trespass for the same Cause ; and now the Party being also libelled against in the Spiritual Court for the same Fact, (*viz*) for Soliciting her Chastity, moved for a Prohibition to the Proceedings in the Spiritual Court. And it was urged for the Jurisdiction of the Spiritual Court, that they may punish for the Solicitation, and Incontinency, and that this Suit was *pro salute animæ,* the other for Fine and Damages. *Sed per Cur':* A Prohibition was granted ; for it being an Attempt and Solicitation to Incontinency, coupled with Force and Violence, it does, by Reason of the Force, which is Temporal, become a Temporal Crime *in toto.* Salk. 522. Far 78, 79. *le mesme Case.*

Solicita-

Solicitation of Chastity. *5 Co. De Jure Regis. Eccl. 9. 4.*

XV. *Fornication.*

A Woman having a Bastard is punishable by the Statute 18 *Eliz.* yet Fornication, or Advowtry, is not examinable by our Law, as they are Deeds in Secret. *4 Co. 17. a.*
Vide Hale's Hist. Law 31. *5 Co. De Jure Regis Eccl. 9. a.*

XVI. *Incest.*

1. ALL Marriages between Cousin Germans and other collateral Cousins are lawful by the Statute 32 *H.* 8. *c.* 28. and if any such should be questioned, as incestuous in the Spiritual Courts, a Prohibition lies *sur le Stat.* Vaugh. 218. Hale's Anal. 42.

2. A Widow's Estate upon an incestuous Marriage is due to her, if she was never divorced *a Vinculo Matrimonii;* though there was Cause. *Hob.* 181.
Vide 5 Co De Jure Regis Eccl. 9 *a Etiam sub* Division of *Matters Matrimonial,* see also *Schism,* what, Case 3.

XVII. *Adultery.*

BY *Holt* C. J. If one commit Adultery, and the Husband brings Assault, this shall not hinder the Spiritual Court; for it is a Criminal Proceeding there, and no Indictment lies at Common Law for Adultery. *Salk.* 552. Farest. 78, 79. *le mesme Case.*
Vide

Vide Hale's Hist. Law 31. 5 *Co. De* ~~Man within the~~
Jure Regis Eccl 9. *a.*   *Godolp. Reper.*   ~~Degrees prohibited is~~
~~406~~   ~~not null till a Divorce —~~

XVIII. *Divorce.*

1 IF a Man marry his Cousin *infra Gradus
Marriages,* who have Issue, and are divorced in their Lives, the Espousals are a-
voided, and the Issue is Bastard , *econtra,* if
either die before Divorce ; for the Divorce
had after, shall not bastardize the Issue ; for
the Marriage is determined by Death before,
and not by the Divorce, *&c.* **Litt. Bro.**
Case 48

2. But note for Law, that where Baron
and Feme are divorced, where she is an In-
heritrix, yet mesne Acts executed shall not
be reversed by the Divorce, as Waste, Re-
ceipt of Rent, *&c.* unless in some particular
Cases. **Lit. Bro. Case** 175   *Vide* 5 *Co.* **De**
Jure Regis Eccl 9. *a.*

XIX. *Perjury.*

1. 3 *H* 2. IT is ordained, that it shall not
be lawful for the Bishop to
punish any one for Perjury, or Breach of
Faith **Rol. Abr. Prohibition,** F. 13.

2 If the Indictors in Felony are perjured ;
yet if they are sued therefore in the Spiritual Court, a Prohibition lies ; for this Perjury arose upon a Temporal Cause. 13 *H.* 7.
Kel. 39 *b*   **Rol. Abr Prohibition** (R) *Case* 8.
So if a Jury give false Verdict, *Case* 9.

3 The Ecclesiastical Courts may punish
Perjury committed in their own Courts, and
Matters

Matters Spiritual, as Matrimony , but not in a Temporal Contract 3 *Cro* 788.

4 The Ecclesiastical Court may punish for Perjury, in their own Courts, for a Matter Spiritual; but not for a Temporal Matter. *Watson*, Bishop of St. *David*'s Case, *Salk.*

5. Perjury in Court Christian, though it be not a Court of Record is still Perjury, for which the Party may be punished at Common Law by Indictment. *Syd* 454. *Vide* 1 *Vent.* 296. *seems contrary, tamen quære. Telv.* 72

6. If one wage his Law untruly in an Action of Debt upon a Contract in the King's Courts, he·shall not be sued for the Perjury in the Spiritual Court, and yet no Remedy lieth for the Perjury in the King's Court; for the Prohibition lieth not only where a Man is sued in the Spiritual Court for such Matter, as the Party might have Remedy in the King's Court, but also where the Spiritual Court holdeth Plea in such Case where they by the King's Prerogative, and by the antient Customs of the Realm ought not to hold any Plea *Doct.* & *Stud. lib* 2. *c* 24 *fo.* 105 *b.*

7. Subornation of Perjury in the Ecclesiastical Court, cognizable in the Court of King's Bench, and accordingly the Court directed, that the Parties who were complained against for Subornation of Perjury should shew Cause why an Information should not be granted against them on that Account. ——— against *Venetia Constantia Phillips,* otherwise *Dellafield,* otherwise *Muleman.*

XX. *Pro Læsione Fidei.*

1 IF one swear to me to infeoff me of Lands, if I sue him in Court Christian, he shall have a Prohibition against me, or the Judge, or both *Stath Prohibition.*

2 If Baron and Feme sell the Wife's Land, and she swear not to bring her *Cui in vita,* yet if after she do, and the Purchaser sue her in Court Christian on this Oath, she shall have a Prohibition. *Stath Ali Prohibition*

3 If a Woman hath Right to sue a *Cui in vita,* and she make Oath that she will not sue it, and yet does, for which she is sued in Court Christian *pro Læsione Fidei,* she shall have a Prohibition; because the Oath concerned a Temporal Matter, as Land. *Fitz N B* 42 I.

4 If a Man acknowledge in Court Christian that he owed another 100 Shillings to be paid to him at a Day certain, and after doth not pay it, &c. and is after sued for it in Court Christian, he shall have a Prohibition and Attachment *fur ceo,* so if he acknowledge in Court Christian that he ought to pay to such a one 100 Marks at such a Day, &c he may not be sued in Court Christian for the Debt, and if he be, he may have Prohibition and Attachment. But if one for Matrimonial or Testamentary Cause acknowledge in Court Christian that he ought to pay 100 Marks or other Sum, at a Day certain, &c there, if he do not pay it according to Conusance, he may be

I   sued

fued in Court Chriftian for it, and no Prohibition. *Fitz N. B* 41. B C D

5. If one acknowledge in Court Chriftian
to pay Money at a Day, and do not pay
it, fo that he is excommunicated, he may
have a Prohibition. *Fitz. N B* 41. C

6. If one fwear to me to infeoff me before fuch a Day, *&c* and do not, yet I may
not fue him in Court Chriftian *pro Læfione
Fidei*; for that the Act to be done is Tem
poral and triable at Common Law; and
therefore if he be fued in Court Chriftian, a
Prohibition lies. *Fitz. N B* 43. D

7 If one make Oath to pay a Debt, or
make a Feoffment, or the like, and he is
fued in the Spiritual Court for Breach of this
Oath, a Prohibition lieth, elfe he fhould be
compelled to perform his Oath, and fo Lay
Contracts be determined in Court Chriftian.
Rol. Abr. Prohibition, F. 11.

8 For *Læfione Fidei*, upon a Promife to
pay ten Pounds by fuch a Day, if the Spiritual Court interfere, a *Præmunire* lieth.
Lit. Bro. 11. *a Cafe* 57

9. Though an Action lieth by the Canon
Law *pro Læfione Fidei*, yet none lying at
Law, none fhall lie in the Spiritual Court
in this Realm, if the Promife be of a Temporal Thing; but if they will meddle in
fuch Matter, a Prohibition or a *Præmunire
facias* lieth. *Doct. & Stud. lib* 2 *c* 24
fo. 105 *b.*

I

XXI. *For-*

XXI. *Forgery.*

1. *General.*

1. IT was refolved, that he who fued in the Ecclefiaftical Court for the Forgery of a laft Will and Teftament, incurred the Danger of a *Præmunire*, becaufe the Party grieved might have had his Remedy by the Common Law. *Anno* 17 *H.* 7.

2 Forged Deeds or Writings are not to be ordered to be torn, or defaced, but to be kept, fo that the King may proceed a-gainft the Criminal. 1 *Vern.* 292.

2. *Where to be fued, and how pu-nifhed, if irregularly profecuted.*

1 HE who fues in the Spiritual Court for Forgery of a Will or Teftament in-curs a *Præmunire*; becaufe the Party grieved might have had Remedy at Law. 3 *Inft.* 121.

2 It was refolved, that he who fued in the Ecclefiaftical Court for the Forgery of a Laft Will and Teftament incurred the Danger of a *Præmunire*; becaufe the Party grieved might have his Remedy by the Common Law : And in the fame Year 17 *H.* 7. Juftice *Spelman* alfo reporteth, that one *Turbervile*, as well for the King as for him-felf, fued a *Præmunire* againft a Perfon for fuing for Tithes in the Ecclefiaftical Court, alledging the fame to be fevered from the

nine

nine Parts, and Judgment was given against the Defendant 3 *Inst* 121   *So that, as it seems to me, where Remedy may be had at Law, a Man endangers a* Præmunire *for seeking Redress in the Ecclesiastical Courts, as it draws the Matter* ad aliud examen, *and to be discussed* per aliam Legem.

XXII. *Schism.*

1. *What,* &c.

1. SCHISM is a Separation from the Unity of the Church, as Sedition is a Separation from the Unity of the Commonwealth, &c. but Schism alone is not Heresy. *Append to Rush. Coll In such Case*

2 A Man is not bound to answer upon Oath Matters concerning his Faith, for that there is a Statute by which he might be punished, if he published any false Doctrine. *Mich* 18 *Ja. Jenner's* Cafe. *Rol Abr. Prohibition,* (T.) *Case* 5.

3. If one convicted of Heresy, Schism, or erroneous Opinions, recant, he shall never be punished by the Ecclesiastical Law, yet in *Fuller's* Cafe they imprisoned and fined him 200 *l.* wherefore he had a *Habeas Corpus.* 12 *Co* 44.

Vide 5 *Co. De Jure Regis Eccl* 9 *a.*

2. *Where*

2. *Where to be tried, and in what Cases.*

OF Necessity a Thing of Ecclesiastical Cognizance or Jurisdiction shall be examined in a Collateral Action, as Schism, &c. or Sufficiency of a Clerk where he is dead, &c. *Skin.* 468.

XXIII. *Heresy, or Miscreancy.*

1. THE Statute made 2 *H* 5. *c.* 7. whereby the Forfeiture of Lands in Fee Simple, and Goods and Chattels were given, in Case of Heresy, standeth repealed by *Stat.* 1 *Eliz c.* 1. So *Belknap's* Opinion never allowed or taken for Law, because the Proceedings in such Case is meerly Spiritual *pro Salute Animæ*, &c. 3 Inst. 43.

2 A Miscreant is one who is perverted to Heresy, or a false Religion *Bro. Presentation* 54 *Termes del' Ley* Tit. *Miscreant.* See *Godb.* 33. *where a Bishop was deprived for Miscreancy.*

3 If one be a Miscreant his Lands were forfeitable, and the Lord shall have the Escheat; the Reason is, for that, if a Man who is out of the Faith of the King shall forfeit his Lands for the same, *a fortiori,* he who is out of the Faith of God. *Gob.* 34. *Bellew* 194. *Forfeiture* Lord *Coke* differs from *Belknap,* as to the Forfeiture. 3 *Inst.* 43.

4. One convicted of Heresy, if he abjure, forfeited not Goods; but if delivered into Lay Hands he did, but his Lands were not forfeited therefore till his Death. *Doct. & Stud lib.* 2. *c.* 29

5. It belongeth to the Church to determine Heresies *Doct. & Stud. lib* 2 *c* 29.

6. *Sur le Stat.* 2 *H* 4 *c.* 15 If an Heretick Convict will recant, he should be received and not punished, but if he relapsed, he was to be burnt without more ado. So the Law of God wills not the Death of a Sinner, but rather that he should repent and be saved, therefore it would be contrary both to Reason and the Law of God, not to receive an Offender upon his Repentance, or to deprive him of the Benefit of his Repentance. *Nullum iniquum in Lege præsumendum est. Hard.* 64, 65. See 12 *Co* 56, 57, 58.

If an Heretick though he be convicted and Excommunicated repents of his Crime, he should be restored to the Church, which ought to imitate the Example of God, who Punishes the greatest of Sinners by the death of the Body, and not by Destruction of the Soul, and as soon as a Sinner repenteth of his Heresy, the Complaint ought to cease, the Cause being removed *Father Paul's Rights of Sovereigns.*

XXIV. *Blasphemy.*

1. BLasphemy contains an Insult upon God, and Scandal to our Neighbour. *Father Paul's Rights of Sovereigns* 306.

2. Blasphemy is triable in Court Christian *Ha. Anal.* 98 *Vide* 5 *Co. de Ju Reg Eccl* 9. *a.* See before *Tit. Schism,* what, *Case* 3.

XXV. *Apostacy.*

A *Postata capiendo* is a Writ, directed to the Sheriff, for the taking of the Body of one, who having entered into or professed some Order of Religion, leaves his said Order, and departs from his House, and wanders in the Country; upon a Certificate of this Matter made by the Sovereign of the House to the Chancery, and praying the said Writ, he shall have it directed to the Sheriff for the taking him and delivering him to the said Sovereign of the said House, or his lawful Attorney *F. N. Br.* 233. *Vue la le forme del Breve, & sur cest il port aver Al & Plur. & un Attachment si le Vic. ne voil server le Breve.* F N Br 234. A. *vue le Forme del Breve* Ditto B; and tho' the Vagrant do not change his Habit, yet if the Sovereign certify, &c he shall have his Writ, notwithstanding the Words *spreto habitu, &c.* for they are but Words of Form, and not of Substance, &c. *Ditto C. Vue le Reg. fo.* 71 & 267. *But this Offence is now gone together with the regular Clergy.* See also 5 *Co de Ju. Reg Eccl.* 9. *a.*

XXVI. *Matters belonging to the Church.*

1. *Bells.*

SUIT in the Spiritual Court for taking away two Bells out of the Steeple, and a Prohibition was granted; for the Church

Warden is a Corporation, and the Property
is in him, and he may bring Trover at Common
Law. *Salk* 547. *Vide Comb.* 132. *Du.
Ch. Ufes* 131.

2. *Seats, or Pews.*

1. THE Difpofal of the Seats *in Navi
Ecclefiæ* belongs, of common Right,
to the Ordinary, *&c. Rol Abr.* Tit *Prohibition,* 288, 289. 12 *Co.* 104, 105.

2 *Per tout le Court de Bank le Roy,* agreed
that a Seat in a Church claimed by Prefcription is triable here, by Action *fur le
Cafe,* and not in the Spiritual Court, fo
Prohibition was granted. *Palm.* 424. 12 *Co.*
104, 105.

3 Action at Law lies for a Seat in a
Church by Prefcription. *W. Jo.* 3, 4. 12
Co. 104, 105

4. Refolved, if any Inhabitant and his
Anceftors only have ufed, Time out of
Mind, to repair an Ifle in a Church, and to
fit there with his Family to hear divine Service, and to bury there ; this makes the Ifle
proper and peculiar to his Houfe, and he
cannot be difplaced nor interrupted by the
Parfon, Church-Warden, or Ordinary, *&c
Cro. Jac.* 366. 12 *Co.* 104, 105.

5. Church-Wardens were ufed Time out
of Mind, to difpofe of the Seats in the
Church, and according to fuch Ufage, difpofed to one, and the Bifhop granted the
fame Seat to another and his Heirs, and excommunicated all others, who after fhould
fit there, and a Prohibition was granted,
for

for the Grant to one and his Heirs is not good, for the Seat belongeth not to the Person, but to the House; else when he goes out of the Parish he should retain the Seat, which is contrary to Reason: And there is no Reason to excommunicate all others who should sit there; for such great Punishments should not be imposed upon so small Offenders, an Excommunication being *Traditio Diabolica.* Poph. 140.

6 *Boothby,* as Executor of *Gilbert,* brought Prohibition against *Baily,* and surmised that Sir *Barnard Whetstone* was seised of the Manor of *Woodford Hall,* and that he and those, whose Estate he hath in the same, had used, Time out of Mind, to have a peculiar Pew in the Body of the Church, and that the Defendants sought in the Ecclesiastical Court to dispossess them of the same, but held, this no good Cause of Prohibition; for the Church and Church-Yard be the Soil and Freehold of the Parson, yet the Use of the Body of the Church, and the Repair and Maintenance of it is common to all the Parishioners, and for avoiding Confusion, the Distribution of Seats, and Charges of Repairs belong to the Ordinary; and therefore no Man can challenge a peculiar Seat, without a special Reason. But if it had been prescribed, that Sir *Barnard, &c* had used, Time whereof, *&c.* and used, at their own only Costs, to maintain that Pew, and had therefore had the sole Use of it, the Prescription had stood and warranted a Prohibition, tho' the Pew was in the Body of the Church: And so it is in the like Case of an Isle, or Chapel adjoining to the Body of the

R 3 Church,

Church, upon the fame Difference, whether it hath been maintained by the whole Parifh, or by fome particular Perfons, like unto the Reafons of a Chappel of Eafe. *Hob* 69. *See Hard.* 378 fame Cafe. *Szd* 89, 203, 361. 2 *Lev* 241. *Mod.* 283. 2 *Mod* 283 5 *Mod* 436. 6 *Mod.* 230 *Salk.* 167 2 *Ven.* 226. *Lutw.* 1033 8 *H* 7. 12 2 *Rol. Abr.* 288. 12 *Co* 105 *Mo.* 878. *Godb.* 200. *Poph.* 140. 2 *Bulft.* 151. 2 *Ro. Rep* 24, 139. *Keb.* 345, 498. 2 *Keb.* 92, 342. *Tiy. per Pa.* 362. *Palm* 424.

3. *Way to Church.*

1. IF a Suit be in the Spiritual Court, *ex Officio*, or otherwife, for an Highway to Church for the Parifhioners, a Prohibition lies, upon a Surmife that it is a common Highway; for it is to be tried at Common Law, whether an Highway or not. *Rol. Abr.* Tit. *Prohibition, Cafe* 47.

2 If the Church-Wardens fue in Court Chriftian for an Highway to the Church, which they claim to belong to all the Parifhioners by Prefcription, a Prohibition fhall be granted, for it is Temporal. 16 *Jac.* in *B. R.* enter *les* Church-Wardens *de Bithorne* and *Bowe* Prohibition grant accordant *Rol. Abr. Prohibition, fo.* 287. *Cafe* 48.

4. *Where*

4. *Where Churches united, and the Parishioners are sued in the Ecclesiastical Courts to come to one Church.*

IF two Churches are united by Patron, King, and Ordinary, by the *Stat* 37 *H.* 8. on Surmise that they are not above a Mile distant, and the Parishioners are sued in the Spiritual Court to come to one Church, a Prohibition lies on this Surmise *Mich.* 10 *Car* B. R. inter *Dobson* and Sir *Robert Mordant* The Churches united were *Wellesborough* and *Waltondevel* in *Com Warwick*; but after *Paf.* 11 *Ca.* B. R the Prohibition was denied; for that there was no Suit depending against the Parishioners, nor any other Suit in the Spiritual Court to be prohibited. *Rol. Abr. Prohibition* 393. *Cafe* 8. *Fi Ley.*

5. *Repairs of the Church.*

1. *Where to be tried.*

1. THE Conusance of the Repairs of the Body of the Church belongs to the Court Christian. *5 Co. Jefferies's Cafe* 66. *b* 67. *a b.* 68. A.

2. The Ecclesiastical Court hath Conusance of the Repairs *Navis Ecclesiæ. Rol. Abr.* Tit. *Prohib.* 289, 290, &c. as appears by *Britton*, who wrote 5 *E.* 1. *lib.* 1. *c.* 4.

fo. 11. and in the Stat. *Circumfpecte agatis, &c.*
5 *Co.* 67 *a*

Paf 8 *Geo.* 2.   *B. R*   *Burton* and *Weldon*

This was upon a Rule to fhew Caufe, why a Prohibition fhould not go to the Confiftory Court of *Litchfield* in a Suit there for a Rate for the Repairs of the Church of *Mansfield* Mr *Abney* faid, that the Motion for a Prohibition was founded upon a fuppofed Cuftom, which the Defendant below had pleaded, fetting forth that there were four Vills in *Mansfield*, namely, *Atherfton*, *Mansfield*, *Hartfel*, and *Oldbury*, and that the Cuftom was, that *Atherfton* fhould pay two Thirds of the whole Rate, and that the three other Vills fhould pay but one Third   To this Plea the Plaintiff had replied, that true it was indeed, that there was fuch an Ufage, but that it was abfolutely void, for that the Lands in the three Vills are of greater Extent, and of greater Value, on Account of Inclofures which have been made than the Lands in *Atherfton*; upon which Mr *Abney* fubmitted it, that the Rule ought to be difcharged, he owned that where a Cuftom is denied, a Prohibition fhall go for Want of Trial; but in the prefent Cafe, the Cuftom is confeffed and avoided.   'Tis admitted that there is fuch a one, but fhewed, that it is unreafonable, and therefore if this had been the Cafe even of a *Modus*, he fubmitted it that the Ecclefiaftical Court fhould have been admitted to proceed, and the prefent Cafe, he fubmitted it, was much ftronger, becaufe the Suit below is for a Church Rate and the Ecclefiaftical Court has a greater
Lati-

Latitude allowed them in those Cases than in any other; and for this Purpose cited the Case *Goodfee* and *Foulden*, *Mich.* 1710. where the Suit was for a Rate for Building a new Gallery, and tho' it was doubted, whether a Gallery was not only an Ornament to the Church, yet the Suit was allowed to proceed. So in the Case of *How* and *Chidmore*. *Mich* 1 of his present Majesty, there was a Suit for a Rate for the Church of St. *Martin in the Fields*; the Defendant pleaded, he had only a Shop in the Change, and that he was not rateable, but notwithstanding this, the Prohibition was refused, and he further cited 3 *Cro* 659 and *Pop* 197. Mr

on the same Side, said, that the Custom was absolutely unequal and void, and wherever such Custom is set forth, it is the same as if no Custom had been set forth at all, for which Purpose he cited *Het.* 203 *Lat.* 217. & *Lev.* 116. My Lord Ch. Just. said, that wherever a Custom does clearly appear to be void upon the Face of it, the Court indeed will not grant a Prohibition; but in the present Case, the only Colour of its being void ariseth from an Allegation of the Plaintiff himself, that the Lands in the three Vills are of greater Value than the Lands in *Atherston*, and that too only by Inclosures; for which Reason his Lordship said, he thought that the Prohibition clearly ought to go He said, that Questions about the Validity of a Custom belong meerly and only to the Common Law to determine as well as Questions of the Truth of them, in Point of Fact, belong to a Jury; and that, he said, was the Reason, that where a

Modus

Modus was pleaded in the Ecclefiaftical Court, in a Suit for Tithes, and the *Modus* admitted, the Ecclefiafticcl Court can decree for the *Modus* only. The Reft of the Court were of the fame Opinion; accordingly the Rule was made abfolute.

2. *Who an Inhabitant to contribute thereunto.*

1. The Inhabitants of any Town may make By-Laws, without Cuftom, for the Repairs of the Church or Highways, *&c.* which are for Publick Good, and the greater Part fhall bind all the Reft, and that *fans* Cuftom. 5 Co 62. *b.*

2. Tho' he live in another Parifh, yet for that he had Lands in that Parifh in his Poffeffion and Manurance, he is, in Law, *Parochianus*, for where he lies, fleeps, or eats, do not only make him a Parifhioner, but alfo his Manurance of Lands; and therefore he is a Parifhioner as to the Purpofe of contributing to the Repair of the Church, for if he fhould not, no Body elfe can for thofe Lands he occupies; but if there was a Farmer, he only who receives Rent is not a Parifhioner, becaufe there is an Inhabitant and Parifhioner who may be charged, and the Charge is upon the Perfon, and not upon the Land; though it is upon him in Refpect of the Land, for the greater Equality and Indifference; and fuch Occupier might come to their Meetings, if he pleafed, when they met to fettle the Repairs 5 Co. 66. *b.* 67. *a. b.* See the *Regifter, fo.* 44. *b.*

3. In Prohibition in *B. R.* held, that none fhall be charged for his Land by Contribution

tribution to Church Reckonings, if he do not inhabit there, or affent to it; and a Prohibition lies, if the Ordinary cite him. See 49 *E* 3. *fo.* —— *Brooke,* Tit. *By-Laws.* *Mo.* 554.

4 If all the Parifhioners are not rated for the Reparation of the Church, but only fome, and they fued in the Ecclefiaftical Court, a Prohibition fhall be granted *Rol. Abr Probibition,* 291. *I apprehend it rea-fonable, that every Parifbioner contributing to the Repairs of the Church, or paying Church-Dues, fhould be feated in the Church fuitable to their Rank or Degree; for that thefe Pay-ments feem to me to be the Confideration of fuch Seats, or Pews in the Church, when fuch Inhabitants attend Divine Service there.*

Vide 5 *Co.* De *Jure Regis Eccl.* 9 *a.*

6. *Ornaments of the Church.*

1. *Who, and how, to be rated thereunto.*

1 IF one, not an Inhabitant, but hath Lands in the Parifh, is rated for Orna-ments of the Church, according to the Law, a Prohibition lieth ; for the Inhabitants ought to be rated for them. *Rol. Abr. Pro-hibition,* 291.

2. If a Man be rated for the Ornaments of the Church, according to the Lands which he hath in the Parifh, a Prohibition lies, for he ought to be rated according to his perfonal Eftate *Rol. Abr. Probibition,* 291.

2. *Who, and in what Cases, bound to contribute.*

1. If the Majority of a Parish, where are four Bells, agree to have a Fifth, and have it accordingly, and they make a Rate to pay for it, it shall bind the lesser Number, though they did not agree to it, otherwise any one obstinate Person might hinder any Thing intended, and which is done for the Ornament of the Church. *Rol. Abr Prohibition,* 291.

2. Church-wardens sue one whose Lands lie contiguous to the Church-yard, that he and all those, *&c.* used to repair all the Fences, *&c.* a Prohibition lies. *Rol. Abr. Prohibition, fo.* 287 *Cafe* 52.

3. *Pollyxfen* moved for a Prohibition, on Denial of a Custom on a Libel against a Chapel of Ease for a third Part of Repairs of the Mother-Church, which was granted 3 *Keb.* 729

4. Prohibition to the Ecclesiastical Court of *Durham,* suggesting that they had a Parochial Chapelry within another Parish in *Northumberland,* and that the Inhabitants thereof, Time out of Mind, had a Parochial Chapel, and Divine Service, and Sacraments, *&c.* and were exempt from Repairs, Bells, *&c.* of the Parish-Church, and in Consideration that they were charged with the Repair of, and had repaired, *&c* their own Chapel ; notwithstanding which the Church-wardens of the Parish Church sued them for Repairs of the Parish Church and Bells, and a Prohibition was granted, and

after

after a Confultation was moved for; becaufe
this Matter was pleaded and Sentence given;
and cited the Cafe of *Chapel-Brimige*, *Hob.*
66 where a Confultation had been granted.
Whereto it was anfwered, that in the Cafe
of *Chapel-Brimige*, Sepulture was referved
to the Parifh Church, (which was not here)
and it was a Refervation of antient Right;
and on Examination of the Court, the Suggeftion appeared untrue, and tho' it was decreed there againft the Plaintiff in the Prohibition upon Plea of the Cuftom, yet it was
to try a Matter there *dehors* their Jurifdiction, for they may not try a Cuftom, their
Law and ours differing upon the Nature of
Cuftoms *Lat* 48 Cuftom alledged in the
Ecclefiaftical Court, if denied, Prohibition
fhall go *Lat.* 200. A *Modus* is fuable there,
but if denied, a Prohibition fhall go. Bounds
of a Parifh not triable there. 3 *Cro.* 228. adjudged, and *Het.* 133 and 3 *Bulft.* 241.
Suit for a *Modus* there, and another *Modus*
pleaded, Prohibition granted; the Court
ruled the Prohibition to ftand. 2 *Lev* 102,
103 2 *Rol* 265. *Vide* 3 *Mod.* 264. *&* *Rol.*
Rep. 126.

7. Repairs and Ornaments of Churches, both.

1. Where to be tried.

1 IF the Church-warden fue a Vill for
Reparation of their Church, fuppofing
the Vill to be an Hamlet within their Parifh, and the Vill infifts, that it is a Parifh
of

of it self, and not an Hamlet of the other, a Prohibition shall be granted; for now the Bounds of the Parish come in Question. *Trin.* 16 *Ja.* B R. *enter Perry* and *Thomas Plaintiffs* v. —— Prohibition granted *Rol Abr. Prohibition,* 291, 292.

2. If the Church-wardens of the Parish of *Steevenage* libel in the Ecclesiastical Court against *J. S* Farmer of the Farm called *D.* for Contribution to the Reapirs of the Church; and alledge, that Parcel of the Farm lies in *Steevenage,* and Parcel in *Walborn,* another Parish; and alledge a Custom, that the Farmers of the said Farm have used, Time whereof, &c. to contribute to the Reparations of the Church of *Steevenage* for all the said Farm: If the Defendant say, that Parcel of the Land lies in the Parish of *Walborn,* and that he and those, &c have used, Time whereof, &c. to contribute for it to the Church of *Walborn,* and not *Stevenage,* and deny the Prescription, it shall not be tried in the Ecclesiastical Court, but by the Common Law, and therefore a Prohibition lies, for they may not try the Custom in the Ecclesiastical Court, by which the Inheritance is to be perpetually charged, yet note, that it is but in Effect a Denial of the Prescription. *Trin* 16 *Ja.* B. R. *The Church-wardens of Stevenage* and *Green,* Rol. Abr Prohibition, fo. 308. Case 20.

3. *Trin* 6 *Geo.* 2. in B. R. *Ray* and *Marriford*

The Plaintiff declared in Prohibition, that the Defendant libelled against him in the Ecclesiastical Court, as Church-warden of the Parish of *Holling cum Withringsey* in

the

4

the County of *York*, upon a Rate for the Repairs of the Parish Church there; he set forth that the Lands, for which he was so rated contained so many Acres of Meadow, so many Acres of Pasture, and averred, that those Lands did not lie in the Parish of *Holling cum Withringsey*, but that they lay in the Parish of *Hampton* in the said County; he also alledged the Trial of Bounds of Parishes to belong to the Temporal Courts, and not to the Ecclesiastical, and thereupon prayed the Prohibition might stand. The Defendant for Consultation pleaded, that true it is, that the Lands mentioned in the Declaration did lie in the Parish of *Hampton*, but agreed that the Plaintiff occupied other Lands, which lay in the Parish of *Holling cum Withringsey*, and set forth, that the Plaintiff was actually rated for such other Lands lying in the Parish of *Holling cum Withringsey*, and not for those lying in *Hampton* aforesaid. To this Plea the Plaintiff demurred, and shewed especially for Cause, that the Defendant had shewed for Cause Matter not traversable. Mr *Robinson* argued in Maintenance of the Demurrer, and said, he did agree, that the Plaintiff had alledged in his Declaration, that the Lands, for which he was rated, lay in the Parish of *Hampton*; but the alledging that they lay in *Hampton* was merely Matter of Form, in whatsoever other Parish they lay, so that they did not lie in the Parish of *Holling cum Withringsey*, it was the same Thing to the Plaintiff; and therefore the Traverse was bad; for it is confining the Plaintiff to prove that they lay in this particular

Parish

Parish of *Hampton.* He said, the Defendant ought only have pleaded, that the Plaintiff occupied other Lands in the Parish of *Holling cum Withringsey,* for which he was rated, and there he ought to have rested, and then the Traverse, that he had other Lands in the Parish of *Holling cum Withringsey,* would naturally have come on in the Replication, which was the material Point to be put in Issue. To this Purpose he cited *Saund.* 206. *Syd.* 227, 405. *Lev.* 43, 263. *Plow* 95 & *Carth.* 116. Mr. *Agar* argued, on the other Side; but *Page* and *Lee,* Justices, inclined to be of Opinion that the Traverse was bad; however this Matter stood over. *Probyn* J absent.

8. *Arms, Monuments and Grave-stones.*

1. IF a Nobleman, Knight, Esquire, &c. be buried in a Church, and have his Coat, Armour, and Pennions, with his Arms, and such other Ensigns of Honour, as belong to his Degree or Order set up in the Church, or if a Grave-stone be laid, or made, &c. for a Monument of him; though the Freehold of the Church be in the Parson, and that these are annexed to the Freehold, yet cannot the Parson, or any, take them, or deface them; but he is liable to an Action by the Heir and his Heirs, in Honour and Memory of whose Ancestor they were set up: And some hold, that the Wife, or Executors who first set them up may have an Action against those who deface them, in their

4

their Time. *Co Litt.* 18 *b* 3 *Inst.* 202. 12 *Co* 105. *Mo* 878. *Godb.* 200, 279. *Rol. Rep* 57 *Lamb* 496 *Noy* 104

2 Coats of Arms placed in any Window, or Monument in the Church, or Church-yard, cannot be beaten down, or defaced by the Parson, Church-warden, or Ordinary, or any other, and if they be, the Heir by Descent interested in the Coat, may have an Action upon the Case, for the Heir is inheritable to the Arms, as to Heir-loom. *Cro. Jac.* 366 *Std* 206. *Salk.* 347. *Rot Abr.* 625. 12 *Co.* 104, 105.

XXVII. *Poor's Rates.*

1 **M**ICH 4 *Geo.* 2. *in B R. Anonymus.*   *
A Prohibition was moved for to the Consistory Court of *York* to stay Proceedings there, in a Suit upon a Poor's Rate, upon a Suggestion, that the Party's Lands did not lie in that Parish where the Rate was made, which Matter they had pleaded below, but still the Court below was proceeding, and by this Means would try the Bounds of Parishes. The Court said, the Party ought not only have pleaded that the Lands did not lie within the Parish, but also that they lay within some other, for *Non con-stat* upon this Plea, that the Party has any Lands, and if so, this would be Matter proper for Appeal: However, as the Counsel said, the Truth of the Fact was, that the Lands lay in the next adjoining Parish. Rule to shew Cause; but *Hill.* following the Rule was discharged; for that he had not

pleaded that he had not Lands in this Parish which the Libel had charged, his Plea was only, that he had no Lands in this Parish rated at this Rate, which was far from alledging, that he had no Lands at all in this Parish; but is rather a Confession that he had, and is only a Denial of their being set at this particular Rate

2 *Paf* 5 *Geo.* 2. *B. R. Hall* and *Godley.*

This was upon a Rule to shew Cause why a Prohibition should not go to the Ecclesiastical Court Mr *Fazakerly* urged, that the Suggestion set forth, the Plaintiff below had libelled upon a Rate, whereby the Inhabitants, who lived in the Parish *anno* 17 9, are required to pay a certain Pound Rate towards the Building of the Church finished *anno* 1716. He said, the Suggestion further set forth, that a Suit was in the Exchequer by the Workmen against some of the Inhabitants, wherein there was a Decree against such Inhabitants, and that the Rate further was, that the other Inhabitants should contribute to the Expence of that Suit, and upon that Part of the Rate they libel Upon each of these Parts of the Libel, he submitted it, that the Ecclesiastical Court had Jurisdiction, but the Court were of a contrary Opinion, and so the Rule was made absolute.

XXVIII. *Parish Offices.*

1. *Who privileged from serving.*

1. THE King's Officers are privileged from serving Parish Offices, tho' they trade besides 2 *Rep. Ch* 196, 197. 1 *Vol* 86, 140, 189, 278, &c.   2. *Stamp*

2. *Stamp*, a Clerk of the King's Bench, was elected a Church-warden *de Kingston*, and had a Writ of Privilege to the Ecclesiastical Court, that they should not swear him, and for that they obeyed not the Writ, a Prohibition went. *Palm.* 292

3. If a Clerk of his Majesty's Court of King's Bench, *or any of the other Courts of Westminster*, be appointed Church-warden, a Prohibition lieth. *Palm.* 292.

XXIX. *Bounds of Parishes.*

1. *These Courts may not try.*

IF a Suit be in the Spiritual Court to try the Bounds of a Parish, a Prohibition shall be granted ; for they cannot try it. 14 *Ja. B. R. Fisher* and *Chamberlayne.* Resolved *Hill.* 41 *Eliz. B. R.* between *Piper* and *Barnaby*, and a Prohibition was granted. *Hill.* 13 *Ja. B. R.* between *Foster* and *Hide* adjudged. *Rol. Abr.* 291. *Prohibition.*

2. If the Vicar of a Parish libel against another to avoid his Institution to a Church, which he supposeth to be a Chapel of Ease belonging to his Vicarage ; if the Defendant suggest it to be a Parish Church of it self, and not a Chapel of Ease, a Prohibition shall be granted ; for they may not try the Bounds of a Parish. *Mich* 4 *Ja. B. R. Fisher* and *Chamberlene*, for the Church of *Oakely* and *Clapham* ; and yet there it was alledged *subdolè libellando.* *Trin* 31 *Ja Les Gardens de St. Sampson*'s Case *in Cornubia.* *Pas* 9 *Ja B R. enter Elie, Vicar de Alderburne en Com. Wilts*, and *Cooke*, a Prohibition

S 2 tion

tion granted. *Rol. Ab. Prohibition, fo.* 291. L. *Case* 2, 3.

3. If the Suit be in the Spiritual Court by a Viscount to avoid an Institution of another, who is instituted to *A.* his Chapel of Ease, as he pretends ; if the other suggests that *A.* is a Parish Church by itself, a Prohibition shall be granted to try, whether it be a Parish by it self, because they may not try the Bounds of a Parish ; but not for the Institution, because that appertains to them to examine whether good or not *Mich.* 14 *Ja. Fish* and *Chamberlayne* ; but *Haughton* said, that they might not try Institution, without trying the Bounds of the Parish. *Rol. Abr. Prohibition, fo.* 314, 315. (E) *Case* 2.

4 If a Suit be in the Spiritual Court for Tithes, where the Question is, whether the Lands out of which, *&c.* be within the Parish or out of it within the King's Forest, *even* after Sentence for the Plaintiff and an Appeal for the Defendant, a Prohibibition shall be granted ; because it is all utterly out of their Jurisdiction to try the Bounds of a Parish ; and also it concerneth the King ; for if it be within the Forest of the King, he shall have the Tithe, *& nullum tempus occurrit Regi* Vide *Hill* 9 *Car. Rol. Ab. Prohibition,* M *Case* 1, 2.

B. The

B.

The Person.

4. Re=

I. *Laying*

I. *Laying violent Hands on a Clerk.*

1. *General.*

1. IF one sue a Priest, or Monk, or Canon, or Clerk, in the Temporal Law, in Debt, or Trespass, and cause him to be arrested by his Person, if the Plaintiff at Law be for this Cause cited in the Spiritual Court *de Violenta Manuum injectione in Clericum,* the other shall have a Prohibition directed to the Judge. *F N. B* 42 *E.*

2 An Information in the Spiritual Court for laying violent Hands upon a Clerk in the Church, and Costs given, and the Defendant is excommunicated for Non-payment; but because it was not at the Suit of the Party, but on Information, in which Costs are not grantable, the Court awarded a Prohibition. *Mo.* 540.

3. Prohibition, and surmiseth that the Defendant was a Clerk, and made an Assault upon his Servant, and he coming in Aid of his Servant, and to keep the Peace laid his Hands peaceably upon h m; whereupon the Defendant made an Assault upon the Plaintiff, who defended himself, and then the Clerk sued him in Court Christian *pro Violenta Injectione Manuum super Clericum,* where he pleaded all this Matter, and that if the Defendant had any Hurt, it was *de son Assault demesne,* but the Court Christian would not allow this Plea; but proceeded to

S 4 Sentence

Sentence against him, and fined him 10*l*. and awarded Damages to the Clerk; whereupon he brought the Prohibition. The Defendant confesseth the Plaintiff pleaded this Plea in the Spiritual Court; but shews that the Plea was condemned there for Non-Attendance upon the Suit, and traverseth the Refusal of the Plea; and it was thereupon Demurred. *Godfrey* moved for a Consultation, for the Suit was well begun in the Spiritual Court, it being for beating of a Clerk by *Stat. Artic. Cleri, vide Nat. Br.* 51, and this Plea pleaded there was well triable there, as 1 *R.* 3. 4. 46 *E.* 3. 32. And then the Allegation for taking away the Jurisdiction of that Court is well traversable; as where a Cause alledged for removing of a Suit out of ancient Demesne Court, it is traversable, as 6 *H.* 4. 1. and 27 *H.* 6 4. Wherefore, &c. *Gaudy* held, that this Case was out of the Stat of *Artic. Cleri* and of *Circumspecte Agatis*; for here the Party had good Cause to beat the Clerk: And as to the Traverse it is not good; for the Surmise is not traversable, but he agreed the Case in Ancient Demesne; for otherwise the Lord should lose his Franchise; but it is not so in the other Case, as in the Case alledged to move a Plaint in a *Recordare*, it is not traversable; and of that Opinion were all the Court, wherefore it was adjudged for the Plaintiff. *Cro. Eliz.* 655. See 5 *Co. De Ju. Reg Eccl* 9 *a.*

4 If a Man lay violent Hands upon a Clerk and beat him, for the beating Amends must be in the King's Court, and for the Laying violent Hands upon him, Amends may

may be in Court Chriſtian ; therefore if the Judge in Court Chriſtian award Damages for the Beating, he does againſt the Statute. *Dr. & Stud. lib.* 2. *cap* 32. *fo.* 118. *b.*

2. *Pleas in.*

A Prohibition was awarded, upon Surmiſe that the Defendant, a Clerk, had aſ-ſaulted the Plaintiff's Servant, for which the Plaintiff in the Prohibition peaceably put his Hands upon him, which he alledged in Court Chriſtian ; but they would not allow it, wherefore Prohibition, notwithſtanding the Stat. *De Articulis Cleri, & Circumſpecte Agatis* See *Fitz. Nat. Br. fo.* 51. 1 *R.* 3. 4 46 *E.* 3. 3. *Mo.* 915.

II. *Where Clerk* Criminoſus.

1. THE Eccleſiaſtical Decree, that all Clerks in any Orders, Greater, or Smaller, ſhould be exempt *pro Cauſis Criminalibus* before Temporal Judges, never was received, ſo never could have any Force here for Want of ſuch Reception , and for that it was againſt the Laws of the Land, as appears by infinite Precedents, as well as the King's Prerogative and Sovereignty, that any of his Majeſty's Subjects ſhould not owe Obedience and pay Obſervance to the Laws made for the Government of the Realm. See 5 *Co. De Ju. Reg Eccl.* 32. *b.* 33. *a.* *When Kings themſelves and their Miniſters, Judges, and Magiſtrates muſt ſo obſerve the*
Laws

Laws as to govern and determine by them, I take the liberty to fay, it furpaffeth Lay Affurance, or indeed of any other but confirmed Papifts, and their Mercenary, or blind and befotted Adherents, and Tools of Church Ufurpation and Oppreffion, (tho' it has been ftrongly laboured by the Clergy heretofore, as well Archbifhops and Bifhops as all others of that Body) to fay, any Ecclefiaftic whatfoever, and much more fo to contend, that every petit and inconfiderable Church Cleric fhould be exempt from all, or any, the Obedience due to the Municipal Laws of our Country, fure none will have the Countenance to pretend this, who have at all confidered and weighed the difmal Effects of fuch an Exemption; tho' exercifed only by church Incroachment, and that but for a fhort Time, when the greateft Wickedneffes, even Murder itfelf, were not only fuffered to go unpunifhed, but alfo countenanced, nay, even juftified and maintained in Clericks by Guarding, Defending, and Supporting fuch being Murderers, &c. in Bifhops Palaces, Religious Houfes, and Sanctuaries, from the juft Refentment of an offended Sovereign, and his moft juft, equal, and merciful, Temporal Laws, made and provided againft fuch heinous Offences, and that becaufe the Offenders were Clerks, &c Scoffing the Rule, Intereft Reipublicæ ne maleficia remaneant impunita.*

2. In the reign of *H* 2. The ancient Law was revived, (*for tho' it had been, by Means of Difloyal and Traiterous Church-Men, for a time fuppreffed, it always was the undoubted Law of this Realm*) That if any Clerk fhould commit Felony, that he fhould be hanged, if Treafon, that he fhould be drawn and quartered. *Da.* 91, 92 *a b*

3. The

3. The Ecclesiastical Court may not examine any Capital Crime, as Felony, or the like, not even for Purposes examinable there; and therefore they may not examine such Crimes, though in Order to prove a Man *Criminosus*, much less, when he is so proved in the proper Superior Court, *to which the Spiritual Courts are but inferior, may they* impeach the Sentence or Judgment in a proper Court, in a Court improper, *as their's, in such Case, is;* but yet they may build a Sentence of Deprivation upon such a Conviction, and they are bound by it, and it is dangerous for any Ecclesiastical Judge to come against it *Hob* 121. *Searle's Case.*

4. Regularly the Ordinary, at Common Law, had no Power over a Clergyman in a Crime or Offence touching the Crown; but where such Power was given to him by the Common Law *Hob* 290; and therefore when the King's Court delivered the Offender to the Ordinary, it implied a Power, or a Permission of the Law, that he might deal with him to convict, or discharge him, according to the Form of their Laws; but since the Statute hath forbidden the Delivery of him to the Ordinary, it retains all Power itself, and denies the Ordinary's, and therefore if he, at Common Law, would have convened a Church-Man to have deprived or degraded him, for Felony before his Trial at Law, a Prohibition would have lain for holding Plea of a Cause of the Crown and prejudging the King's Court *in eadem.* Much rather then in the Marquis of *Winchester's Case,* 6 *Co.* 23. where a Prohibition was

granted,

granted, to stop the Probate of a Will for Goods, because the said Will did also give Lands; for tho', in Truth, the Will be made *uno flatu*, and interlaced within one Continent or Writing; yet in Effect they are two Wills, and of diverse Natures and Effects, and Cognizances, whereas in the other Case, the Crime is all Temporal *idem Individuo*, and the End of the Conusance is only divers: That is, with us Capital, with them Deprivation, or Degrading, or the like. *Hob.* 290. *Cro. Jac.* 430, 431, same Case.

5. If a Clerk in Felony was found not guilty, and discharged, notwithstanding which the Ordinary would convene him again, and admit new Proof, that he was guilty, in Order to deprive him, they were to be prohibited; or if upon a Clerk's being delivered, *Absque Purgatione*, to the Ordinary, they would admit him to his Purgation, a Prohibition would lie, yea and a *Præmunire* too; and yet these Offences are not so highly a Plea of the Crown, as Criminal Causes; as amongst Criminal Causes there are Degrees, as Treasons, and even some against the King's own Person, also if they would proceed betwixt Conviction and Clergy, a Prohibition would lie for Prevention; for that the Cause is not yet finished in the King's Court: But if they would not controvert nor re-examine the Acts of the King's Courts, but build their Sentences upon them, they were not to be prohibited; as if they deprived a Man by Sentence, because he was convicted or attainted

tainted of Felony, Murder, or Manslaughter, at Common Law. *Hob.* 290, 291. *Cro. Jac.* 430, 431, same Case. 2 *Inst* 637.

III. *Scandalous Words spoken of a Clerk.*

Vide ante, *Scandal, Slander, or Defamation.*

1. IF a Parson call *A* a Drunkard; whereupon *A.* answereth, Thou lieft, if the Parson sue him in the Ecclesiastical Court for giving him the Lie, a Prohibition lieth; for that the Cause for which he gave him the Lie, was not Spiritual, but depended upon a precedent Temporal Matter *Mich.* 7 *Jac. Simpson* and *Water.* *Rol Abr.* 295. *Case* 5.

2 If a Man call a Minister Knave, Searjeant *Roll* says, he may be sued for it, in the Ecclesiastical Court, and no Prohibition should be granted. *Prohib* 295 *Case* 8. *sed quere de ceo. Sur* 1 *Vent.* 2. *ou un Prohib. fuit grant en tiel Case.*

3 If *J B* say to *J D* it is reported that *J N* did or doth keep in his House a Man or a Boy to bugger, whereto *J. D* answereth, the vile Villain would have done as much to me If *J N* sue *J. D* averring himself to be a Minister, a Prohibition lieth; because it is no Spiritual Defamation, and is Felony by Statute *Mich* 8 *Car* B. R. *Higgon* & *Coppinger, introtur Hil* 8 *Car Rol* 129. *Rol. Abr. Prohib.* 296, 297. *Case* 20.

4. If a Man libel for saying of him, thou art fitter for the Pillory, than for a Preacher, and that he spoke the Words in Time of Divine Service; and hereupon Sentence is given, that he should recant the Words, &c if the Defendant shew to the Temporal Court, that he spoke them of a certain Release, &c saying that the Plaintiff had forged the said Release, and on that Account the Words were spoken, so that he might have had an Action at Law for the Words, in such Case, tho' the Suit be maintainable in the Ecclesiastical Court for speaking the Words in Time of Divine Service, yet because Sentence is given that he should revoke the Words, which is for all, a Prohibition shall go for all. *Mich.* 38 & 39 *Eliz. Butler* and *Bartlet, Rol. Abr. Prohib* 316. *Case* 7

5. Prohibition, because the Plaintiff *Parlor* was convened before the High Commissioners, for saying to *Butler*, being a Minister, that he was fitter to stand on the Pillory than preach in the Pulpit, and that he had taken two Orders already, that he lacked but taking the third, which was, to have his Ears cut off; *Parlor* justified, because *Butler* had forged an Acquittance, and shewed it in certain; the Commissioners would not allow of this Justification; but censured him to ask Forgiveness, whereupon he brought the Prohibition, and it was adjudged maintainable; because the high Commissioners had nothing to do with this Cause, unless it was in Time of Divine Service. *Mo. fo.* 460. *Case* 639

6. Dr *Parsons* libelled against *Coxeter*, for saying of him, *He had no Sense, was a Dunce,*

I

Dunce, and a Blockhead, and he wondered the Bishop would lay his Hands upon such a Fellow, and that he deserved to have his Gown pulled over his Ears, a Prohibition was granted; for a Parson is not punishable in the Spiritual Court for being a Knave or a Blockhead more than another Man; and whereas it was urged, that a Parson might be deprived for Want of Learning; the Chief Justice said, if that be the Case he must bring his Action at Law; for that was a Temporal Damage, and a Prohibition was granted. *Salk* 692. See 1 *Ven* 2

7 A Prohibition was prayed and granted, upon a Suit in the Ecclesiastical Court, by a Parson for calling him *Fool, Ass,* and *Goose,* for they are but Words of Heat, and do not touch him in his Profession 2 *Lev.* 49.

8 If a Clergyman be a Bailiff of a Manor to *J S.* and he oppress the Tenants, and one of them says to him, *Thou art a Knave, and fitter to wear a white Cloak than a black one,* if the Parson sue him for these Words in Court Christian, a Prohibition shall be granted. *Rol. Ab. Prohibition,* 295. *Case* 6.

9. *Hill* 6 *Geo.* 2. *Bovey* and *Busby.*
The Parties being both Clergymen, the Plaintiff libelled against the Defendant in the Ecclesiastical Court for these Words, *You are an old Rogue, and a Rascal, and a contemptible Fellow, despised and hated by every Body;* and likewise for saying of him at another Time, *You are a Liar.* Mr. *Filmer* now moved for a Prohibition, notwithstanding the first Set of Words were said to be spoken against the
Plaintiff

Plaintiff in his Eunction. The Lord Chief
Juſtice doubted, whether, in ſuch Caſe, the
Ecclefiaſtical Court had not a Jurifdiction,
however a Rule was made to ſhew Cauſe.
Juſtice *Page* abſent.

IV. *Ecclefiaſtical Officers.*

1. *Scandalous Words ſpoken of.*

IF *A.* a Surrogate ſue *B.* in the Spiritual
Court *ex officio, pro ſalute animæ, & morum
reformatione, ex promotione C* becauſe that *C*
being a Proctor of the Spiritual Court, and
a Maſter of Arts, the ſaid *B* ſaid to him,
Thou art or *he is a ſcabbed Knave, and a
pickerel Bum-Bailiff,* vel ſic, *I ſcorn to be
abuſed by ſuch a ſcabbed Knave,* or *ſuch a
pickerel Bum-Bailiff, as thou art,* and avers
that it was ſpoken to defame *C* and in
Contempt of the Ecclefiaſtical Jurifdiction,
a Prohibition lies; for it is not any Spiritual
Slander, nor any Defamation to the Court.
Mich. 8 *Car. B R. Cory* and *Ward, Rol. Ab.
Prohibition,* 297. *Caſe* 22.

2. *Their Offices Temporal, and there-
fore, as ſuch, triable in the Temporal Courts.*

1. *Chancellors.*

1. IF a Biſhop grant the Office of Chancellor to *A* and *B.* and after *A* releaſeth
to *B.* and then *B.* dies, and the Biſhop
gives

4

gives it to *R.* against whom *A.* sues in the Ecclesiastical Court, suppossing the Release void, a Prohibition shall go; because the Office is Temporal, though he exercise the Office in Spiritual Matters. *Rol Abr. Probibition,* F. 38 8 *Ja.* But if the Knowledge of the Chancellor in the Canon Law be the Question, no Prohibition to go; for they are the proper Judges. 39. *tamen quære.*

2. Assise was brought by Sir *John Bennet* for the Office of Chancellorship of the Archbishop of *York;* the Defendant endeavoured to gain an Injunction, out of the Star-Chamber, to stay his Suit, he being by Sentence and Decree there, (for Bibery and other Misdemeanors in his Office of Judge of the Prerogative Court) fined 20000 *l.* and censured to be imprisoned and made incapable of any Office of Judicature, by Reason whereof, being disabled to hold that Office in Question, the Defendant obtained it, and pretended this Assise was brought by Sir *John Bennet,* that he might injoy the said Office, contrary to the Decree; he therefore prayed to stay his Proceedings; whereupon Sir *John Bennet,* having Day given him to shew Cause, why an Injunction should not go, shewed then a Pardon from the late King, after the said Sentence, wherein was recited all the Bribery, and Offences contained in the said Decree, and all Punishments and Penalties by Reason thereof, and all Disabilities, and Incapacities, and all Things concerning the said Sentence, except the said Fine of 20000 *l.* and and thereupon the Court of Star-Chamber requested Sir *John Waller,* Chief Baron, and

Sir *Francis Harvey*, third Justice of the Common Pleas, to call to them all the Justices and Barons, and to consider of the said Decree and Pardon, and to certify their Opinions, whether it were fit to permit the Proceedings in the Assise or not; and all the Justices and Barons being assembled at *Serjeants-Inn Hall*, the Sentence and Pardon were read before them, and the Case argued by Counsel on both Sides, and it was resolved by the Justices and Barons, that this Pardon hath taken away all Force of the Sentence in the Star-Chamber, except the Fine of 20000 *l.* and all Inabilities are discharged thereby, and that the Sentence never took from him the Office, but the Execution thereof; neither gave Authority to put in another, but if the Archbishop, before the Pardon, and after the Sentence, had appointed him to execute his Office, and he durst not do it, then, peradventure, the said Archbishop for his Non-attendance, might have seised the said Office, and granted it to another; but the Sentence of itself could not take away the Office, being a Freehold : And the Pardon having taking away all the Offences, they therefore conceived it convenient to permit him to proceed in the Assise ; and if doubtful, it may be found specially, and so receive a judicial Hearing. *Cro Car. fo 55, 56.*

2 *Surrogate.*

1. *Who to be, and his Duty.*

1 No Chancellor, Commiſſary, Archdeacon, Official, or any other uſing Eccleſiaſtical Juriſdiction, ſhall at any Time ſub-
ſtitute, in their Abſence, any to keep any
Court for them, except he be, either a
grave Miniſter, and a Graduate, or a li-
cenſed publick Preacher and a beneficed
Man, near the Place where the Courts are
kept, or a Bachelor at Law, or a Maſter
of Arts at leaſt, who hath ſome Skill in the
Civil and Eccleſiaſtical Law, and is a Fa-
vourer of true Religion, and a Man of
modeſt and honeſt Converſation, under Pain
of Suſpenſion for every Time that they offend therein, from the Execution of their
Offices, for the Space of three Months, *to-
ties quoties*; and he likewiſe who is ſo deputed, being not qualified as aforeſaid, and
yet ſhall preſume to be a Subſtitute to any
Judge, and ſhall keep any Court, as is a-
foreſaid, ſhall undergo the ſame Cenſure, in
Manner and Form, as is before expreſſed.
Can 128.

2 In *Canc.* 1 *May* 1740 *Havers* and *Havers.* ✳
If the Court of Chancery ſee the Exerciſe of a Juriſdiction by a Surrogate, be to
an Infant's Prejudice, where the Adminiſtration is but a limited one, as *durante minoritate*, and the Adminiſtrator a Truſtee
for the Infant, it is incumbent on Chancery
to interfere, and take Care that the Infant
be not prejudiced, in ſuch Caſe, eſpecially

T 2 where

where the Administration was, as my Lord
Chancellor said, in the principal Case it
had been, granted in a careless, slovenly, and
scandalous Manner, and where it was incumbent on the Surrogate to have taken
Care, as the Estate was considerable, the
Administration should have been granted to
a responsible Person, and not to a poor and
indigent one, as was the principal Case.

3. *Proctor.*

1. *How retained, and his Duty.*

1. None to procure in any Cause, unless
thereto constituted and appointed by the
Party himself, either before the Judge, and
by Act in Court, or unless in the Beginning of the Suit, he be by true and sufficient Proxy thereunto warranted and enabled, we call that Proxy sufficient, *saith this
Canon*, which is strengthened and confirmed
by some authentical Seal, the Party's Appro-
bation, or at least his Ratification there-
withal concurring, all which Proxies shall
be forthwith by the said Proctors exhibited
into the Court, and be safely kept and preserved by the Register, in the publick Re-
gistry of the said Court; and if any Register offend therein, he is to be secluded
from the Exercise of his Office, for the
Space of two Months, without Hope of
Release or Restoring. *Can* 129.

2. For lessening and abridging the Multitude of Suits and Contentions, as also for
preventing the Complaints of Suitors in
Courts Ecclesiastical, *who many Times are
over-*

overthrown by the Overſight and Negligence,
or by the Ignorance and Inſufficiency of Proc-
tors, and likewiſe for the Furtherance and
Increaſe of Learning, and the Advance-
ment of Civil and Canon Law, following
the laudable Cuſtom heretofore obſerved in
the Courts of the Archbiſhop of *Canterbury,*
it is willed and ordained by that Canon,
That no Proctor exerciſing in any of them,
ſhall entertain any Cauſe whatſoever, and
keep and retain the ſame for two Court-
Days, *without the Counſel and Advice of*
an Advocate, under Pain of a Year's Suſpenſion from his Practice ; neither ſhall the
Judge have Power to releaſe, or mitigate
the ſaid Penalty without expreſs Mandate
and Authority from the Archbiſhop. *Can* 130.

3. No Proctors ſhall conclude any Cauſe
depending, *without the Knowledge of the*
Advocate retained and feed in the Cauſe,
which if any Proctor ſhall do or procure to
be done ; *or ſhall, by any Colour whatſoever,*
defraud the Advocate of his Duty or Fee ;
or ſhall be negligent in repairing to the
Advocate and requiring his Advice, what
Courſe is to be taken in the Cauſe, he ſhall be
ſuſpended from all Practice for the Space of
ſix Months, without Hope of being thereunto
reſtored, before the ſaid Term be fully com-
pleat. Can. 131.

4. As it is found by Experience, that the
loud and confuſed Cries and Clamors of
Proctors in the Courts of the Archbiſhop,
are not only troubleſome and offenſive to
the Judges and Advocates, but alſo give Occaſion to the Standers-by of Contempt and
Calumny towards the Court itſelf ; that

T 3 more

more Respect may be had to the Dignity of
the Judge than heretofore, and that Causes
may more easily and commodiously be han-
dled and dispatched, all Proctors in the
said Court, are specially to intend that the
Acts be faithfully ordered, and set down by
the Register, *according to the Advice and
Direction of the Advocate*, that the said
Proctors refrain loud Speech and Brabling,
and behave themselves quietly and modestly,
and that when the Judges or Advocates, or
any of them, shall happen to speak, they presently be silent, upon Pain of silencing for
two whole Terms then immediately following every such Offence; and if any of them
shall a second Time offend, and after due Monition shall not reform himself, let him be
for ever removed from his Practice　*Can*
133.

4 *Register.*

1. *Is a Temporal Officer.*

1. If there be a Question between two
Persons upon two several Grants, which
shall be the Register of the Bishop's Court,
it shall not be tried in the Bishop's Court;
but at Common Law; for though the *Sub-
jectum circa quod* be Spiritual, yet the Office
is Temporal. *Rol. Abr. Prohibition*, T. 35
or 36. F. *Case* 43

＊　　2. *Hill.* 8 *Geo.* 2. B. R. *The King* and
Wheeler.

Mr. *Strange* moved for a *Mandamus* to
the Deputy-Register of *Durham*, to deliver
over to his Principal all publick Books relating

lating to that Office, the Deputation being expired; and the Cafe of *Herne* and ——— *Paf. 6 W. 3* was cited, where, after the Right to the Office of Regifter of *Hereford* was tried in an Affife, the like Motion was granted; and accordingly Rule was to fhew Caufe, and now in *Eafter* Term Mr *Fenwick*, coming to fhew Caufe, he laid down the Fact to be thus, That the Deputy was *Auguft* 1731 appointed Deputy to one *Trotter* for three Years, and that in *December* following the Regifter and his faid Deputy, the Defendant, came to another Agreement, that after the Expiration of thefe three Years the Defendant fhould injoy this Office four Years longer This Agreement, tho' in Writing, was not under Seal, hereupon the Defendant brought his Bill in Chancery againft *Trotter* to enforce a fpecifick Execution of this Agreement, and in that Court Proceedings had been therein to Publication, and on this State of the Cafe, he fubmitted it, the Rule ought to be difcharged, he faid, *Mandamus's* of this Sort were not due *ex debito juftitiæ*; and as there was a Suit depending concerning this Office, that was a fufficient Reafon for the Court's refufing it, to which Purpofe was cited the Cafe of *The King* and *Vincent* Mr. *Strange* argued, on the other Side, that *Mandamus's* ought to be granted by the Court *de jure*, and faid the Difpute in Chancery is merely relating to an equitable Intereft, but the Books ought to be granted to him who has the legal Poffeffion of the Office My Lord Chief Juftice declared, he did not think thefe Writs were to be granted *de jure*, but that the proper Rea-

T 4   fon

son and Occasion for granting them is, where otherwise the Course of Justice would be obstructed, he did not think, that where-ever a Person was in Possession of an Office, that the Court ought always, for that Reason only, to give him Possession of the Books also, by a Writ of *Mandamus*. Suppose a Man is a Disseisor of an Office, the Court will not do it And *Vincent*'s Case cited his Lordship thought a Case in Point, and a full Authority to the present Purpose, and there his Lordship observed, the Court refused to grant a *Mandamus* to the Bishop of *London*, to grant a Licence to a Lecturer, on this Reason only, that a Suit was then pending in the Court of Exchequer con-cerning the Lectureship, so in the principal Case the Rule was discharged. In *Hill.* 9 *Geo* 2. Mr *Fenwick* came again and of-fered for Cause why a *Mandamus* should not go to the Defendant to deliver the Books over to his Principal He agreed indeed, that the present Case had some Appearance of Variance from what it was on the former Motion, for now it is insisted upon in the first place, that a Decree has past against *Wheeler*, and in the next place, that he is run away, and deserted his Office; however he submitted it, those Objections might both of them receive a very proper Answer, as to the first of them, he said, though his *Honour of the Rolls* had decreed against *Wheeler*; yet an Appeal from that Decree is now pending. And to the second he said, *Wheeler* had delivered over the Custody of the Books to a Person of known Ability and Reputation. My Lord Chief Justice said, had

had this Matter of the Party's Deserting the
Office appeared on the former Motion, he
should even then have been for granting the
Mandamus, though no Decree was at that
Time; and said further, there being a Decree now pronounced, though appealed from,
was certainly an additional Circumstance for
granting the *Mandamus;* the rest of the
Judges according with his Lordship, the Rule
was made absolute.

3 8 & 9 *Geo* 2. *B. R. Stephens* and
Rooding

This was a Motion to supersede a *Man-*
damus, to restore *Richard Stevens* to the Office of Register of the Archdeaconry of *Leice-*
ster, said by Counsel, that *anno* 1710. a Grant
was by the Archdeacon of this Office to one
Rooding in Reversion expectant on a former
Patent to *Stephens,* afterwards *Rooding* came
to the Possession of this Office, and continued 21 Years in it, during which Time he
appointed *Richard Stevens,* his Deputy; and
anno 1731 the Archdeacon granted a Patent
to *Richard Stevens,* that he might be able to
try the Validity of *Rooding's* Grant; and
thereupon *Richard Stevens* insisted on keeping the Possession of this Office in his own
Right, whereupon *Rooding* applied for and
obtained a *Mandamus* from this Court to restore him, and the Validity of his Grant received a Determination for him by Verdict,
since which, there hath been a Writ of Error in the Exchequer-Chamber upon that
Judgment, which was affirmed; and thereupon another Writ of Error was brought
before the House of Lords, whereon was a
Non-pros; wherefore he submitted it, that
it

it was not reasonable that this Matter should go through any farther Examination on a second *Mandamus*. But my Lord Chief Justice said, that the former *Mandamus* was granted to the Archdeacon, and not to *Richard Stephens*; so that this Case is no more than the common one, where two Persons are contending about the Right to an Office; as of Capital Judges, one of them brings a *Mandamus*, the Corporation submits to it, yet the other may have a new *Mandamus* notwithstanding; and *Page* Justice said, the Court did the same Thing, in the Case of Mr. *Barcoat*, concerning the Office of a Clerk of Assise; and the Rest of the Court were of the same Opinion, and accordingly the Motion was refused.

2 *His Duty.*

1. *General to.*

If any Register, or his Deputy, or Substitute whatsoever, shall receive any Certificate without the Knowledge and Consent of the Judge of the Court, or willingly omit to cause any Person cited to appear upon any Court-Day, to be called, or unduly put off or defer the Examination of Witnesses to be examined by a Day set and assigned by the Judge, or do not obey and observe the judicial and lawful Monition of the said Judge, or omit to write, or cause to be written, such Citations and Decrees as are to be put in Execution, and set forth before the next Court-Day, or shall not cause all Testaments, exhibited into his Office, to be
registred

regiftred within a convenient Time, or shall set down or enact as decreed by the Judge any Thing false or conceited by himself, and not so ordered or decreed, or in Transmission of Proceffes to the Judge *ad quem*, shall add or infert any Falfhood, or Untruth, or omit any Thing therein either by Cunning or grofs Negligence; or in any Caufes of Inftance, or promoted of Office, shall indirectly, with either Party in the Suit, or in the Execution of their Office, shall do ought elfe malicioufly or fraudulently, whereby the faid Ecclefiaftical Judge or his Proceedings may be flandered or defamed, *it is by this Canon ordained* fuch Regifter, or his Deputy, or Subftitute offending in all or any of the Premiffes, shall by the Bishop of the Diocefe be fufpended from the Exercife of his Office, for the Space of one, two, or three Months, or more, according to the Quality of his Offence, and that the faid Bifhop shall affign fome other Publick Notary to execute and difcharge all Things pertaining to his Office during the Time of his faid Sufpenfion. *Can.* 134.

2 *Proctors*, Proxies of Retainer are to be fafely kept and preferved by Regifters, on Pain of Sufpenfion. *Prout in the Canon* 129.

2. To fet up Tables of Fees.

It is appointed, that the Regifter belonging to every Ecclefiaftical Judge, shall place two Tables containing the feveral Rates and Sums of all the faid Fees, one in the ufual Place, or Confiftory where the Court is kept, the other in his Regiftry, and both

of

of them in such Sort that every one concerned may, without Difficulty, come to
the View and Perusal thereof, and take a
Copy of them, and if any Register fail
therein, he is to be suspended, till he cause
the same to be done: And the said Tables
being once set up, if he shall at any Time
remove or suffer the same to be removed,
hidden, or any Ways hindered from Sight,
contrary to the true Meaning of that Constitution, he shall for every such Offence be
suspended for six Months. *Can.* 136.

5. *Apparator.*

1. *What.*

He is the Messenger who cites Offenders
to appear in the Spiritual Court, and he
serves the Processes thereof. *Blo. Law Dict.*
sub hoc Tit.

2. *His Office.*

1. *His Duty therein.*

For the Redress of such Abuses and Ag-
grievances as are said to grow by Summoners
or Apparators, and that the Multitude of
Apparators be (as much as is possible) a-
bridged or restrained, it is by this Canon ordained, that no Bishop or Archdeacon, or
their Vicar, or Officials or other inferior Ordinaries, shall depute or have more Apparators to serve in their Jurisdictions respec-
tively, than either they or their Predecessors
were accustomed to have thirty Years before the Publishing of these Constitutions
or

or Canons, *anno* 1603. all which Apparators are orderly themselves to execute their Offices, and that they do not by any Colour or Pretence whatsoever, cause or suffer their Mandates to be executed by any Messenger, or Substitutes, unless upon some good Cause to be first known and approved by the Ordinary of the Place; moreover they are not to take upon them the Office of Promoters, or Informers for the Court, neither to exact more or greater Fees than are in the said Constitutions prescribed. And if either the Number of the Apparators deputed shall exceed the aforesaid Limitation, or any of the said Apparators shall offend in any of the Premisses, *the Persons deputing them,* *Nota diver-* *if they be Bishops, shall, upon Admonition* *sitatem.* *of their Superior, discharge the Persons ex-ceeding the Number so limited. If inferior Ordinaries they shall be suspended from the Execution of their Office, until they have dismissed the Apparators by them so deputed,* and the Parties themselves so deputed shall for ever be removed from the Office of Apparators, and if being so removed they desist not from the Exercise of their said Offices, let them be punished by Ecclesiastical Censures, as Persons contumacious. Provided, that if, upon Experience, the Number of the said Apparators be too great in any Diocese in the Judgment of the Archbishop of *Canterbury,* for the Time being, they shall by him be so abridged, as he shall think meet and convenient. *Can.* 138.

2. *Is*

2. *Is Temporal.*

* *Pasch.* anno 1727. *B. R. The King* and *Betsworth.*

Mr *Reeve* moved for a *Mandamus* to be directed to Dr. *Betsworth*, Judge of the Prerogative Court, to admit *Folke* to the Office of Apparator General, he said the Office was a Freehold, and that he remembered the like Motion made by the Predeceffor of the prefent Gentleman, and allowed. *Reynolds* and *Probin*, Juftices, only fitting, Juftice *Reynolds* faid, that *Mandamus's*, had been denied in the Cafe of a Proctor, and therefore, as they were not clear in the Point, they made a Rule to fhew Caufe *Vide Salk* 468. 3 *Mod.* 335.

6. *Parifh-Clerks.*

1. If the Church-wardens have ufed, Time out of Mind, to elect the Clerk, and a Suit is in the Eccleffaftical Court to remove him, and put in another at the Nomination of the Parfon, a Prohibition lieth. *Rol Abr. Prohibition,* F 42. *Mich* 22 *Ja* Cafe *Walpole* and *Coldwell*, a Prohibition by Confent to try a Cuftom. *Hill.* 22 *Ja.* & *Paf.* 19 *Ja;* & *Paf.* 11 *Ca.*

2. If a Parfon libel in the Spiritual Court againft feveral of his Parifhioners, for Interruption in placing a Clerk, and, upon Suggeftion, that the Parifhioners by Prefcription, Time whereof, &c were ufed, to elect a Clerk, a Prohibition was granted:

I
And

And so had been granted before, 19 *Ja.* in *Crashaw's* Case, Parson of *Whitechapel,* and in several other Cases. *Palm.* 379.

3. If the Clerk of a Parish claims by Custom to have so much Bread of every Inhabitant at *Christmas,* and sue for it in the Spiritual Court, a Prohibition lieth , for it is not like a Pension due to a Parson. *Rol. Abr. Prohibition,* F. *Case* 43.

4. *Trin* 1727 *B R Townsend* and *Thorpe.* Motion was for a Prohibition to stay Proceedings in the Ecclesiastical Court, who was there proceeding to deprive the Plaintiff of the Office of Parish-Clerk, whereto the Parson had appointed him, and this Motion was intended to be grounded upon a Charge of Sodomy, but the Motion was rejected ; for that it was, as the Court said, unfit that a Man should be suffered to remain in such Office who was guilty of so great a Piece of Bestiality, and rather denied the Prohibition ; for that the Temporal Courts had no Way of depriving him ; and the Court said, they grounded themselves upon a like Case, 1 *Lev.* 138. where a Prohibition was moved for, and refused, to stop the Spiritual Court from proceeding to deprive one for forging Orders, (the same Case is in 1 *Sid.* 217) they said further, that the Office of a Parish-Clerk, even when he came in by Election ; *and therefore, as I conceive, even in such Case, they would have refused the Prohibition;* That a Man coming into an Office by Temporal Hands, would not change the Nature of the Office. *As I take it, this Case is not unlike some Cases of Seamen's Wages, where the Temporal Courts will*

will allow the Admiralty to take Cognizance of Matters which do not strictly fall within their Jurisdiction, on Account of the Aptness of the Remedy, which, in such Cases, are there gi-

* ven. *Vide* Case *Buck* and *Atwood*, B R.

* *Pasch.* 1727. *Newcomb* and *Higgs*, B. R. *Hil.* 4 *Geo.* 2. *The King* and *The Bishop of Litchfield* and *Coventry, concerning Rushworth Usher of* Coventry *School, under this Title, Division* School-Masters, *as to this Court's suffering the Ecclesiastical Courts proceeding in such particular Cases on Account of the Fitness of their Remedy.*

* 5. *Mich.* 4 *Geo.* 2. B. R. *Speak* v. *Born & al'.*

Dr. *Andrews* came now to shew Cause why a Prohibition should not go to the Commissary of St. *Paul's*, to stay proceeding there in a Suit by the Church-Wardens of St. *Giles's Cripplegate*, to compel the now Plaintiff, *Speak*, to take a Licence from the Ordinary in order to qualify him to act as Deputy to *Venn*, a Clergyman, appointed Clerk, according to Canon, he said there were two Points, which would properly fall out in this Inquiry; one was, whether a Clerk of a Parish can make a Deputy; the other was, that admitting he may, whether such Deputy may be obliged to take a Licence? To the first Point, he submitted it, a Parish Clerk could not make a Deputy' The Exercise of this Office related to Matters meerly Spiritual; and therefore the Office was to be considered, as Ecclesiastical, especially when supplied by a Parson, as this Case is, the Consequence of which was, that such Officer could not make a Deputy, for

I   the

the Rule of the Civil and Canon Law is,
that all Perfons fhall exercife their Offices
themfelves, in proper Perfon, and not call in
Aid the Affiftance of any other To the
other Point, he allowed there was no exprefs
Canon which required thefe Officers, that
even act in Perfon, as Parifh Clerks, to take
a Licence, but the Canons 1603 do appoint the Bifhops *Præordinator omnium*, and
the Conftruction of this Canon has been,
That Clerks of Parifhes fhall be under the
Regulation of the Bifhop, and fhall take
Licences, and then he argued, that, as this
was reafonable that the Clerks themfelves
fhould take Licenfes, there was equal Reafon that their Deputies fhould do it alfo.
Mr *Reeve*, on the other Side, urged, that
this Office was confidered in Law, as Temporal, and to the Purpofe cited 13 *Co* 70.
18 *E* 3 27. *Mar*. 101. 1 *Keb*. 286, and if
this was fo, then he fubmitted it, as a Confequence, that the Clerk might make a Deputy; he faid, it's determined that a Conftable may, and fo it was of all other Officers.
And, as another Confequence, he fubmitted
it, there's no Occafion for a Licenfe. The
Court at prefent inclined to think the fettled
Diftinction was, that this Office is confidered,
as Temporal, when fupplied by the Parifh
upon a Cuftom, but Spiritual, when fupplied by the Parfon, according to the Canon, however they thought proper to grant
a Prohibition, that the Party might declare
in it, and gave a Week's Time, though
Serjeant *Chapple* faid, that four Days was
the ufual Time. The Plaintiff having declared in Prohibition, this Matter now came

on again upon Demurrer to the Defendant's
Plea this prefent *Easter Term*, and Serjeant
Eyre, for the Plaintiff, argued, that there
were divers Authorities in the Books, which
declared a Parifh Clerk, a Temporal Officer,
and he particularly cited *Palm.* 379. Cro.
Jac. 670, and faid, no Difference was taken
as to the Manner of his coming in; but if
that Point was to be given up, ftill upon the
general Nomination of the Parfon, he has
an Eftate for Life in the Office, and then
this Court has a Right to grant its Prohibition, and prevent the Spiritual Court from
depriving fuch Officer, and to this Purpofe
cited 2 *Brownl.* 11. in the Cafe of a Chancellor of a Diocefe; and fo it is in the Cafe
of a Regifter. He further infifted, that the
Ecclefiaftical Court had no Power or Authority to require a Clerk to take a Licenfe.
Serjeant *Chappel*, on the other Side, fubmitted it, that whatever was the Authority of
the old Books, that a Clerk is a Temporal
Officer in its Nature; yet the Court has, of
late, taken a Difference between the Manner
of coming into this Office; and this, he infifted, appears from the Cafe of *Townfend*
and *Thorpe*, where the Court allowed the
Spiritual Court to proceed in depriving a
Parifh Clerk, where he was nominated by
the Parfon, which, he faid, he apprehended
they would not have done, had he been
elected by the Parifh, he then faid, the Nature of this Office made it unfit, that it
fhould be fupplied by a Deputy. Perfonal
Qualifications are required in a Clerk of a
Parifh by the 91 *Can Anno* 1603. as he muft
be 20 Years of Age, able to read and write,

and

and of a competent Understanding in Singing, if it may be; and *Gibson* in his Construction upon that Canon, says, they were originally Assistants to the Minister; he also observed, that these Inferior Officers, in general, could not make Deputies; a Constable, he said, could not; but in Necessity, as extreme Sickness, or Infancy, or the like, as where a Woman is, and so, he said, was 2 *Keb* 309, 355. Then as to the Taking a License, he agreed, that indeed he knew no direct Authority for it; but a Lecturer is certainly obliged to do it; and he submitted it, that the present Case was within the same Reason. My Lord Chief Justice said, he did not remember any express Resolution, that a Clerk was a Spiritual Officer; and as to the Case of *Townsend* and *Thorpe*, he did not remember what that Case went upon; but as to the License, he questioned whether it was necessary. *Probin Ju.* now Lord chief Baron, said, he well remembered the Case, *Townsend* and *Thorpe*, and that it went upon that Point singly; that the Clerk there was a Person absolutely unfit to execute the Office; and therefore this Court would not hinder the Ecclesiastical Court's depriving him, as this Court had not an ordinary Method of doing it themselves. And he thought the Court made no Sort of Distinction between the different Methods of the Clerks coming in. And as a further Authority, that a Parish Clerk is considered a Temporal Officer, he cited the Opinion of my Lord *Holt* in 6 *Mod.* 253, *Lee* Just. also cited a Case out of *Salk.* 536, where it is held a Clerk of a Parish, tho' named by the Par-

U 2 son,

son, gains a Settlement within the Stat 9 & 10 *W.* and *M.* as executing a Temporal Office; and as to the Lecturer's taking a Licenfe, he faid, that is abfolutely by Statute. *Page* Juft. alfo was of Opinion, that a Parifh Clerk was in all Cafes to be confidered a Temporal Officer: The Matter however ftood over to *Mich* Term, when Mr. *Reeve*, for the Plaintiff, argued, that there were in the prefent Cafe three Points proper for the Determination of the Court. 1ft, Whether a Parifh Clerk can make a Deputy? 2dly, Whether a Parifh Clerk is a Temporal Officer? And 3dly, Whether a Licence is neceffary? To the firft Point he faid, that in *Rol.* 274, and in *Mo* 845, it is refolved, that a Conftable may make a Deputy, and fo may a Dean; and yet in 13 *Co.* a Dean is held to be a Spiritual Officer; and he fubmitted it, that the general Diftinction in the Books was, between Judicial Officers and thofe who were Minifterial only. To the fecond Point, he agreed, that in fome of the Books a Parifh Clerk is taken to be a Spiritual Officer, but faid, that wherever this Queftion has come judicially before the Court, they have always confidered him as a Temporal Officer, whereto he cited 13 *Co* 70. *Ma.* 101. 1 *Keb* 286, he faid, he apprehended that the different Manner of appointing a Parifh Clerk could not poffibly make the Office itfelf different, in one Cafe, from what it was in the other. In fome Places, he obferved, Church-Wardens are chofen by the Parifh, in others they are nominated by the Parfon; but yet the Nature of the Office does in all Cafes continue the fame. In the prefent Cafe, he agreed,

agreed, that the Exercise of this Office really was *circa Spiritualia*, but yet he submitted, it by no means would follow, but that the Right and Title to the Office may be of Temporal Cognizance: And in the Case in Question, he observed, the Libel complained, that the Plaintiff intrudes upon the Defendant, by which it plainly appears, that the Title to this Office is really in Dispute, and on this Score cited 2 *Rol. Abr.* 285. 2 *Brownl.* 11. *Mandamus's* have been often granted to admit these Officers, as appears from 1 *Lev.* 75. 2 *Lev.* 18. *Ven.* 143. To the third Point, he said, the Proof of that lay upon the Defendant, and it will not be enough neither, for them to shew that there was a Canon which required a Licence; but they must shew further, that such Canon has been received and allowed by the Common Law, &c Mr *Marsh*, on the other Side, argued and said, as to the Case cited out of *Rol Rep* of a Constable's making a Deputy, it has been questioned, and said, so it was in *Sid.* 355 and as to the Case of a Dean's making a Deputy, he agreed, in some Places there is a Vice-Dean, but he believed that depended only upon Local Statutes, and he apprehended, it was never received for Law, that he could make a Deputy; at least, he submitted it, the Law at this Day is taken to be otherwise; he also submitted it, that the Distinction taken between Judicial and Ministerial Officers must not be received in so large a Latitude; for that there's a Difference between some Ministerial Officers and others, those that require Skill and Judgment cannot make a

U 3   Deputy

Deputy without exprefs Words in their Patents; though others might, and cited 2 *Rol. Abr.* 154. that the Marfhal of *England* cannot and in *Dy.* 278. it appears, that there was a Claufe in his Patent giving him a Power fo to do, and he relied upon 3 *Cro.* 187 *Plow.* 379 *b.* and to fhew that the Senfe of the Legiflature has lately been, that a Parifh Clerk cannot make a Deputy, he faid, in a late Act of Parliament, which paffed the third of his now Majefty, and which was made for creating the Parifh of *St. Nicholas, Deptford,* it is provided by an exprefs enacting Claufe, that the Parifh Clerk fhall have this Power of making a Deputy: Then, as to the Queftion, whether his Office was Spiritual or not, he fubmitted it, that the whole Employment was fo; he faid too, it was well known that anciently Parifh Clerks were of the Order of the Clergy, and not of the Laity; and he faid, in 2 *Rol Abr.* 227 it appears, that by the Canon, the Parfon has a Right to appoint him · And as to *Mandamus's* going to admit Parifh Clerks, he faid, he believed the Court did not grant thofe Motions, but on Affidavit that they were elected by the Parifh, and for the Purpofe cited *Salk.* 468. To the laft Point, he agreed, that he could find no Canon making thefe Licenfes neceffary, but the innumerable Inftances of them, he fubmitted it, was an Evidence that fuch Canon has been received and allowed; tho' cannot now be found; and faid, that the Ecclefiaftical Courts are governed by the *Lex non Scripta,* as well as ours My Lord Ch. Juft. faid, that the Marfhal was confidered partly as a

Judicial

Judicial Officer; for wherever Battle is joined, he is to determine that Matter; and said, it was certain, that even a Ministerial Office, which requires Skill, cannot be executed by Duty, without Words in the Grant for that Purpose; he said, he had some Doubt, how that was to be understood as to the Constable, for if a Justice of Peace directs his Warrant to a Constable, he questioned whether the Constable could appoint by Word of Mouth, that another should execute it. As to the Nature of the Office, he said, he was well satisfied, that the different Methods of appointing this Officer, could not make his Office different in one Case from what it was in another; the Case of *Townsend* and *Thorpe*, he said, was determined intirely upon its particular Circumstances: The Temporal Court permitted the Ecclesiastical Court to deprive the Party there singly, by Reason of the Enormity of his Crimes. As to the Matter of the Licence, he said, he could not see how it could be maintainable, and his Lordship also observed, the Suit below was principally instituted to deprive the Party for his not obtaining one; and therefore his Lordship said, he was of Opinion, the Prohibition must stand. *Page* Just. was clearly of Opinion, that the different Methods of coming into an Office, could, in no Case, make the Office itself to be different. In the Case of St *Clement's*, the Court was of Opinion, that this Office of a Parish-Clerk was Temporal, if so, this Court would not suffer the Court below to deprive him *Lee* Just. said, that the Question, whether this Office is Spiritual, or not, strikes at the

whole.

whole; he agreed, that the Busineſs of the Office was *circa ſpiritualia*; but yet ſaid, he could not ſee but the Office muſt be conſidered Temporal: A Cuſtom for the Pariſh to chuſe ſuch Officer is agreed, on all Sides, to have been good: If this Office had been conſidered as Spiritual, he could not ſee how the Lay-Gents could have any Thing to do with it; and therefore he thought the Canon ſeemed, in this Reſpect, to be an Innovation upon the Common Law: As to the Office of Dean, he ſaid, it was certain, that it was many Times, till Queen *Mary*'s Time, executed by Laymen. The Court was of Opinion, that the Prohibition ſhould ſtand, yet, at the Deſire of the Defendant, gave Leave for another Argument: And now Mr. *Filmer*, for the Plaintiff, firſt ſubmitted it, that the Office of Clerk of a Pariſh was merely Temporal, he obſerved, that there were ſeveral Authorities cited upon the former Argument to prove it, and he craved Leave to cite a few more, and accordingly cited *Godb.* 163. *Hill.* 22 *Ja* in the old Edition *Benl.* 142. 1 *Leon.* 94. *& Fitz. Abr* Tit. *Annuity*, 40 which Caſe is alſo in *Hugh's Parſon's Law* 279 and ſaid, if this Office in the Nature of it was conſidered as Temporal, he conceived, there could not be any Difference, whether he was nominated by the Parſon, or elected by the Pariſh. If this Point was with him, he apprehended, that the clear Conſequence would be that he might make a Deputy, and for this Purpoſe cited *Mo.* 885. 3 *Bulſt.* 77. 9 *Co.* 48. yet ſuppoſing, for Argument's Sake, it were admitted, that the Office was Spiritual; yet no Caſe has been cited, on the

the other Side, to shew it necessary to take
a Licence, and if that Point was with the
Plaintiff, the Prohibition must necessarily
stand; for the whole Tenor and Pursuit of
the Libel is upon that Matter singly Mr. *Fazackerly*, on the other Side, argued, that all
the Citations, which have been made, to
shew that this was a Temporal Office, were
only *obiter* Sayings of Judges pretty much
about the Times of *Jac.* 1. except the Case
in *Fitz Ab.* but he apprehended that Case
went a great deal too far; for that it is there
held, that a Parish-Clerk is an Officer at
Will only; and he said, he conceived, that
general Experience shews this to be otherwise, and it having been held, that such
Office gains a Person a Settlement, proves it
to be otherwise; he observed also, that the
Case *Mallard* and *Smith, Hill.* 8 of the late
Queen, was a much later Case than any
cited, and was an Authority directly on
the other Side, there a Clerk of a Parish
sued in the Ecclesiastical Court for a Pension, on Motion for a Prohibition, the Court
held, that a Suit would well lie; for that he
was a Spiritual Officer : And in the Case
Townsend and *Thorpe*, cited on former Argument, the Court was expressly of Opinion,
that he was to be considered as a Spiritual
Officer, when he came in at the Nomination
of the Parson, which was enough for the
present Purpose. But, admitting that he
was to be considered as a Temporal Officer;
yet this was an Office of Skill; and therefore as there were no Words in his Nomination, giving him a Power to make a Deputy, he could not do it. It cannot be denied, but the Matters which a Clerk exer-
cifeth

ciseth himself in, are Matters relating to
the Church; wherefore he submitted it, it
could not be denied, but that the Ecclesiastical Court had a general Jurisdiction over
him; and a Suit therefore against him, in
that Court, for Matters relating to the Execution of his Office, could not be said, but
to be rightly instituted; and if there are
any Matters thrown into the Libel, which
are, of themselves, of a Temporal Nature,
yet if they relate to him in the Execution of
his Office, he apprehended, this Court would
not grant their Prohibition, and cited 1 *Lev*
138. 1 *Sid*. 217. 1 *Cro* 65 1 *Ven*. 64. *The*
Lord Chief Justice: A Clerk may make a
Deputy, and that, whether he come into
this Office by the Nomination of the Parson, or by the Election of the Parish, the
Office must be considered the same in the
one Case as the other; and of the same O-
pinion was *Page* Justice; and *Lee* Justice
thought there was no Occasion to determine,
whether this Office was Temporal, or not,
but the Common Law Books were very
strong on that Side of the Question, and he
said, he had a Note from a Gentleman at
the Bar, in Lord *Holt*'s Time, where a Suit
was instituted, in his Lordship's Time, by a
Clerk in the Ecclesiastical Court for his Salary; and on Motion, the Court granted a
Prohibition. Yet what the Court in general
grounded their Opinion upon, in this Case,
seemed to be, the plain Tenor of the Libel
against the Plaintiff's being for his not taking a Licence, which they could not see
any Law obliging him to; wherefore Rule
was that the Prohibition should stand.

6. *Pas* 6 *Geo* 2 *B R Austin* and *Jarvis.*

The Case was thus, There being a Vacancy of Parish-Clerk of St *Anne's Limehouse*, the Plaintiff and Defendant, together with one *Harry Babstock*, were Candidates, and the Election came on the sixth of *October*, when the Vestry, who had the Nomination, agreed to proceed by Balloting, and accordingly every Vestryman put his Vote or Ballot into the Hat of *Graves*, then Church-warden, and on telling them out, there were thirty-four for the Defendant, two only for the Plaintiff, and thirty-two for *Babstock*, *Graves* the Church-warden, who espoused *Babstock*'s Interest, objected to the Vote of one *Ackard*, who had voted for the Defendant, (though he after allowed *Ackard* to be a good and sufficient Voter) also *Graves* insisted, that, as Church-warden, he himself was intitled to two Votes, and accordingly voted a second Time for *Babstock*, and then under Pretence that *Ackard*'s Vote was not good, and that he the said *Graves* had a double Vote, as aforesaid, he the said *Graves* insisted, that the Defendant and *Babstock* having equal Number of Votes, the Vestry should proceed to another Election, which the Defendant and his Friends absolutely refused, and insisted on the Defendant's being duly elected, and demanded his Admittance to the said Office, which *Graves* refusing, several of the Defendant's Friends left the Vestry, and the Defendant, by the Advice of his Friends, went directly and entered a *Caveat* in the Ecclesiastical Court against any one's being sworn in, or having a Faculty. And on the *Sunday* next following the Election, having taken the above previous

vious Steps, the Defendant, and his Friends
of the Veſtry with him, went to the Church
and applied themſelves to *Graves*, as Church-
warden, and tendered the Defendant as
Clerk, and demanded of *Graves* to deliver
him Poſſeſſion of, and to admit him into,
the Clerk's Desk, which *Graves* abſolutely
refuſed ; and on the 15th of the ſame *October*, *Graves* being ſtill Church-warden, called
another Veſtry, and being, in Combination
with *Legbone*, the Parſon and others, againſt
Jarvis, before the Veſtry-Book was brought
to the Veſtry-Room, he (*Graves*) at his
own Houſe cauſed one *Richard Dunne*, who
was Son and Clerk to *Dunne*, the Town-
Clerk, to make an Entry in the Veſtry-
Book, purporting an Appearance of *Jarvis*
at the Veſtry, and conſenting to withdraw
his Licence, and to abide the Event of another Election, which Entry was not only
made before the Veſtry aſſembled, and before
Jarvis had, or could have, appeared, for
that, at the Time of the Entry of this Matter,
there was not any Veſtry congregated, before
whom *Jarvis* could poſſibly appear, but alſo
was without either his Conſent or Privity, and
not only ſo, but alſo contrary and directly op-
poſite to what he and his Friends had all along,
and at that very Veſtry did, inſiſt upon,
but notwithſtanding theſe being the true
Circumſtances of the Caſe, the ſaid *Graves*,
on the 31ſt of *December* following, called
another Veſtry, (being the third called on
that Account) and though the Defendant
and his Friends alſo did inſiſt, as before, on
his being duly elected, and his Right to the
ſaid Office in Virtue of ſuch due Election;
and abſolutely refuſed to ſubmit to any further

ther or other Election, or to ftand again, as a Candidate, for the faid Office; yet the faid third Veftry, (by the Influence of *Graves*, and all, or fome of his, Confederates) proceeded to another Election, and (the Defendant difregarding their Proceedings, as having declared againft them, as aforefaid) the Majority fell upon *Auftin* the now Plaintiff, who addreffing himfelf to the Ecclefiaftical Court to be fworn in, they refufed him, (the Defendant's Caveat being ftill pending). Whereupon the faid *Auftin* the Plaintiff inftituted a Suit, in the Ecclefiaftical Court, againft the Defendant to take off this Caveat After a tedious and expenfive Litigation of above two Years there (to almoft the Ruin of the Defendant) and examining Witneffes on both Sides, that Court fentenced the Defendant duly elected, and decreed him to be admitted and fworn in, and condemned the Plaintiff in Cofts; and the Defendant was accordingly admitted and fworn in by the Ecclefiaftical Court or Judge, but before his Faculty made out, the Plaintiff appealed to the Court of Arches, and proceeded there till the Caufe was ripe for Trial, but then thought fit to drop the Profecution of that Suit, and to refort to this Court for a Prohibition, and obtained a Rule to fhew Caufe, why a Prohibition fhould not go to the Ecclefiaftical Court, on Account of their not having Jurifdiction of this Matter, as it concerned a Right to a Temporal Office; and Mr. *Fazakerly* coming now to fhew Caufe againft the Rule, fubmitted it, that the Ecclefiaftical Court had Jurifdiction, but faid, admitting they had not, yet the Plaintiff could not move for a Prohibition to ftay a

Suit

Suit which he himself had begun and instituted, besides he apprehended, that *Jarvis*
had a good Right to be admitted, and that
the Ecclesiastical Court could not refuse
him; and so the Court were of Opinion, in
a Case, where a *Mandamus* went to admit
a Church-warden, that the Ecclesiastical
Judge was but Ministerial in this Case, and
was bound to admit the Party in Possession
of the *Mandamus*, and that he could make
no Return to excuse himself from doing it
Mr *Strange*, on the other Side, agreed, that
the Office of a Parish-Clerk was exercised
about Spiritual Matters; but notwithstanding, he insisted, that the Office itself was a
Temporal Office, wherefore, he apprehended, the Ecclesiastical Court had no Jurisdiction concerning it, and for this Purpose he
cited 2 *Rol Ab* 285 in the Case of a Register, and if that was so, he insisted it
would be no Objection, that the Plaintiff
himself had begun in the Court below, and
he said, this Court was of that Opinion in
Dr. *Wilmot*'s Case, last *Mich.* Term. *The
Court* declared, they were of the same Opinion, in the present Case, and as to what
was said, by Mr *Fazackerly*, concerning the
Mandamus, they agreed that there was one
Case to that Purpose, but said, all the
Cases since have been against it; and now
they said, it was settled, that the Ecclesiastical Judge may return, that the Party was
not elected　Upon which M. *Fazackerly*
proposed, that the Ecclesiastical Judge should
admit *Austin*, as well as he had admitted
Jarvis, and that the Parties should try the
Merits of their Elections in a feigned Issue,
which Proposal being agreed to, the Court

　　　there-

thereupon ruled *Auſtin* to receive a Declaration for Money had and received to *Jarvis's* Uſe, and to go to Trial of the Elections, and the Poſſeſſion was directed to go according to the Verdict, on ſuch Trial. On the Trial, Verdict was for *Jarvis*, who accordingly was admitted, and ſtill enjoys the Office having duly qualified himſelf by taking the Oaths, as a Temporal Officer, in the Court of King's Bench, *&c. as others have done ſince on this Determination.*

7 *Paſ* 8 *Geo* 2

Mr *Lacy* moved for a *Mandamus* to Dr. *Henchman*, to grant a Licenſe to one *Trot*, he having been choſen by the Pariſhioners, into the Office of Pariſh Clerk, and to this Purpoſe cited *Mo* 101. My Lord Ch. Juſt. ſaid, he did not know that a Licenſe was neceſſary; Mr. Juſtice *Page* ſaid, that the Eccleſiaſtical Court claims a Right of granting a Licenſe to Surgeons, but he firmly believed they had none; and Mr. *Juſtice Lee* ſaid, that in the Caſe of *Speak* and *Borne*, on Demurrer to the Prohibition, the Court were of Opinion, that ſuch Licenſe was not neceſſary However the Court granted a *Mandamus* to Dr *Henchman*, requiring him to admit the Clerk. *Pariſh Clerks by whom to be choſen, their Qualifications, Duty, how to be paid, &c.* See *Mo* 908. *Can.* 91.

I clearly think, after ſo many Adjudications againſt theſe Eccleſiaſtical Encroachments, as the Clergy's, and particularly Ordinaries, inſiſting on Pariſh Clerks, *&c* and citing them to take Ordinary Licenſes, as what they ought and are compellable *de Jure* to do, is a Matter derogatory to the Prerogative Royal, and to the ſettled and eſtabliſhed Common Law, and prejudicial to the Liberty of the Subject, as well as repugnant to the Oaths taken by all Ordinaries, on their being received into Office, and therefore (*poſſibly may*) juſtly challenge a due Reſentment, Correction and Reſtraint.

7 *Sextons*

7. *Sextons.*

1. T*RIN.* 8 *Geo.* 2. *B. R. Pritchard's Cafe.*

A *Mandamus* was moved for to the Church-Wardens of *St Mary* in *Chefter*, to admit one *Pritchard* to the Office of Sexton, and an Affidavit was produced, that *Pritchard* was duly elected by the Majority of the Inhabitants; but notwithftanding that, the Church-Wardens kept the Keys of the Church, and refufed to deliver them, and *Vern* 143. was cited for the Motion. My Lord Ch Juft faid, that he had indeed known *Mandamus's* granted to reftore Perfons to the Office of Sexton, but his Lordfhip faid, it did not appear, by the Affidavit in the prefent Cafe, that the Church-Wardens were to admit the Sexton; and therefore his Lordfhip further faid, he did not fee that this Court could compel them to do it' However *Mandamus* went, that a Return might be made to it.

2. On a Motion for a *Mandamus* to admit a Sexton, the Court asked, whether he came in by Nomination of the Parfon, or by Election of the Parifh; and though it was allowed that he came in by the Nomination of the Parfon; yet a Rule was made to fhew Caufe. *One of the Judges faid, in another Cafe, and I think, it was* Mr *Juftice* Lee, *now Lord Ch Juft. that fince Lord* Holt's *Time,* Mandamus's *had been frequent to admit Sextons.*

2

8. *Church-*

8. *Church-Wardens, Sides-Men,* &c.
Vide *the Matter* XXIII.

1. *General to.*

1 IF the Church-Wardens of a Church sue in the Ecclesiastical Court *J. S* for that he, and all those who have been seised of such an House, &c. at the Perambulation of the Parishioners of the Parish, &c. have used to find Refreshment, *scil.* Bread and Services, and to rest themselves there, a Prohibition shall be granted; for that they claim it in Nature of a Corody, and if that should be suffered, great Inconvenience would follow, &c *Rol. Abr Prohibition, fo.* 287 *Case* 49.

2. If a Man be defamed for a Bastard, *per un Meretrice,* and the Church-Wardens of the Church oblige him to give Bond to discharge the Parish, according to the Statute, and hereupon the Party defamed libel in the Ecclesiastical Court against the Church-Wardens for the Defamation, a Prohibition lies. *Mich* 10 *Jac. Berrie's Case, Rol Abr. Prohibition, R Case* 5.

Mich. 8 *Geo* 2   B. R.   *Cumberbach* v.

3 A *Mandamus* had been granted to the Archdeacon of ——— to swear in two Persons Church-Wardens, and the Archdeacon swore them in accordingly; notwithstanding which a Suit was instituted in the Ecclesiastical Court of the Bishop of *Litchfield* and *Coventry,* by Way of Appeal, to what the Archdeacon had done, and an Inhibition was

granted to the Church-Wardens to prevent
their Acting; whereupon Mr. *Strange* moved
for a Prohibition, and said, the Church-Wardens were Temporal Officers, and that the
swearing them in, by the Archdeacon, was
meerly a Ministerial Act, and that he had
nothing to do with their Election, which is
the Reason it has been determined, that *non*
fuit electus is not a good Return to such
Mandamus, he said, that if what the Archdeacon did was Ministerial, he could not
conceive, that an Appeal could lie from it,
at least, it could not after this Court had in-
terfered by Way of *Mandamus*. Justice *Lee*
said, he did not think that a *Mandamus* being
granted could make any Difference in the
Case; however (absent the Lord Ch. Just.)
Rule was to shew Cause in Order that it
might be considered, whether the Appeal lay;
and now Mr *Parker* came to shew Cause, and
said, that the *Mandamus* being granted could
be no Objection to the present Proceeding is
the Ecclesiastical Court; because that does
not give the Party any Right, but only is a
Means of putting him into Possession, the
single Question therefore will be, whether
the Ecclesiastical Court can inquire into
the Right of Election of Church-Wardens,
or not; and as to that, he did submit it,
that Church-Wardens were Spiritual Officers, and in the present Case there is no
Pretence to say, that there is any Custom
in Dispute concerning the Choice of them;
and he, for Authority, cited *Ray.* 246.
1 *Mod* 22 & 3 *Mod.* 69 Mr *Strange* argued
on the other Side, and agreed, that Sides-
Men were Spiritual Officers, they being
created

created by Canon, since the Reformation; but Church-Wardens were a Lay Corporation known to the Common Law In the Case of —— and *Preston*, *Paf* 3 of the late King, in the Common Pleas, it appeared that there had been a Suit in the Spiritual Court against a Church-Warden, for not taking the Oath of Office being duly Elected, and upon Debate, the Court granted a Prohibition, he said, he did agree that So far the Archdeacon may inquire into the Manner of the Election of a Church-Warden as to return *Non fuit electus*, (though there has been Authorities to the Contrary, even in that Point) but he submitted it, that the Spiritual Court was never yet allowed to proceed to determine the Right of this Officer to his Election, and thirdly, he submitted it, that there being a *Mandamus* obtained and executed was a Circumstance in Favour of the present Application. My Lord Ch Juft. thought, that the Circumstances of the present *Mandamus* ought to be put out of the Case; for if a *Mandamus* should go to the Spiritual Court, or Judge, to give Judgment, there was no Pretence to say, but an Appeal or Writ of Error would lie, after that the single Question, his Lordship said, would be, whether the Spiritual Court could inquire into the Right of Election of such Officer, and he thought they could not; for a Church-Warden he took to be a Temporal Officer; and therefore his Right might be tried, either upon an Action for a false Return to a *Non fuit electus*, or else in a Consultation *Page* and *Probin*, Justices, of the same Opinion; but

Lee Justice doubted, as to the Return of *Non fuit electus*, which he inclined to think was a good Return, and that the Ecclesiastical Judge might proceed in this Enquiry, however the Rule was made Absolute, and the Plaintiff directed to declare in Prohibition in three Weeks Time.

Anno 10 *Geo.* 2   *B. R.   Stoughton* & *Dr. Reynolds.*

4. The 89 Canon of 1603, which gives Direction about the Choice and Duty of Church-Wardens, &c does not bind the Laity, but is subject to and controuled by the Custom of particular Parishes, as in *Cro. Jac.* 523   *Cro. Car* 551, 670.   2 *Rol. Abr.* 287   *Hard* 378   *Carth* 118, &c The Rector, or Vicar, of a Parish has no Right of presiding at the Election of Church-Wardens, or in Vestries, much less, of adjourning them, unless by Custom or Act of Parliament, but this Right is in the Assembly, and though the Vicar had a Right to preside, yet that doth not give him Title or Power to adjourn, for he presides only, as a Speaker. Where the Parson Nominates one Church-Warden, and the Parishioners chose another, or the like, he having nominated his Church-Warden has no Business any longer at the Assembly. *Vide Noy* 123.

2. *Who to chuse.* Vide Case *Stoughton* and *Dr Reynolds,* supra.

1 If the Parishioners have used, Time whereof, &c to elect one Church-Warden, and the Vicar another, and then a Canon is made,

made, that the Vicar shall elect both, and he does so accordingly, and the Parishioners elect one, according to their Customs, and the Ordinary disallow him, and establish the two appointed by the Vicar, a Prohibition shall be granted. *Pas. 5 Jac.* 1. The Parishioners of *Rowlden* in *Kent*, adjudged. *Rol Abr Prohibition, fo.* 287 *Case* 50, 51.

2 *Evelin* being elected by the Parishioners of St *Thomas's*, to be Church-Warden there, with another, the Parson pretending that, by the Canons he had the Nomination of one, named *Hill* to be Church-Warden, and procured Dr *Clark* the Official, to swear in the said *Hill*, and to refuse *Evelin*; whereupon the Parishioners surmising that they had a Custom within the Parish, Time whereof, *&c.* to elect both the Church-Wardens, and that the Canon cannot take away their Customs, prayed a Writ to Dr *Clarke* to admit the Church-Warden, elected by them, and to swear him in, and amove the Church-Warden, elected by the Parson, and a Precedent was shewn in 1 *Jac.* where such a Writ was granted, and it was said, there were divers others the like Precedents, and because the Church-Wardens in *London* are, for the greatest Part, Corporations, and Owners of Lands to them devised, the Writ was granted; and the Court (being informed that the said *Hill*, elected Church-Warden by the Parson, sued the said *Evelin*, elected by the Parish, in the Ecclesiastical Court, granted a Prohibition, to the Intent it might be tried, whether there was such Custom, or not *Cro Car* 551, 552.

X 3　　　　3 *Pas*

3. *Paf.* 1727. *B R. Thomas* Berry &
Jackman v. *Crofs & al'.*

The Plaintiffs were chofen Church-Wardens by the Inhabitants, and the Defendants
were chofen by the Occupiers of the Lands
in the fame Parifh; the Plaintiffs had a Cuftom to fupport them, the Defendants Common Right; and on thefe Matters feveral
Sentences had been in the Ecclefiaftical
Court for the Defendants, whereupon á Prohibition was moved for, and on Queftion,
whether the Cuftom was properly fuggefted?
To which the Counfel *pro Def.* faid, it
was true, that in the firft Article of the Sug-
geft on, the Plaintiff had alledged all Cuftoms
to be triable in the King's Temporal Courts,
and in the fecond and third Article, they
had mentioned Cuftom; but then in the
fourth Article, which is the principal one,
they had only fuggefted, that the Inhabitants had a Right to chufe Church-Wardens
fole, without, or exclufive of the Outliers.
But the Court faid, that the Occupiers of
Lands have all, of Common Right, equally
a Voice in fuch Elections; and therefore the
Inhabitants, fole, could not have fuch a
Right, but by Cuftom, accordingly the Prohibition went. The Rule is, that in all
Cafes where, upon the Face of the Proceedings, it appears the Ecclefiaftical Courts have
no Right, or that they have not ufed their
Right, according to the Rule of the Common Law, a Prohibition goes, after Sentence, and in no other Cafe. The fame Law
is of Prohibition to the Admiralty Court.
Vide Hob 79. 1 *Ven* 115. *An.* 20 *b Salk.*
547, 548 Church-Wardens and Sides-Men,
by

by whom to be chosen, their Duty, &c.
Can. 89, 90.

3. *Their Accounts.*

1 *Paf.* 7 *Geo.* 2. *B. R. Wainright* and
Church v. *Bradshaw.*

On a Rule to shew Cause why a Prohibition should not go to the Ecclesiastical Court
of *Litchfield,* Mr *Abney* said, this Suit was
instituted below, in Order to compel the Defendants, who are Church-Wardens, to bring
in their Accounts before the Parishioners.
To this the Defendants pleaded their being a
Parish Meeting, and that they there delivered in their Accounts of Receipts, Expences and Disbursements, according to the
Ancient Usage and Custom of the Parish,
and that the said Accounts were examined
and allowed by the Parson, and a great Majority of the Inhabitants and Parishioners
there then present, according to Law, and
that such Inhabitants and Parishioners subscribed their Names thereunto. He also
said, that by the 89 Canon *Anno* 1603, the
Ecclesiastical Court has Jurisdiction of compelling Church-Wardens to bring in their
Accounts before the Parson and Parishioners,
and no other Person has a Power of allowing
those Accounts, but themselves; however, in
the present Case, the Church-Wardens have
pleaded, that their Accounts were allowed
by the Inhabitants at large, as well as the Parishioners, and the Inhabitants at large have
nothing to do in this Matter. Mr *Strange* and
Mr. *Denison* (now Mr Justice) argued, on the
other Side, and said, it was certain, that the

X 4   Eccle-

Ecclesiastical Court could do no more than compel the Church-wardens to bring in their Accounts before the Vestry, and so the Point was determined, on solemn Argument, in the Case of *Hutchins*, Church-warden of *Hammersmith*, against *Robinson* and *Carew*, *Mich* the 1st of his present Majesty, and in that of *Hortrey* and *Kendrick*, *Easter* Term last, both which Cases were in the Court of Exchequer; and therefore the single Question must necessarily depend upon the Defendant's Plea: And as to that, it might well be understood, that no other Inhabitants were meant, but those who were Parishioners, and the Court declared their Opinions to be so; and so made the Rule absolute.

Mich. 8 *Geo.* 2. *B. R. Hopkins & al'* v. *Keir & al'.*

2 On Appeal to the Court of Arches, in a Suit against the Church-wardens of St. *Botolph without Aldgate*, to compel them to account; the Defendants pleaded, that their Accounts were already settled and adjusted by the Parson and Parishioners at a Vestry; which Plea the Ecclesiastical Judge thought fit to reject, and proceeded to examine the *Items*; whereupon Mr. *Abney* moved for a Prohibition, and contended that the Vestry had a Power to adjust the Accounts by the 89th Canon, *anno* 1603. My Lord Chief Justice said, that it was certain, that the Ecclesiastical Judge might examine into the Truth of the Fact, whether such Accounts were settled by the Vestry, or not, but they could not inquire into the *Items* of that Account, accordingly (*Probyn* Justice absent)

fent) Rule was to fhew Caufe. And Mr. ——
applying for Liberty to infpect the Publick
Books of the Parifh, faid, thefe Motions are
common in Informations, in the Nature of
a *Quo Warranto*, as foon as a Rule is made
to fhew Caufe, but my Lord Chief Juftice
faid, that this Cafe differed from that, becaufe here the Prohibition can only iffue
upon the Face of the Proceedings; wherefore the Motion was denied. Mr. *Marfh*
coming now to fhew Caufe why the Prohibition fhould not go, he owned, it was
fet forth in the Plea, that it was ufual in
this Parifh for the Parifhioners to nominate
the Minifter, one of the Church-wardens,
and twelve of themfelves, to examine into
the Accounts of the old Church-wardens,
and when they have fo examined them,
then to lodge them in the Hands of fuch
Church-warden, for one and forty Days, to
be reftored and in the mean Time infpected
by any of the Parifhioners; and after the
Report of this felect Number, is to be confirmed at a Veftry; but this Ufage had
been no longer than the Year 1733, and
then an Order of Veftry was made for this
Purpofe, but he fubmitted it, that this Order was, by no Means, binding, or to be
called an Adjuftment of Church-wardens
Accounts, according to the Canon, but the
prefent Cafe, he faid, was much worfe;
for even this Order had been by no Means
complied with, the Defendants only fetting
forth, by their Plea, that this felect Number figned their Accounts, and not that this
Signing was confirmed by that Veftry. Mr.
Abney, on the other Side, argued, that there
was

was no Pretence for the Ecclesiastical Court to examine into the *Items* of the Account, accordingly the Rule was made absolute, that a Prohibition should go, as to the *Items*, and be, as to the Rest, discharged.

* 6. *Trin.* 9 *Geo* 2. *C. B Griffin* and *Foster*. This was upon a Libel against Church-wardens to account; they pleaded, that the Accounts were passed before a Vestry, notwithstanding which the Court below sentenced they should pay Part of the Money, whereupon Serjeant *Wynn* moved for a Prohibition, and insisted, it had often been determined, that after such Accounts were passed before the Vestry, they could not be re-examined in the Ecclesiastical Court; and accordingly the Rule was to shew Cause. Serjeant *Chappel*, on shewing Cause, said, no Custom having been pleaded, he conceived, the Ecclesiastical Court had a Right to proceed, which Serjeant *Wynn* denied, saying, it had been often determined expresly to the contrary, and cited the Case of St. *Botolph's* Parish lately in the King's Bench, and he also cited the Case of *Wainwright* and *Bradshawe*, and also *Bullock* and *Dunbar*, but last Term; and accordingly the Rule was made absolute.

4. *Who to present.*

1. The Church-wardens of *Ridgewel* in in *Essex* presented to the Arch-deacon, that one *Pannel* was a Railer, and Sower of Discord amongst Neighbours, the Archdeacon thought fit to injoin him Purgation, and the Court awarded a Prohibition; for the Cause belongs

belongs to the Leet, and not to them, except in the Church, or the like. *Hob.* 246, 247.

2. If any offend their Brethren, either by Adultery, Whoredom, Inceſt, or Drunkenneſs, or by Swearing, Ribaldry, Uſury, or any other Uncleanneſs, or Wickedneſs of Life, the Church-wardens, or Queſtmen and Sideſmen, in their next Preſentments, ſhall preſent all and every the Offenders, to the Intent they may be puniſhed : And ſuch notorious Offenders are not to be admitted to the Holy Communion, till reformed. *Can.* 109 *Sure, if there be any ſuch, as is more than to be feared, amongſt the very Clergy themſelves, they ought with much higher Reaſon to be preſented as they act therein, not only againſt the ordinary Duties of Chriſtianity, but alſo, as they are therein guilty of the moſt heinous Perjury, by breaking their ſolemn Vows and Engagements, made at their ſeveral Ordinations, and not only ſo, but as a ſtricter Regard to all Sobriety and Religion ought to be paid by them, as Paterns to the Laity; therefore they muſt needs offend abundantly more by their Vice, as thereby perſuading the People, round them, that they themſelves do not believe in that Religion they preach to others, and if the Church-wardens, &c. fail in the Duties required of them by this Canon, I conceive, that by the* 113 *Canon, as well as* ex officiis ſuis, *not only Miniſters of Pariſhes, but even Curates are in Conſcience bound to preſent ſuch; and therefore to the Canons aforeſaid, and their own Conſciences, I refer them: With this further Obſervation, that I muſt hold it to be the Duty of all the Clergy, in general, to be moſt*

parti-

*particularly cautious, in their Lives and Con-
versation, and that they ought particularly to
admonish the Church-wardens, &c. with all the
Persuasions they are Masters of, to a strict Observance of their Duties, as they would avoid
Perjury, and discharge their Consciences to
their Neighbours.*

5 *Their Duty.*

1. *As to Strangers Preaching in their Churches.*

1. That the Bishop may understand (if
Occasion so require) what Sermons are
made in every Church of his Diocese, and
who presume to preach without Licence,
the Church-wardens and Sidesmen shall see,
that the Names of all Preachers which come
to their Church from any other Place, be
noted in a Book, which they shall have ready
for that Purpose; wherein every Preacher
shall subscribe his Name, the Day when he
preached, and the Name of the Bishop, by
whom he had Licence to preach *Can 52.*

2. If any Preacher shall in the Pulpit
particularly, or namely of Purpose, impugn
or confute any Doctrine delivered by any
other Preacher in the same Church, or in
any Church near adjoining, before he hath
acquainted the Bishop of the Diocese therewith, and received Order from him what to
do in such Case; because upon such publick
Dissenting and Contradicting there may grow
much Offence and Disquietness unto the
People; the Church-wardens, or Party
grieved shall forthwith signify the same to
the said Bishop, and not suffer the said
Preacher

Preacher any more to occupy that Place which he hath once abused, except he faithfully promise to forbear all such Matter of Contention in the Church, until the Bishop hath taken further Order therein, who shall with all convenient Speed so proceed therein, that publick Satisfaction may be made in the Congregation, where the Offence was given. Provided, that if either of the Parties offending do appeal he shall not be suffered to preach, *pendente lite* Can 53.

6. *Their Attendance on the Ecclesiastical Courts.*

By Canon, no Ecclesiastical Judge ought to cite any Church-warden to the Court, but so as he may return home again to his own House the same Day. 12 *Co.* 112.

9. *School-Masters.*

1. *Whether need the Ordinary's Licence.*

1. If a Man hath a Calling, as a School-Master, &c. which any Layman may follow, by the Common Law, no Canon can restrain him of the Liberty the Law gave him, for the Common Law or the Custom of the Realm cannot be abrogated, but by Act of Parliament; and therefore no Canon, which is of mean Authority in Comparison of the former, can possibly do it, not though the same be an Act of what some have weakly called an Act of Ecclesiastical Legislature, and that though ordained by the King's Royal Licence, and after affirmed by his Royal Authority.

rity. 12 Co. 72. *See also* 2 Inst. 94, 642, 643, 657. Rol. Abr. 454. Mo. 782. *A Parson himself exercising the Imployment of a School-Master, Head of a College, Minister of an Impropriation, Donative, or Free-Chapel, or other Exemption, is clearly discharged of all Canonical Obedience, as no Party to the Passing of those partial Laws.*

2 *Pasch. & Hill.* 10 & 11 *W.* 3. *Betsham* and *Barnardiston*

The chief Question was, whether a School-Master might be prosecuted in the Ecclesiastical Court for not bringing his Scholars to Church, contrary to the 79th Canon, *anno* 1603. And it was the Opinion of *Treby* Chief Justice, and *Powel* Just. and the Court, That the School-Master, being a *Note;* This Layman, was not bound by the Canons Doctrine will 1 *Peer Will fo.* 32. Margin. See *Salk* 672. appear esta- *Mathews* and *Burdet's* Case. blished, past

Contradiction, under the Divisions of *Parish-Clerks, Sextons, Appropriations, or Impropriations, Donatives, Heads of Colleges and Hospitals,* and under this Division, and in several other Parts of this Work, for he must not only be a Clergyman, to be bound, but it must also be in a Matter merely Spiritual, and of Spiritual Cognizance, &c

3 *Cox* was libelled against in the Spiritual Court at *Exeter,* for teaching School *sans* Licence from the Ordinary, and the 14th *December* 1699, an Order was on Motion, that Cause should be shewn the first Day of next Term why a Prohibition should not go, and in the mean Time, that all Things should stay, which Order had been from Time to Time inlarged to this Day, *Term. S. Mich* 1700. when the *Attorney General* and Dr. *Waller* moved to discharge the said Order,

4

der, alledging, that before the Reformation, this was assuredly of Ecclesiastical Jurisdiction, and in Proof cited the 11th Canon of the Counsel of *Lateran*, which Canon (as well as that for making Tithes Parochial) has been received by Custom into this Kingdom, and so made Part of our Ecclesiastical Laws. The Statute 1 *Eliz. c.* 1 having restored the Spiritual Jurisdiction to the Crown, which had been usurped by the Pope; thereupon the Queen immediately set forth Ecclesiastical Injunctions, the 40th whereof is, that no Man shall take upon himself to teach School, but such as is allowed by the Ordinary; the making of which Injunctions by the Ecclesiastical Power of the Crown shews them to be of an Ecclesiastical Nature, and consequently cognizable in the Ecclesiastical Court. It must be admitted, that these Injunctions were not confirmed by any Act of Parliament, but their being referred to and mentioned 5 *El c.* 1. was an Argument, that the Legislature did approve of them. That in the 12th Year of that Queen the said Injunction, and (*inter al'*) this against Teaching without Licence by the Ordinary, were by the Convocation, then fitting, turned into Canons; that afterwards 23 *Eliz. cap.* 1. was the 1st Statute which prohibited it, since which, two others had followed, 6 *Ja. c* 4. & 14 *Ca.* 2. *c* 4. but none of them tended to destroy the Ecclesiastical Jurisdiction, only by making the Offence punishable in both Courts, gave a Remedy where there was none before. 1 *Jac.* the Convocation met, and reduced all the Canons into one Body,

Body, and then particularly made this Canon, that none should teach School without Licence from the Ordinary; and though it might be difficult to prove, that these Canons were directly confirmed by Act of Parliament, yet there was a Sort of Confirmation of them 4 *Jac* 1 *c.* 7 for the Founding and Incorporating a Free Grammar-School at *North-Leeche* in *Com' Gloucester*, whereby the Provost and Scholars in Queen's in *Oxford* were to nominate the School-Master and Usher of the said School, and to make such Ordinances for the Government thereof, as they should see meet, so as the same were not repugnant to the King's Prerogative, to the Laws and Statutes of the Realm, or to any Ecclesiastical Canons, or Constitutions of the Church of *England* But, on the other Side, it was answered, that there could not be one Canon or Precedent, before the Reformation, cited to prove the keeping School of Ecclesiastical Cognizance, for that supposing the Council of *Lateran* to have been in every Part thereof received in *England*, yet the Canon cited did not prove the Point for which it was produced; that Canon only appointing School-Masters in every Cathedral Church, Salk. 672. and such School-Master to be licensed by the Bishop; which was but reasonable, (*viz.*) that he who taught in the Bishop's Church should be approved of by the Bishop That teaching School was not in the Nature thereof Spiritual, and it would be hard to affirm that it was of Ecclesiastical Jurisdiction or cognizable there by the old Ecclesiastical Laws of the Kingdom, received by

4

common

common Use, at the same Time that not one single Precedent of any such Law or Usage, before the Reformation, was to be found; and that as to the Canons made since, they did not bind a Lay-man, as *Cox* was suggested to be, because that the Laity are not represented in Convocation, and it was a fundamental Maxim of our Government, that what bound all must be assented to by all; neither could a Reference to the Canons, in a private Act of Parliament, add any greater Weight to them than they had before. That this was a Case which deserved great Consideration, having before been in the other Courts of *Westminster-Hall*, where several Prohibitions had been granted on this very same Point, in Order that it might receive a judicial Determination, but the other Side would never venture to go on, as in the Case *Betsham* and *Barnardiston* in *C. B* and in *B. R. Oldfield*'s Case, *Mich.* 9 *W.* 3. *Chadwick*'s Case, 10 *W.* 3. *Scorrie*'s Case, *Trin.* 11 *W.* 3. and 12 *W.* 3. one *Davison*'s Case, *Salk.* 105. who being brought to the Bar, on *Habeas Corp.* it appeared, that he was committed on an *Excom. Cap.* being excommunicated for teaching School, without Licence, and the Court holding it to be a doubtful Point bail'd him during their Consideration thereof; which Practice of the other Courts of *Westminster-Hall* shewed it to be a Matter not fit to be determined on a Motion, but in a judicial Way, but supposing it to have been originally a Spiritual Crime; yet being now made a Temporal one, by several Acts of Parliament, it was thereby drawn from the Spiritual to the

Temporal Jurisdiction. *Lord Keeper Wright:*
Both Courts may have a concurrent Jurisdiction, and a Crime may be punishable
both in the one and the other. The Canons of a Convocation do not bind the Laity, without an Act of Parliament; but I always was, and still am, of Opinion, that
keeping of a School, by the old Laws of
England, is of Ecclesiastical Cognizance, and
therefore let the Order for a Prohibition
be discharged; whereupon it was moved by
Williams, that this Libel was for Teaching
School generally, without shewing what
School, and Court Christian could not have
Jurisdiction of Writing-Schools, Reading-Schools, Dancing-Schools, &c. To which
Lord Keeper assented, and granted a Prohibition as to the Teaching of all Schools,
excepting Grammar-Schools, which he
thought to be of Ecclesiastical Cognizance.
1 *Peer Will.* 29, 30, 32, 33. *See* Baldham
and Barnardiston's *Case before, and* Rushworth's *Case following*; & qu *for thereby
as well as many other Cases, too many to particularize here, the Opinion of Lord Keeper*
Wright *seems to be over-ruled, or rather never
to have been Law; unless in the Days of Popery there might be such a Jurisdiction exercised here; and if so, it was not a lawful,
but an usurped Jurisdiction, and an Incroachment on the Superior Temporal Laws, and
Courts, by a pretended Church Authority, no
Ways binding upon the Laity, the Canons being Nullities as to them, as they never have
been confirmed by Act of Parliament, or otherwise had the Consent of the Laity, to give
them a binding Force upon them; for no Law
can possibly bind any, who have not assented to*
such

such Law, the Rule being, that a Law to bind all, must be consented to by all

4 *Mich* 7 Geo. 2 *B R.* The King and The Bishop of *Litchfield* and *Coventry*

Mr. *Parker* now Judge obtained a Rule for superseding a Writ of *Mandamus*, directed to the Ordinary, commanding him to grant a License to *Rushworth*, then lately appointed Usher of the free Grammar School of *Coventry*, founded by *John Hale* in *H 8* Time, for the teaching in the said School He said that by 77 Canon *Anno* 1603. the Bishop of the Diocese is trusted with these Licenses, and in this Case, he said, he acted Judicially and not Ministerially, and therefore he conceived the present *Mandamus* was not proper, for in Case the Bishop refuse a License, without Reason, the Party may appeal, and of this Opinion the Court was, in the Case *Turton* and *Reynolds*, *Mich* 10 *W.* 3. and in *Policie's* Case afterwards, he said, My Lord *Macclesfield* and *Eyre* and *Powis* Justices inclined to be of Opinion a *Mandamus* would not lie. He said the Business of a Shool-Master is not an Office, but an Imployment; but the present Case is not even so strong as that, for *Rushworth* is only appointed Usher; he also observed, that the present School is but a private one, and not a Royal Foundation. Then came Serjeant *Birch* and another Counsel, and moved to discharge this Rule, and said they took it, that it was never yet settled, That an Usher was bound to take a License, and therefore it was proper that the Ordinary should make a Return to this *Mandamus*, that that Point might be fully settled: And if a License was

necessary

neceffary they conceived a *Mandamus* the proper Remedy to obtain it, and to the Purpose cited 1 *Sid.* 94, 107, 169. 4 *Inft.* 309. 3 *Keb.* 855. *Ven.* 155, 187, 143, 153, 335, and the Serjeant faid, that a *Mandamus* had been before moved for againft this very Bifhop, requiring him to grant a Licenfe to one to teach the School of *Broomefield* in *Com. Derby*, indeed it was not granted becaufe the Affidavit, whereon the Motion was made, was not fufficient, but faid he took the Opinion of the Court to be, that a *Mandamus* would lie. My Lord Ch Juft did not think it a clear Point, that a Licenfe was neceffary in the prefent Cafe, and therefore faid, that it was proper that a Return fhould be made in Order that that Point might be fettled, but if it was neceffary he did not fee that a *Mandamus* was the proper Remedy. His Lordfhip agreed, that the Bufinefs of a School-Mafter was only an Employment; but yet it is a Temporal Employment; and therefore this Court might interfere. In the Cafe *Coleful* and *Newcombe*, *Mich.* 4 of the Queen, the Opinion of Mr. Juftice *Powel* was, that the Court might grant a *Mondamus* in Cafe of a Licenfe for a Preacher by the Stat. 13 and 14 *Char.* 2 4. and in the Cafe of *Vincent*, Lecturer of St *Dunftan's Fleetftreet*, this Court actually did grant a *Mandamus*, for a Licenfe to Preach at that Lecturefhip, though after, for particular Reafon, the Rule was difcharged; he faid, no Inftances had been produced that ever an Appeal lay in thefe Cafes: And if a *Mandamus* would lie, in the Cafe of a School-Mafter he thought it would,

would, in the Cafe of an Ufher equally
Lee Juft. faid, he remembred *Policie's* Cafe
cited by Mr. *Parker*. *Prat* Juft. was ftrongly
of the other Opinion, on the firft Argument,
and on the fecond, the other Judges came
over to his Opinion, and accordingly the
Rule was difcharged for fuperfeding the *Mandamus*. And this Matter coming on again
Paf 7 *Geo*. 2. upon the Return Serjeant *Birch*
prayed, that a Peremptory *Mandamus* might
be granted: The Return, he faid, fet forth,
that there was a Reprefentation drawn up
by feveral Inhabitants of the Town of *Coventry*, fetting forth great Immoralities to be
in *Rufbworth*, and that there were Affidavits
charging him with great Misbehaviour, and
a Certificate to the fame Effect. The Return further fet forth certain Articles, *in bæc
verba*, exhibited againft him in the Bifhop's
Court for feveral Spiritual Offences: That a
Caveat was entered in Purfuance of them:
That *Rufbworth* appeared to thefe Articles,
by his Proctor, and that they were now depending againft him. 'Twas further alledged,
that by one of the Canons in 1603, which
was confirmed by the King's Letters Patents
on 6 *Sep*. 20 *Jac* 1. it was neceffary for every
School-Mafter to take a Licenfe from the
Bifhop, and that the old Canons made before that Time, required the fame. That
Rufbworth was a Clergyman, and that for
the Reafons above, the Ordinary fufpended
granting him this Licenfe; this Return, the
Serjeant fubmitted, was infufficient, he faid,
in *Salk* 432 the Law required the moft exact certainty in thefe Returns, but in the
prefent Return it is not fet forth, with any

Y 3   Cer-

Certainty, what the Purport of the Affidavit was, neither that it was sworn before a competent Authority, and if this was in the Case of an Indictment of Perjury, the setting forth of an Affidavit, in this Manner, would not be sufficient, as is *Lat* 39, 133 and the same Objection may be made to the Certificate, and as to the Articles against *Rushworth*, he said, that would be no Objection in his Way, for that a Charge can be of no Force against any one till he is convicted upon it, he observed further, that it was not set forth in this Return, that the Bishop ever gave *Rushworth* Notice to appear and answer these Charges And in the Case of Dr *Bently*, who was degraded by the University of *Cambridge*, he took the clear Opinion of the Court to be, that in a Suspension, as well as a Degradation, it was necessary that the Party should have an Opportunity to be heard The objections he submitted, might well be made to shew, that the Cause returned by the Bishop was not sufficient; and were it not that *Rushworth* hath applied for a *Mandamus*, and so had, in some Measure, admitted, that a License was necessary, he could produce many Authorities in the Law, to shew that no License at all was necessary, and for this Purpose he named 1 *Vent.* 41 and he said, there were divers others to the same Purpose M. *Parker* argued, on the other Side, and submitted, it was very certain that in these Cases Licenses are necessary *Stat.* 1 *Jac* 1 4, 9 & 13 & 14 *Car.* 2 4, 8 take Notice of them to be so. In the old Canons, made by the Popes, this is required. 1 *Mod* 3

the

the Cafe in 1 *Ven* 41, is reported contrary and the Authority of the 2 *Lev* 222 is full in Point   The granting fuch Licenfe is a Judicial Act, and may well be compared to a Bifhop's refufing to admit a Perfon to a Living who is prefented, and in fuch Cafe it is held in 5 *Co* 57 that no *Mandamus* will lie, and he conceived, that there was the fame Reafon, in the prefent Cafe, that it fhould not, and in Support of this Opinion cited 1 *Keb* 5 *Sid* 40. *Sty* 457, but fuppofing it fhould be faid, that the Return, was a full Excufe for the Ordinary's Non-compliance with the Writ: The Return has fet forth the Reafons, why the Ordinary at prefent fufpends granting this Licenfe Articles are actually exhibited againft the Party, he appears to them, by which he himfelf takes Notice of them, and till he has acquitted himfelf of the Charge, it is highly reafonable the Licenfe fhould be fufpended, and to fhew that fuch general Returns have been allowed, he cited 5 *Co* 158 and *Show Parliament Cafes* 88.   My Lord Ch Juft. it's faid, that the Return fet forth the Party applying for the Licenfe to be a Clergyman, and his Lordfhip faid, he at prefent thought it muft be admitted, that a Licenfe was neceffary, becaufe the Canons in 1603 require it, and it muft be admitted that they bind the Clergy; but his Lordfhip alfo faid, he did think they did not bind the Laity; as they never were confirmed by Parliament his Lordfhip faid alfo, it has not been made to appear that thofe ancient Canons, which had been mentioned, were ever allowed of by the Courts of Common Law; therefore

he

he could not fee, that by any Canon, it could be made appear, that a Layman could be obliged to take fuch Licenfe, and faid, that with Regard to the General Queftion of taking thefe Licenfes, he thought it very material to be eftablifhed, that the Laity were not bound to take them by the Canon Law; for if they were, a *Mandamus* could never lie, requiring them to be made to any one particular Perfon; but an Appeal would be the proper Remedy. If, on the other Hand, this Obligation arifeth fiom the Stat. Law; though the Ordinary may be, in fome Meafure, fuppofed to act Judicially, yet a particular *Mandamus* may be granted; the principal Queftion therefore in the principal Cafe reforts to this, whether the Ordinary has not fet forth a fufficient Excufe, for re-fufing to grant this Licenfe, at prefent, and as to that, his Lordfhip thought, he clearly had; upon Account of the Articles con-taining a Criminal Charge being exhibited againft the Party, he having appeared to them; and that Matter not being yet deter-mined. The reft of the Judges concurring, a Peremptory *Mandamus* was refufed, yet the Matter ftood over till *Mich.* the 9. of his pre-fent Majefty, when the fame coming on again, Mr *Wynne* now Serjeant, argued for *Rafh-worth*, and faid, he fhould not contend, but that School-Mafters are obliged to take Licenfes from Bifhops, in fome particular Cafes, but he apprehended, that this Authority of granting Licenfes, was only *fub modo*, and that it was only of Minifterial and not Ju-dicial Authority; and if this was fo, then he apprehended, that Bifhops have no Right

to

to examine the Qualifications of those to
whom they granted them, and to the Purpose cited ———— 200 or 203. 11 *H* 4. 47.
20 *H.* 6 13. *Sty.* 457. Mr. *Abney* now Judge
on the other Side, said, that if *Rushworth* had
been a Layman, he should not have contended, that even a License was necessary,
but as it's set forth in the Return, that he
is a Clergyman, he conceived, that not
only a License was necessary, but that
the Bishop had a Right to examine his Qualifications before he granted it.   And this Distinction between the Laity and Clergy he
apprehended was fully warranted: The Canon which requires this License, he said,
was one of them in 1603, but those Canons
being only confirmed by the King's Letters
Patent, he conceived it to be certain, that
they bound the Clergy only; but the Clergy, he apprehended, were bound by all of
them, whether they related to Ecclesiastical
Matters, or not; and for Authority, he cited
1 *Keb.* 5. 2 *Keb.* 538 2 *Lev.* 222 & *Salk.*
372. My Lord Ch. Just said, that he
thought, that the single Question for the
Court to consider was, whether the Matter
returned was a sufficient, temporary, Excuse
for not granting the License at present; he
said, he did not think, that *Rushworth's*
being a Clergyman made the Case any ways
different from what it would have been if
he had been a Layman; for he could not
think that the Canons in 1603, made in
Convocation, and confirmed by the Crown,
without being confirmed by Parliament,
bound even the Clergy in any Matter, but
in re Ecclesiastica; if this were otherwise,
his

his Lordship observed, there would be this
Consequence, that if a Clergyman were
Head of a College, he might be bound in
Matters relating to him in that Capacity,
and so in any other Temporal Right, he
said likewise, that he did not think it material, in the present Case, to consider, whether Bishops have any Jurisdiction to grant
Licenses of this Sort in general, for, in the
present Case, the *Mandamus* supposes that
he has this Power; the *Mandamus* suggesting,
that *Rushworth* was duly appointed and chosen Usher of the Free Grammar School,
founded by *Thomas Hale* in the Reign of
H. 8. and that, before his Admission, he
ought to be licensed by the Bishop, but
whether that License was necessary by the
particular Foundation of the School, or by
the general Rule of Law, was not material
to enter into; but thus much, he said, he
did think, that however ministerial the
Bishop might be, in granting a License of
this Sort, yet he had a Right, in some
Measure, of examining into the Qualifications of the Person, to whom he granted
this License. And, in the present Case,
his Lordship further said, he thought that
the Bishop had set forth a sufficient Excuse
for not obeying the Writ, in the Manner as
he had returned, for the Return set forth,
we further certify that we never utterly re-
fused, but only suspended granting our License,
till we should receive Satisfaction touching the
Morals and Sufficiency of the Party. And then
the Return set forth some Charges of Im-
morality in *Rushworth,* others of his Deficiency and Quarreling in the Church and
Church-

Church-Yard with his Parishioners, his Excess in Drinking, and his being guilty, or suspected to be guilty of a lew'd Behaviour. And, on the Court's refusing a peremptory *Mandamus*; for this Reason, his Lordship said, they were well warranted by the Case of *Lupton* and *Wallis*, which was cited on the former Argument *Page*, Justice said, that he was always of Opinion, that no Canons bound the Clergy, unless confirmed by Parliament, but in Ecclesiastical Matters, but said, there was no Occasion to inquire into that Matter at present, that he intirely agreed with my Lord Ch. Justice *Lee* Justice said, that in *Salk* 572 the Foundation of a *Mandamus* going is resolved to be, the requiring the Party to do some Act in Execution of Law; but it never was yet determined, that a *Mandamus* of this Sort lies at all· In the Case of *Turton* and *Reynolds*, my Lord *Holt*, said, that it does not lie to a Lecturer, but, in another Case, there was the Opinion of a single Judge, that it would lie Where *Mandamus*'s have been applied for, requiring Justices of Peace to grant a License, he said, the Act of granting the License has been looked upon, as discretonary, and for that Reason has been refused, but where such License has been once granted, the Justice cannot, *ad Libitum*, revoke it, and so that Point has been determined In the present Case, he thought it could not be said, that the Bishop was bound to grant the License, at all Events, and this fully appeared by the Act of Uniformity, 13 & 14 *Ch* 2. The only Point remaining
then

then to be considered was, whether there

'Tis true, the was not a sufficient Excuse returned for not
Canon says, granting the Licenfe at present, and said,
None shall he was clear of Opinion, that the Excuse
teach in Pub- returned was sufficient, and accordingly the
lick Schools, Rule pronounced by the Court was, that
or private the Return should be allowed.
House, but
such as shall

be allowed by the Bishop of the Diocese, or Ordinary of the Place, un
der his Hand and Seal, being found meet, as well for his Learning and
Dexterity in Teaching, as for sober and honest Conversation, and also
for right Understanding of God's true Religion, and also except he shall
first subscribe to the first and third Articles simply, and to the two first
Claufes of the second Article *Can* 77. And Curates, desirous to teach,
are to be licensed before others, under the Terms in *Can* 78 All School
Masters shall teach in *English*, or *Latin*, as the Children are able to bear,
the larger, or shorter, Catechism, heretofore, by publick Authority, set
forth ; and as often as any Sermon shall be upon Holy and Festival Days,
within the Parish where they teach, they shall bring their Scholars to the
Church where such Sermon shall be made, and there see them quietly
and soberly behave themselves, and shall examine them at Times convenient, after their Return, what they have born away of such Sermons.
Upon other Days, and at other Times, they shall train them up with
such Sentences of Holy Scripture, as shall be most expedient to induce
them to all Godliness, and teach them the Grammar, &c And if any
School Master being licensed, and having subscribed, as aforesaid, shall
offend in any of the Premisses, or either, speak, write, or teach, against
any Thing, whereunto he hath formerly subscribed, (if upon Admoni
tion by the Ordinary he do not amend and reform himself,) let him be
suspended from teaching School any longer *Can* 79 But yet I con
ceive, that a School-Master, though he be of the Clergy, is not bound,
as a School Master, by these, or any other, the Canons, for this is a
Temporal Imployment, though exercised by an Ecclesiastick, and he is
extra all Ecclesiastical Conusance or Jurisdiction, and only accountable to
his natural Visitor, or such other as such natural Visitor has thought fit
to put him under the Government of; and I think, I am well supported
in this Notion by the preceding, and many other, Cases in the Books

2 *Not removeable at the Ordinary's Plea-*
sure.

2. If a Town erect a common School,
and make an Allowance to the School-Master, the Bishop may not remove him, and
put in another, at his Pleasure; but if he be
a Recusant, he may, by the *Stat.* 23 *Eliz.*
c. 1. *Rol. Abr. Prohibition,* F. 7. *Mich.* 13
Ja The Bishop of *Carlisle's* Case.

3 *As to licensing Dissenters to teach Schools.*

Hill 2 *Geo.* 2. *B R. Dodridge* v. *Rand* & al'.
Mr *Marsh* moved for a Prohibition to the
Bishop of *Peterborough,* to stay Proceedings
against one *Dodridge* for keeping an Acade-
my and dissenting Meeting-House at *Nor-*
thampton, sans Licence, which the Canons
1603 require. Suggestion was, in the first
place, that those Canons do not bind the
Laity, and, in the next place, that *Stat*
1 *Ja* 1. 4. hath given a Penalty for this Offence; accordingly he cited *Carth* 464. Rule
to shew Cause On shewing Cause, Serjeant *Eyre* observed, that two Matters are
contained in the Objection, 1st, that the Canons in 1603 do not bind the Laity, and
2dly, that since the Statute requiring a Licence, the Ecclesiastical Courts have no Jurisdiction; but he said, he apprehended,
that the Suggestion in both Parts were
wrong, and to that Purpose cited 2 *Lev.*
222 However the Court made Rule absolute, and gave the Party to the first Day of
next Term to declare.

8. *Mid-*

8. *Midwives,* &c. &c. &c.

A Suit is in the Ecclesiastical Court for exercising the Trade of a Midwife, *sans* Licence *del'* Ordinary, as an Offence against the Canon, a Prohibition lies, for it is no Spiritual Function. *Rol Abr. Prohibition, Case* 44. 9 *Ca.* B. R. The Canons do not bind the Laity.

C.

Both.

342. — I. *Spoliation.*
— II. *Church and Church Livings.*

1. *By whom founded.*
2. *When began, and how may be obtained.*

3. *Whether Dignities, or not.*
4. *Void, or not.*

1. *Where to be tried.*

5. *The Profits thereof.*

1. *The Ordinary not to meddle with.*
2. *Where to be sued for.*

III. *Cole-*

1. *The*

1. *The* Duties *of* Ordinaries *to* Patrons *in* such Cases.
2. By *the* Patron.
3. By Lapse.
4. Where *the* Right *to be tried.*

2. Admission.

1. What.
2. Who *to be admitted.*

3. Institution.

1. What *it is, and its Effect.*
2. Where Admission *and* Institution *may be* refused.

4. Induction.

1. What, *how performed, and its Effect.*
1. General.

2. Where triable.
3 Where delayed.

5. General *to* Admission, Institution *and* Induction.

1. Who may be a Priest or Deacon, when, where, by whom, and before whom to be ordered, or ordained.
2. The Office of Bishops in these Cases Vide ante Presentation, the Duty of Bishops to Patrons in such Cases.
3. Where to be tried.

4

X. Ability.

1. *By Acceptance of another in-compatible without Dispensation,* &c.

1. *General.*
2. *The Patron's Right to present in such Cases.*

XIX. *Wherefore a Clerk may be removed.*
XX. *Deprivation.*

1. *What it is.*
2. *The Sorts.*
3. *Wherefore one may be deprived, and who must do it, and in what Cases.*
4. *How to be tried.*

XXI. *Where a Clerk is ousted or disturbed.*

1. *Ousted.*
2. *Disturbed.*

XXII. *Chaplains.*

1. *The King's.*

1. *Their Residence.*

2. *Other Chaplains,* vide *Court of Faculties* antea.

XXIII. *The*

C.

Both.

I. *Spoliation.*

1 SPoliation is a Suit for the Fruits of a Church, or the Church itself, and is to be sued in the Spiritual Court, and not in the Temporal, and this is a Suit for one Incumbent against another, where they both claim by the same Patron, and the Right of Patronage doth not come in Question, as if a Parson be created a Bishop, and hath a Dispensation to hold his Benefice, after which the Patron presents another, who is instituted and inducted, in such Case the Bishop may have a Spoliation against the Incumbent in the Spiritual Court; for they both claim under the same Patron, and the Right of Patronage is not drawn in Question, and because the other Parson came into the Possession of the Benefice by the Course of the Spiritual Law, namely, by Institution and Induction, so that he hath Colour thereto by the same Spiritual Law; for if he were not instituted and inducted, no Spoliation lieth, but rather Trespass or an Assise of Novel Disseisin, &c (*which means some other Temporal Remedy*) The Law is the same, where a Parson that is beneficed already accepts another Living with Cure of Value, who is instituted and inducted; in such Case one of them may

V. ugh 24.

may have Spoliation againſt the other, and then, whether he hath a ſufficient Plurality, or not, will neceſſarily come in Queſtion, and ſo it is of Deprivation, &c. The Law is the ſame where the Patron, on Suppoſition the Clerk is dead, preſents another, in which Caſe the firſt Clerk, who was ſuppoſed dead, may have a Spoliation againſt the other, and ſo it is in many other like Caſes, whereof ſee *Fitz N. B* 36 G &c *Terms del' Ley*, ſub hoc Tit. Vide *Secular Clergy, where ouſted, the Remedy.* Vide ante *The Matter, Preſentation.*

2 If an Husband poſſeſſed of Goods, in Right of his Wife, as Adminiſtratrix, grants them to *J S* and then the Wife dies, and after another Adminiſtration is granted to *J D* who ſues the Grantee of the Goods for a Spoliation in the Eccleſiaſtical Court, a Prohibition lieth *Mich* 11 *Car. B R Clark* and *Daniel, Rol Abr. Prohibition, fo.* 302. *Caſe* 21

3. If an Husband poſſeſſed of Goods in Right of his Wife as Adminiſtratrix, waſte them, and the Wife dies, if the Husband be ſued in the Spiritual Courts for a Spoliation, or Waſte of theſe Goods, a Prohibition lies *Mich.* 11 *Ca B R. Clark* and *Daniel* Juſtice *Jones* ſaid, it was ſo reſolved, though the Spiritual Court complained of it to be very hard. *Rol Abr. Prohibition, fo.* 302. *Caſe* 22

Z 4 II. *Church*

II. *Church and Church Livings.*

1. *By whom founded.*

THE King and his Lay Subjects were the Donors of all Benefices to Ecclesiastical Persons, and therefore Church Benefices are called *Eleemofynas Laicorum* Dav 81

2. *When began, and how may be obtained.*

1 *Parochia est Locus in quo degit populus alicujus Ecclesiæ* 5 Co 67 a

2 Parochial Right before the Council of *Lateran.* Cro Car 422

3 A Church may be filled these several Ways, by Presentation, Collation, &c Sec Case *Archbishop Armagh* v *Le Roy*, before House of Lords, *Feb.* 1728. and again *April* 1730

4 One may come, without Presentation, Institution, or Induction, these several Ways to a Parsonage, or Church Living 1 By Way of Appropriation. 2 By Way of Union 3 By Way of Permutation 4. By Way of *Commendam*, and in past Times, when the Pope usurped Jurisdiction in *England*, there was a fifth Way, by Way of Provision. *Dav.* 81. *b.*

3. *Whether*

3. *Whether Dignities, or not.*

1 SOME Promotions are merely Admini-
ſtrations, as Prebendaries and Parſons,
and are not Dignities not having Juriſdiction *Palm* 461 11 *H* 4. *So that it would
ſeem it is Juriſdiction which makes a Dignity.*

2 *Beneficium Eccleſiaſticum* extendeth not
only to Benefices of Churches Parochial,
but to Dignities, and other Eccleſiaſtical
Promotions, as to Deaneries, Arch-deaconries, Prebends, &c. and it appeareth in our
Books, that Deaneries, Arch-deaconries,
Prebends, &c. are Benefices with Cure of
Souls, but they are not comprehended under the Name of Benefices with Cure of
Souls within the Statute 21 *H* 8 by Reaſon
of a ſpecial Proviſo, which they had been,
if no ſuch Proviſo had been added, (*viz*)
*Deans, Arch-deacons, Chancellors, Treaſurers,
Chanters, Prebendary,* or a *Parſon, where there
is a Vicar endowed.* 3 Inſt. 155.

4. *Void or not.*

1 *Where to be tried.*

1 IF *A.* be preſented by *J S* to a Benefice,
and be admitted, inſtituted and inducted, and after the King preſent his Clerk to
the ſame, on a Suppoſition that *A* was preſented by Simony, and his Clerk is inſtituted
and inducted, whereupon *A* ſues in the Eccleſiaſtical Court againſt the King's Clerk,
on Suppoſal that he himſelf did not come in
by

by Simony, and therefore prays, that the Superadmission, Institution and Induction, may be repealed; a Prohibition shall be granted for the Clerk of the King, upon his Suggestion, that *A* was presented by Simony; for now the sole Question betwixt them is, whether the Church was void, or not, at the Time of the King's Presentment, which is only triable by the Temporal Courts *Trin* 16 *Ja inter Scrison* and *Bathoe*, *Rol Abr Prohibition*, 292 M 1, 2

2 If *A* recover in a *Quare impedit* against the Ordinary and Incumbent, and the Incumbent bring Error, whereon the Judgment is affirmed, and a Writ to the Bishop is granted to *A* upon which *A.* presents his Clerk to the Bishop, before any actual Removal of the first Incumbent, and his Clerk is admitted and instituted; upon which, the first Incumbent appeals to the Audience for a Superinstitution before that he was removed, a Prohibition shall be granted, for the first Incumbent was removed in Law by the Judgment, though he continued Incumbent, *de facto*, till the last Incumbent was presented, and the last Institution was by Force of the King's Writ, and therefore no Appeal may be of it. M 12 *Ja inter Wostler* and *Singleton* adjudged, and Prohibition granted *Rol Abr. Prohibition*, 292 M 3.

3 Plenarty shall be tried by the Bishop, where the Plenaity is made by Institution; for that Institution is a Spiritual Act, but where there is no Plenarty till Induction, then full, or not, shall be tried, by Verdict of twelve Men, according to the Common Law, for Induction is a Thing notorious,

and

and shall not be tried by the Ordinary *Vide* 22 *H*. 6 27, *&c* And yet in some Cases a Jury shall inquire of Plenarty, as in the principal Case; and in all *Quare impedits*, one of the three Points inquirable is, if the Church be full, or not. 6 *Co*. 49 *a*

5. *The Profits thereof.*

1. *The Ordinary not to meddle with.*

THE Ordinary has nothing to do to intermeddle with the Church, or the Fruits thereof. *Hob* 316, 317.

2 *Where to be sued for*

If a Man sues in Court Christian to have an Account for the Profits of a Benefice, a Prohibition lies; for that it belongeth to the Common Law. *Hill.* 3 *Ja.* adjudged *Rol. Abr Prohibition, fo.* 293. *Case* 6. But for Profits taken in Time of Sequestration, *alter, Case* 7.

III. *Celebration of Divine Service.*

BEfore all Sermons, Lectures, and Homilies, the Preachers and Ministers shall move the People to join with them in Prayer, in the Form, or to the Effect, therein mentioned. *Can.* 55. See 5 *Co De Jure Reg. s Eccl.* 9. *a*

IV. *Parish*

IV. *Parifh and Parifh Churches.*

* IF an Act of Parliament make a particular Diftrict a particular feparate and diftinct Parifh, the Jurifdiction of the Ecclefiaftical Court does not attach upon it for this clear Reafon, that it was not fuch immemorially, and ftill more fo, where it is not a Parifh Church Parifh St. *John, Clerkenwell,* 9 Geo. 2. *B R.*

V. *Sacraments.*

1. *Baptifm.*

1. *Fees for.*

1 SUggeftion, that by Law, *&c.* no Perfon ought to pay any Thing for the Sacrament of Baptifm againft his Will, a Prohibition was granted. *Lutw. Anderfon* and *Walker's* Cafe

2 *Burdeaux,* a *French* Proteftant had his Child baptized at the *French* Church in the *Savoy,* and Dr *Lancafter,* Vicar of St *Martin's,* in which Parifh it is, together with the Clerk, libelled againft him for a Fee of two Shillings and fix Pence due to him, and one Shilling the Clerk, a Prohibition was moved for, and *Levinz* urged, this was an Ecclefiaftical Fee due by Canon *Holt* C. J Nothing can be due, of common Right, and how can a Canon take Money out of Laymen's Pockets *Lindwood* fays, it is Simony to take any Thing for Chriftening, or Burying,

ing, unless it be a Fee due by Custom ; but then a Custom for any Person to take a Fee for Christening a Child, when he does not christen it, is not good, like the Case in *Hob.* (175, 176) where one dies in one Parish, and is buried in another, the Parish where he died shall not have a burying Fee. If you have a Right to christen, you should libel for that Right, but you ought not to have Money for Christening, when you do not. *Salk.* 332.

2. *The Lord's Supper.*

A Citizen of *Bristol* had a Country House, and frequently received the Sacrament in the Parish Church in the Country, likewise he received it frequently at the Cathedral Church in *Bristol*, notwithstanding which he was cited into the Ecclesiastical Court and admonished, and afterwards, for not obeying and receiving in his Parish Church, according to the Monition, he was excommunicated, though one of the Surrogates of the Court, but the *Sunday* before, had with his own Hand given him the Sacrament, and that, though he there pleaded this, and likewise his receiving in the Country, at his own Parish, they would not allow of it : Upon this Matter appearing to the Court (*B R*) a Prohibition went. *Skin.* 101, 176

VI. *Church*

VI. *Church Dues.*

1. *For Churching Women.*

IN *Banco Regis.* *Naylor* & *Scot.*
Libel was in the Confiftory Court of
York, founded upon a Cuftom, that every
one keeping Houfe, and having Children in
the Parifh fhould pay Ten Pence *per* Child
to the Parfon, at the Time the Wife is, or
ought to be, Churched; the Counfel apprehended it to be an unreafonable Cuftom,
that the Parfon fhould have Money for doing
of nothing, and fo moved for a Prohibition,
for they faid, the proper Way was, if the
Wife would not be Churched, at the proper
Time, to force her to it by Ecclefiaftical
Cenfures, upon which the Court made a
Rule to fhew Caufe; and Mr. *Reeve* coming
to fhew Caufe upon the above Rule, Mr. *Fazakerley* faid, that, fince that Time, they
had pleaded below, and denied the Cuftom,
notwithftanding which the Plaintiff in the
Ecclefiaftical Court was there going on,
and faid, if the firft Matter fhould go againft
them, they fhould move upon this other
Footing; and therefore it would a good deal
fhorten the Bufinefs, if the Suggeftion was
amended by Confent, and made, as he had
then opened it, whereupon it was amended
by Confent   Then the Plaintiff having declared in Prohibition and Verdict had for
the Cuftom, Mr *Bootle* moved in Arreft of
Judgment, that the Cuftom was void, and
accordingly the Court ordered Judgment to
be

be stayed, till the *Postea* brought in, and the *Postea* being brought in, the Court made a Rule to shew Cause why the Judgment should not be arrested, and Serjeant *Cheshire* and Mr *Reeve*, who came to shew Cause, said, the Words of the Custom were, that an Housekeeper having Child or Children born in the Parish of *Wakefield* in *York-shire*, at the Time of the Churching the Mother, or at the usual Time after her Delivery, when she should be Churched, have, Time out of Mind, paid Ten Pence to the Vicar, for and in Respect of such Churching, or at the usual Time when the Mother of such Child should be churched To that two great Objections were made, that this Custom is unreasonable in itself and uncertainly set forth· To the first it was observed, that Religion requires a Woman should return Thanks to God, in a publick Manner, for so great a Deliverance, and therefore it is but fit, that he who assists her in such Office should have some Requital To the other, they said, there are other Cases where these Courts allow the Ecclesiastical Courts to set forth Matters equally uncertain, as in the present Case, even upon Libels upon Customs, and have not granted their Prohibitions, to which Purpose they applied a Case, where a Libel was upon a Custom, that the Farmers of such a Farm have always laid out Eight Shillings, *aut eo circiter*, for Cakes and Ale in the Perambulation, and yet held good , and besides they said, if the Court was in Doubt, whether the Proceedings in the Courts below were usually in so uncertain a Manner, the proper Method

I   would

would be to write to them to certify how
their Proceedings are there; and to this
Purpose they applied a Cafe, *Palm* 296.
where a Libel was for a Woman not coming
to be churched in a Veil; whereupon a Prohibition being moved for, the Court wrote
to the Archbishop to certify how the Canons
in that Cafe were, and he certified the Canon to require it. They obferved further,
that tho' indeed the Woman's Fitnefs to be
churched is unknown to our Courts, yet to
thofe Courts it is well known, and therefore they might well have proceeded upon
it below The Canon Law fays, that a
Month is a reafonable Time for Women's
coming to be churched, after their Deliverance, unlefs in Cafe of great Weaknefs,
that Standard is the proper one to regulate
this Cuftom by; and therefore the Court
below ought to be allowed to go on in their
Proceedings; but the Court faid, they were
of Opinion, that they were not to confider
the Methods by which this Fee might be afcertained, they were only to confider that
it was not certain, as it ftands upon the Libel; and therefore upon the Libel they
ought not to fuffer them to proceed; for
they obferved, according to the other Doctrine, that this Matter may be made right in
the future Parts of the Proceedings, they may
refufe to grant Prohibitions at any Time,
but they faid, that the Rule they founded
themfelves upon was fettled in the Cafe of
Wood and *Hicks*, and *Whittle* and *Offley*,
where a *Modus* was fet out imperfectly, and
they granted a Prohibition. But the Court
obferved, that the proper Method, in this
Cafe,

I

Cafe, would have been for the Plaintiff to fet forth in the Libel the proper Time when Women ufually are fit to be churched, and then to have averred, that the Defendant's Wife was not churched within that Time. Upon the whole Matter the Court made the Rule abfolute for arrefting the Judgment. *Vide Salk* 332.

2. *For Burials.*

1. EDward Topfal, Clerk, Parfon of St. Bo- tolph without *Alderfgate,* and the Church-Wardens of the fame libelled in Court Chriftian againft Sir *John Ferrers* Knight, and alledged a Cuftom within the City of *London,* and efpecially within that Parifh, that if any Perfon die within that Parifh, being Man or Woman, and be car- ried out of the fame Parifh and buried elfe- where, that there ought to be paid to the Parfon of this Parifh, if he be buried elfe- where, in the Chancel fo much, and to the Church-Wardens fo much, being the Sums that they alledged were by Cuftom payable to them for fuch as were buried in their own Chancel, and then alledging, that the Wife of Sir *John Ferrers* died within the Parifh, and was carried away and buried in the Chancel of another Church, and fo de- manded of him the faid Sum ; whereupon, for Sir *John Ferrers,* a Prohibition was prayed by Serjeant *Harris,* and granted ; for that Cuftom is againft Reafon, for that he who is no Parifhioner, but may pafs through the Parifh, or lie in an Inn for a Night, fhould

be forced to be buried there, or to pay as if he were, and so upon the Matter to pay twice for his Burial. *Hob* 175, 176.

2. Serjeant *Hooper* shewed Cause against a Rule for a Prohibition to the Spiritual Court to stay a Suit there for a customary Fee of Ten Shillings, due to the Dean and Chapter of *Exeter*, for burying in the Cathedral Church; *sed non allocatur*, for no Fee is due for Burial, of Common Right, but where a License is necessary, the Person giving it may stand upon his own Price; and if there be such a Custom it is triable at Common Law. *Vide* 3 *Keb.* 527, 523. If the Custom be not denied, the Spiritual Court shall proceed, for there is no other Remedy; but if the Custom be denied, a Prohibition shall go, not *propter Defectum Jurisdictionis*, but *Triationis*; and Burials at Common Law ought to be in the Church-Yard, and without Fee *Salk.* 334.

3. If the Parson of *B* in *London* libel in the Ecclesiastical Court on a Custom, that if a Parishioner of *B* die in *B.* and is carried and buried in another Parish in *London*, and there are given to the Parson a Gown, a Pulpit Cloth, and a Pair of Gloves, &c. that the same Things ought to be given to him, a Prohibition lies to try this Custom, if it be denied; for a Custom might be made in the Ecclesiastical Law by a shorter Time than at Common Law. *Trin* 15 *Ca* B. R *Cooker* Parson of *St Thomas Apostle's* & *Goale.* Prohibition granted. *Rol Abr. Prohibition* (N) *Case* 18 *Vide Lutw. Anderson* & *Walker's* Case, *which, with the Cases above, seem to me to determine this Demand of the Parson to have a Gown,*

4

a Gown, &c. and what not, for nothing, to be very unconscionable, especially when it shall be considered, that no Fees are due, of Common Right, for Burial; and if there be a Custom, the Question, I confess, with me is, whether it is not to be feared such Custom may have had it's Foundation in Incroachment on the Ignorance, or Compliance, of the Laity, or an Abuse of Power; for if the Clergy are to be severally paid for Burials, &c. what are the Considerations of Tithes, Glebe Lands, &c. but if they are to be doubly paid for one and the same Duty, and they can make good their Right thereto, tho' I cannot, at present, reconcile that Matter to myself, I will leave it, but, to return to our present Case, to me it would seem very extraordinary to say, because a Man hath done either an Act of real Charity perhaps to a poor needy Parson; or but of Bounty and Generosity, on the most proper Occasion, that for so doing he shall be mulcted or fined at the Will of an unconscionable Priest. In the present Case, what has this Parson done to give him Title to this Gown, &c. why nothing; but notwithstanding he has a Title, and I suppose, thus makes it out; you freely, and of Favour, gave them to one who discharged the Offices of his Function for you, and at your Request, and therefore (which is a most clear, as well as upright Consequence) you shall, of Force, and against your Will, give the same Things to another who has done nothing for them, but endeavours to pick your Pocket, by making so iniquitous a Demand. This Case brings to my Mind a Story, which I firmly believe having several Times heard it from one or more Persons of undoubted Character and Reputation, and is.

A a 2   of

of a reverend Doctor of our Church, since dead, (tho' he has not been many Years so) who held a Living in this Town, not inferior, as I have heard, to very many in it : He was a Person eminent for a fine Preacher, and one esteemed as a great Example of Religion and Piety, yet, as none are without Faults, it is to be feared he had a Taint of Avarice, for having a Curate (a young Gentleman, who behaved himself greatly to the Satisfaction of the Parish) at a certain Stipend or Salary of 20 or 30 l. or some other yearly Wages, where it was Part of the Agreement, that the Doctor (as, it seems, is usual in these Cases) should have the Surplice Fees; tho' the Curate did the Duty. This being the Case between the Doctor and his Curate, a young Lady of Fortune and Figure in the Parish, being to be married, and both she and the Gentleman, as well as all the Lady's Family, having an extraordinary Opinion of the Curate, it was resolved that they would be married at this Parish Church, and the young Gentleman, and not the Doctor, should perform the Ceremony, which being done, the Bridegroom made the Curate a Present of a Purse of Guineas, desiring him to pay the Doctor's Fees, and to accept the rest himself; but notwithstanding this was the Case, and the Doctor informed of the whole of it ; yet the Doctor very equitably and conscienciously insisted upon the whole, as being the Reward for the Performance of this Office, which the Doctor, by his Art of distinguishing, demonstrated he himself did by his Deputy; and so insisted on the Premium; for the Labourer is worthy of his Hire, which occasioned the Bridegroom's Certificate of his own Act and Intention, which unluckily

turned

turned out for this Twig of Divinity against the full grown Doctor; but who carried off the Purse my Memory fails me, but I think the young Gentleman lost his Curacy, so he was Loser, whoever got.

3. *Baptism.* Vide *Sacraments.*

VII. *Dilapidations.*

1. *Rules.*

MEliorem Conditionem Ecclesiæ facere potest Prælatus, deteriorem nequaquam. 11 Co. 49. b.

2. *Where and how punished.*

1. Dilapidations and Diminutions of Ecclesiastical Livings are Torts, and are *quodammodo* punishable at Law, for the Master, Dean, &c for Dilapidation and Waft or Diminution of the Revenues of their Houses might be deprived as appears in 29 E. 3 16. 2 H. 4 3 11 H. 6 20 H. 6. 46. 9 E. 4. 34. 35 E. 1. 1 Co 72. b.

2. *Anno* 14 H. 3. *Archiepiscopus Dublin fecit finem de* 300 *Marcis pro de efforestatione forestæ Archiepiscopatus sui* 11 Co. 49 b.

3. If a Bishop or Archdeacon abate and cut down all the Trees which he has, he shall be deposed, as a Dilapidator of his House. 11 Co. 49. b.

4. *Prosternant Arbores in Cœmeterio.* Vide 11 Co. 49. b.

A a 3 5. Stat.

5. Stat. *ne Rector prosterneret Arbores in Cœmeterio* made *Anno* 35 *E.* 1. *Anno Domini* 1307 Parsons to fall Trees in Church-Yards for Repair of the Chancel, &c. *Vide* 11 *Co* 49 *b*

6. The Ecclesiastical Court may punish for Dilapidation. *Watson* Bishop of St *David's* Case. *Salk. Rep.* Vide 5 *Co. De Ja Reg. Eccl* 9

7. In Prohibition the Case appeared to be this; a Vicar lops and cuts down Timber-Trees growing in the Church-Yard; the Church-Wardens hinder him in carrying the same away, and they being in Trial of this Suit, the Church-Wardens Counsel moved for a Prohibition to the Vicar to stay him from felling any more. *Coke* Ch. Just this is a good Cause of Deprivation, if he fell down Timber-Trees and Wood, this is a Dilapidation, and by the Resolution in Parliament, a Prohibition by Law shall be granted if a Bishop fell down Wood and Timber-Trees, and the whole Court agreed to grant a Prohibition to the Vicar to inhibit him not to make Spoil of the Timber, this being (as it is called in Parliament) the Endowment of the Church. *Coke,* we will also grant a Prohibition to restrain Bishops from felling Wood and Timber-Trees of their Churches, &c. 3 *Bulstr.* 158. 2 *Bulstr.* 279 1 *Ro* 86. *Mo.* 517.

8. It was held in this Case, being the Bishop of *Salisbury's* Case, that if a Bishop, Parson, or other Ecclesiastical Person do cut down Trees upon the Land, save for Reparation of the Ecclesiastical Houses, or do, or suffer to be done, any Dilapidations, that
they

they may be punished for the same in the Ecclesiastical Court, and a Prohibition will not lie in the Case, and that the same is a good Cause of Deprivation of them of their Ecclesiastical Livings and Dignities; but yet for such Waste done, they may be also punished at Common Law. (*Vide* 2 *H*. 4 3) *Godb.* 259. Case 357.

9. The Vicar of *Alesbury* in *Devon* had fallen Timber and had not repaired the Church with them, and on Suggestion of this Matter to the Court and that he was about to fell more, a Prohibition was granted by the Court by the Common Law. 31 *E*. 1. The Bishop of *Durham* fell'd Trees for Iron Works, and a Prohibition was granted in Parliament. It was moved this Term (*Hil.* 13 *Jac.*) by *Thomas Crew*, that after a Judgment in *Quare impedit* by the King against *Sacker*, and a Writ to the Bishop, *Sacker* continued Possession and wasted the Vicarage-House, and therefore he prayed a Prohibition, *quod fuit concessum per Cur.* for that it is the Dowry of the Church, as Lord *Coke* said, and any Body may bring this Writ against him; for it is the King's Writ. The Prohibition was not to waste. 1 *Rol. Rep.* 335. 3 *Bulst.* 158.

10. *Note*; By *Coke*, C. J. a Bishop is only to fell Timber for Building, for Fuel, and for his other necessary Occasions. The Woods of a Bishoprick are called the Dowery of the Church, and are always carefully to be preserved, and if he fell and destroy, on Motion to us made, we will grant a Prohibition; and to this Purpose his Lordship said there was a great Case, which concerned

the

the Bishop of *Durham*, who had divers Coal-Mines, and would have cut down his Timber-Trees for the Maintenance and Upholding of his Works, and on Motion in Parliament thereupon for the King, Order was thereupon made that the Judges here should grant a Prohibition for the King, and we will here revive this again; for there a Prohibition was so granted, and so we will do in the like Case for the King by the Statute 35 *E* 1. If a Bishop fell Timber and sell to a Stranger, a Prohibition shall go, the same of a Dean and Chapter. The whole Court agreed with his Lordship therein 2 *Bulst.* 279. 2 *Rol Rep.* 335. 2 *Rol Abr.* 813. *Mo. Rep.* 917 1 *Rol Rep.* 199, 252. 3 *Bulst.* 116, 119, 158. 1 *Keb* 354. 1 *Show* 353. *Het* 30 *Far.* 127 *Parl Ca.* 6^. 1 *Vent.* 307, 316, 323. Vide postea *Deprivation*

3. *Who to have Remedy for.*

1. *General.*

1. IF the Parson of a Church will waste the Inheritance of his Church for his own private Use, the Patron may have a Prohibition; for the Patron is seised, as in Right of his Church, and the Glebe is the Dowry of the Church 11 *Co* 49 *a*

2. My Lord *Coke* said, any Body may have this Writ; for it is the King's Writ. 1 *Rol. Rep.* 335. *Vide* 3 *Bulst.* 158.

2. *Against whom.*

Agreed by all the Justices, that a Prohibition is awardable against any one pulling down the Houses of any Incumbent, or felling his Trees, or any other Waste. *Mo. fo* 917.

4. *How to be pleaded.*

AT *Bury St. Edmund's* Assises Lent, 3 *Geo.* 2. *Pithern* and *Ellis.* This was in Trespass by a Parson against the Executor of his Predecessor for Dilapidations. Held by the Court, that it was incumbent upon the Plaintiff to prove his declaring his Assent and Consent to the Articles, and taking the Oaths, in as much as he was but compleat Incumbent *February* last, and the Court would not suffer any Proof of his taking the Oaths, but Matter of Record: However the Court said, it was not necessary to prove Institution and Induction, and the Reason of this Distinction is, that in the first Case an Act of Parliament has declared the Church to be void, where these Ceremonies are not performed, in the other, not. The Judge observed further, that even this is not necessary to be proved where the Parson has been in several Years, and this, he said, was the constant Practice in the Exchequer. Tamen quære *of this last Part, since the Act of Parliament vacates the Living for want of these Qualifications, after any Number of Years, &c.*

VIII. *The*

VIII. *The Clergy may punish their own Members.*

1. *General.*

1 EVERY Parson of a Parish ought to be *persona idonea*, as appears by the Words of the Writ of *Quare impedit, quod permittit præsentare idoneam personam, &c.* where *Idonea* includes Ability. 1. In Learning. 2. In Doctrine. 3. In Honesty. 4 In Conversation. 5. In Diligence in his Function ; and all this to instruct the People of God in true Religion, good Conversation, and to avoid Contention, &c 6 *Co.* 49. *And I submit it, that if so, then Bishops and all Governors of the Church and Churchmen are to visit and inquire into and reform these Defects ex debito, and that it must be at the most important Peril that they omit so essentially necessary a Duty.*

2. Felony or other Capital Crimes are not examinable in the Ecclesiastical Courts, no, not for Purposes examinable even there, as in Case of Deprivation ; and therefore they cannot originally examine such a Crime, to prove a Man *Criminosus*, much less when he is so proved in the proper Court, impeach the Sentence in a Court improper; but they may build a Sentence of Deprivation upon such a Conviction, and they are bound by it, and it is dangerous for a Judge Ecclesiastical to come against it *Hob.* 121.

3. In a Parliament holden 1 *H* 7. (*cap* 4.) for the more fure and like Reformation of Priefts, Clerks, and Religious Men culpable, or by their Demerits openly noifed of incontinent living in their Bodies contrary to their Order, it was enacted, ordained, and eftablifhed, by the Advice and Affent of the Lords Spiritual and Temporal, and Commons in the faid Parliament affembled, and by Authority of the fame, that it be lawful to all Archbifhops and Bifhops, and other Ordinaries having Epifcopal Jurifdiction, to punifh and chaftife Priefts, Clerks and Religious Men, being within the Bounds of their Jurifdiction, as fhall be committed before them, by Excommunication and lawful Proof, requifite by the Law of the Church, of Advowtry, Fornication, Inceft, or any other flefhly Incontinency, by committing them to Ward and Prifon, there to abide for fuch Time as fhall be thought to their Difcretions convenient for the Quality and Quantity of their Trefpafs : And that none of the faid Archbifhops, Bifhops, or Ordinaries aforefaid, be thereof chargeable of, to, or upon, any Action of falfe, or wrongful, Imprifonment ; but that they be utterly difcharged thereof in any of the Cafes aforefaid by Virtue of this Act　5 *Co.* De *Jure Regis Eccl.* 27. *b.* 28. *a.*

4. The Statute 1 *H.* 7. gives Bifhops, &*c.* Power to commit Priefts convicted of any Incontinency to Prifon, and that no Bifhop, &*c.* fhall be chargeable for fo doing in any Action of falfe Imprifonment. 4 *Inft.* 329.

5. **By**

5. By the Act 1 *Eliz.* there is referved to Archbifhops and Bifhops, &c. and other Ordinaries, *having peculiar Ecclefiaftical Jurifdiction,* to inquire, &c. within the Limits of their Jurifdiction, and to punifh the fame in like Manner, as had then before been ufed in like Cafes by the Queen's Ecclefiaftical Laws. *5 Co. De Jure Regis Eccl.* 6. *b.*

6. *Anno* 7 R. 2. *Spencer,* Bifhop of *Norwich,* and others, punifhed for receiving of Money, &c. of the *French* King, which drew them without the King's Licence to yield up Caftles and Forts in *France* committed to their Cuftody, punifhed by Fine and Imprifonment. 3 *Inft* 144.

7. The Ecclefiaftical Court may punifh for foreign Orders *Watfon,* Bifhop of St. *David's* Cafe in *Salk.* and *Keb.* 39.

8. The Spiritual Court may punifh a Bifhop, for any Offence whatfoever, done againft the Duty of his Office, as a Bifhop, and as it relates to that ; for Ecclefiaftical Perfons are fubject to the Canons; and tho' thofe of 1640 have been queftioned, yet thofe of 1603 never were, and as the Clergy are under different Rules and Duties, it is reafonable, if any of them offend, in his Ecclefiaftical Duty, he fhould be punifhed for it in thefe Courts ; and that more fo, if it be for a Matter not punifhable at Law, and it is reafonable and fit that the Clergy fhould have a Power to cleanfe their own Body from fcandalous Members. *Vide Cawdry's* Cafe, 5 *Co* 1 *Part,* 6 and *Watfon,* Bifhop of St. *David's* Cafe, reported in *Salk. And as it is reafonable and fit they fhould thus do, it is unpardonable if they do not ufe this Power to fo good*

good Purpose ; but how much more so must it needs be, if any in Holy Orders, and especially if any Dignitaries, or beneficed Clergy, know, or have any Reason to suspect, within their several Districts, and suffer to continue, without informing their Superiors thereof, any Places of Resort for such wicked Clerks to act their Wickedness in · Sure it must needs redound to the Disparagement of Men of Holy Orders, to the Offence and Endangering the Salvation of the Laity, and to the Dishonour of Religion, to have so necessary a Duty as the Reformation of the wicked Part of the Clergy neglected. What must the World and Enemies to our most happy Establishment in Church say, to see most gross Faults in the Clergy winked at, whilst an inconsiderate Layman, hardly arrived at the State of Man, is to be excommunicated and damned, as far as in them lies, for simple Fornication, bare Solicitation of Chastity, a brawling Word, or a meer Contempt without any previous Crime at all.

9. A Prohibition was moved for to the Spiritual Court *sur* Suggestion, that he was sued for forging Letters of Ordination ; but the Fact was, that they sued him there, in order to Deprivation, *quia mere Laicus*, wherefore Court would not grant the Prohibition. 1 *Sid.* 217. 1 *Lev.* 138. Same Case

10. *Watson*, late Bishop of St *David's*, was taken on an *Excommunicato Capiendo*, and brought into B. R. by *Habeas Corpus*, and pleaded to the Writ, that he was a Lord of Parliament, and moved to be bailed, while the Return was under Consideration, *Powel* said, tho' it had been done, it was in
their

their Discretion, and contrary to the Statute of *Westminster*; and he did not think it Discretion, in such a Plea, which every Body knew to be false, he being deprived by Commissioners of Delegates (of which *Powel* himself was one) on the Appeal. *Holt* Ch. Just. agreed and said, tho' they could not take Judicial Notice of the Frailty of his Plea; yet it should lead their Discretion, so he was not admitted to Bail. *Salk.* 106. *Far.* 56, 117. The short Case was thus, this Bishop was sued at *Lambeth*, at a Court held there, before the Archbishop of *Canterbury* himself in Person, for *Simony*, and several other Offences, and now he moved for a Prohibition, on Suggestion, that he was cited to *Lambeth*, and not to the Arches, and that before the Archbishop himself, and not his Vicar General, and the Proceeding against him was in Order to a Deprivation. *Et per Cur.* 1. the Archbishop hath a Provincial Power over all his Bishops of his Province, and may hold his Court where he pleases, and may convene before himself and sit Judge himself, and even so may any other Bishop; for the Power of a Chancellor or Vicar General is only delegated, in Ease of the Bishop. 2. That the Spiritual Court might punish for any Offence whatsoever done against the Duty of his Office, as Bishop, and as it relates to that; for Ecclesiastical Persons are subject to the Canons. Indeed those Canons of 1640 have been questioned; but there hath never been any Doubt made as to those of 1603; and as the Clergy are under different Rules and Duties, it is reasonable, if any Ecclesiastick offend in
his

his Ecclesiastical Duty, he should be punished for it in those Courts, and that more especially, if it be for a Matter not punishable by Common Law, and it is reasonable and fit the Clergy should have a Power to purge their own Body from scandalous Members. *Cawdry's* Case, *5 Co.* 1 *Part* 6, was remarkable; for he was deprived for Preaching against the Common Prayer; and yet being the first Instance, there was another Punishment appointed by the Statute. *Vide* 31 *E.* 1. *c.* 4. 2 *Inst* 586. The Ecclesiastical Court may Punish an Ecclesiastical Officer, *&c.* for Extortion; they may punish for foreign Orders. *Keb.* 39. They may punish Perjury committed in a Spiritual Court and a Matter Spiritual, as Matrimony, but not in a Temporal Matter, as Contract. 3 *Cro.* 788. Simony is determinable in the Spiritual Courts, but not in *B R.* for it was not supposed at the Common Law; and therefore there was no Damages in a *Quare impedit.* 4 *Co* 49. *b.* 3 *Inst.* 204. Bishop deprived for Dilapidations. A Prohibition being in the Principal Case denied, the Archbishop proceeded to give Sentence of Deprivation; wherefrom the deprived Bishop appealed to the Delegates, suggesting, that by the Common Law the Archbishop alone could not deprive a Bishop; but his Allegations being rejected by the Delegates, he moved *B R* for a Prohibition, suggesting that all Bishops were Barons, and, *inter se,* Peers, *& quod par in parem imperium non habet*, and that, tho' a Bishop may be censured, yet he cannot be deprived by an Archbishop; because of their Temporalties, which are protected by the

Common

Common Law, are concerned; *vide* 14 *E* 3.
c. 3. but it ought to be done by Convocation
(which *Holt* Ch. Juft. called a new Fancy of
Sir *Barth. Shower's*) or by the Eccleſiaſtical
Commiſſion. *Holt* Lord Ch. Juft. and thereſt
held, an Archbiſhop had Power over his Suffragans, and might deprive; that Biſhops are
co-ordinate, or *Pares*, *Jure Divino*, but not
Jure humano, otherwiſe their Inſtitutions
would be to no End: And as to their Peerage,
it was by Reaſon of their Barony: That
ſeveral Abbots ſat in the Houſe of Peers in
former Times, and it might as well be pretended they were exempted; and therefore
could not be deprived: That by the Common Law the Archbiſhop hath a Metropolitical Juriſdiction, and Archbiſhops are over
Biſhops, as Biſhops are over the other Clergy: That his Power was diminiſhed and
uſurped upon by the *Pope*, but reſtored to
it's Extent by the Stat. *H.* 8. That by allowing his Power to viſit all is admitted, for
he who may viſit may deprive, as well as
cenſure, theſe being but ſeveral Degrees of
Puniſhment by the 26 *H* 8. and 1 *Eliz c.* 1.
the only Power given to the Eccleſiaſtical
Commiſſioners was to viſit without one Word
of Deprivation; yet they were always
allowed a Power to deprive; from the Time
of *H* 2. till *H.* 8. there hardly is an Inſtance
of Deprivation of a Biſhop, and it is true,
that before the 17 *Car. cap.* 11 confirmed
by 13 *Car.* 2 which takes away the Court of
High Commiſſion inſtituted by Queen *Eliz.*
the Deprivations that are of Biſhops are by
the Court of Eccleſiaſtical Commiſſioners;
but the Reaſon thereof was only, as that
was
4

was the eafier and fhorter Way; but it cannot be queftioned, that a Bifhop may be deprived for Dilapidations. 2 *H.* 4. 3 *Godb.*
259 3 *Bulft.* 158. 2 *Bulft.* 279 1 *Ro*
Rep 86. *Mo.* 917. And it is as plain, the
Law takes no Notice of any other who can
deprive him. If Iffue be, whether a Parfon
be deprived or not, the Court muft write to
the Bifhop, and if Iffue be, whether a Bifhop be deprived, or not, this Court (*B R*)
muft write to the Archbifhop to certify;
and to what Purpofe fhould the 23 *H* 8 *c.* 9.
againft citing out of the Diocefe fave the
Power of the Archbifhop over his Bifhops if
he had no Power. *Vide* to the fame Purpofe
29 *Car* 2 *c.* 9. 13 *Car* 2 *c* 11. The Prohibition was denied, and ordered the Suggeftion be entered on Record, that the Court
might enter their Reafons of Denial. *Et*
per Holt Lord Ch Juft. if it be infifted upon
a Prohibition cannot be moved for, till the
Suggeftion be entered on a Roll Afterwards
Holt, Ch. Juft. faid, that the Bifhop of
St. David's moved the Houfe of Lords for a
Writ of Error on this Denial, where it was
held, no Writ of Error lay Bifhopricks in
England anciently were donative by the
King, and with good Reafon ; for the King
was Patron; he endowed them with thofe
Lands and Baronies, and then the Ceremony
was Inveftiture *per Annulum & Baculum* , the
one a Simbol of the Spiritual Marriage with
the Church, the other of the Paftoral Care
and Charge over *Chrift's* Flock After many
Scuffles between the Kings of *England* and
the *Pope*, it was at laft fettled in King *John's*
Time. 1 That the King fhould fuffer a free

Election; but that that should be founded on his *Conge d'eslier.* 2. That the Bishop should not have his Temporalties, till he had sworn Allegiance to the King; but that Confirmation and Consecration should belong to the *Pope,* by which Means he gained, in Effect, the Disposal of Bishopricks, till the 25 *H.* 8. took away the Papal Jurisdiction Afterwards by 1 *E.* 6 *c* 1. all Bishopricks were made donative; but the 8 *Eliz.* c.4. hath restored the Stat. 25 *H.* 8 and thereby hath made them elective in *England,* but in *Ireland* they are donative, by Letters Patent at this Day. Note, by the Council of *Lateran* and the Decrees of *Alexander* 3d, no Man was to take a Benefice from Lay Hands. *Per Whitlock Witherington* 69. *b. per Doderidge.* That the Original Letter of Agreement is to be found in *Mathew Paris* and *Eadmerus. Vide* 1 *Jo.* 160. *Lat.* 37, 233. *Palm.* 457. The Manner of making a Bishop, as well, in Case of Translation, as mere Creation, is this: When a Bishop dies, the Dean and Chapter certify the King in Chancery, and pray his License to elect; whereupon the King gives his *Conge d'eslire,* and thereupon they elect, and then certify the King, Archbishop, and Party; and then the King by his Letters Patent gives his Royal Assent, and commands the Archbishop to confirm and consecrate him, whereupon the Archbishop examines the Election and the Party, and then confirms the Election and Consecration himself. This is the Manner of Proceeding in Creations, and it holds also in Cases of Translation, save that he is not consecrated, for a Consecration is like an
Ordi-

Ordination, *Character indelibilis*, and suffices for ever. See 1 *Jones* 100. When a Bishop is translated, the old See is not void by Election, till it be confirmed, for tho' he be elected, the King may not consent, nor the Archbishop confirm, and it is not reasonable he should lose his old, before he gains the new Presentment. 1 *Jo.* 162. And in Case of Creation, not till Consecration. *Per Doderidge, Withrington* 69. *b.* As there are four Things required to compleat a Parson, *sc* Presentation, Admission, Institution, and Induction; so there are four Things analogically requisite in the making a Bishop, Election, which resembles Presentation, Confirmation, which resembles Admission, Consecration, which resembles Institution, and Installation, or *Inthronization*, as in the Case of an Archbishop, which resembles Induction. *Per Doderidge, Witherington* 69 *b.* —— Heretofore when a Bishop was to be translated, there was no Election; for the Rule of the Canon Law was, *Electus non potest eligi*; and because it was pretended he was married to the first Church, which Marriage could not be dissolved, but by the *Pope*, thereupon Petition was made to the *Pope*, and upon his Consent the Party was translated, this was said to be by Postulation *With.* 48. *b. Sed per Cur.* this was an Usurpation and against Law, and restrained by 16 R. 2 & 9 H. 4. *c.* 8. and Translations are ever by Election, and not by Postulation (1 *Jo.* 160.) *Salk* 134, 135, 136, 137. The Bishop, being thus in Custody in *Newgate*, at another Day prayed an *Habeas Corpus*, and was thereupon brought into

Court,

Court, and it appeared by the Return, that the Writ of *Excom Cap.* was not returnable, and the Court held, 1ft, That one taken on a Writ of *Excom Cap* cannot come into this Court, but by *Hab. Cor Farest.* 56, 117 and if he be brought in before the Writ is returnable, he fhall not be allowed to plead to quafh the Writ. 2. The Writ of *Excom Cap.* recites the *Significavit,* which is in Chancery; but the Writ is brought into this Court, and is inrolled here before it goes to the Sheriff, which Inrollment is to inform the Court, that at the Return of the *Excom. Cap.* they may award further Procefs, as the Cafe may require. 3 If by the Recital of the *Significavit* it appears that there was no Caufe for the Writ the Court of King's Bench may quafh it, and the Court of Chancery cannot, tho' the *Significavit* he there. *Salk* 294.

2. *Rules in.*

AS the Clergy are under different Rules and Duties it is reafonable, if any Ecclefiaftick offend in his Ecclefiaftical Duty, he fhould be punifhed for it in thofe Courts, and that more efpecially, if it be for a Matter not punifhable at the Common Law, and it is reafonable and fit the Clergy fhould have a Power to purge their own Body from fcandalous Members. *Watfon* Bifhop of St David's Cafe, *Salk. Rep.*

IX. *Pre-*

IX. *Presentation, Admission, Institution and Induction.*

1. *Presentation.*

1. *The Duties of Ordinaries to Patrons in such Cases.*

1 THE Law presumes, that every Bishop who hath the Cure of Souls of all People within his Diocese, for which he must answer at the last Day at the grand Tribunal (on which Account he ought to watch and keep them against all Hereticks, and Schismaticks, and other Ministers of the Devil) will neither do himself nor assent to any Tort to be done to their Patronages, which is of their terrene, or worldly Possessions, but if the Church is litigious, that he will inform himself of the Truth *de Jure Patronatus*, and so do what is right and just. 6 Co. 49 *b*

2. The Ordinary hath no Interest in the Church, but an Office only, and he ought So that the Ordinary is bound in Duty to take no Sides, but to

B b 3

act uprightly between Party and Party, and to enquire of the Right of Patronage, where the Church is litigious, with all possible Impartiality, and that, as he will answer the same, at the grand Tribunal, at the last Day; and as he is in Duty thus bound to do no Wrong himself; so he is also forbidden to suffer any others to do it. The Ordinary has no real Interest in the Church, but a bare Office only; in the Discharge whereof he ought to be found faithful, always abounding in the Work of the Lord, and not exercising himself, as heretofore, from the Books has often been the Case, in Usurpation on the Prerogative of the Crown, and undoubted Rights and Liberties of the Subject He ought not to take any undue Advantage of any Neglect, neither of the Ignorance of the Laity, nor of his Authority and Power over their Clerks, much less to scheme

and

and contrive to be indifferent to all Patrons, and maintain
how to perpe- no Sides. *Hob.* 319.
trate and effect
such wicked and unjust Usurpations, for which he must one Day give an
Account; but on the contrary, he is bound in Conscience to know where
his Right and Authority is bounded, and not strain either And I can
make no Sort of Doubt, but he is bound also in Conscience to inform Pa
trons and others in their several Rights, where he finds them ignorant of
them, and that Ignorance, which is not to be presumed, may not be his
Plea, neither this Duty shuffled off to his Chancellor, or other Official,
I crave Liberty to insist, as the Acts of such Officials are the Acts of the
Ordinary, so are their Neglects, also the Neglects of the Ordinary And
as to the Plea of Ignorance, St *Germain* is most indisputably right, when
he, speaking of Ecclesiastical Judges, as all Ordinaries are, says, if they
know not what in the particular Case is their Business and Duty to do,
they must inform themselves from those who are learned in such Matters,
and it will not admit of a Question, but it is also their Duty to know
and be acquainted with all such Temporal Laws, as any ways clash or
interfere with the Laws Spiritual, for in such Cases, they are to be ruled
by the Temporal Laws And to say, that they need not give themselves
this Trouble; for that they judge in their Courts by Officials, or Depu
ties, who are Gentlemen learned in the Laws of Holy Church, I say,
thus to say, is saying nothing, or no more, in Effect, than that they
who are to be Guides to others are to be led blindfold by others, and see
with other Men's Eyes, and hear with other Men's Ears, and to judge
and determine with other Men's Hearts, and according to other Men's
Understandings Sure this is pinning of one Man's Faith on another's
Sleeve with a Witness.

2. *By the Patron.*

1. *Though Presentation is a Temporal Act,
and performed by a Layman, and, as such,
may be thought not so proper to this Division,
yet as the same is the first and most essential
Step to the introducing an Ecclesiastical Person into a Spiritual Benefice, or Living, and
as it must precede Admission and Institution,
which are Spiritual Acts done by and to Spiritual Persons, I hold it convenient here to speak
to Presentation, previous to Admission, Institution and Induction.*

2 Pre-

2. Presentation is a Temporal Inheritance, and shall descend, as Lands, and shall be Assets, as Lands. *Doct. & Stud. lib.* 2. *c.* 26, 36

3. Presentation, *Præsentatio*, is used properly for the Act of the Patron presenting his Clerk to the Ordinary to be instituted in a Benefice, where such Patron hath the Patronage, or Gift thereof, or Right of Nomination, or Appointment of a Clerk to fill such a Church; as in *Blo Law Dict.* And if the Bishop refuse to give Institution and Induction upon such Presentation, an Action lies, for the Bishop is but a Kind of an Attorney made by Law to do that for the Patron, which it is supposed he would do for himself, were there not some Let or Hindrance; and therefore the Bishop's Collation by Lapse is in the Patron's Right, and for his Turn, and he shall lay it as his Possession. *Hob.* 154, 155.

4 The Patron's Right was never subject to Churchmen, nor their Officers Ecclesiastical. The Act of the Ordinary himself is but in Execution of the Patron's Right, like as the Admittance of a Copyholder; and the King himself, and much more the Ordinary, is only in Trust to provide for the Patron's Neglect, that is, for him, and to his Use, and not otherwise. The King cannot, much less can the Ordinary, transfer this Trust. The Metropolitan, or immediate Ordinary, whoever of them presents by Lapse, is but *negotiorum Gestor*, or Attorney, appointed by Law, to do that for the Patron, it is to be presumed, were there not some Let, he would do for himself;

and therefore it can be no otherwife than
in his Right, and is rather an Adminiftration than an Intereft. The Patron's Prefentment takes place, even after Lapfe, a-
againft the Ordinary, Metropolitan, or even
the King himfelf, fo it be before Prefentment on Lapfe; and the King can have no
Lapfe, but where the Ordinary might have
had it before. Prefentment is the firft and
moft worthy Act, and the Patronage is both
granted and pleaded by the Name of *libera difpofitio Ecclefiæ*, 14 *E. 4.* 2 & 7 *E* 3 4
and the *Quare impedit* is *quod permittat præ-
fentare ad Ecclefiam, &c. quæ vacat & ad
fuam fpectat Donationem*, and the Acts of
the Ordinary are but in Execution of it
13 *E 4* 3. 43 *E.* 3 11. 11 *H 4* 80. The
Patron's Right and Part to the filling of a
Church, and making an Incumbent, is *prior
tempore & potior jure*, both in Time and
Dignity; and therefore the Ordinary's Act
cannot be good to perfect and finifh that
Act which the Patron ought to begin *Hob
Colt and Glover* v. *Bifhop of Coventry and
Litchfield's Cafe.*

5. If a Man prefent to a Church, he
may revoke it, and prefent another, and if
the Bifhop will inftitute the firft, a *Quare
impedit* lieth againft him. *Palm.* 475.

6. Admiffion, Inftitution, and Induction,
without Prefentation, are merely void. *Cro
Jo.* 255

7. The Patron's Prefentation takes place
againft the Ordinary after Lapfe incurred,
and before Collation. *Hob.* 152 *Vide* 13
E 4 3. 43 *E.* 3. 11. 11 *H.* 4. 80.

8. The

8 The Ordinary's Collation by Lapse, or before the Lapse incurred, though it be wrong, doth not displace the Patronage; but shall be said to be done in Right of the very Patron, being nothing but Institution and Induction, which are his Office, as Ordinary, as well upon Presentation as without, though he doth them out of Season, he hath no Meddling with the Church or the Fruits of it   *Hob.* 316, 317.

3 *By Lapse.*

1. When *Quare impedit* is brought against the Disturber and the Bishop, and six Months pass, the Bishop may not collate by Lapse; the same of the Metropolitan; for he shall never present by Lapse, but where the inferior Ordinary might have had Collation by Lapse, and surceases his Time, and herewith agrees 11 *H.* 4 8   6 *Co* 52. *a.*

2. The Ordinary and King are only in Trust to provide for the Patron's Neglect, and that for him, and to his Use; but this Trust is not transferrable, shall not go to the Executor of Ordinary, but to his Successor. He who presents by Lapse *est negotiorum Gestor*, or Attorney, appointed by Law to do that for the Patron, it is presumed, were there not some Let, he would do for himself; and therefore it is in his Right, and in Pleading the Patron calls it his Presentation. *Hob.* 154, 155.

3 Presentation by Lapse thereof, the Crown maintaining the Right of the true Patron, and does not gain a Patronage against him. *Palm.* 311.

4. If

4 If the Bishop collate to a presentable Living, and his Clerk is inducted, yet it shall not put the rightful Patron out of Possession; for it is no more than a Provision that the Celebration of Divine Service in the mean Time, till the Patron present, be performed; and this belongs to his Office, and therefore does not put the Patron to his *Quare impedit;* but his Presentee ought to be received; and therefore in such Case no Plenarty by Collation could be pleaded against the Patron; for no Plenarty is available in Law against him who hath Right, but only Plenarty by Presentation, and with this agree the Words of the Statute *W. 2. c. 5. Cum aliquis, &c. præsentaverit ad aliquam Ecclesiam;* but forasmuch as Bishops will admit and institute Presentees, without informing themselves (as they ought) of the Right of him who presents, many Patrons have lost their Presentments, without any Regard to Infancy, Coverture, &c. wherefore the Statute *W. 2. c 5* was made, giving Remedy. *6 Co. 50. a.* See much excellent Matter to this Purpose.

5. Institution and Induction are merely void against the lawful Patron. See Case *Archbishop Armagh* v. *Attorney General,* on Error, 21 *April* 1730, before the House of Lords.

6. The King's Turn which accrued to him by his promoting the Incumbent, is satisfied by another's dying in Possession; for after he comes too late; else the Executor of such Incumbent, who so held, tho' by Mistake, yet without Intention of Wrong, might be accountable. See Case *Archbishop Armagh*

Armagh and Dr. *Whaley* v. *Le Roy*, in the
Houfe of Lords, *Feb.* 1728, and *April* 1730.

7. *Prefentation is the firft and moft worthy
Act*, and the Acts of the Ordinary are but
in Execution of it, and therefore the Ordinary's Act cannot perfect and finifh that
which the Patron ought to begin. *And fo it
is, as I take it, that Induction and Inftitution,
without Prefentation, are, not only, mere Nullities and void, but injurious and unjuft Acts;
for Collation without Title does not make an
Ufurpation.*

4 *Where the Right to be tried.*

1. If the Parfon of *B* take a fecond Benefice, *deins le Stat. fans* Difpenfation, whereby the firft Benefice is void, which is of the
King's Patronage and after *ad uberiorem Can-
telam & ad tollendum omne dubium*, he ob-
taineth a new Prefentation from the King;
and thereupon requires the Bifhop to admit
and fuperinftitute him, the Bifhop take Time
to advife, and in the mean Time the King
prefents another, who is inftituted and inducted, and then the firft Parfon fues the
Bifhop for Injuftice in the Spiritual Court,
a Prohibition fhall be granted; for the Spiritual Court may not examine the Right of
Prefentation. *M.* 3 *Ja. B. R. William's*
Cafe, *Rol Abr. Prohibition*, 293. *Cafe* 5.

2 A Clergyman, fuing for a Right by
Prefentation, needs only to prove he is Incumbent. See Cafe *Archbifhop of Armagh
and Dr. Whaley* againft *Attorney General*, 21
April 1730, in the Houfe of Lords. Cafes
cited 6 *Co.* 29. 2 *Cro.* 252, and *Hob* 302. *pro.*
2. *Ad-*

2. *Admission.*

1 *What.*

ADmiffion. In Propriety of Speech, Admiffion is, when the Bifhop, upon Examination, admitteth him to be able, and faith, *admitto te habilem* ; but fometimes in a more large Senfe, *admiffus* doth include *inftitutus* alfo. *Cujus præfentatus fit admiffus, i. e. inftitutus.* Co. Lit. 344. a. Vide 5 Co. De Jure Regis Eccl. 9.

2. *Who to be admitted.*

1. Forafmuch as the antient Fathers of the Church, led by the Examples of the Apoftles, appointed Prayers and Fafts to be ufed at the folemn ordering of Minifters, and to that Purpofe allotted certain Times, in which only Sacred Orders might be given or conferred, we, following their Holy and Religious Examples, do conftitute and decree, that no Deacons or Minifters be made or ordained, but only upon the *Sundays* following *Jejunia quatuor temporum,* commonly called *Ember-Weeks,* appointed in antient Time for Prayer and Fafting, purpofely for this Caufe at their firft Inftitution, and fo continued at this Day in the Church of *England :* And that this be done in the Cathedral or Parifh Church where the Bifhop refideth, and in the Time of Divine Service, in the Prefence not only of the Arch-deacon, but of the Dean and two

Prefen-

Prebendaries, at the least, or if there shall happen to be any lawful Cause to be let, or hindred, in the Presence of four other grave Persons, being Masters of Arts, at the least, and allowed for publick Preachers. *Can* 31. And none to be ordained both Deacon and Minister the same Day. *Can.* 32

2. No Bishop shall ordain any, but of his own Diocese, unless he be of one of the Universities of this Realm, or bring Letters dimissary from the Bishop of whose Diocese he is, and desiring to be a Deacon is twenty-three Years old, and to be a Priest twenty-four Years complete, and hath taken some Degree in either of the Universities, or at least except he be able to yield an Account of his Faith in *Latin*, according to the Articles of Religion approved in the Synod of the Bishops, &c. *Anno Dom* 1562, and to confirm the same by sufficient Testimonies out of the Holy Scriptures; and except moreover he shall exhibit Letters Testimonial of his good Life and Conversation under the Seal of some College of one of the Universities of this Realm, where before he remained, or of three or more grave Ministers, together with the Subscription and Testimony of other credible Persons, who have known his Life and Behaviour by the Space of three Years next before. *Can.* 34.

3 Upon Consideration had of the Statutes 3 R 2. 7 H 4 1 H. 5. *Rot Pail* 6 H. 4. *Nu.* 48. & 4 H 6. *Nu.* 29 if an Alien or Stranger born be presented to a Benefice, the Bishop ought not to admit him, but may lawfully refuse him. 4 *Inst* 338 So a Bastard

Baſtard cannot be admitted *ſans* Diſpenſation. Vide poſt *Refuſal of Clerks.*

3. *Inſtitution.*

1. *What it is, and its Effect.*

1. INſtitution is, when the Biſhop ſaith to the Clerk, *inſtituo te Rectorem talis Ecclesiæ cum cura animarum, & accipe Curam tuam & meam.* Co. Lit. 344. a. 5 Co. De Ju. Regis Eccl. 9.

2 By Inſtitution, *Ecclesia plena & conſulta exiſtit,* againſt all Perſons, except the King; for when the Ordinary, on Examination, admits him able, then he inſtitutes him, and ſaith, *inſtituo te ad tale Beneficium, & habere Curam Animarum* of ſuch a Pariſh, *& accipe Curam tuam & meam.* Vide 3 H. 6. 13. 4 Co. 79. a Dy. 346

3. The Biſhop to inſtitute in twenty-eight Days. *Can.* 95.

4. No Biſhop ſhall inſtitute any to a Benefice who hath been ordained by any Biſhop, except he firſt ſhew him his Letters of Ordination, and bring him a ſufficient Teſtimonial of his former good Life and Behaviour, if the Biſhop ſhall require it, and ſhall appear, upon due Examination, to be worthy of the Miniſtry. *Can.* 39.

2. *Where Admiſſion and Inſtitution may be refuſed.*

The Biſhop refuſed one preſented to him for Inſtitution and Induction, becauſe he was an Haunter of Taverns, and a Player at

unlawful

unlawful Games, *ob quod & diversa alia Crimina* he is *Criminosus & non idoneus*, the particular Causes were adjudged not sufficient, for they were not *Mala in se*, but *Mala prohibita*, & *ob quod & diversa alia Crimina*, he was *Criminosus & non idoneus* are too general and uncertain. *5 Co. 58. a. Dy. 254. b. Hob. 296 2 Rol. Abr. 355. (40, 45.)*

4. Induction.

I. What, how performed, and its Effect.

1 *General.*

1. THO' Induction be a Matter of *Temporal Cognizance*, and therefore may be thought not to be so properly introduced here, yet as it cannot be properly dealt with, but together with Presentation, Admission and Institution, I have adventured to consider something of it in this Place, and I hope, not with the greatest Impropriety.

2 Induction, *Inductio*, or Leading into, is a giving an Incumbent Livery and Seisin, as it were, of his Church, by leading him into it, and delivering him the Keys of it, by the Arch-deacon, or Bishop's Deputy, and by his ringing one of the Bells. *Blo. Law Dict*

3. Induction is performed by Delivery of the Ring, or Bell-Rope, to the new instituted Clerk, that he may toll the Bell, &c. to shew he hath taken Possession, &c. and though Institution makes the Parson complete Clerk as to the Cure of Souls; yet, as to the Temporalties, he hath nothing till Induction,

Induction, and so hath no Remedy for any Matter due to his Church till then, &c. and this is triable by Jury, and not by the Ordinary, &c.

4. As to the Temporalties of an Ecclesiastical Benefice, as the Glebe, &c the Parson hath not the Freehold thereof till Induction. *Vide Hare* and *Bulkley's* Case, *Plow. Com.* 528. 4 *Co* 79. *Dy.* 346.

5. Induction is a Thing notorious, and shall not be tried by the Ordinary, &c. 6 Co. 49.

6. The Archdeacon inducts on the Bishop's Mandate, but that, *de communi jure.* Vent 319.

7 Induction is a Ministerial Act *in jure Episcopi*, and like a Letter of Attorney to deliver Seisin, which cannot be executed but in the Life of him who made it. 1 *Vent.* 320. Note, *There is a* Quære *in our Reporter, whether this Judgment was not after reversed in the Exchequer Chamber, as is said in Sir* William Jones's Rep 78, 79

2. *Where triable.*

1 If *A.* be instituted and inducted to a Church, and then is sued in the High Commission Court, for that before *B* was instituted and inducted, and that after he *A.* was superinstituted and inducted, and is to be punished, as an Intruder. *A.* answers, that he knows not that *B* was instituted and inducted before him, by which he excuses himself of any Crime, a Prohibition shall go, for that they shall not try which of them hath the better Right, after Institution

4

tion and Induction, but it shall be tried at Law, &c. *Mich* 16 *Car.* B. R. *Maddox* &c *Corval, Rol Abr. Prohibition* 292, 293. M 4

2 If a Man, presented to the Bishop, on Refusal, sue to the Metropolitan who, after Monition, Citation and Default of the Bishop, admits and institutes the Incumbent, whereupon he is also inducted, and after the Bishop sues *for* double Quarrel, appealing from the said Sentence to the Delegates to disannull the said Admission and Institution, a Prohibition shall be granted; for that, after Induction, the Admission and Institution may not be drawn in Question in the Spiritual Court. *Mich* 12 *Jac* Sir *Timothy Hutton* and *The Bishop* of *Chester*, per *Cur*. *Rol. Abr. Prohibition* 393 *Ca* 10.

3. If one, pending a *Quare impedit* libel in the Spiritual Court to avoid the Institution of the Clerk of the same Church, after he is inducted, a Prohibition shall go, else he would prevent the *Quare impedit*. *Mich* 14 *Jac Fisher* & *Chamberlene, Rol Abr. Prohibition* 294. *Ca* 12. So it shall be, if after Induction, where there is no *Quare impedit* pending, if the Suit be to avoid Institution, a Prohibition shall be granted, because, by the Induction, it is become Temporal, which draws the Spiritual to it, for if he should avoid the Institution, he would necessarily avoid the Induction *Ca.* 13

4 If I present my Clerk and he is admitted and instituted, and, before Induction, a Caveat is entered by a Stranger into the Spiritual Court, that he may not be inducted, and thereupon an Inhibition is there granted to the Archdeacon, that he do not induct

him; in this Case, a Prohibition shall be granted; because that being instituted, he hath an Inception to the Lay Fee, and the Church is full against all *præter le Roy*, and if this should be suffered, all Trials by *Quare impedit* should be ousted. *Hil* 14 *Jac* B R Prohibition granted. *Rol Abr.* 294 Ca 14

5. Induction is a Temporal Act, and triable by the Temporal Law, and is not to be avoided, but by a Suit of *Quare impedit*, or the like, at the Common Law, and not to be undermined by alledging Insufficiency in the Institution in the Ecclesiastical Court, for that Matter may come in Question upon the Trial of the Induction at Common Law, which will not be good, if the Institution was defective, whereupon it was granted, but if this Course might be admitted, they might avoid all Plenarties in the Ecclesiastical Courts, or question them, at least upon Quarrel to the Institution. *Hob* 15

3 *Where delayed.*

If a Patron present *A.* his Clerk, to his Church, and the Bishop, by Examination, delay him above two Months, contrary to the last Canons, whereupon *A* fearing lest a Lapse should incur, sues a *duplex Querela* in the Court of Audience, by which the Bishop is inhibited to present, and after the six Months, the Court of Audience gives Judgment for him, and after the Bishop, notwithstanding collates, and upon this Matter to the Court of King's Bench prays a Prohibition to the Court of Audience, the Prohibition shall be granted, for now, if it
be

be a Lapfe, the Ecclefiaftical Law may not remove him, the Church being full, and if the Bifhop be a Difturber, then his Clerk fhall be removed, notwithftanding the Plenarty for fix Months before the Writ purchafed, for Collation, *fans* Title, does not make an Ufurpation; and therefore, *quacunque via data*, it does not belong to the Ecclefiaftical Law to proceed in the *duplex querela Tr. 3 Jac B R inter Palmer & Smith* Prohibition granted, and Confultation denied *Rol Abr. Prohibition* 294. *Cafe* 16

5. *General to Admiffion, Inftitution and Induction.*

1 *Who may be a Prieft or Deacon, when, where, by whom, and before whom to be ordered, or ordained*

VIDE the Canons to thefe Purpofes, & *poftea*, for what may be refufed, and before under the Divifion *Admiffion.*

2 *The Office of Bifhops in thefe Cafes* Vide ante *Prefentation, the Duty of Bifhops to Patrons in fuch Cafes*

1 If any Bifhops fhall admit any Perfon into the Miniftry that hath none of the Titles in the faid Canon mentioned, he (*fuch Bifhop*) fhall keep and maintain him with all Things neceffary, till he do prefer him to fome Ecclefiaftical Living; and if the faid Bifhop fhall refufe fo to do he fhall be fufpended by the Archbifhop, being affifted by

another

another Bishop, from giving of Orders, by the Space of a Year. *Can.* 33.

2 The Bishop is diligently to examine every Candidate for Orders, in the Presence of those Ministers who shall assist him at the Imposition of Hands; and if he have any lawful Impediment, he is to cause such Ministers carefully to examine every such Person, so to be ordered, provided they, who assist the Bishop in examining and ordering, be of his Cathedral, if conveniently may be had, else other sufficient Proctors of his Diocese, to the Number of three at least, and if any Bishop, or Suffragan, shall admit any to sacred Orders, who is not so qualified and examined, the Archbishop of his Province having Notice thereof, and being assisted therein by one Bishop, shall suspend the said Bishop, or Suffragan, so offending from making either Deacon, or Priest, for the Space of two Years *Can* 35. *I do not doubt a religious Observance is paid to this Canon, and that there are no private Ordinations, &c contrary to or inconsistent with it*

3 *Where to be tried*

1. The Ecclesiastical Courts may try Institution, but the Temporal Courts must try Induction *Alisb 14 Fa Lisb* and *Cl bertone, Ro Abr Prohibition, Jo* 314, *H..* (E) *Cafe* 2

2 In a *Quare Impedit,* Admission and Institution shall be tried by Certificate of the Ordinary, but Induction shall be tried *per pais* Bro Abr Trials, 109, but if the Bishop be Party, Admission and Institution are triable

triable by the Metropolitan; but Induction and Installation shall be tried *per pais* Bro. Abr Trials, 117

3. Issue upon an Induction was tried *per pais*, and not by the Bishop *Bro Abr Quare impedit*, 54. *Trials*, 28

4 In *Quare Impedit*, if the Issue be upon the Admission, Institution and Induction, it shall be tried *per pais, ratione de l' Induction*, which is by the Arch-deacon, *eadem Lex* of Institution and Installation, for Installation is also by the Archdeacon, which lies in the Notice of the Country, but where Issue is upon the Admission and Institution only, it shall be tried by the Bishop, and because the Bishop was Party, it was tried by the Metropolitan, and a Writ made to him accordingly to certify the King's Court. *Bro. Abr Trials*, 44. *Vide etiam* 43

5 Where has been Institution and Induction, if Suit be to avoid Institution, a Prohibition shall be granted; because by the Induction it is become Temporal, which draws the Spiritual to it, for if he should avoid Institution, he would necessarily avoid the Induction. *Rol Abr. Prohibition, Case* 13

6 If a Man be admitted, instituted and inducted to a Church, and after is sued in the Spiritual Court for the Institution, supposing it was not good, for that by the Induction the Parson hath the Church, as a Lay Fee; and forasmuch as the Common Law shall be prefer'd before the Spiritual Law, it draws the Trial of all to it, else *Quare impedits* should be overthrown; for they, by this Means, might try all Rights of Patronage in the Spiritual Court. *Rol. Abr.*

Abr. Prohibition, fo. 3 *Trin* 15 *Ja* B R. *enter Hitchen* and *Glover, refolve per tout le Cure. Vide Rol. Abr Prohilition, fo* 4

7 If a Man be inftituted and inducted, and after is deprived, for that he was inftituted contrary to, and againft, the Courfe of the Ecclefiaftical Law, this Sentence of Deprivation is void, becaufe it is become a Lay Fee by the Induction. *Rol Abr. Prohibition, fo.* 5. *Hutchin* and *Glover, Trin.* 15 *Ja* B. R.

8. Induction is but a Formality, and therefore not to be ftrictly examined. *Vent.* 320.

9 Sir *Timotby Hutton* brought *Quare impedit* before the Judges of *Lancafter,* where the Truth of the Cafe was, he had prefented *Boothe,* his Clerk, to the Bifhop of *Chefter,* being O dinary, who refufed him, whereupon he complained to the Archbifhop of *York,* who fent his Monition to receive the Clerk within Time, or elfe to appear before him and anfwer, who doing neither, the Archbifhop received the Clerk, and inftituted him, and by his Warrant he was alfo inducted. Now the Bifhop and one *King,* a great Scholar, prefented by the King fued in the Delegates on Suppofition the Inftitution by the Archbifhop was void, and, by Confequence, meant to avoid the Induction too, as being *fans* Warrant, whereof the Reafon was, becaufe the Archbifhop did inftitute, &c here at *London,* being up in Parliament Time, and they pretended, thefe Acts of his being then out of the Diocefe were Nullities, whereupon Serjeant *Hutton* prayed a Prohibition, and
this

this Court was of Opinion, that this Suit ought to be prohibited, for fince, by Induction, which is a Temporal Act, and triable by Temporal Law, the Church is full, it is not to be avoided, but by a Suit of *Quare impedit*, or the like, at the Common Law, and not to be undermined by alledging Infufficiency in the Inftitution, in the Court Ecclefiaftical, for that may come in Queftion, upon the Trial of the Induction at Common Law, which will not be good, if the Inftitution was not good, whereupon it was granted; but if this Courfe might be allowed, they might avoid all Plenarties in the Ecclefiaftical Court, or queftion them, at leaft, upon Quarrel to the Inftitution. But it was faid to Serjeant *Hutton*, that he did not pray his Prohibition in Refpect of his *Quare impedit* hanging, becaufe, of his own fhewing, the *Quare impedit* muft abate, for the Church is full of his Prefentation, but he muft make his Surmife, that the Church being full (*ut fupra*) that they feek (*ut fupra*) without Mention of the *Quare impedit*, and though this Advowfon and Church were in *Lancaflire*, and the *Quare impedit* ought there to be brought, and not here, and there alfo a Prohibition might be had, yet the Opinion was, that Prohibition might be granted alfo in this Court; becaufe the Title of the Advowfon is not hereby queftioned; but the Intrufion *fur le* Common Law (whereof this Court hath general Care) is to be reftrained: And the Prothonotaries faid, that they have commonly Prohibitions into *Chefter* upon it. This Act of the Court was complained of to the King, and he signified his Pleasure, both by Sir *Thomas Lake*, and the Archbishop of *Canterbury*, that he would have a Confultation granted, but we answered his Majesty by Letter, that we could not do it by Law; and it was left, and so it stood. *Hob* 15, 16.

10 Plenarty, or not, of a Church shall be tried by the Bishop, if the Plenarty was by Institution, for that Institution is a Spiritual Act; but in Case where there is no Plenarty, till Induction, then Full, or not, shall be tried *per pais*; for Induction is a Thing notorious, and shall not be tried by the Bishop *Vide* 22 *H* 6 27, *&c* And yet in some Cases a Jury shall inquire of Plenarty, as in the same Case; and in all *Quare impedits* one of the three Points inquirable is, whether the Church be full or not. 6 *Co* 49. *a.*

X. *Ability, and Nonability, of Clerks.*

1. *Where to be tried.*

1 WHERE the Ordinary refufeth the Clerk for Nonability, which is put in Issue in *Quare timped t*, and the Ordinary is Party, it shall not be tried by him, because a Party, but by the Metropolitan; if the Clerk be alive, but if he be dead, then it shall be tried *per pais* Bro. Abr Trials, 52

2 In *Quare impedit*, able, or not able, is triable by the Certificate of the Guardian
of

of the Spiritualties of the Archbishoprick ;
but if the Clerk be dead, it shall be tried
per patriam 2 Bro Abr 301 8.

3 *Quare Impedit* against the Bishop, who
saith that he refused the Clerk for Disabi-
lity. the Plaintiff saith he was able, it shall
be tried *per pais*, for the Clerk is dead *Bro
Abr Tisne, 61*

4. Ability of Clerk, where he is dead,
is to be tried *per pais*. Skin. 468

XI. *Refusal of Clerks.*

1. *Wherefore may be.*

1. BAstard, Villeinage, *Criminofus*, within
Age, & *non* able, are good Causes
to refuse a Presentee. *Bro Abr Quare Impedit, 119, 120*

2 If the Presentee was perjured, it was
good Cause of Refusal, tho' no Conviction;
so if he hath killed a Man. 2 Rol Abr.
Presentment, Refusal, Z

XII. *Ordinaries Licences.*

1. *Whether absolutely and essentially necessary.*

1. *Where such Clerk hath been licensed before.*

1. DOCTOR Watson, *in his* Clergyman's Law, *himself allows, that where
one licensed before takes Ecclesiastical Preferment*

ment in another Diocese, it is not necessary to take another Licence from the Ordinary, in whose Diocese the second Living is Fol 147, 174. And so it is of a Donative, which indeed is a much stronger Case, as the Bishop has nothing to do with it, and very little, or rather nothing with the Clerk See 1 Mod. 90. 3 Salk 141.

2. Mich. 3 Geo. 2 in Scacc', Price v Piat & al'.

In this Case the Lord Chief Baron said, that every Curate must take a Licence unless Fellows of Colleges, &c And Carter Baron said, that no Curate is obliged to take a new Licence upon a bare Translation of a Bishop; and that though this is frequently done, it has been complained of in Parliament.

XIII. *The Subscription of Clerks.*

1. THERE are several Statutes directing Subscription to the Articles of the Church after having read them, and also directing what Oaths, and in what Manner, Time, and Places to be taken, but these are Matters so well known, that I need not take much Notice of them in this Place, and therefore the following Cases shall suffice

No Person shall hereafter be received into the Ministry, nor, either by Institution or Collation, be admitted to any Ecclesiastical Living, nor suffered to preach, to catechise, or to be a Lecturer, or Reader of Divinity,

2. A Subscription by a Clerk (as to the *Canons and Articles of the Church*) to all that the Laws and Statutes of the Realm require, is not sufficient, because he is to subscribe

subscribe generally, and not with any Reservation By Lord Chancellor, the two in either Uni-
Chief Justices, and Chief Baron. *Moor*, versity, or in
Jo 783 dral or Colle-
giate Church,
City, or Market-Town, Parish Church, Chapel, or in any other Place
within this Realm, except he be licensed either by the Archbishop, or by
the Bishop of the Diocese, where he is to be placed, under their Hands
and Seals, or by one of the two Universities, under their Seal likewise,
and except he shall first subscribe to the three Articles (*contained in this
Canon*) 1 The King's Supremacy, and that no foreign Prince, Person, Prelate, State or Potentate, shall, or ought to, have any Jurisdiction,
Power, Superiority, Preheminence, or Authority Ecclesiastical or Spiritual
within his Majesty's Realms, Dominions and Country. 2dly, That the
Book of Common Prayer, &c containeth in it nothing contrary to the
Word of God, and that it may lawfully be used, and that he himself
will use the Form in the said Book prescribed in publick Prayer and
Administration of the Sacraments, and none other 3dly, That he al-
loweth the Book of the Articles of Religion, agreed upon by the Archbishops, &c (*Canon* 1562) besides the Ratification to be agreeable to
the Word of God And such Person is to subscribe in the precise Form
in this Canon prescribed And if any Bishop shall ordain, admit, or license any as is aforesaid, except he first have subscribed, as aforesaid,
shall be suspended from giving Orders and Licences to preach for the
Space of twelve Months, but if either of the Universities shall offend
therein, they are left to the Danger of the Law, and his Majesty's Censure *Can* 36, 37

If any Minister having subscribed, as aforesaid, shall omit to use the
Form, &c prescribed in the said Book, let him be suspended, and if,
after a Month, he do not reform and submit himself, let him be excommunicated, and then, if he shall not submit himself within the Space of
another Month, let him be deposed from the Ministry *Can* 38. *And
if a Clergyman is thus to be punished for an Omission, how ought he to be
punished for broaching any Antichristian, or Heretical, Notions contrary to
the Principles he has avowed and sworn in most solemn Manner, with all
his might to defend and maintain, or for a vicious Life to the Scandal of
Religion, and the Loss of Souls ; for the Clergy, I hold, must be either the
best, or worst of Men, and that there is scarce any Indifferency in the
Case, as to others, though there may comparatively amongst themselves be
some*

XIV. *When*

XIV. *When one may be said to be Compleat Incumbent.*

1. *General.*

VIDE *Dispensations, in what Time to be,* Case 1.

2. *What Interest he hath in his Benefice.*

1 ECclesiastical Offices, as Bishopricks, Deaneries, Rectories, which are instituted for the Government of Holy Church, should continue in Course of perpetual Succession, *usque ad finem Seculi*, and therefore no Man may take such Office in his natural Capacity; but every such Ecclesiastical Officer is a Body Politick *ipso facto*, as a Parson is incorporate by the Common Law. 40 *E*. 3. 27. So Bishops, Deans, &c have their Offices in Politick Capacity, and in Course of Succession. *Dav* 45 *b*.

2 Whenever the King gives a Bishoprick in *Ireland*, where all Bishopricks are given and granted by the King's Letters Patent, by the *Stat.* 2 *Eliz* c. 14 there needs no Limitation of Estate in the Donation, no more than in the Investiture *per annulum & baculum*, made by the antient Kings of *England* before the *Norman* Conquest, and after, for King *John* was the first King, who, by his Charter dated 15th *January Anno* 16th of his Reign, granted Power and Liberty to all Churches, Cathedral and Conventual, in *England* to make Canonical Election of
their

their Prelates, *petita prius*, of him, his Heirs and Succeffors, *Licentia eligendi, &c.* which Charter is found in *Mat Paris Hift. Mag Fo.* 253. *Dav 46 a.*

3 A Bifhop, a Dean, *&c* may not have an Eftate at Will for Years, or Life, or Intail, in his Bifhoprick, or Deanary ; but they have Eftates in Fee in their Hands; but not to them, and their Heirs, but only to them and their Succeffors. *Davis* 45. *b.*

4 In the Grant of a Deanary made by the King, there needs no Limitation of Eftate, or if a particular Eftate be limited, as for Life, or Years, *&c* it fhould be repugnant and contradictory to the Grant; for the Dean may not take the Deanary, other than to him, and his Succeffors, which is an Eftate in Fee, and therefore thefe Sorts of Limitations are void. *Dav* 46. *a.*

5 Alfo a Deanary, which is Donative, may not be granted for Years, or at Will, by Reafon of a very great Inconvenience, which would follow, for that the Freehold of the Lands, which the Dean hath in Right of his Deanary, fhould be, by this Means, in perpetual Abeyance, which Inconvenience the Law will not endure. *Dav.* 46. *a.*

6. Another Reafon why a Deanary, or Bifhoprick may not be granted *pur Vie tantumis*, on Account of another Inconvenience ; for a Dean, or a Bifhop may have a Writ of Right. *Lit.* 143. *b.* which Writ may not be brought by him, who hath no more than a bare Eftate for Life, and by that Means the Church fhould be difinherited, and that without Remedy, which the Law will not fuffer *Da·. 46 a.*

7 Tho';

7 Tho', upon Presentation, Institution, and Induction, of a Parson to a Rectory, there is no Limitation what Estate the Parson shall have in the Rectory; yet the Law creates his Estate before, and gives to him a Fee *in Jure Ecclesiæ.* Dav. 46. a.

XV. *How Clerks are privileged.*

1. HOLY Church shall enjoy her Liberties in Quietness. Stat. 14 *E.* 3. *cap* 1

2 Priests not to be arrested doing divine Service. Stat 50 *E.* 3 5 *Stat* 1 *R.* 2. 15

3. Doctor *Lee,* having Lands within the Level, was made an Expenditor by the Commissioners of Sewers; whereupon he prayed his Writ of Privilege in this Court, and it was granted; for the Register is *Vir militans Deo, non implicetur secularibus negotiis,* and the antient Law is, *quod Clerici non ponantur in Officio.* F N. B. Clergymen are not to serve in the Wars. 1 *Vent.* 105 Dr *Lee's* Case. 1 *Mod.* 282. S. C. *Vide* 1-*Lev* 303. 2 *Keb.* 693.

XVI. *How restrained.*

1. *From Secular Concerns.*

1 IT is enacted, that no Spiritual Person, Secular, or Regular, beneficed with Cure, by Authority of any License, Dispensation, or otherwise, shall take any particular Stipend, or Salary to sing for any Soul; nor have or occupy by himself, or

I   any

any other to his Use, any Parsonage, or Vicarage in farm, nor take any Profit, or Rent thereof, on Forfeiture of forty Shillings a Week, *prout in le Stat*   Provided that no Deanary, Archdeaconry, Chancellorship, Treasurership, Chantership, or Prebendary, in any Cathedral, or Collegiate Church; nor Parsonage that hath a Vicar endowed, nor any Benefice perpetual appropriate, be taken as comprehended under the Name of Benefice with Cure in any Article in the said Act   Stat 21 *H* 8 *cap.* 13

2 No such Spiritual Person of what Estate, Degree, or Condition, shall have, use, or keep by him, or themselves, or to their Use, or Commodity, any Tan-House or Brew-House (other than for their Families) on Pain of Ten Pounds a Month, *prout in le dict. Stat.* save as in the said Statute is provided. *Stat.* 21 *H.* 8 *cap.* 13.

3 Ecclesiasticks are prohibited to traffick, in any Places, in any Cattle, Corn, Lead, Tin, Hides, Leather, Tallow, Fish, Wool, Wood, or any Manner of Victual, or Merchandize, on Forfeiture of treble Value, and such Bargain to be void, save as in the said Act is excepted.   Stat. 21 *H.* 8. *cap.* 13.

4. No Spiritual Person, Secular, or Regular, shall take to Farm, to himself, or to his Use, by any Manner of Means, any Manors, Lands, Tenements, or other Hereditaments, for Life, Years, or at Will, on Pain of Forfeiture of Ten Pounds for every Month, one Half to the King, the other to every such Person, as will sue for the same, as in the Act is mentioned, and such Leases to be void   21 *H* 8. *cap* 13   *Vide* 27 *H* 8. *sc* 21,

fo. 21, 23. alfo Serjeant *Exer's* Read. upon the two firft Branches in *Gray's Inn Hell,* Lent Anno 1637 *Dy* 27, 28, 358.

5. *Scot* brought Debt againft *Laws* Clerk *fur le Stat.* 21 *H* 8. the Writ was *Præcipe Will'o* Laws *quod reddat nolis & Job'i Scot, qui tam pro nobis, quam pio fe ipfo fequitur,* 110*l quas nobis & præfat. Job'i debet, &c.* and declares for taking to Farm fix Acres of Land, and holding the fame fix Months, *per quod Actio, &c.* for 50 *l.* The Defendant pleadeth, *quod ipfe non debet præfato Job'i qui tam, &c præditt.* 110 *l nec aliquem inde Denarium in formâ quâ, &c* whereupon Iffue, and the Jury found, that the Defendant did owe 30 *l.* and for the reft, *quod non debet. Henden* in Arreft of Judgment, took two Exceptions ; 1 That the Verdict expreffeth not for which Farm, nor for which of the Months the 30 *l.* was due. This Exception was not regarded by the Court, becaufe the Demand and Iffue was for 110 *l* in general, tho' it had been more formal to have diftinguifhed it better. 2. Exception was, that the Defendant had not anfwered the Writ and Declaration ; for the Plea ought to have been, as the Demand is, *quod ipfe non debet ditto Domino Regi & præfeto Job'i qui tam, &c.* which the Court regarded the rather, becaufe the Statute of *Jeofailes* excepts penal Statutes *Hob* 327, 328

6 *Una Ecclefa unius Rectoris,* as one Wife to one Husband , that the Parfon fhould not farm, graze, *&c.* nor mingle himfelf with fecular Affairs, that might withdraw his Mind *Hob* 157

I

XVII. *Residence.*

1 REsidence and Non-residence, what is, & econ. *Ma* 540. 6 *Co* 21. *b.*

2 A Parson or Vicar is called Incumbent, because he is supposed to be resident, and if he is disturbed in his Office, for his Remedy, *vide Stat* 2 & 3 *E* 6. *c* 1. also Stat. 1 *W & M sess* 1 *cap* 18.

3 By Stat 21 *H.* 8. *c* 13. None is to procure a License for Non-residence, contrary to the Statute, under the Penalty of 20 *l.* for every Time they put such License in Execution.

4 Every Spiritual Person promoted to any Archdeaconry, Deanary, or Dignity, in any Monastry, or Cathedral Church, or other Church Conventual, or Collegiate, or being beneficed with any Parsonage, or Vicarage, shall be personally resident and abide in, at, and upon, his said Dignity, Prebend, or Benefice, or at one of them, at the least; and in Case any such Person keep not Residence at one of his said Dignities, Prebends, or Benefices, &c. but absent himself wilfully by the Space of one Month together, or for two Months, to be accounted at several Times, in any one Year, and make his Residence and Abiding in any other Places by such Time, that then he shall forfeit, for every such Default 10 *l.* Sterling, save such as in the said Act are exempted from Residence. Stat. 21 *H* 8 *cap.* 13

5 A Parson shall be intended by the Law resident upon his Benefice for the Cure of

the Souls he hath there; for a Parson who hath Cure of Souls, and is Non-resident, *non est Dispensator, sed Dissipator, non Speculator, sed Speculator;* and therefore Non-residence is not to be presumed, *nor countenanced.* 11 Co. 70 b.

6. On special Verdict, it was resolved, that a Parson ought to reside upon his Rectory, upon the Parsonage House, and not in another, tho' within the same Parish; for the Statute doth not only intend for serving the Cure and Hospitality; but also for the Maintenance of the House for Habitation of the Parson, and that, not only for himself, but for his Successors, that they also might maintain Hospitality there · Yet lawful Imprisonment, or Want of a Parsonage House, are good Excuses for Non-residence, for *Impotentia excusat Legem,* and these Cases are excepted out of the Statute by Construction of Law Sickness also, without Fraud, a good Cause; so if removed, by Advice, for better Air, and for the Recovery of his Health 6. Co. 21. b. Mo 540.

7. No Construction can be too liberal to make Parsons reside, and take Care of their Parishes, *&c Gilb.* 230. *Veu le Livre*

XVIII.

XVIII. *How an Incumbent may vacate his Ecclesiastical Benefices.*

1. *By Acceptance of another incompatible without Dispensation,* &c.

1. *General.*

1 A Cardinalship at *Rome* made a Parsonage at *Durham* void. *Palm* 459.

2 If a Bishop in *England* be made a Cardinal, the Bishoprick becomes void, and the King shall name the Successor; because the Bishoprick is of his Patronage. 4 *Inst* 357. If an Incumbent be made a Bishop, or accept of another Cure, the first is void. *Vau.* 20, 21.

3. A Bishop taking another Bishoprick, the first is void, by the Consent of the Superior *Palm.* 462, 464. *Vau.* 21.

4 It was agreed by all, as well Justices, as those at the Bar, that if a Parson, or Dean, in *England*, take a Bishoprick in *Ireland*, that this makes the first Church void, by Cession, and *Whitlock* gave the Reason, for that there is but one Common Law for all the Church. *Nemo potest habere duas Militias, nec duas Dignitates.* It is impossible a Man should be in two Places at the same Time, &c *Palm* 458, 469 *Vaug* 21.

5 A Prebendary made Dean, the Prebend is void, by Cession 5 *E* 2. *Breve* 800 attendant *Palm.* 461

6. A

6 A Man having a Benefice with Cure, to the Value of 10 *l.* or more, receives another Benefice with Cure, and is inducted into it; now the first is void, *ac si esset per Mortem vel Resignationem, & hoc per* 21 H. 8. Dy. 255. Vau 21.

7. The Bishoprick of *Man* made a Cession of a Benefice in *England. Palm.* 459

8. A Man, beneficed in the Diocess of *Peterborough,* which was of the Value of 8*l* or more (and yet is valued in the Records of the Exchequer for First-Fruits and Tenths at 6 *l* a Year only) accepts a Benefice with Cure in the Diocess of *Gloucester,* and is inducted thereto, by this the first is void *Dy* 237. *a Vaug* 21.

9. It is said in *Hob* if a Man, having a Benefice, take another, *sans Dispensation,* tho' he be not inducted, and so not within the Statute 21 *H* 8 yet the Patron of the first Church may take it, as void, and present presently, or may leave it, as full, till Sentence of Deprivation *Hob* 166 *Vau* 21

10. Upon Issue, *utrum Ecclesia vacavit per mortem, &c.* in *Quare impedit,* the Case was, a Man had a Benefice compatible, and *sans* sufficient Dispensation, took another compatible, but did not subscribe to the Articles of Religion, according to the Statute 13 *Eliz.* and yet was admitted, and instituted, and inducted to the second Benefice *Quere,* upon the Evidence, if this made the first Benefice void, by the *Stat.* 21 *H* 8. or not *Et per Opinionem Curiæ* held, that the first Benefice *vacavit per Mortem,* and not by Reason of taking the second Benefice, and that he was never lawful Parson of it by Force of the
Statute

Statute of 13 *Eliz* *Dy.* Laſt Caſe. *Vide Hob.* 168.

11 No Eccleſiaſtical Perſon, having a Benefice, with Cure, of 8 *l.* a Year, or above, ſhall accept or take any other with Cure of Souls, and be inſtituted and inducted in the ſame, but the firſt ſhall be from thence void, and the Patron may from thence preſent, except as in the Statute is provided. Stat. 21 *H.* 8 *cap* 13.

12 Parſon made Biſhop, Parſonage void. *Palm* 345 11 *H* 4 60 & 74. *Dy* 159. 4 *H* 4 2 32 *H* 6 5 *E* 4 19 24 *Palm.* 348, 349 ———— Biſhop what. *Palm* 345.

13 Plenarty by Collation is good againſt another Parſon, but not againſt the Patron. *Palm* 346.

14. One, collated to one Benefice, is after collated to another, the firſt is void. *Palm.* 346, 347

15. *Quare impedit ad præſentondum ad Ecclefiam Vicariæ de Ichingſtoke,* and makes Title by Stat 21 *H.* 8. for that one *Shilſton,* being Vicar there, which was a Benefice with Cure above 8 *l* a Year, *Anno* 15 King *Jac* took another Benefice, *viz* the Vicarage of *Holcombeburnel in Com Devon,* being alſo a Benefice with Cure, and was thereto admitted, inſtituted, and inducted, ſo that thereby the firſt Benefice became void, and ſo remained two Years, and ſo Title of Preſentation accrued to King *James,* and from him deſcended to the King that now is, (*King Charles*) and therefore belongs to him to preſent The Archbiſhop claims nothing, but as Ordinary, the Defendant pleads and confeſſeth the King's Title from the Accep-

tance

tance of the second Benefice, whereby the first was void, and so remained 21 *Jac* and pleads the general Pardon 21 *Jac.* and that *Shilton* was a Person not excepted in the said Pardon, nor the said Cause of Lapse excepted, and that *Shilton*, being the Incumbent, resigned *Ichingstoke*, and gave Title to *Fayle* to present, who presented the Defendant, who was presented, instituted, and inducted before the King's Writ, *&c.* The Attorney Gen. replies, shewing the Exception in the Pardon, wherein is excepted all Titles and Actions of *Quare impedit*, other than such Actions of *Quare impedit*, which the King had, or might have, *ratione Lapsus*, incurred *ultra* three Years last past, for or concerning any Benefice, whereof any Incumbent then was, or the last Day of the Parliament, should be, in Possession by Presentation of any Patron, or the Collation of any Ordinary, and that the said Church being so void *Fayle* presented, *&c.* and traverseth, that the said Vicarage of *Ichingstoke vacavit per resignationem* of *Shilton*, the Defendant demurred to this Replication, and, after several Arguments at the Bar, and twice at the Bench in *Com. B* and the Judges being both Times divided, *viz. Richardson*, Ch Just. and *Harvey pro Quer.* and *Hutton* and *Yelverton pro Def* and after Sir *Robert Heath*, Ch. Just of the Com. Bench and *Harvey* for the Plaintiff, and *Hutton* and *Vernon* for the Defendant; and afterwards Sir *Robert Heath*, by Reason of this Difference in Opinions it was adjourned into the Exchequer Chamber, and argued there at the Bar, and after Trial, the Justices of both Benches and

Barons

Barons of the Exchequer, *viz* Sir *Thomas Richardson* Ch. Juft. of the King's Bench, Sir *Robert Heath*, Ch Juft of the Com. Bench, Sir *Humphrey Davenport*, Ch. Baron, and all the other Juftices and Barons, and two main Queftions were made 1 If an Avoidance of a Church, happening and continuing void divers Years, fo as the King hath Title to prefent by Lapfe, and the King doth not take Advantage thereof, but dies, whether the fucceeding King may take Advantage of the Lapfe, or be barred by the Stat. 25 *E.* 3 *cap* 1. and that refted only upon the Expofition of the faid Statute, the Words whereof are (" And touching Pre-" fentments to be made by the King, or his " Heirs to any Benefice, in another's Right, " by old Titles, the King granteth, that, " from henceforth, he, nor any of his Heirs, " fhall not take Titles to prefent to any Be-" nefice, in another's Right, of any Time " of his Progenitors; nor that any Prelate " is bound to receive, &c but that the King " and his Heirs be for ever hereafter clearly " barred of all fuch Prefentments, faving " always to him and his Heirs all fuch Pre-" fentments in another Right, fallen, or to " fall, of all his Time, and of the Time to " come ") It was ftrongly urged at the Bar and Bench both, for the Defendant, that this Statute extends to all the Succeffors and Heirs of King *E.* 3. that none of them may prefent to a Church, in another's Right (as they argued that this Church is) becaufe the King hath not that Title, as to his proper Advowfon, but in Right of him, who hath the

Inhe-

Inheritance to any Church which falls in Time of his Progenitors, and the rather, for that in the Abridgment of the Statute in the Book of the Statutes, this Saving is altogether omitted; fo they conceived the King was bound by the exprefs Words of the Statute, and that there is not any fuch Saving, and of this Opinion *Vernon* Juft continued, but *Hutton*, who argued in the Com. Bench for the Defendant, in this Point, that the Title of the King was bound by the Statute, and that he might not have Title to prefent to a Church, fallen in the Time of his Predeceffor, by Reafon of his Title of Lapfe fallen in the Time of his Predeceffor, now changed his Opinion, and all the other Juftices and Barons, befides *Vernon*, argued for the Plaintiff in this Point, that the King hath good Title to prefent by Lapfe, incurred in the Time of his Predeceffor, and is not reftrained by the Stat. 25 *E*. 3. for thereby all Rights and Titles to prefent in his own Time, until before the Statute, and in his Time after, and all his Heirs, after the Death of *E*. 3 are faved, and it fhall not bar the Title which the King had in another's Right, fallen, or to fall, in his own Time, or in the Time of his Heirs; and that there was fuch a Saving appeared by the Copy out of the Parliament Roll, and by an antient Book in the Exchequer, writ in Parchment, where it is writ with a Saving; and they held that thefe Words of Old Titles are intended in the Time of the Progenitors of King *E* 3. and not of any Titles of Prefentments to fall in the Time of *E*. 3. or his Heirs, but intended to exclude King *E*. 3. and all his

Heirs

Heirs from Titles of Presentation in other's Right, fallen before the Time of that King, whereof any Church was full, and which Title is only another's Right, and that was the express Intent of the Statute, *viz.* to take away the Stat 14 *E.* 3. *c.* 2 in this Point And *Berkley,* and some of the Justices doubted, whether a Presentment by Lapse should be said to be in another's Right, but only Presentments by Reason of Guardianship and Temporalties in the King's Hands, but all the other Justices agreed, that it shall be said to be in another's Right; for tho' he presents *Ratione Præerogativæ,* yet he presents in Right of the Patron: So it is where one presents, by Reason of a Church being void after Forfeiture for Alienation without License, or for Outlawry, and for that was cited 14 *E.* 3. *Quare impedit* 54. 22 *H* 6 29. 21 *Eliz.* Dy. 364, *(which last is denied to be Law)* and for the principal Point, they relied upon 11 *H.* 4. 7 where it is resolved, 7 *H.* 4 25. 18 *Eliz* Dy 347. 7 Co. 28 and many Precedents, where the King makes Title to present by Lapse and Title in another's Right; wherefore for this Point, *Richardson* Ch. Juft (who argued alone one Day) said, it is to be taken for clear Law, that the King hath good Title to present, and the Declaration was good notwithstanding that Objection. The second Question was, if *Shilton* was Incumbent and might refign, whether, by his Refignation, the Church is become void: And that rested upon the Exposition of the Stat. 21 *Jac.* of the general Pardon, and Stat 21 *H* 8. of Pluralities, whether the Church was absolutely

lutely void, by the Acceptance of a second
Benefice, being both with Cure; and if the
Pardon unto him, being in Poffeffion, may
make him Incumbent? And this Point was
argued ftrongly in the Common Bench by
Telverton and *Hutton*, and afterwards by *Vernon* and *Hutton*, and by both of them in the
Exchequer Chamber for the Defendant, that
this Church by *Stat.* 21 *H* 8. was not abfolutely void *in facto*, but is voidable, *quoad*
the Patron; that he may prefent by the
Statute; but until he prefents, the other
remains Incumbent; and then, he remaining Incumbent, and for three Years being in
Poffeffion of the Church, as Incumbent, until the Pardon 21 *Ja* and the Pardon then
coming, he being in Poffeffion, eftablifheth
him in Poffeffion, and continues him Incumbent, and he cannot after be oufted by the
King, or any other, and then he is Incumbent until he refign; and therefore his Plea
is good; for he is out of the Exception of
the Pardon; for he was in for three Years
before the Pardon; and therefore they faid
he remained Incumbent, and that he might
plead as Incumbent by the Statute 25 *E* 3.
as he pleads here; alfo he is Incumbent as to
all Strangers, but not as to his Patron, for
he may prefent before any Deprivation, tho'
a Stranger cannot, becaufe the Church remains full againft him, and he is Incumbent,
fo as to take a Releafe of any Annuity iffuing out of the Parfonage, and is chargeable in an Annuity, and is chargeable to the
Payment of Subfidies and Fifteenths; and
may have an Action of Debt againft any of his
Parifhioners for not fetting out their Tithes,

And

And many other Reasons they alledged, and said, that the penning this Statute differs much from the Statute 31 *Eliz* of Simony, and from 13 *Eliz.* for not reading the Articles; wherefore they concluded, that Judgment ought to be given for the Defendant: But all the other Justices and Barons argued against it, holding that the Church was absolutely void *in facto & jure*, by taking the second Benefice, and that by the express Words of the Statute 21 *H.* 8 for at the Common Law, before' the said Statute 21 *H* 8. by Reason of the Canons and Constitutions Ecclesiastical, the first Church was *in jure* void; so as the Patron might present thereto, if he would; but because it was but an Ecclesiastical Constitution, the Patron was not compellable to take Notice of that Avoidance, until Deprivation and Notice thereof given him; and then, after Deprivation, the Church is void *in facto & jure*, and the Patron, at his Peril, ought to present, and this appears by the Books 9 *E.* 3 2 5 *E* 3 9. 10 *E.* 3 1. 24 *E* 3 30. 11 *H* 4 37. *Fitz. N B* 34. 14 *H.* 7. 28. Now by the Statute 21 *H* 8 it was absolutely void after Admission, Institution and Induction, so it is void *facto & jure*, and the Patron, at his Peril, ought to take Notice thereof, and so present within the six Months; otherwise a Lapse incurs; and that it was void to all Purposes absolutely, appears by the Manner of pleading in this, and all other such Cases; that by the Admission, Institution and Induction to the second Benefice, *prima Ecclesia vacavit de persona* of the Incumbent, *& vacans*

conti-

continuavit; so the Church is absolutely void
by the Pleadings and Confession of the Defendant, and this appears by the Books,
since the Statute 21 *H* 8. that by the Acceptance of a second Benefice, the Church is
void *facto & jure, quoad* the Patron and all
others. 18 *Eliz* Dy. 347. 5 *Co* 75 *Hol-
land*'s Case, and *Digby*'s Case, and *lib.* 6.
fo 29. *Green*'s Case, and 23 *Eliz* Dy. 377.
and *Co. Ent* 368. And for the Reasons before alledged, on the other Side, *viz* that he
may plead, as Incumbent, that is, because
he is admitted by the Writ of the Incumbent, and his pleading, as Incumbent, is not
contradicted; and for the taking of a Release, it is much to be doubted; and if it
be good, it is because he is in Possession, as
an Intruder, to whom a Release may be a
Discharge of such Things; and for his being charged with Subsidies, that is, because
he hath the Profits, and therefore reasonable he should bear and pay the Charges.
And *quoad* his having Debt for not setting
out of Tithes, it was denied by all those
who argued on the other Side: And as to
the Pardon of 21 *Jac.* all the other Justices
and Barons held, that the Pardon doth not
help him; first, because it is no Offence
within the Body of the Act; for it is not
any Offence or Contempt against the King
2dly, Because it never was the Intent of
the Pardon to dispense with Pluralities, nor
are there any Words therein to make him
an Incumbent, or to make a Plenarty of a
Church, which was absolutely void. And
divers of the Justices and the Chief Baron
held, that a special Pardon, after such an
abso-

absolute Avoidance, with Words, *that he may retain*, or whatsoever other Words he may have, cannot make him Incumbent. So the general Words in the Pardon shall not enure to make a Dispensation, and the Church being since void, shall not be full without a new Presentation, Admission and Institution. And for the Words in the Exception of the general Pardon, *Of all Titles and Actions of* Quare Impedit, *other than such Titles and Actions of* Quare Impedit, *as have incurred by Lapse, above three Years before the first Day of this Parliament, whereof any Incumbent is in actual Possession, by any Presentation, or Collation,* &c. the last Parts of this Exception do not extend to the said *Shilton*; for that extends only to those who are in as Incumbents, (which he is not) and not to those who are in by Usurpation and Wrong, who are removeable by *Quare impedit*: And it was said, that since the Statute 21 *H*. 8 there have been divers general Pardons, and no Pluralities were ever conceived to be within them; wherefore they concluded, that Judgment should be given for the Plaintiff, and it was adjudged accordingly. *Cro. Car. fo* 354 *to* 355 *inclusive.*

16. Taking of a second Living, or Benefice with Cure, above Value, by the Statute 21 *H* 8 makes the first absolutely void *in facto & jure*, and that be the express Words of the Statute; for at Law, before the Statute, by the Canons and Constitutions Ecclesiastical, the first Church was void *in jure*, so as the Patron might present thereto, if he would; but because it was but an Ecclesiastical Constitution, the Patron

was

was not compellable to take Notice of the Avoidance, till Deprivation, and Notice given him ; but, after Deprivation, the Church is void *in facto & jure*, and the Patron, at his Peril ought to present ; and this appears by the Books 9 *E.* 3. 2. 5 *E* 3 9 10 *E.* 3. 1. 24 *E.* 3. 30. 11 *H* 4 37. *Fitz N. B.* 34. 14 *H.* 7. 28. But now by this Statute of 21 *H* 8. it is made absolutely void after Admission, Institution and Induction ; so it is void *facto & jure*, and the Patron is to take Notice, at his Peril, (and it is void to all Men, as it appears by the Books 18 *Eliz. Dy.* 347. 4 *Co.* 75 & 78. 6 *Co* 29. *Dy* 377. *Co. Ent.* 368.) *Cro. Car.* 357.

17. A Church may be vacated by Cession, or Incumbent's becoming a Bishop. See Case *Archbishop Armagh* v. *Attorney General*, in the House of Lords, 21 *April* 1730.

    2 *The Patron's Right to present in such Cases.*

A Parson beneficed in a Living above Value, taking another Benefice, both being with Cure, *sans* Dispensation, the first is void ; yet, as is said in *Dy* 255, 129 the Ordinary is not bound to give Notice of this Avoidance, of which the Patron may take Notice, as well as the Ordinary, being by Act of Parliament, whereof every one is to take Notice, *but quære if this Case is not over-ruled, if the Law ever was so, by subsequent Cases, where it has been adjudged, that the Patron may, at his Pleasure in such*

  I

Case,

Cafe, take the Church as void, and prefent in-
ftantly, or confider it as full, and fo leave it
till Sentence of Deprivation be formally pronounced Vide Fitz N. B 34 L. Dy 377.
Hob. 166, 168. 6 Co 29. 30. 4 Co. Hol-
land's *Cafe*, and Digby's *Cafe*. Vaugh. 131.

XIX. *Wherefore a Clerk may be removed.*

1 LEcturer removed for not officiating in
Perfon, as the Foundation required.
See *Phillips* and *Walter*, in Houfe of Lords,
anno 1720. See 2 *Chan. Ca* 19.

2. In the Exchequer, the Chief Baron
faid, that all Curates are, at Common Law,
removeable at Pleafure, though by the Ecclefiaftical Law, they are for Life. *Price
againft Pratt and others, Mich.* 3 *Geo.* 2.

XX. *Deprivation.*

1. *What it is.*

1. DEprivation is, when an Abbot, Bifhop, Parfon, 'Vicar, Prebendary,
&c. is deprived, or depofed, from his Preferment, for any Matter in Fact, or in Law ;
as if a Mifcreant or Schifmatick be prefented, admitted, and inducted, there is good
Caufe of Deprivation, *&c. Terms de l' Ley*,
Title *Deprivation.*

2. Deprivation, *Deprivatio*, a Depriving,
Bereaving, or Taking away, with the Lofs
or Deprivation of all the Spiritual Promotions,

tions, whereof, &c. as of Bishops and Deans, &c. *Blount's Law Dict.* Tit. *Deprivation.*

2. *The Sorts.*

1. *D*Eprivatio a Beneficio is, when for some great Crime a Minister is wholly, or for ever, deprived of his Living

2 *Deprivatio ab officio* is, when a Minister is deprived of his Orders, which is also called *Depositio,* or *Degradatio,* and is commonly for some heinous Crime, meriting Death, and is performed by the Bishop in solemn Manner. In *Godb.* is Mention made of a Bishop deprived for Miscreancy. See *Bellewe, fo.* 194. *&* 3 *Inst.* 43

3. *Wherefore one may be deprived, and who must do it, and in what Cases.*

1. *T*HEY may build a Sentence of Deprivation upon a Conviction of Felony or other Capital Crime; for such they are bound by. *Hob* 121.

2. *Per generale Concilium Lattarense tentum sub Innocentio, Papa, tertio, statutum est quod quicunque receperit aliquod Beneficium habens Curam Annimarum annexam, si prius tale Beneficium obtinebat, eo fit jure ipso privatus, & si forte illud retinere contenderit, alio etiam spolietur: Is quodque ad quem Prioris spectat Donatio, illud post receptionem alterius conferat cui merito viderit conferendum,* which Council was held *Anno Dom.* 1215 By

I   which

which it appears, that by taking a second Benefice the first is void *ipso jure*, and the Patron may present, and on this general Council are the Books 9 *E.* 3 22 10 *E.* 3. I (*where the Council is mentioned*) 24 *E.* 3 30 *a.* 11 *H.* 4. 37. 14 *H.* 7 28. 14 *H.* 8. 17. *Fitz N. B.* 27. L. 4 *Co.* 79 *a.* Dy. 346 *a b.*

3 Regularly the Ordinary, at Common Law, had no Power over a Clergyman, in a Crime or Offence touching the Crown, but where that Power was given him by the Common Law. *Hob.* 290. And therefore when the King's Court did deliver the Offender to the Ordinary, it implied a Power or Permission of the Law, that he might deal with him, to commit, or discharge, him according to the Form of their Laws, but since the Statute hath forbid the Delivery of him, to the Ordinary, it retains all Power to itself, and denies the Ordinary's, and therefore if the Ordinary, at Common Law, would have convened a Churchman to have deprived or degraded him **for** Felony, before his Trial at Common Law, a Prohibition would have lain for holding a Plea of a Cause of the Crown, and prejudging the King's Court *in eadem.* Hob. 290.

4. If a Clerk were found Not guilty of Felony, and discharged, and the Ordinary would convene him again, and admit new Proof to find him guilty, in Order to deprive him, a Prohibition shall go, or if a Clerk delivered *absque Purgatione* to the Ordinary, they would admit him to his Purgation, a Prohibition lieth, yea, and a *Præ-*

munire too ; and yet thefe Offences are not
fo highly Pleas of the Crown, as in Criminal
Caufes, there are Degrees, as Treafon, and
fome even againſt the Perfon of the King
himſelf. Alfo if they would proceed between Conviction and Clergy, a Prohibition
lies for Prevention ; for that the Caufe is
not finifhed in the King's Court; but if they
would not controvert, nor re-examine the
Acts of the King's Court, but build their
Sentences upon them, they were not to be
prohibited ; as if they deprived a Man by
Sentence, becaufe he was convicted or attaint of Felony, Murder, or Manflaughter,
at Common Law. *Hob.* 290, 291. See 2 *Inſt.*
637.

5. If a Parfon of a Church be convicted
of Manflaughter, and hath his Clergy allowed, according to the Statute 18 *Eliz* and
is delivered out of Prifon; if he be after
fued in the Ecclefiaftical Court, in Order
to Deprivation for this Offence, a Prohibition lieth for him; becaufe by the Allowance of his Clergy, by the Statute, he is
purged and acquitted of the Felony, and of
all Penalties and Damages incident to it, in
the Nature of a Pardon. *Mich.* 27 *Eliz.*
Rot. 2574. *Nichol's* Cafe accordant. *Rol. Ab.*
Prohibition, S. C. 3 *Hob* 288, *&c. Searle* and
Williams Cafe, and 2 *Inſt.* 673.

6. A Prohibition was prayed by *Richardfon* Serjeant; for that *Searle,* a Parfon, having been convicted of Homicide, and allowed his Clergy, was now fued in the Spiritual Court by Libel, that whereas he was
convicted of Homicide, *&c.* it fhould be
Caufe to deprive him of his Benefice. *Per*
totam

totam Cur': No Prohibition ought to be granted, and *Mountague*, Chief Justice, said, that though the Statute 18 *Eliz. cap.* 7. ordains, that after Clergy, the Party shall be set at large, and shall not be put to his Purgation, yet that doth not disaffirm the Judgment; whereto *Crooke* and *Doderidge* accorded. As to the Objection, that the Libel in the Spiritual Court was not against him, as an Homicide, the Court held it, so much the better; for if it had been so, a Prohibition ought to have gone, but it is, *quod convictus fuit de Homicidio,* as it ought to be, for without Conviction there is no Cause of Deprivation, and if it were against him, as an Homicide, it should be contrary to the Verdict given; but here they proceed only to deprive him, by Reason of his Conviction, and so thereby do affirm the Verdict. And as to the Objection, that as the Statute 18 *Eliz* hath disabled him that he shall not make his Purgation, he shall now not be taken to be, as if he had made his Purgation before the Statute, and before the Statute he could not have been deprived. It was answered, that antiently by the Conviction he was to undergo two Punishments, the one of Death, the other of Defamation, and that the first was discharged by the Allowance of the Clergy, *Pœna potest dirimi, culpa perennis erit.* Afterwards in the Time of *Anselme,* Archbishop of *Canterbury,* it was ordained by a general Council, *quod Clerici non tradentur manibus judicis temporalis,* which Council, in the Time of *Thomas de Becket,* was by Usurpation received here in *England,* and so far

E e 2 prevailed,

prevailed, that if any such Person prayed his Clergy, and was delivered to the Ordinary, they then re-examined him by twelve Spiritual Persons; and if he were acquitted, he should not be deprived; but this Trial, by twelve Clerks, was only *de Credalitate*, so as the first Conviction remained and the Purgation did not disaffirm the Verdict, for he is delivered to the Ordinary, by the Judgment of the Common Law, and the Entry thereof is, *quod traditur Ordinario, &c.* and the Law was, that if he did not make his Purgation, he ought to remain perpetually in Prison, and have slender Diet, *viz.* every Day Bread and Water only; and if the Ordinary refused to accept of his Purgation, then he might have a Command to the Ordinary to do it: And note that the Writ is, *satis habetur suspectus*, so as the Stat. 18 *Eliz.* 27 makes no Purgation for the taking away what was before, and the Purgation before the Statute did not defeat, but affirm the Verdict; and it is a Rule not to grant a Prohibition, where the Proceedings in the Ecclesiastical Courts are not against the Laws of the Land, nor the Liberty of the Subject; and so the Prohibition was denied *per Cur Cro. Jac* 430, 431. *Hob.* 288. S C. *Keil.* 7 *H.* 8. 181.

7. A Bishop may be deprived for Dilapidations. 2 *H* 4　3 *Godb.* 259. 3 *Bulst* 158. 2 *Bulst* 279. 1 *Ro. Rep* 86. *Mo.* 917. *Watson* Bishop of *St. David's* Case. *Salk. Rep*

8. An Archbishop hath Power over his Suffragans, and may deprive. *Watson,* Bishop of *St. David's* Case in *Salk.*

9 By the Common Law an Archbishop hath a Metropolitical Jurisdiction, and Archbishops are over Bishops, as Bishops are over the other Clergy. *Watson*, Bishop of *St David's* Case in *Salk*.

10 The Archbishop must deprive a Bishop *Watson* Bishop *St David's*. *Salk Rep.*

11. A Bishop offending in the Ordering of Priests or Deacons, contrary to several of the Canons ——————— is to be deprived by his Provincial in such Manner as the said Canons direct. See the Canons 1603.

12. For Dilapidations may be deprived. 29 *E* 3 16. 2 *H* 4 3 11 *H* 6 20 *H* 6. 46 9 *E*. 4. 34 25 *E* 1. 1 *Co*. 72. *b* *Vide* Division, Dilapidations, how punished. *Vide etiam* may punish their own Members

13 *Cawdrey's* Case 5 *Co* 1 *Part* 6 was remarkable, he being deprived for Preaching against the Common Prayer.

14. *Prohibition* A Layman forged Orders and obtained a Benefice, for which he was prosecuted in the Ecclesiastical Court, in Order to Deprivation, he prayed a Prohibition, for the Forgery is triable at Law, but rejected, for the Forgery is concerning an Eccle-

When any Minister is complained of in any Ecclesiastical Court belonging to any Bishop of his Province for any Crime,

E e 3

the Chancellor, Commissary, Official, or any other having Ecclesiastical Jurisdiction, to whom it shall appertain, shall expedite the Cause by Processes and other Proceedings against him, and upon Contumacy for not appearing, shall first suspend him and afterwards, his Contumacy continuing, shall excommunicate him; but if he appear and submit himself to the Course of Law, then the Matter being ready for Sentence and the Merits of his Offence exacting by Law, either Deprivation from his Living, or Deposition from the Ministry, no such Sentence shall be pronounced by any Person whatsoever, but the Bishop, assisted by his Chancellor, the Dean (if they conveniently may be had) and some of the Preben-

Prebendaries, Ecclesiastical Matter, and he is sued for it if the Court there in Order to Deprivation only. *1 Lev.* be kept near *138.* *1 Sid* 217. Same Case. the Cathedral Church, or of the Archdeacon (if he may be had conveniently) and two others of, at the least, grave Ministers and Preachers to be called by the Bishop, when the Court is kept in other Places. *Can.* 122.

4. *How to be tried.*

1. IF Issue be, whether a Parson be deprived or not, the Court must write to the Bishop, and if the Issue be, whether the Bishop be deprived or not, they must write to the Archbishop to certify. *Watson,* Bishop of *St David.* *Salk. Rep.*

2. Court Christian may not examine Felony, or other Capital Crime, tho' for Purposes examinable there; as in Case of Deprivation. *Hob.* 121.

XXI. *Where a Clerk is ousted or disturbed.*

1. *Ousted.*

3 ANNO 28 *H.* 6. in the Exchequer Chamber; where an Incumbent ousted by his Patron, upon a Suggestion, that he is created a Bishop, or hath resigned, or hath accepted another Living, the Patron presented another Clerk, who is admitted, he shall not have a Spoliation, but where another Person claims the Patronage, he may, for then the Right of Advowson seems in Debate. *Stath Abr.* Consultation *ult. Vide the Remedies, Spoliation.*

2 *Tith.*

2 *Trin.* 4 *Jac. in Canc.* The Case was, that *Smith* was deprived by the High Commissioners for not conforming to the Canons of the Church; the Reason given in the Deprivation was, *quod fuit refractorius, &c* but mentions no Canon; upon which Deprivation the King presented *Bird* to the Church, who was instituted and inducted, and yet *Smith* would not yield Possession; but he himself being in Prison, his Wife and Servants kept the Possession of the Parsonage House, whereupon a *vi laicâ amovendâ* was awarded out of Chancery; whereupon the Sheriff came to the Parsonage House, and the others thereupon fled, so that he could not apprehend them, and *Bird* finding the House open, entered peaceably, after which *Smith* made Affidavit in the King's Bench, that he was ousted by the Sheriff with Force, and *Bird* put in Possession; and upon this Affidavit the Court of King's Bench awarded a Writ of Restitution, he having an Appeal pending *del* Deprivation. And *Bird* exhibited his Bill in *Canc.* from whence the Writ *de vi laica amovenda* was awarded, and there returned, praying that *Smith* might be injoined from the Possession, till he had defeated the Deprivation; and upon Day given to both Parties, the Lord Chancellor called to his Assistance the Lord Ch. Just. *Popham*, *Coke*, Ch. Just of the Common Pleas, and *Flemming* Chief Baron, and they all concurred in Opinion, that a Decree ought to be pronounced for *Bird*'s Possession, till *Smith* had undone the Deprivation. *Mo. fo* 781, 782, 783.

E e 4   3. *He*

3. *Hil.* 39 *Eliz* A Leafe was made of the Rectory of *Chebington* in *Com. Bucks,* and a Parfon was prefented to it, who came into Chancery, and fuppofed he was held out by Force , whereupon he had a *vi laica removenda* returnable in *B. R.* Whereupon the Sheriff returned *non inveni vim laicam neque armatam Potentiam;* and now it was moved, that the Leffee in Truth was put out of Poffeffion, notwithftanding the Return of the Sheriff, and therefore Reftitution prayed, and upon Affidavit of it, a Writ of Reftitution was awarded out of the King's Bench, and a Precedent fhewn of it between *Arkinfal* and *Palmer* in *Com Cambridge.* 35 *Eliz. rot.* 66. *inter Placita Coronæ* accordant *Mo fo* 462.

2. *Difturbed.*

1 IF two feveral Patrons prefent feverally to the Ordinary, and thereupon one fues a *Quare impedit,* or Affife of Darreign Prefentment againft the other, and recovers, and his Clerk is admitted; whereupon the Clerk of the other fues the Clerk of him who recovered by Way of Appeal, or otherwife in the Court of the Archbifhop; for that he was not admitted to the Prefentment of his Patron, there the Patron who recovered fhall have a Prohibition to the Archbifhop, &c or againft the Clerk who fued for this Caufe to furceafe, &c. And fo if the Patron be difturbed by the Prefentment of another Stranger, and he who difturbed fue in Court Chriftian the Clerk of the true Patron, or
econtra

contra the Clerk of the true Patron sue in Court Christian the Clerk of the Disturber, the Party aggrieved shall have a Prohibition. *Fitzb. N Br* 42 K.

2 If the King collate to a Prebend, or recover such Collation and his Clerk is admitted, and after the Clerk is vexed, or sued in Court Christian, by means of Appeal, Commission, or other Cause, by which the Title of Collation might come in Question, the King shall have a Prohibition to the Judge, *&c.* commanding him not to proceed, and if the King recover his Collation, or Presentation to a Church, and after the Execution of the Judgment is disturbed by Appeal, or Citation, or other like Means, or if, after the Clerk inducted, he is disturbed in Court Christian, the King shall have a Writ directed to the Sheriff and other Officer to attach the Bodies of them, making such Impediments, and another to the Bishops, and their Officials, *&c* and also he may have a Prohibition to the Parties that they pursue not, *&c* neither suffer the same, to their Knowledge, and the King may have an Attachment *sur ceo* to the Sheriff, if the Party will pursue, *&c Fitzb. N Br* 43. L. M.

XXII. *Chaplains.*

1. *The King's.*

1. *Their Residence.*

IF the King's Chaplains, *&c.* are compelled by the Ordinary to Residence, when they are attendant on his Majesty and his Service, a Pro-a Prohibition lies. *Fitzh. N. Br* 44. G Of Chaplains, *vide ante* Court of Faculties.

2. *Other Chaplains,* vide *Court of Faculties* antea.

XXIII. *The Duty of the Clergy.*

The Introduction.

PErhaps it may be thought this Chapter of the Faith and Duty of the Clergy, is a *Transition* from my Purpose, but I conceive it to be otherwise; for if any Clerk of Holy Church broach any anti-christian or Heterodox Opinion, or is scandalously Immoral in his Life and Conversation, tho' it be undoubtedly the Duty of Ecclesiastical Governours to punish and reclaim such, to a found Faith and regular Life; yet if they neglect this so necessary Duty, I hold, the Temporal Courts may compel them thereto, or punish their Neglect, and correct the Delinquent, according to his Demerit. And what these Gentlemen are bound to believe and do, as also what are the Matters and Things they are bound to refrain from, appears from their Ordination Obligations, or Engagements, as is elsewhere mentioned, as well as from the Articles, and Canons of the Church; and I may also add, that every Thing required by holy Scripture, to be believed, or done, or is there forbidden to be done, are by them in most serious and solemn Manner to be believed, done or avoided accordingly; and not only so, but there are several other Duties required and commanded them to do, by several of the Statute Laws, as well as several other Things thereby forbidden them

them, as appears, amongst others, by the Stat.
1 H. 7. 21 H 8. 32 H 8. 1 Eliz. 9 & 10
W 3. and several other Stat for Subscription
and Oaths by them to be taken, &c. therefore
these Scriptural, Temporal, and Ecclesiastical
Laws, and Constitutions, are the several Oracles
from whence Churchmen are to receive Instruction and Information in their several Duties,
and to these they owe Observance, namely, to
Scripture, as the Law of God, to the Temporal
Laws, for Conscience Sake, for the Peace of
Society, and as they are farther obligated thereunto by Oaths taken to secure their Obedience
thereunto, &c. and to the Last, as the Laws of
holy Church strictly binding them; to which I
think it necessary to observe that every Church
Clerk, at his Entrance into every of his Orders,
hath, in most solemn Manner, in the Presence
of God, in his Temple, at his Altar, before his
Prelate, or Prelates, Clergy assistant at these
holy Offices, and before an Assembly of Christians congregated on such Occasion, promised
and vowed thus to believe and do, according to
these Doctrines and Rules, and that in their
common received and known Sense and true
Meaning, without any Mental Reservation,
framed Constructions, or Sense of his own put
upon them. Now should any one make these
Sacred Vows, in such solemn Manner, as the
Church requires, and further subscribe, according to Rubrick, and Receive the holy Sacrament of the Lord's Supper, in Evidence of his
Sincerity, when he is an Unbeliever in any of
the Doctrines, or intends not to be ruled by any
of the Directions there laid down for his Rule
and Governance, I think at least, it can be no
Breach of Christian Charity, to determine such
an

an one, an Hypocrite to God, and a Darer of his
Vengeance, an Enemy to that Religion he has
avowed, and to the Souls of Men, as well as a
Traitor to the Laws, both Temporal and Ecclesiastical, of the Realm. And tho' he were
sincere at his Ordination; yet if after he take
up Notions, contrary to, or govern himself by
other Rules, or lives as without God or Religion in the World, I submit it, such an one is
to be considered in the same Light, or as one
not much better, unless he quit his Order and
Profession, with all the Emoluments and Advantages appendant, in which Case, I leave him
as not worth following; and therefore, to return
to the rest, I apprehend the Question is not whether all and every these Things are strictly and
to a Tittle true, (which, for my own Part, I
will not presume to doubt) yet these are the
Doctrines and Rules the Clerk has, in such
solemn Manner, vowed, to God and Men, to
believe and observe; and therefore these he has
(over and above being bound to some of them,
as a Christian) obliged himself to, and therefore from these he cannot regularly depart.
These are the Terms on which he received and
holds his Office and Benefits. Upon the whole
these are the Doctrines he is to maintain against
all Gainsayers, and propagate and inculcate to
the People, these are the Rules, by which he is
to govern himself and guide those committed to
his Charge: But to say, that thus to believe
and do are too difficult, will, I fear, be no Excuse when he comes to make his great Account,
for these ought well to have been considered in
Time. If he either inconsiderately ran into
these Engagements, or even suffered himself
precipitately to be hurried into them, or was
actuated

actuated by worldly Profit only; and not by Divine Impulse; or disbelieved their binding Quality, I will not presume to say his Punishment, but without Divination I may venture to pronounce the beginning of his Sin as a Clerk was his starting or setting out with a Lye both to God and Man.

1. *As to their Faith, &c.*

VIDE *antea,* the Introduction.

2. *To be regular and sober in their Lives and Conversations.*

1. *Donea Persona* includes, not only Ability, 1. In Learning 2 In Doctrine, but also 3. In Honesty 4. In Conversation. I observe, at 5. In the ordering, or ordaining, of Deacons, the Bishop upon the Archdeacon's, or his Deputy's, presenting the Candidates at the Altar, very solemnly, in Presence of the Clergy and Congregation, cautions the Presentor, That he take Heed, That the Persons, whom he presents, be apt and meet, *for their Learning, and Godly Life, to exercise their Ministry duly, to the Honour of God, and the Edifying of his Church* Then I observe that the Bishop demands of, and charges the Congregation, that if any of them know any of the Parties to have any Impediment, or to have been guilty of any notable Crime, that they shew the same Then I find that the Bishop, with the Clergy and Congregation present, in the first Collect, peculiar to the Occasion, devoutly prays to Almighty God, mercifully to behold the Candidates, and that he would replenish them so with the Truth of his Doctrine, and adorn them with Innocency of Life, that both by Word and Good Example, they may faithfully serve God in their Office, to the Glory of God, and the Edification of his Church Then I observe, that the Epistle for this solemn Occasion, which is Part of the 3d Chapter of the 1 *Tim* is an Exhortation, and Charge to the New Doctors, and indeed to all others adorned with this Sacred Character, that they be grave, not

5 In Diligence in his Function And thef
not double-
tongued, not to inftruct the People in true Religion, good
given to much
Wine, not   Con-

greedy of filthy Lucre, holding the Miniftry of Faith in a pure Confcience, and that they be found blamelefs, and ruling their Children and
their Houfes well And I further obferve from the 12 Chapter of the *Acts*
of the holy Apoftles, which is a Portion of Scripture alfo appointed on
this Occafion to be read, That the Men, whom the Apoftles direct the
Difciples to chufe for this Sacred Function, fhould be Men of honeft Report, full of the Holy Ghoft and of Wifdom After this, the Bifhop
examines every one of the Candidates for this order, whether they have
Confidence, that they are inwardly moved by the *Holy Ghoft* to take on
them this Office, and Miniftration, to ferve God, for the Promoting of
his Glory, and the Edifying of his People, and he alfo demands of them,
if they think themfelves truly called, to all which they are to anfwer,
they truft, or think fo After which, he demands of them, if they believe *all the Canonical Scriptures,* whereto they anfwer, they do, whereupon the Bifhop takes their folemn Promife feverally, in the Prefence of
the Clergy and People congregated, *diligently to read the Scriptures to the
People where they fhould be appointed, and to do faithfully their Office,*
and, (amongft many other Matters) *diligently to fearch for the fick, poor,
and impotent People of the Parifh,* which they promife in moft folemn
Manner, by God's help, to do: *And alfo,* that they will apply *their Diligence to frame and fafhion their own ard Families Lives, according to the
Doctrine of Chrift, and to make themfelves, as much as in them lies, wholefome Examples of the Flock of Chrift,* and alfo, *that they will reverently
obey their Ordinary and other Chief Minifters of the Church, and them, to
whom the Government over them is committed, following with a glad Mind
and Will their godly Admonitions* All which they in fuch folemn Manner,
as hath been mentioned, *Promife, God being their Helper.* Whereupon
the Ordinary delivers to them their Sacred Commiffion ; and then, I
conceive, in further Obligation, they receive the Holy Communion of
the Lord's Supper (the ftrongeft Obligation a Chriftian can take) after
which is a Prayer to Almighty God, to make the new ordained Parties,
*Modeft, Humble, and Conftant in their Miniftry, and to have a ready Will
to obferve all Spiritual Difcipline* In the ordering of Priefts, I obferve,
is the like Caution to the Prefentor, and Charge to the People, and alfo
the like Collect, That God would replenifh them *with the Truth of his
Doctrine ; and adorn them with Innocency of Life,* for the Ends mentioned in the former Collect in the Ordering of Deacons. In the Exhortation, the Bifhop admonifhes them to be ordained Priefts of *their Great
and Important Charge, and to ufe all their Diligence in it,* and lays before them the Direful Confequence of Negligence therein, *and alfo the
Horrible Punifhment that will crue fuch Negligence* And then he proceeds

4

Converſation, and to avoid Contention. ceeds to ex-
6 Co 49. hort them,
that no Place

be left amongſt them, either for Error in Religion, or for Viciouſneſs of
Life, and that they neither offend themſelves, nor be Occaſion that others do;
but to be ſtudious in Reading and Learning the Scriptures, and in framing
the Manners both of themſelves, and thoſe who appertain unto them accordingly, and, to that End, to ſet aſide all worldly Cares and Studies, and
to draw all their Care and Study to the faithful Diſcharge of their Holy
Office, and to make themſelves and Families wholeſome and godly Examples
for others to follow, and to obey their Superiors · All which they ſolemnly
promiſe And then, after the Veni, Creator Spiritus, and ſeveral Prayers,
the Biſhop gives them the Sacred Truſt, and concludes with the Prayers,
which the Church, in her great Wiſdom, and Piety, hath compoſed for
this Holy Purpoſe From hence it is eaſy to perceive what a Candidate for the Orders of Prieſts or Deacons ought to be, at his Entrance
into Orders, and as no Doubt can reaſonably be made, I hope none will,
but theſe Gentlemen having made theſe Vows, and entered into theſe
Engagements are ſtrictly bound to a religious Obſervance of them for the
reſt of their Lives, and that if any are found groſly faulty, the Spiritual
Governors of the Church will take ſuch Means, as they ought, to reduce them to their Duty What is the Duty of theſe Gentlemen, in
Point of Faith, hath been briefly hinted at already, as alſo the Reſort
they are to have to learn the ſame, but I cannot omit reminding them,
it is not the leaſt of their Duty, to inform themſelves, what the Temporal Law has to ſay to them, though I have ſome Apprehenſions this
has not had its proper Attention, but however that be, I think proper,
in Juſtice to the Care, Wiſdom, and Piety of the Church, to take Notice, that beſides what has been mentioned, that no impious, prophane,
or looſe Livers, or others unworthy, might thruſt or intrude themſelves
into the Miniſtry, the Church has ſtill further provided, by the 34th
Canon, that every Candidate for Holy Orders bring a Teſtimonium of his
good Life and Converſation, and by the 39th Canon the like is required
before Inſtitution, (which ſhew what their intermediate Lives ought to
be) and that he appear a Perſon worthy of the Miniſtry, and becauſe
Men may loſe their Learning by Diſuſe, I think it not altogether un-
neceſſary to put the Clerk in Mind, that though, at his Ordination, or
at a former Inſtitution, he has been found and paſſed as ſufficient; yet the
Temporal Courts have determined, that the Ordinary, on every Inſtitution, may, nay, and for this Reaſon ought, to examine every to be inſtituted Clerk, whether he be, at the Time, able, or not, for Learning,
as well as for a ſound Faith, and good Morals, for Inſtitution

2 The

2 The Statute 1 *H.* 7 for the more sure Reformation of Priests, Clerks, and Religious Men culpable, or by their Demerit openly reported of incontinent Living, enacteth, that it be lawful for all Ordinaries to chastise Priests, Clerks, and Religious Men, within their several Jurisdictions, by the Law of the Church, of Advowtry, Fornication, Incest, or any other fleshly Incontinency; and the Statute 32 *H.* 8. makes all such Forfeitures as therein is mentioned, and the Statute 21 of the same King prohibits them farming, *&c.* for these laudable and pious Ends, namely for the more quiet and virtuous Increase and Maintenance of Divine Service, Preaching and Teaching the Word of God, godly and good Example, and the better Discharge of Churchmen's
I hold myself Duty, the Maintenance of Hospitality, the
bound to de- Relief of the Poor, the Increase of Devotion,
clare it my
Opinion, at and the good Opinion of the Laity towards
least, that as Spiritual Persons, *&c.*
the Temporal
Laws have thus strengthen'd Spiritual Governors Authority over their own
Members when they give just Cause of Suspicion, that this is an additional Obligation on them to take Care to the Discharge of this Office; for as now they stand protected by the Civil Authority from all Redress against their just Procedure in these Matters, they cannot so much as pretend the Excuse made for their Omissions before the Civil Interposition, and I confess, to me this seems, in Conscience, a Command to them to see to this *Duty*.

3. By the 75 and 76 Canon it is required, that no Ecclesiastick, at any Time, other than for their honest Necessities, resort to any Tavern or Ale-house, neither board or lodge in such, neither give themselves to any base or servile Labour, or to Drinking, or spending their Time idly by
4 Day

Day or by Night, playing at Dice, Cards, or Tables, or any other unlawful Game, but at all Times convenient to hear or read somewhat of Holy Scripture, or occupy themselves in some other honest Study or Exercise, always doing the Things which shall appertain to Honesty, and endeavour to Profit the Church of God, having always in Mind, that they ought to excel all others in Purity of Life, and should be Examples to the People, to live well and christianly ; and these Things are injoined them under Pain of Ecclesiastical Censures, to be inflicted with Severity *according to the Quality of their Offences.*

3. *As to their Habit.*

1. *In general.*

1. EVERY Minister, saying the publick Prayers, or ministring the Sacrament, or other Rites of the Church, shall wear a decent and comely Surplice, with Sleeves, &c. and furthermore such Ministers as are Graduates, shall wear upon their Surplices, at such Times, such Hoods, as by the Orders of the Universities, are agreeable to their Degrees; which no Minister shall wear (being no Graduate) *under Pain of Suspension,* notwithstanding it shall be lawful for such Ministers as are not Graduates, to wear upon their Surplices, instead of Hoods, some decent Tippet of Black, so it be not Silk. *Can* 58.

By the for-
mer of these
Canons, I ob-
serve, that
Ministers are
so to apparel
themselves as

2. Decency in Apparel injoined to Ministers; in short, *they are always, and in all
Places, and on all Occasions so to apparel
themselves,* that they may be known for what
they are. See *Can.* 74.

becomes their Order and Degree, and particularly, that being Graduates,
they are to wear the Hoods of their respective Degrees; which no Minister shall wear, being no Graduate, under Pain of Suspension, and by
the latter of these Canons, Decency of Apparel is injoined Parsons, and
therefore sure as they are directed how to habit themselves, (at Home
and on Journies) by the Canons of the Church, they are, in a Word,
always to be so apparelled as their Profession, at least, if not their Degree may be known; and they respected accordingly, but how are these
Canons (though they are certainly binding to the Clergy) neglected, dif-
pised, and set at nought, by many of the Clergy themselves, whilst not
only in our Streets here, but all the Kingdom over many of these Gentlemen appear, as they daily do, in such various, and uncertain Lay
Dresses, as not to leave so much as Room to guess or suspect their being
of Sacred Order, whilst, on the other Hand, though it be confessed, that
no one Degree whatever is essentially necessary to the taking all or any
the Orders of the Church; yet we may see every Day Clerks walking
the Streets, *&c* in Scarves, as Doctors, or Chaplains, or others qualified,
who have no Manner of Title thereto, and others strutting in Masters
of Arts Gowns, who never took even the first Degree, or so much as
ever were matriculated in, or made Members of, an University; nay,
perhaps, never so much as ever saw one, or never may, in all their
Lives The Graduate Clergy sometimes complain of Discouragements
from the Laity to the Universities, but these hinted at are (amongst
many more, and it is at least to be feared, some worse) amongst themselves, and as Clergymen, where it would not be improper to begin a Reformation, Canons they have vowed to obey, and Canons thus require,
if they have made an indifferent Matter a Duty, it was their own Choice
so to do, and was a deliberate Act done with their Eyes open, and in
full Sense of what they were about.

2. *In Cathedral and Collegiate Churches.*

In Time of Divine Service and Prayers
in all Cathedral and Collegiate Churches
when there is no Communion, it shall be sufficient to wear Surplices, saving that all
Deans

Deans, Masters and Heads of Collegiate Churches, Canons, and Prebendaries, being Graduates, shall daily at the Time both of Praying and Preaching, wear with their Surplices, such Hoods as are agreeable to their Degrees. *Can. 25.*

4. To keep their Orders.

1. NO Minister or Ministers shall, without Licences and Direction of the Bishop of the Diocese, first obtained and had under his Hand and Seal, appoint or keep any solemn Fasts, either publick, or in private Houses, other than such as by Law are, or by publick Authority, shall be appointed, nor shall be wittingly present at any of them, under Pain of *Suspension* for the first Fact, and of *Excommunication* for the second, and of *Deprivation* for the third; neither shall any Minister, not licensed, as is aforesaid, presume to appoint or hold any Meetings for Sermons, commonly termed by some Prophesies, or Exercises, in Market-Towns, or other Places, under the said Pains; nor, without such Licence, to attempt, on any Pretence whatsoever, either of Possession or Obsession, by Fasting and Prayer, to cast out any Devil or Devils, under Pain of the Imputation of Imposture or Cousinage, and Deposition from the Ministry. *Can. 72.*

2. No Priests or Ministers of the Word of God, nor any other Person, shall meet together in any private House, or elsewhere, to consult upon any Matter or Course to be

taken by them, or upon their Motion, or Direction, by any other, which may any Way tend to the Impeaching or Depraving of the Doctrine of the Church of *England*, or the Book of Common Prayer, or of any Part of the Government and Discipline now established in the Church of *England*, under Pain of *Excommunication ipso facto* Can. 73

3 No Man being admitted a Deacon, or Minister, shall from thenceforth voluntarily relinquish the same, nor afterwards use himself in the Course of Life, as a Layman, upon Pain of *Excommunication*, and the Names of all such Men so forsaking their Calling, the Church-wardens of the Parish, where they dwell, shall present, to the Bishop of the Diocese, or to the Ordinary of the Place, having Episcopal Jurisdiction. *Can.* 76.

4. If a licensed Minister should refuse to conform to the Laws, Ordinances, and Rites Ecclesiastical established, he is to be admonished by the Bishop, or Ordinary of the Place, to submit himself to the due Use and Exercise of the same ; and if he do not, on such Admonition, conform in a Month, his Licence is void. *Can* 57.

5. *Marriages.*

1. *When, where, and with what Caution, to be celebrated.*

1 MAtrimony is to be celebrated publickly in the Parish Church, or Chapel, where one of them dwelleth, and in

no

no other Place, and that, between the Hours of Eight and Twelve in the Forenoon *Can* 92, 104.

2. No Minister, on Pain of *Suspension, per triennium ipso facto,* is to celebrate *Matrimony,* but *sub modo, Can.* 62 not even those of exempt Churches. *Can.* 63. *And at Law, where a Clerk of an exempt Church had married against this Canon in his exempt Church, yet having another Living, which was presentable, a Prohibition was denied to restrain the Ecclesiastical Censure,* quoad *the presentable Living, though the Offence was committed at his Church exempted, and though the Minister or Curate of such an exempt Church is not to be censured in the Ecclesiastical Court; yet I think no Doubt can be made, but that such Offence is a good Cause for the Impropriator, or Donator, to visit and censure, as his Conscience shall direct, and I further think that such Lay Incumbent or Visitor may well make the Canon the Rule and Measure of his Censure, and yet he is not by Law bound by this, or any other Church Law; and therefore not obliged to judge, as the Canon does, whether he thinks it suitable to the Offence, or not*

3 For the *Terms* of *Licences for Marriage,* see Can. 92, 93, 104 *And for who may, and who may not marry by the Canon Law,* see Can. 99, 100. *And for and concerning the Matter by whom these Licences are to be granted,* see Can. 101.

6. *The*

6. *The Sacraments.*

1. *Christening Children*, &c.

1. I Must repeat, that every *Minister*, at his *Ordination*, promised to be diligent in his Office, &c. as hath been shewn; and therefore he is not to neglect this particular Office on Account of *Fee*, or other *Consideration* whatsoever, if he would stand clear of *Offence* against his *Ordination Vow*. But to hear what the *Canons* say, as to this necessary and charitable Duty.

2 No Minister shall refuse or delay to christen *any Child*, according to the Form of the Book of Common Prayer, that is brought to the Church to him, on *Sundays*, or Holidays, to be christened   *Can.* 68.

3. If any Minister being duly, without any Manner of Collusion, informed of the Weakness and Danger of Death of any Infant unbaptized, in his Parish, and thereupon desired to go, or come, to the Place, where the said Infant remaineth, to baptize the same, shall either wilfully refuse so to do, or of Purpose or of gross Negligence, shall so defer the Time, as when he might have conveniently resorted to the Place, and have baptized the said Infant, it dieth, through such his Default, unbaptized, the said Minister shall be suspended (*prout* the *Canon*) and before his Restitution shall *acknowledge his Fault, and promise before his Ordinary, that he will not, wittingly, incur the like again,* provided that where there is a Curate, or Substitute, this Constitution
                                                              shall

shall not extend to the Parson, or Vicar, himself, but to the Curate, or Substitute, present. *Can.* 69. *As to the Excuse, in this Canon, extended to the Parson, or Vicar, I apprehend it is to be understood of Non-residents only, for if resident, I submit it, in Reason, and Conscience, it is his Duty to do it himself, or see that his Substitute do.*

From these Canons, as well as from the Ordination Obligations, the Office of the Clerk to christen Children, I conceive to be exceeding plain and clear, but had they not particularly obliged themselves at Ordination, to the Performance of this Duty, and had the Canons been also silent in the Matter; yet sure they had been bound in Conscience to it upon their own Notions of it. It must either be of Consequence, or not, and they tell us it is so essentially necessary, that the Salvation of the Souls that die without it there is no Promise for in Scripture. And Dr *Bennet*, in particular, labours hard this Point; and if the Argument be with them, as we must suppose, they are persuaded, then it cannot be doubted, but they ought to perform this Office on Request, and without any Delay, for sure a Soul is neither to be lost nor hazarded for a *petit Loss* to the Priest of a Fee, perhaps founded in Tort, which if they have any Right to, by Custom or otherwise, they ought first to discharge the Office, to intitle themselves to the Reward for doing it, (in which Case they have good Remedy at Law, if they can establish the Right) but sure not till then; for it would be hard, if not unjust, and highly unbecoming a Pattern of Justice and Equity, &c to force Money out of Mens Pockets for doing of nothing, as is the following Case.

4 A Custom to take for christening a Child, when, in Fact, he does not do it, is not good; like the Case in *Hob.* of a Burial Fee, demanded by the Parson where he died, when he was buried elsewhere. If you have a Right to christen, libel for it; but you ought not to have Money for christening, when you do not do it. *Salk.* 332.

2. *The*

2. *The Lord's Supper.*

1. *How often in the Year the* Parson *is to communicate himself, and to administer to others, and where.*

1. In every Parish Church and Chapel, where Sacraments are to be administred, within this Realm, the Holy Communion shall be administred by the Parson, Vicar, or Minister, so often, and at such Times, as every Commoner may communicate, at least, thrice in the Year (whereof the Feast of *Easter* to be one) according as appointed in the Book of Common Prayer Every Minister, as often as he administreth the Communion, shall first receive that Sacrament himself, after having instituted, *consecrated*, the Bread and Wine. *Can* 21.

2 Every Minister is required to give Warning to his Parishioners, publickly in the Church, at Morning Prayer the *Sunday* before every Time of his administring that Holy Sacrament, for their better Preparation of themselves. *Can.* 22.

3 In all Cathedral and Collegiate Churches, the Holy Communion shall be administred upon principal Feast-Days, sometimes by the Bishop, if he be present, and sometimes by the Dean, and sometimes by a Canon or Prebendary, the principal Minister using a decent Cope, and being assisted with the Gospeller and Epistler agreably, according to the Advertisement published *anno* 7 *Eliz.* The said Communion to be administred at

such

such Times, and with such Limitations, as is specified in the Book of Common Prayer, provided that no such Limitation, by any Construction, shall be allowed of, but that all Deans, Wardens, Masters or Heads, of Cathedrals, Collegiate Churches, Prebendaries, Canons, Vicars, Petit Canons, Singing-Men, and all other of the Foundation, shall receive the Communion four Times yearly, at the least. *Can.* 24.

4. Every Minister, being possessed of a Benefice with Cure, though he chiefly attend to Preaching, and hath a Curate under him, to execute the other Duties for him; and also other Stipendary Preacher who readeth any Lecture, or catechiseth or preacheth in any Church, or Chapel, shall administer the Sacrament of the Lord's Supper, in such Manner and Form, and with the Observation of all such Rites and Ceremonies as are prescribed by the Book of Common Prayer, in that Behalf, which if he do not accordingly perform, then shall he who is possessed of a Benefice be suspended, and he who is but a Reader, Preacher, or Catechiser, be removed from his Place by the Bishop of the Diocese, until he, or they, shall submit themselves to perform all the Duties in the said Canon, in such Manner and Form, as therein is prescribed See *Can.* 56.

5. Ministers not to administer the Holy Communion in any private House, except in Times of Necessity, when any being either so impotent, as he cannot go to Church, or very dangerously sick, are desirous to be Partakers of the Holy Sacrament, upon Pain of Suspension for the first Offence, and
Excom-

Excommunication for the second, provided that Houses are here reputed for private Houses, wherein are no Chapels dedicated, and allowed by the Ecclesiastical Laws of this Realm; and provided also, under the Pains before expressed, that no Chaplains do preach or administer the Communion in any other Places, but in the Chapels of the said Houses, and also that they do the same very seldom, upon *Sundays* and Holidays, so that both the Lords and Masters of the said Houses, and their Families, shall at other Times resort to their own Parish Churches, and their receive the Holy Communion, at least, once every Year. *Can.* 71.

2. *Who not to be admitted to the Sacrament, or not till when.*

Vide *Canons* 26, 27, 28, 57.

7. *To the Sick.*

1. WHEN any Person is dengeroufly sick in any Parish, the Minister or Curate is to visit him (if the Disease be not suspected to be infectious) to instruct and comfort them in their Distress, according to the Order of the Communion Book, if he be no Preacher, or if he be a Preacher, then as he shall think most needful and convenient. *Can.* 67.

2. When any is passing out of this Life, a Bell shall be tolled, and the Minister shall not then slack to do his Duty, and after the Party's Death, there shall be rung no
more

more, but one short Peal, and one other be- It is true, the
fore the Burial, and one other after the Bu- Canon seems
rial. See *Can.* 67. to leave the
Minister in

some Measure, at Discretion to judge, whether the Disease be infectious, and if it is to wave going; but I take the Liberty to put him in Mind, at Ordination he solemnly vowed and promised *diligently* to search out the sick, &c without any express Condition And I cannot see how one can be supposed to be implied · I dare believe a Physician would scarce refuse to attend his Patient, because his Distemper was imagined infectious, and yet I have more than once heard a Clergymen say, and declare, in publick Conversation, that if he thought the Distemper in any Degree infectious, he held himself bound neither by the Laws of God, or Man, to visit such sick Person; but I am strongly persuaded, that every considerate, good, Christian, Clerk, having duly weighed the Matter, will agree with me, the Nature of the Distemper can be no Excuse for a Neglect of this important Duty; for admitting the Hazard apprehended to be real, which I conceive, can hardly be allowed, without Dishonour to Providence, yet the Clerk, even in such Case, ought to attend his Duty, at any Hazard, rather than a Soul should go out of the World into an eternal and unalterable State, in Want of the last and most important Offices; suppose a Soul, by this Neglect, to be eternally and irretrievably lost, alas ! no Recompence or Attonement can be made for it, by the over cautious, timerous, and distrustful, Clerk; but on the contrary, he has certainly the Loss of that Soul to answer; but says the Clerk I am not to hazard my Life, no, not even to save Souls; but I conceive, for the Reasons aforesaid, he clearly is, and even should he lose a short transitory *Life*, in the Discharge of so necessary and charitable a *Duty*, he cannot be supposed but to have an eternal, beneficial Account in it But I can by no Means allow, there is, in this Case, any such Danger, or not to be taken into Consideration; for God's Care is over all his Works; by his Providence we are preserved from innumerable Dangers daily and hourly, he is with us wherever we go, and whatever we do, or suffer, not a Hair of our Head falls to the Ground, without him, by him it is we live, move, and have our Being; and no Doubt can be made, that the Souls of Men are precious in his Eyes infinitely more than the Body, as they are of infinite greater Estimation and Value; and is it then possible for one, who is so strongly bound to make Religion and the Attributes of God, &c. his Study, to doubt either the infinite Power or Mercy to protect and keep him or reward his Labour of Love I confess sincerely from my Heart none, in my Thoughts, at least, would hesitate upon this Duty, who is what his Character requires he should be; and I think he who acts contrary has the greatest Reason to apprehend the supposed Danger, or a worse Evil is the best that can befall him for his Antichristian Scruple, &c.

8. *As*

8. *As to Burial of the Dead.*

1. L *Inwood* makes it Simony to take any Thing for burying the Dead, unless due by Custom, like the Case in *Hob.* where one dies in one Parish, and is buried in another, the Parson where he died, *notwithstanding any pretended Custom,* shall not have a Burial Fee *Salk.* 332.

2. No Minister shall refuse or delay to bury any Corps that is brought to Church, or the Church-yard, (convenient Notice being given to him thereof before,) in such Manner and Form, as is prescribed in the said Book of Common Prayer, and if he shall refuse to christen (*pro it* in the Canon) or to bury the Dead, except the Party deceased were denounced Excommunicate *Majore excommunicatione*, for some grievous and notorious Crime (and no Man able to testify of his Repentance) he shall be suspended, by the Bishop of the Diocese, from his

If this be so, how shall those Ministers be excused, who either refuse Burial to the Dead, because the poor Relations cannot pay a paultry Fee, or, what is worse, a scandalous *extra* twelfthpenny Exaction, for not bringing the Corpse to the Minute, the Minister has, as arrogantly, fixed for the Purpose Or where the poor Relations cannot without neglecting their Business, and starving their Families attend the Times appointed by the Minister, (though he has nothing to do with the Appointment, further than to have reasonable Warning thereof) being perhaps at the Hours of their highest Labour, for the Interment of their deceased Relation It is plain, from Canon, as well as common Sense, and all Religion, that the Conveniency of the Relations of the Deceased is in such Case, altogether to be consulted, and so it is, that they are allowed by the Canon to appoint the Time, giving convenient Warning to the Minister, as aforesaid so affixed by them, for that Purpose And would our Clergy consider themselves the Servants of *Christ* and his Church, the

his Miniftry by the Space of three Months. they would
Can 68. act other-
wife in this
Particular, on the Rich, where are Perquifites attendant on their Atten-
dance, they will wait at any Time, or Place, or in any Manner, but
the Poor muft fuit themfelves to the Conveniency of thefe Men, though
the Canon be exprefly againft them as aforefaid, but then fays the Clerk,
there will be more Labour, then he cannot cut his Work fhort, by burying four, five, fix, feven, eight, nine, ten, more or lefs, with one Office
or Service, as is too frequent, efpecially in and about this Town.

9. *Bound to keep Regifters.*

IN every Parifh Church and Chapel within this Realm, fhall be kept a Regifter,
of the Marriages, Chriftenings, and Burials,
prout the *Canon* 70.

10. *In Relation to Recufants and Excommunicates.*

1. MInifters folemnly to denounce Recufants and Excommunicates, that
others may be thereby both admonifhed to
refrain their Company, and excited to procure out a Writ *De Excommunicato Capiendo*,
thereby to bring and reduce them into due
Order and Obedience Likewife the Regifter of every Ecclefiaftial Court fhall yearly,
between *Michaelmas* and *Chriftmas*, duly certify the Archbifhop of the Province of all
and fingular the Premiffes aforefaid. *Can* 65.
2. Every Minifter being a Preacher, and
having any Popifh Recufant or Recufants,
in his Parifh, and thought fit by the Bifhop
of the Diocefe, fhall labour diligently with
them,

them, from Time to Time, thereby to reclaim them from their Errors, and if he be
no Preacher, or not such a Preacher, then
he shall procure, if he can possibly, some
that are Preachers, so qualified, to take Pains
with them, for that Purpose; and if he can
procure none, then he shall inform the Bishop of the Diocese thereof, who shall, not
only appoint some Neighbour, Preacher, or
Preachers, adjoining to take that Labour
upon them; but himself also (as his important Affairs will permit) shall use his best
Endeavour by Instruction, Persuasion and all
good

The Duty of
the Clergy is
hereby clearly
seen in this

Particular, and how far this Duty is neglected is not my Province to determine; but if it be a necessary Office for every Parish Priest, &c. as
most certainly it is, then assuredly it ought not to be omitted And I
conceive, there are others who, tho' not within the Letter, yet, as being
within the Reason of this Constitution, challenge the Care of the Clergy,
who are appointed to the Cure of Souls, in the several Parishes, Pre-
cincts, Districts, Chapelries and other Divisions, where any of these
wretched Creatures are, I mean Atheists, and Deists, the first denying
God himself, and the others denying, sporting at, and profanely jesting
upon all revealed Religion making the Mysteries of Godliness the Matter
whereon to whet and exercise their Blasphemous Wit; these I must needs
think the very worst of Men in Christian Society; but however, I must
needs believe, that Charity and the Love of Souls, should (however others
may think) be Considerations with our Clergy to Labour the Recovery of
such Men to the Confession of the Truth. Our Saviour tells us himself he
came not to call the Righteous but Sinners to Repentance, and that the
Sick are the People only who want the Physician, his Command to his
Disciples was, go and Preach to all Nations, this is a Command of a
most general and universal Extent; and therefore these People are not to
be given up as Castaways, and left to ride on Post, in their own Way,
to eternal Destruction, but should, by the peaceable and mild Means of
the Gospel, Kind Treatment, Sound Reason, and good Argument, be
reclaimed to a true Sense of Religion. I am far from being for the Use
of what some Men call wholesome Severities to compel Men to come in,
but I think it strongly the Duty of the Ministers of Christ to use all possible fair Means for the Recovery of these to the Truth, and by such
Means enlarging the Dominions of Christ But should it be yielded
that these Men, as Apostates, or what else, have forfeited all Title to
the

z'

good Means he can devise, to reclaim both them, and all others within his Diocese so affected. *Can.* 66.

granted, which I think no good Christian will or can allow, another Consideration of itself, must sufficiently evidence the Necessity of this Duty, namely, the Mischief that these Men do, and the Havock they make in the Church, by tainting the Principles, and corrupting the Morals of unwary Christians: Amongst them, it is to be feared, are not a few of the Learned, and of others who profess themselves such, thro' a Vanity of being thought more learned, and having searched further than their Neighbours, and this Vanity alone, as well as that Desire which is in our very Nature, to wish all of our Minds, must needs urge them on to broach and propagate their destructive Opinions, wherever they come; to the Loss and Scandal of Religion, the Hurt of Souls, and the Disturbance of the Peace and Quiet of Society.

11. *Bound to instruct the Ignorant, and teach them the Catechism,* &c.

EVERY Parson, Vicar, or Curate, upon every *Sunday* and *Holyday*, before Evening Prayer, *shall for Half an Hour or more*, instruct the Youth and Ignorant Persons of his Parish, in the Ten Commandments, the Articles of the Belief and the Lord's Prayer, and shall diligently hear, instruct, and teach them, the Catechism set forth in the Book of Common Prayer, &c. and if any Minister neglect his Duty herein, let him be sharply reproved upon the first Complaint, and true Notice thereof given to the Bishop or Ordinary of the Place: If after submitting himself, he shall, willingly, offend therein again, let him be suspended; if so the third Time, there being little hope, that he will be therein reformed, then ex-
com-

communicated, and so remain, until he will be reformed, &c Can. 59 I further conceive him obliged diligently from House to House, to search out the ignorant, and to instruct them; and were this done, there would be less Room left for the Clerk, either to offend himself, or be a Means that others should, the Canon requires, not only that Children should be catechised, which is the common Case, a few Sundays in the Year; but that every Sunday and Holy Day, not only Children, but all others of their Charges who are ignorant be instructed, and that not only in the Catechism in which our Religion is briefly summed up, but that first, to follow the Course of the Canon, they be taught the Ten Commandments, then that they be instructed in the Articles of the Belief, which I understand from the general Tenor of the Words, not only to mean the Creed, commonly called the Apostles; but all the other Articles of Faith, which the Church teaches to be believed, and then to proceed to the Catechism, as the Sum total of all that's required to be believed or done, and this, as its to be every Sunday and Holyday, so its also to be, for at least Half an Hour, under the Penalty in the Canon.

2

12. Con-

12. *Confirmation.*

1. BIshops are to confirm once in three Years *Can.* 60.

2. Ministers are to prepare Children for it. *Can.* 61.

13. *As to others preaching for them.*

NEither the Minister, Church-Warden, nor any other Officers of the Church, shall suffer any Man to preach within their Churches or Chapels, but such as, by shewing their Licenses to preach, shall appear unto them to be sufficiently authorized thereunto, as aforesaid. *Can.* 50.

14. *How often bound to officiate themselves.*

EVERY Minister being possessed of a Benefice that hath Cure and Charge of Souls, tho' he chiefly attend to Preaching, and hath a Curate under him to execute the other Duties, which are to be performed for him in the Church, and likewise every other Stipendary Preacher that readeth any Lecture, or catechizeth, or Preacheth, in any Church or Chapel, shall, twice *at the least* every Year, read himself the Divine Service, upon two several *Sundays, publickly, and at the usual Times, both in the Forenoon and Afternoon, in the Church, which he so possesseth,*

*or where he readeth, catechiseth or preacheth,
as is aforesaid, and likewise shall as often in
every Year Administer the Sacrament of Baptism, (if there be any to be baptized) and of
the Lord's Supper in such Manner and Form,
and with the Observance of all such Rites and
Ceremonies as are prescribed by the Book of
Common Prayer, in that Behalf; which if he
do not accordingly perform, then shall he that is
possessed of a Benefice (as before) be suspended,
and he that is but a Reader, Preacher, or Catechiser, be removed from his Place, by the
Bishop of the Diocese, until* he or they, shall
submit themselves to perform all the Duties,
in such Manner and Sort, as before is prescribed. *Can 56*

2. Every Beneficed Man, allowed to be a
Preacher, and residing on his Benefice, having no lawful Impediment, shall, in his own
Cure, or in some other Church or Chapel,
where he may conveniently, near adjoining,
(where no Preacher is) *Preach one Sermon
every Sunday of the Year, wherein he shall soberly and sincerely divide the Word of Truth,*
How often *to the Glory of God, and to the best Edification*
these Gentle-
men are re- *of the People.* **Can. 45.**
quired to offi-
ciate themselves, appears from these Canons, and it is observable that
they are to divide the Word of Truth to the Ends proposed in the Ca
non ; but I conceive this last Canon amounts to a Prohibition to meddle
in political Matters, or of Civil Government, whereof they are rarely
the most competent Judges, so as either to stir up the People to Rebellion
or Sedition, or to make them uneasy at, or under, the Civil Power, as
hath been too often the Case with some restless, turbulent and rebellious
Spirits of this Class.

15. *Plu-*

15. *Pluralists.*

1. *Sometimes to reside.*

NO License or Dispensation for the Keeping more Benefices, with Cure than one, shall be granted to any but such, as in the said Canon are, for that Purpose, mentioned, wherein is provided that, such Pluralist, be, by a good and sufficient Caution, bound to make his Personal Residence in each his said Benefices, for some reasonable Time in every Year, &c *Can.* 41.

2. *To have their Cures sufficiently supplied.*

Every beneficed Man, licensed by the Laws of this Realm, upon urgent Occasions of their Service not to reside upon their Benefices, shall cause his Cure to be supplied by a Curate that is a Sufficient and Licensed Preacher, if the Worth of the Benefice will bear it, but whosoever hath two Benefices, shall maintain a Preacher licensed, in the Benefice where he doth not reside, except he preach himself at both of them usually. *Can.* 47.

16. *Their Duty to their Ordinaries.*

1. *General.*

THEIR Duty to Ordinaries, and all other Spiritual Governors and others set over the inferior and subordinate Clergy, is easy,

and

*and ought, as they regard their Ordination
Vows and Promises, and as they tender Canonical Obedience, and the Duty they owe to all
those who have the Government and Visitation
of them; so be sought out by these Gentlemen
and to be strictly observed by them*

　　2. *To their Ordinaries at their first Visitation.*

Every Parson, Vicar, Curate, School-
Master, or other Person licensed at the Bishop's first Visitation, or at the next, after his
Admission, are required to shew his Letters
of Orders, Institution, and Induction, and
all other his Dispensations, Licenses, and
Faculties, to be by the Bishop allowed, or
(for just Cause) disallowed, and being by him
approved, to be, as the Custom is, signed
by the Register, and that the whole Fees
accustomed to be paid, in the Visitation, in
Respect of the Premisses, be paid only in the
whole Time of every Bishop after, but Half
the accustomed Fees, in every other Visitation, during the said Bishop's Continuance.
Can. 137.

It's true
School-Ma-
sters are ex-
pressly named
in this Canon, amongst others, to be Licensed at the first Visitation of the
Bishop; but I cannot avoid taking Notice that School Masters are, by
no Means, bound by this or any other Canon, save the School Master of
Cathedral Churches, who must certainly receive their Power from the
Bishop to teach such School, as every other School Master must, from
the Founder or Governors, or Trustees, appointed by the Founder, as
hath been fully shewn already, but in ordinary Cases of School Masters
the Ordinary hath no more Authority than he hath in Cases of Physi-
cians, Surgeons, Midwives, &c. where he has nothing to do at all

　　　　　　　　　　　　　　　XXIV. *Appu*

XXIV. *Appropriations and Im-*
propriations.

1. *General.*

1 IMpropriation is, when it is in the Hands
of a Layman, as Appropriation is,
when it is in the Hands of a Bishop, College, or others, religious, &c Blount's *Law*
Dict sub hoc Tit See also *Appropriation*, and
2 *Mod* 258.

2 Appropriations are but perpetual *Com-*
mend i's 1 Rol Rep 476 Mo 905. Dav.
81 b Plow. Com

3 A *Commenda perpetua* is, during the
Life of the commendatory *tantum*, but an
Appropriation is a Perpetuity Dav 81 *b.*

4 Appropriations are not dissolved by the
Statute, (for then they would revert to the
first Owners or Patrons who gave them to
the Priory, &c) but they are given to the
King by the Act Sir Will Jones 3

5 Every Appropriation compriseth in it a
Dispensation to the Parson imparsonee, to
have and retain the Benefice in Perpetuity,
wherein the King is always, by the Common Law, to be an Actor, not only as Supreme Patron, but as Supreme Ordinary,
for the King sole, without the Pope, could
make an Appropriation. Dav 73. Plow
Com 503.

6 Though every Parish Church is, *prima*
facie, presumed to be presentative, yet there
may be Prescription that such Church was
appropriate. 11 *Co.* 10 *a*

7. Ap-

7 Appropriations were anciently made to Spiritual Bodies, and not to Bishops, &c 11 Co. 11. b.

8. When a Living is appropriate, it comes in Manum mortuam, and the King for ever hath lost his Title of Lapse. Cro Jac 518

9 Stat 27 H 8 gives the Possession of Appropriations, as they were in the Hands of the Abbots, &c. Sir Will Jones 3

10 The making one Parson makes him Possessor of the Parsonage; for a Spiritual Office draws with it a Right to have all the Possessions; and for that Reason, when one is an Appropriator, he lawfully may intermeddle with the Tithes, as the same are annexed to his Church, &c. Plow. Com 500 a b.

11. The Statute 16 R. 2. c. 6. ordaineth, that in every Licence, from thenceforth to be made in Chancery, of the Appropriation of any Parish Church, that, according to the Value thereof, a convenient Sum of Money be paid, and distributed yearly of the Fruits and Profits of the same, by those who have the same Church in proper Use and their Successors, to the poor Parishioners of the said Church, in Aid of their Living and Sustenance for ever, and also that the Vicar be well and sufficiently endowed

12 In the Statute of Monasteries there is a Saving of Rights, &c. but the Founders, Donors, &c. are excepted out of this Saving, so they are bound by the Body of the Act 11 Co 13. a

13. The Lands, &c given to Abbots, &c. and their Convents, &c. were given in the original Grants, to them and their Successors,

in

in pure and perpetual Alms, or in Frankalmoigne to hold of the Grantor, &c in free
Alms. *Litt* Chap. *Frankalmoigne, fect* 133
and Lord *Coke* in his 1 *Inst.* 94 *a* fays, *Libera Eleemofyna* are Words appropriate to
this Cafe, and diftinguifhes it from other
Tenures, and his Lordfhip further fays, tho'
neither Fealty, nor any other Temporal Service is due, yet it is a Tenure; *that is, if I
may be allowed to comment upon his Lordfhip's
Text, though thefe Tenures carry not with
them the ufual Badges of Dependance on their
Lords, yet they certainly hold of them;* and
his Lordfhip fays 1 *Inst.* 98 *a* all Lands are
holden of fome Body, and again in *Litt.
Ten. fect* 141. none may hold in Frankalmoigne, but of the Grantor and of his
Heirs. It is an Incident to the inheritable
Blood of the Grantor, and can be neither
forfeited nor transferred, no more than the
Founderfhip of an Houfe of Religion, &c.
but the Lord may releafe it. *Co Litt* 99 *a. b.*
Littleton fays, thofe who hold in Frankalmoigne were bound of Right before God to
make Orifons, &c. for the Souls of their
Grantors, &c and their Heirs dead, and for
the good Life and Health of them alive,
and the Reafon why they fhall not do Fealty is, becaufe this Divine Service is better
for the Donors, &c. *Lit. Ten. fect.* 135 And
my Lord *Coke* fays exprefly, they are bound
thereunto, and as his Lordfhip further fays,
tho' the Liturgy be altered, yet the Tenure
remains as it was. In Confideration of the
Prayers of thofe who held in Frankalmoigne,
the Lord is bound to acquit them of all Services to the Lord Paramount. *Litt. fect.* 142.

Co. Lit. 99 *b.* Save what is in Respect of his Person and Resiancy. *Co Lit.* 100. *a* *And therefore, though they are not to pray for the Souls of the Dead, yet, in my Apprehension, they are to go in their Duty as far as the Alteration will allow, that is, they are still to pray for the good Life, Prosperity, and Health of their Lords or Patrons, for this they may lawfully do; and therefore this Part of the original Duty is still obligatory upon them, and though I cannot think the Welfare of the Patron depends on the Prayers of his Clerk, yet I must think the Clerk bound to this Duty for the Reasons aforesaid, as well as for that the same was the Terms of his Tenure by the original Contract, whether he be Vicar indowed, or other Minister, Chaplain, or Clerk, deriving Benefit from these Eleemosynary Endowments I have thought fit to observe thus much, and to refer the same to the Consideration of all Clerks therein concerned, as I have some Reason to fear that some of them, at least, have never dreamed of such a particular Duty.*

2. *How made.*

1. **A**Ppropriations might have been by the Patron and Pope, before the Council of *Lateran*; because, till then, the Patron might give his Tithes to whom he pleased, but since that Council, it cannot be *sans* Consent of the Crown 2 *E* 3 23 For now the King is interested in every Parish, for that it may devolve on him, and that as Patron. 21 *E.* 3. 6. *Palm.* 220. See
11 *Co.*

11 Co *Priddle* and *Napper*'s Case throughout

2. Tho' an Appropriation be by Words
de præsenti tempore, and not *de futuro*, yet
good. 11 *Co* 11. *a b*.

3. *How came to the Crown.*

1 $STAT$. 27 *H*. 8. gave all such Monasteries, whereof the Possessions did not
exceed 200 *l* a Year, so that whatsoever
makes to that yearly Revenue, was meant
to be given to the King Also it was the
clear Purpose of the Statute to give the
King all that those Abbies had, and therefore the Saving doth exclude the Founders,
Patrons, Donors, &c. but if the Appropriation should be dissolved, the Giver should be
restored to his Parsonage; and *Priddle*'s
Case, 11 *Co*. 13 is, that Appropriations in
Reputation pass by the Statutes 27 & 31
H 8 *Hob* 308 *Sir Will Jo* 3.

2. The Inferior Abbies being but of 200 *l*.
a Year Value came to the Crown by the
Statute 27 *H* 8. *Cro Ca*. 423. *Hob*. 307.
Sir Will Jo. 2, 3.

3. *Stat.* 31 *H*. 8. gives the Lands, &c. of
Religious Houses to the King in as large and
ample Manner, as the Abbots, &c. held the
same *Hob* 309

4 They came to the Crown as they were
in the Hands of the Abbots, &c. *Sir Will
Jo*. 3. 11 *Co*. 13. *Hob* 308. *Cro Ja* 252,
600.

5 Lord *Hobart* observeth, that all the Appropriation of Abbies which were surrendered

dered between the 27 & 31 *H.* 8. were, *ipso facto,* diffolved with the Diffolution of the Corporation, and were prefentable, and might have new Incumbents; but as foon as the Statute 31 *H* 8. came, they were re-ftored, and given to the King, and fuch new Incumbents oufted. *Hob* 308

4. *How into Lay Hands.*

1. PArifhes, Patrons, Inftitutions, Advow-fons, *&c* were by the Law of Men, and not by Divine Law, or the Law of God; and therefore Difpenfations might be by human Law; and fo of Appropriations *al les Ley-Gents* No Parifhès were till 267 Years after *Chrift* 1 *Rol. Rep.* 453.

2. Before the Time of *H* 8. no Lay Per-fon could have a Rectory Impropriate. *Pop.* 168.

It is to be ob-ferved, that the Statute gave thefe Li-

3. But the Statute 27 *H.* 8 is, that all Patentees fhall injoy, *&c.* in ample Manner, *&c.* as the King, *&c.* 1 *Rol Rep.* 98.

vings to the Crown, in as ample, full, and abfolute Manner, as they were before in thefe refpective Religious Bodies; and then the Statute gives them to the Patentees of the Crown, in as full, and large a Manner, as they were either in thofe Religious Houfes before the Statute of Diftri bution, or in the Crown, in Virtue of them, fave the Royal Vifitation, which is, indeed, no more than what the Crown had over thefe Livings, even whilft in the Hands of thefe Religious Houfes, and then they we e exempt of all Epifcopal Jurifdiction, and fo they ftill remain, and that indeed with greater Reafon, as they are not only meer Lay Fees, but alfo in the Hands of meer Lay Perfons, who owe no Canonical Obe-dience, nor are bound by Church Laws.

4. The

4. The Intent of the Acts of Dissolution of Religious Houses, and of Exemption from Tithes, &c. were intended to benefit the Crown, and to make the Subject more desirous of purchasing the Appropriations and Lands, exempt from Tithes, &c. 2 *Co.* 47 *a* 48. *a.*

5. Tithes, or the Ecclesiastical Duties, which came to the Crown by the Statutes of 27 *H.* 8. 31 *H* 8. 37 *H* 8. and 1 *E* 6. are, by those Statutes and 32 *H.* 8. and 1 *& 2 Ph & Mar* in the Hands of Laymen, Temporal Inheritances, and shall be accounted Assets, and Husbands shall be Tenants by the Curtesy, the Wife indowed, and shall have other Incidents belonging to temporal Inheritances, only this Ecclesiastical Quality they have, that the Owner or Possessor, may sue for the Substraction of the same in the Ecclesiastical Court. *Co. Litt* 159. *a.*

5. *They are grantable over or transferable.*

1 BY Statutes the King and Lay Persons, are made capable of Parsonages appropriate, and they well pass by Grant from one common Person to another. *Plow. Com.* 501

2. *Stat.* 31 *H.* 8. *c.* 13. makes the King and Laity capable of taking and holding the Appropriations of dissolved Monasteries, &c. and tho' they were not originally grantable over, as Incumbents of Parsonages presentable cannot, at this Day, grant over such Incumbencies, but must resign, if they will be

clear

clear of their Incumbencies, yet now Impropriations, by Act of Parliament, may be passed away, or transferred from one to another; and so the Appropriations of the *Knights Templers,* were to the Priors of *St. John,* by Consent of the Pope, (*though that I think no Ways was available, as he was always an Usurper, and never had any Authority here,* &c) King, and Parliament *Plow. Com. Grendon*'s Case. *Palm.* 219, *&c. Hob.* 307, 308.

6. *How favoured.*

1. *General.*

1. WHether an Appropriation be good or not, cannot now be called in Question, but shall be intended good. *Cro. Ja.* 252.

2. Appropriations or Impropriations are not within the Statute of Pluralities, not being at all in the King's Books, nor being deemed, in Judgment of Law, as Benefices. *Vide Stat.* 21 *H.* 8. *c* 13.

3. The Statute 31 *H.* 4 made all Appropriations Lay Fees, and they are neither presentative nor Spiritual Functions. *Sir Will. Jo.* 3. *Cro. Ja.* 518. *Fitz.* 250. *Keil* 48.

4. A Benefice appropriate is not within the Statute of 21 *H.* 8. of Pluralities. *Hob.* 157, 158

5. An Appropriation is not void by the Clerk's being made a Bishop; but tenable with any other Preferment.

6. Though

6. Though every Parish Church is supposed presentative, and that the Incumbent came in by Admiſſion, Inſtitution and Induction, yet the Plaintiff may prescribe, that the Prior, &c immemorially have been Rectors of the said Church; for this amounts to its having been appropriate, &c and the Commencement of a Matter before the Time of Memory cannot be known, whether it came by Union, Appropriation, or how, &c. 11 Co. 10. a.

2. There can be no Uſurpation of them.

1. There cannot be an Uſurpation upon a Parſon imparſonee; but if a Stranger meddle with his Tithes, &c he may have Treſpaſs or Aſſiſe, but not a Writ of Right of Advowſon, for that is only for him who is out of Poſſeſſion. *The Com.* 500, 501.

3. Preſumptions for, or in Favour of, them.

1. Though defective.

1. *Stat.* 35 *Eliz. c.* ——. That all Manors, Lands, Tenements and Hereditaments, which at any Time thentofore were the Poſſeſſions of any Abby, Monaſtry, Priory, &c which after the 4th of *February, anno* 27 H 8. were granted, or conveyed, or mentioned ſo to be, in or by any Letters Patent whatſoever, made by the ſaid late King H. 8. to any Perſon, &c. were and ſhould be reputed, taken, and adjudged to have been lawfully and perfectly in the real and actual Poſſeſſion of the ſaid King, and of his Heirs and Succeſſors

ceffors, at fuch Time as the fame were
granted by the faid King. In the Purview
of this Statute, four Things are to be obferved. 1. The favourable Penning of it,
mentioned to be granted, though in Effect,
nothing paffeth by the Grant. 2. The Generalty of the Words, 1. Concerning the
Quality of the Letters Patent, *in, or by,
any Letters Patent whatfoever*, be they under
the Great Seal, the Exchequer Seal, the
Court of Augmentation Seal, the Duchy
Seal, &c. 2. Concerning the Eftate, or Intereft, to pafs by fuch Letters Patent, which
is quite at large, and reftrained to none in
certain; and therefore if the Letters Patent
purport a Grant for Life, or Years, the Statute hath as great an Operation, as to the
Purview of the Act, as if the Letters Patent had purported a Grant of an Eftate-
tail, or Fee-fimple. 3. The Generalty of
the Purview; for it doth not only extend to
make the Grant good, but to veft the Manors, Lands, Tenements, and Hereditaments,
of the late Abbots, &c. in the actual and
real Poffeffion of King *H* 8 and not only
fo, but alfo to him, his Heirs and Succeffors,
fo that the Lands fhall as well veft in the
King, his Heirs and Succeffors, when he
grants the Lands for Life, or Years, as where
he grants in Fee-tail, or in Fee-fimple; fo
the Purview extends to three other Cafes.
1. Where any fuch Lands, Tenements, or
Hereditaments, came to the Hands or Poffeffion, of the faid late King *H* 8 2 Or
which were put in Charge to or for his
Highnefs in his Court of Exchequer, or any
other Court of his Majefty's Revenue.
3. Or

3. Or by any Auditor, or other Officer of the said late King. Then follows the Qualification, or Reſtraint, *notwithſtanding*, 1ſt, *any Defect, Want, or Inſufficiency, of, or in, any Surrender, Grant, or Conveyance of the ſaid Manors, Lands, Tenements, or Hereditaments, or any Part thereof, to the ſaid late King* H. 8. *or any other Matter or Cauſe whatſoever, by which his Highneſs was, or might have been, intitled to the ſame*; ſo that the Scope and Purpoſe of the Statute was to veſt in King *H.* 8. all the Lands, Tenements, and Hereditaments, which the Abbots, &c. had, notwithſtanding the Defects aforeſaid. 11 *Co.* 11. *b.* 12 *a. b.* 13. *a.*

2 All Appropriations, howſoever defective, were given to the King, by the true Meaning of the Laws of Monaſteries, which meant to give all, as well in Reputation, as in Truth. *Hob* 148.

3 Though there was a Defect in the Appropriation, yet if the Rectory be in Reputation appropriate, and ſo hath been uſed, it is given to the King, by the Statutes 27 *H.* 8. or 31 *H.* 8. and therefore the 19 *Eliz.* in the Dean of St *Paul's* Caſe, it was adjudged in *B R.* that a Chantery, or College in Reputation, and not in Law, was given to King *E.* 6. by the Statute 1 of that King, by theſe Words, *All and all Manner of Chanteries, Colleges*, &c. 11 *Co.* 13. *a.*

4. 27 *June*, 29 *El. in Canc.* The Caſe was between *The Lord St John* and *The Dean and Chapter of Glouceſter*, for the Parſonage impropriate of *Penmark* in the County of *Glamorgan*; becauſe that the Patron, who had appropriate, was but Tenant in Tail, yet as it always

I   had

had continued as a Church appropriate, it was refolved by Sir *Thomas Bromley*, Lord Chancellor, Sir *Gilbert Gerrard*, Mafter of the Rolls, *Chute* and *Wyndham* Juftices, whom the Lord Chancellor in this Cafe af-fociated to him, That this Rectory in Re-putation was given to the King, by the Sta-tute of Monafteries. 11 *Co.* 13. *a.* The fame of the Church of *Humbalton.* 11 *Co.* 13. *a.*

5. The Parfonage of *Bulbenam* was appro-priate to the Abbot of *Sulby*, and no Vicar indowed, according to the Act 4 *H* 4 and 15 *R* 2. but there had been a Vicar in Re-putation continually, and the Rectory, as appropriate, continued alfo, and it was re-folved, that this Rectory was given to the King by the Statute of Monafteries. 11 *Co.* 13 *a.*

6 Though the Appropriation is defective, or that the Advowfon did not pafs by the Grant, yet it fhall be intended, in Refpect of the antient and continual Poffeffion, that there was a lawful Grant of the King, *Om-nia præfumuntur folemniter effe acta,* which might make the antient Impropriation good; for *Tempus eft Edax rerum,* and Records, and Letters Patent, and other Writings, either confume, or are loft and imbezilled, and God forbid, that the antient Giants and Acts fhould be drawn in Queftion, though that cannot be fhewn, which at firft was ne-ceffary to the Perfection of the Thing; and if the Impropriation had been drawn in Que-ftion in the Life-time of any of the Parties to it, they might have fhewn the Truth of the Matter; but after all Parties dead, and

I   fuch

such a Succession of Ages, in all which the Churches were esteemed and allowed to be rightfully impropriate, if any Objection should now prevail, the longer the Possession of the Owners were, the more difficult it must needs be for them to make out their Title, &c. 12 Co. 4, 5.

If the Law be thus, how ridiculous, as well as iniquitous, must it needs be, for Ecclesiasticks to pretend, or usurp a Jurisdiction over these Things, which in their Beginning were exempt, and in the very Nature of them are *extra* their Jurisdiction and Authority, and with which they cannot, without manifest Injustice, and indangering a Premunire, meddle.

7. And if a Confirmation was necessary, it shall be intended that there was one, *Ex diuturnitate temporis omnia præsumuntur solenniter esse acta.* Hard 382.

8. The Case was thus the Abbot of S. held the Parsonage of L to his own proper Use, which, as a Parsonage appropriate, came to King *H.* 8. by Dissolution of Monasteries *anno* 31 *H.* 8. who in the 37th Year of his Reign granted it in Fee-Farm, under which Grant the Plaintiff claims; the Defendant had got a Presentation from the Queen, and to destroy the Appropriation, shewed the original Grant or Instrument of it 22 *E.* 4 with a Condition in it, that a Vicarage should be compleatly indowed, and alledged, it never was done; and therefore the Appropriation was void; and indeed there was no Instrument nor Proof of any Indowment; but yet as it had all along been reputed and taken to be appropriate, and all along a Vicar had been presented, admitted, instituted and inducted, as a Vicar rightfully indowed and paid his First Fruits and Tenths; it was resolved *per tout le Cure,*

that it shall be presumed that the Vicarage, by Reason of the Continuance, was lawfully indowed, for *omnia præsumuntur solemniter esse acta*, and it would be a dangerous Precedent to examine the Original of Appropriations of Parsonages, and the Endowment of Vicarages, for the Origin, in Time, of them will be lost, and so decreed for the Plaintiff   12 *Co* 4.

9. *Hill.* 4 *Ja in Canc. inter Bedel* and *Bear*; the Church of *K* was appropriate, anno 40 *E.* 3. and the Defect was, that *Humphrey de Bohun*, Earl of *Hereford*, (who granted the Advowson of the Church to an Ecclesiastical Body, to whom the Appropriation was made) was but Tenant in Tail, resolved clearly, that it was given to King *H.* 8. by the Statute   11 *Co* 13 *a*

10. Though every Parish Church is supposed presentative, and the Incumbent to come in by Admission, &c. yet one may prescribe that a Prior, &c. and his Successors, &c. Time whereof, &c. had been Rectors, &c. for that amounts to the same as to say, that it was appropriate, &c. and the Commencement of a Thing before Time of Memory cannot be known, as whether it came by Appropriation, Union, &c and with this agrees 21 *E* 4. 65 *a*   11 *Co.* 10 a.

11. One had gotten a Presentation to the Parsonage of *Gosnal* in *Lincolnshire*, and brought a *Quare impedit*, and the Defendant pleaded an Appropriation, there was no Licence of Appropriation produced, but because it was antient the Court would intend it.   1 *Mod.* 117.

12. Old

12. Old Appropriations shall be presumed to be well and lawfully made. *Trials per Pais* 301, 392.

13 In Things of such Antiquity, *Omnia præsumuntur solemniter esse acta.* Trials per Pais 406. Vide Palm. 427.

14 The Plaintiff brought a *Quare impedit* for the Church of *P.* which Suit was stayed by Aid Prayer, and the Cause removed into Chancery, whereupon the Plaintiff moved for a *Procedendo,* and on Oyer before the Lord Chancellor *Bromley,* in Presence of Sir *Gilbert Gerrard,* Master of the Rolls, *Chute* and *Windham* Justices, and *Popham* Attorney, and *Egerton* Solicitor General, the Plaintiff shewed a Gift in Tail of the said Advowson made to his Ancestor 18 *R* 2. and Verdict for his Ancestor 12 *H* 8. and a Presentation, by his Grandfather, to the said Church of a Clerk, who was admitted, instituted and inducted, with Possession for certain Years, and divers other Matters, to make out his Title ; notwithstanding, as the Defendant, and those from whom he claims, had had the Possession Time out of Mind of the Parsonage as impropriate, (saving Interruption for some small Time) and as it would be of dangerous Precedent to the Queen and other Owners of Impropriations being able to maintain their Titles, in all Points, and Circumstances, perfectly ; it was resolved, by this Court of Chancery, by Advice of the Justices and Counsel learned of the Queen, that no *Procedendo in loquela* should be granted 12 *Co.* 3, 4, 5 *Bedle* and *Beard's* Case *Ley's Rep.* 14. *Stafford's* Case.

15. Whe-

15. Whether Appropriations be good, or not, cannot now be called in Question, but shall be intended good, and to have all Requisites. 2 *Co.* Archbishop *Canterbury's* Case *Cro. Ja.* 252, 517, 292. *Concurrentibus his quæ in jure requirantur.*

7. *Suits concerning.*

1. *To be in the Temporal Courts.*

1. A N Appropriation is not cognizable in Court Christian. *Palm.* 220.

2 If a Vicar sue the Parson impropriate of the same Parish, to shew Cause why a Terrar, concerning the Lands and Tithes, appertaining to the Vicar, should not be allowed, a Prohibition lies. *Rol. Abr Prohibition*, F. 40.

3. Treble Damages are given for predial Tithes, as well to Lay Persons, as to Ecclesiasticks, by the Statute 2 *E.* 6 *c.* 13. but if the Proprietor will sue in the Ecclesiastical Court, he shall recover but double Value, by the express Words of the Statute, wherein it is to be observed, that the Act of Parliament doth give a Temporal Remedy, at the Common Law, to Parsons, and Vicars and other Ecclesiastical Persons, for an Ecclesiastical Duty, and to Laymen, Proprietors of Tithes, the like Remedy; but, as hath been said, they have Election either to sue for the treble Value, at Law, or for the double Value in the Ecclesiastical Court, or And if they for Substraction of Tithes there also. *Co.* will wave the *Litt.* 159. 11 *Co. Priddle* and *Napper's* Case. Penalty, they may sue also in Equity, and compel the Defendant to discover even against himself, as daily Experience shews, these Sort of Bills being frequent.

4. If

4. If a Vicar fue a Parifhioner for Tithes in the Spiritual Court, and the Parfon appropriate appear there *pro intereffe*, and pray a Prohibition, it fhall be granted *Hill.* 14 *Ca. B. R. Robert's* Cafe, Prohibition granted. *Ro. Abr. Prohibition,* fo. 812. *Ca. 5. Vide Cafe* 7. *& quære fur ceo.*

5. If there be a Parfonage appropriate, which came to the Crown by the Diffolution of Monafteries, and after it is granted over to a common Perfon, and there is alfo a Vicarage indowed in the fame Parifh, and by Command of the Vifitor of the Archbifhop in his Vifitation, the Church-wardens of the Parifh make a Terrar of the Tithes within the Parifh, and Glebe, which belongs to the Parfon, and which to the Vicar, and prefer it in the Spiritual Court ; whereupon the Vicar libels in the Spiritual Court againft the Parfon to have it confirmed, and Sentence for him, and the Parfon prays a Prohibition, and fhews, in his Suggeftion, and agrees all the Terrar to belong to the Vicar, but only the particular Tithes, *fcil.* Tithes of Carrots, Coals, and fuch like, being in Lands out of Gardens, and for Burials in the Chancel, and for thefe he prays a Prohibition, a Prohibition lies, for though it be between Parfon and Vicar, and fo the Right of Tithes comes in Queftion between them, yet (becaufe it is not between the Parfon or Vicar, and a Parifhioner, where no Prohibition lies, for that the proper Suit againft fuch is in the Ecclefiaftical Court) the Prohibition lieth ; becaufe the Vicar might have had his Action at Law, againft the Parfon, if he took the Tithes

being fet out by the Parifhioner. *Trin.* 11
Car. Sir *Geo. Winter* and *Perrie*, Vicar of
St. Peter and *St. James* in *Briftol. Mich* 11
Ja it was moved again, and the Court took
a Difference between a Parfon appropriate
and a Parfon prefentable, that the Parfon
appropriate had it as a Lay Fee by the Statute ; and therefore it ought to be tried between him and the Vicar at Law, *&c. Rol.
Abr. Prohibition*, 311, 312. *Cafe* 3.

6 If a Man having a Parfonage impropriate, make a Leafe for Years, of Parcel
of the Tithes by Deed, which Deed is denied in the Ecclefiaftical Court, and Iffue
taken upon it, a Prohibition fhall be granted
Paf 8 *Jac. per Cur. Rol. Abr. Prohibition*,
(U) *Ca.* 5.

Trin 8 *Geo.* 2. *B. R. Charlton* and *Fan-
fhaw*

7 In a Suit for Tithe-Potatoes in the
Court of Arches, the Plaintiff libelled, as
Impropriator, the Defendant, by his Plea,
had denied his being Impropriator, whereupon *Wright* Serj now Mr. Juftice, moved
for a Prohibition, urging that the Ecclefiaftical Court could not try fuch a Matter
of Right, and accordingly a Rule was made
to fhew Caufe. And Mr. *Parker*, now Mr.
Juftice, coming to fhew Caufe, obferved,
this was a Suit for Tithes of a Nurfery in a
Garden, which the Ecclefiaftical Court has
undoubtedly a Jurifdiction of. To this, he
faid, the Defendant had pleaded, that the
Plaintiff is not Impropriator, as is fet forth
in the Libel, and upon this Plea, the Defendant had obtained a Rule to fhew Caufe,
why there fhould not be a Prohibition, without

out making any Affidavit, that the Plea was refused , and he submitted it, that the Ecclesiastical Court were well intitled to proceed, for which Purpose he cited the Case of *How* and *Tidmash, anno* 1. of the King that now is, there a Libel was in the Court of the Bishop of *Litchfield* and *Coventry*, for not repairing and beautifying the Church; the Defendant pleaded, that he was no Inhabitant, whereupon Mr *Strange*, now Solicitor General, moved in that Case for a Prohibition, submitting it, that the Ecclesiastical Court could not try the Bounds of Parishes , but the Prohibition was refused. Mr *Parker* also cited 1 *Ro* 12 The Court said, in as much as the very Title which the Plaintiff hath set forth is, as Impropriator, and the Defendant has denied the Title, a Prohibition ought to go, for Defect of Trial. Mr *Abney*, now Mr Baron, said also, that this Point was so determined in *Wheeler's* Case, in the late Queen's Time , and accordingly the Rule was made absolute.

It is to be noted, that in Case of Impropriations, Remedy is given for Tithes in the Ecclesiastical Courts, in Recompence for the Remedy given there for Proxies, and Procurations, &c which could not be recovered in those Courts, till the Statute provided that Remedy; Impropriators owing no Obedience to the Ecclesiastical Courts, and these Impropriations being mere Lay Fees, and exempt from all Episcopal Jurisdiction ; whereat some Churchmen, and their Lawyers, and some Mercenaries and Tools of Ecclesiastical Power, have (tho' without the least Colour of either Law, or Reason) been much disguited, in Evidence whereof they have in many of their Writings published obsolete, over ruled, and strained Cases, to countenance their Incroachments on the Liberty of the Subject, and Prerogative Royal, and to subject these Exemptions to their Power, or, I should rather say, Usurpations , but that there can be no Usurpation upon an Impropriator, who canno be put out of Possession.

8. *Exemt*

8. *Exempt from Episcopal Jurisdiction.*

1. *General to.*

1 ONE sued a Writ of Contempt for the King and himself, against *W.* Commissary to the Bishop of *N.* for making several Summonses to the Abbot of *E.* who is exempt from all Ordinary Jurisdiction, by the Charter of the King's Progenitors, and after, the same Plaintiff, sued another Writ, against the Bishop of *N* himself for the same Cause, and adjudged, that the Temporalties of the Bishop should be seised into the King's Hands, and that the Plaintiff should recover his Damages, &c. *Fitz Abr. Excommengment,* 9

2. There are many Peculiars in the Hands of Lay People, where neither the Archbishop, or Bishop, have any Thing to do; the Ordinary there hath no Power to visit, but that is not to be intended in the Case of a Prebendary of a Cathedral Church, that he shall be exempt from the Visitation of the Ordinary. 3 *Lev.* 212 Quære, *For I conceive this Case hath been since over-ruled, and that the Case of a Prebendary is the same with that of any other Person, for Appropriations are not cognizable in Court Christian, as is* Palm. 220 *and this, I conceive, extends to all Cases in whose Hands soever the same be, for though he owes Obedience to his Ordinary, as being of his Chapter, or holding any presentable Preferment in his Diocese,*

such

fuch Obedience is in *Matters* Ecclefiaftical; *but* this *of an* Appropriation *being* Temporal, *he ftands in fuch* Cafe *abfolutely exempt from all Duty to the* Diocefan, quoad *that; for he holds as the* Prior, &c *held before the* Diffolution, *and as the* King, *and his* Donor, *have held fince* And there is no fuch Difference, *as* Gibfon *in his* Codex *groundlefly takes, when in the Hands of a Lay* Perfon, *and when of an* Ecclefiaftick, *for in both Cafes the Law is the fame.*

3. *Twifden :* Wherever there is a Cure of Souls the Church is vifitable, either by the Bifhop, if it belong to him, if to a Layman he muft make Delegates, if to the King, my Lord Keeper does it 1 *Mod.* 12. *I prefume the* Judge, *in this Cafe, is to be underftood, as to the Layman's making Delegates, to mean, if he finds himfelf unequal to this Duty, then he is bound in Confcience to delegate Commiffioners qualified for it ; but not that he may not do it himfelf, though he be really able, for it is to be obferved, if his Commiffioners do otherwife than he is convinced in his Confcience they ought, he may ftill undertake and determine it himfelf, according to Confcience, and as he may fo take it up, I conceive, no Reafon can be fhewn, why he cannot do it in the firft Inftance ; for his Commiffioners are but in Aid of him, and I conceive, in this Cafe his Power, though more abfolute, may be compared to the Ordinary's Authority, who, tho' ordinarily he judges by his Chancellor, or other Official, yet he may fit himfelf and determine Matters within his limited Jurifdiction, if he pleafes, and have, as is to be prefumed, Abilities.*

4. Rec-

4. Rectories appropriate being now incorporated into the Common Law, and converted into Lay Fees; they are therefore exempt from the Jurisdiction of the Ordinary. 1 *Mod* 260, 261   2 *Mod.* 257 S C

5. *Procuratio exhibenda est secundum qualitatem personæ Visitantis, & substantiam Visitatorum* Dav. 4. a. as is the Canon Law; and so the same Law says, *Nulla est adversus Procurationem præscriptio.* Dav 6 b And it was resolved *per le Cure*, that Proxies were not extinguished by the Dissolution of Religious Houses, but were well preserved and saved to Ordinaries, as is *Dav* 2 *b* and so it is that an Impropriator pays Synodals, and Procurations, as well as an Appropriation in the Hands of Ecclesiastical Persons 2 *Mod.* 257. What we call Proxies, the Canonists call *procuratio*; for that on every Visitation the Persons visited procured necessary Provisions for the Visitors, which, at first, were very reasonable and moderate, and were made in Victuals, (*viz.*) *in Esculentis & Poculentis*, but that with great Measure and Temperance, *ne Jejunior' Doctrinam Rubentibus Buccis prædicent*, as is said in one of the Canons, but after, when the Pomp, State, Grandure, Delicacy, and other Excess, of *these* Vitors, both in Retinue and Table, became so great and extravagant as to become not only grievous, but intollerable to the Church and Religious Houses, then every Church and House was reasonably taxed, and then *it was, that* Proxies were reduced to reasonable and certain Sums of Money, payable annually, in Nature of a Pension, to the Ordinary, who had the Visitatorial Power

there

there *de mero jure*, as it is called, 10 *Eliz.*
Dy 273 and this Sum certain, payable in
lieu of these Procurations of Victuals and
Drinks shall be paid yearly, though his Vi-
sitations are not annual, and so the Rule,
Cessante causa cessat effectus, doth not hold
here, and so is Sir *W* Capel's Case put in
Lutterel's Case in 4 *Co.* Though Parsonages
now are made Lay Fee, and are come into
the Hands of the Lay-Gents, who are not
visitable; and though the Religious Houses
are dissolved and gone, yet these certain
Sums of Money, which, as hath been said,
came in Lieu of Proxies, and, by antient
Composition, are made Part of the Revenues of Ordinaries, still remain, and are
not extinguished, no more than Annuities,
Pensions, or Portions of Tithes, which remain payable to this very Day out of many
Abbies, and Rectories impropriate; the original Cause wherefore granted, or wherefore paid, may not now be examined or
brought in Question: And to this Day, the
King himself pays and allows Proxies, out
of all the impropriate Livings, which he
hath in his Possession; and therefore in every Lease which he makes of any of his
Rectories impropriate, he takes a Covenant
from the Lessee, that he shall bear, satisfy,
and pay, all Proxies, Synodals, Pensions.
Dav 3 *a b.* The Ignorance and Weakness
of Lay People, who wanted Instruction and
Confirmation in Matters of Religion, was
the original Cause of the Payment of
Tithes; and the Parson of the Church
does not claim Tithes in Respect of the
Land, but in Respect of the Person of the
Pari-

Parishioner (and Unity of Possession does
not extinguish Tithes, *Vide* 30 H. 8. *By* 43.
32 H 8. *Bro. Dismes,* 17.) This Case of
Tithes, is parallel to that of Proxies, and
concurs with it in all Points; for as Instruction was the Cause of the Payment of Tithes,
so Visitation, which always (was accompanied with Instruction, *Litt. cap. De Frankalmoigne,*) was the Cause of Proxies, and as
Tithes are now due and payable to Lay
Persons who have purchased impropriate
Rectories, though they give no Instruction,
so Proxies are due and payable to Ordinaries out of Impropriations, and Religious
Houses dissolved, though their Visitation be
ceased. And as none may prescribe *De non
decimando,* as is commonly said in our Books,
so the Canon Law hath a Rule, *Quod nulla
est adversus Procurationem præscriptio Inst Juris Canonici,* lib. 2. *cap. De Censibus,* and
therefore Proxies, which resembled Tithes,
in other Points, may be well compared with
them in this Point, namely, that they shall
not be subject to Extinguishment by Unity
of Possession. *Dav. 6. a. b.*

6. The Kings of *England* in every Age,
long before H. 8. granted Dispensations in
Ecclesiastical Causes, as the Law of *England*
is, that every Spiritual Person is visitable by
the Ordinary, yet *William,* the Conqueror,
by Charter granted to the Abbot of *Battel,*
that he should be exempted from Visitation,
and Jurisdiction of the Ordinary, in these
express Words, *Sitque dicta Ecclesia libera &
quieta in perpetuum ab omni subjectione Epis-
coporum, & quarumlibet personarum Dominua-
tione, sicut Ecclesia Christi Cantuariensis;* by
which

which he difpenfed with the Laws. *Vide lib. De verâ differentiâ Regiæ poteftatis & Ecclefiafticæ.* Edit. 1534, where all the Charter is recited at large. The like Charter, was granted to the Abbot of *Abingdon*, by King *Kenulphus*, &c Dav 72. b. 73. a.

7 Where the Cafe is, as in Monafteries, by the Grants both of Kings and Popes, that they be free by a general Exemption, from all Ordinary Jurifdiction, Appeals are to the King, by the Statute 25 *H* 8. *c.* 21. *Hob.* 186, 187. *Cro Car.* 97.

8. Peculiars, though in the Hands of Ecclefiafticks, *as Appropriations,* are not to be prefumed to be within the Jurifdiction of the Ordinary, unlefs it appears: And if a Citation had been, in fuch Cafe, it had been out of his Diocefe within the Statute 23 *H* 8. *Skin* 519. *And if this be fo, in the Cafe of an Ecclefiaftick, the Cafe muft be much ftronger ftill, where it is in the Hands of a Lay Perfon, for there can be no Pretence, that be is fubject to the Bifhop, or any other Ordinary; but only to the Crown, as Supreme; for when the Lord High Chancellor, as Vifitor, is to vifit, correct, and order, as he, in his Wifdom thinks fit, fuch Impropriator is, quoad Vifitation, as the Books have determined, as free as his Grace of Canterbury, who is fubject to no Vifitation, but a Royal one; fave that his Grace, perhaps, as bound by Canon, may be fubject to Sentences and Cenfures of Convocation, &c. which Laymen clearly are not.*

9 By the Statute 25 *H* 8 *c.* 21. it is provided always, that the Archbifhop of *Canterbury,* or any other Perfon or Perfons, fhall have no Power, or Authority to vifit, or vex any

any Monasteries, &c or other Places of Religion, which be or were exempt before this Act; but the same shall be had by the King's Highnefs, his Heirs and Succeffors, by Commiffion under the Great Seal, to be directed to fuch Perfons, as shall be appointed, &c.

10. If a Peculiar be free, by general Exemption, from all Ordinary Jurifdiction, which was commonly the Cafe of Monafteries, both by the Grants of Kings, and Popes, the Appeal is to the King, and fo is the Statute 25 H 8 c. 21 *Hob.* 186, 187.

11. The Ordinary by no Act, *whatfoever,* can difappropriate a Church, and therefore the Appropriator is always Parfon *Hob* 152. 2 *Leon.* 80. *Cro Ja.* 252. *F N. B* 35. 38 *H.* 6. 20. 11 *H.* 6. 18. *Rol. Abr* 350, 351. 6 *Co* 29. *b.*

2. *Cannot be fequeftred.*

1. The Rectory being in the Hands of a Lay Perfon is become Lay Fee, and cannot be fubject to Sequeftration, if it fhould, as the Court obferved, the next Step would be, that Bifhops would increafe Vicarages upon them, when in Lay Hands, as well as *when they were* in the Hands of Ecclefiaftical Corporations, which would leffen the Poffeffions of fuch who have purchafed, under the Acts of Diffolution 2 *Mod.* 258. 2 *Vern* 35

2 The Bifhop cannot fequefter; for being made a Lay-Fee, the Appropriation is out of his Jurifdiction, and the Remedy now only againft a Lay Perfon, for not repairing,

2   or

or Dilapidations, &c. 2 Vent 35. 2 Mod.
254. 1 Mod 258 le mesme Case.

3 A Lay Impropriation may not be sequestred, for the Repairs of the Chancel;
though the Repairs of the Chancel was an
Ecclesiastical Cause; yet both the Rectory
and Impropriator are Lay, and not to be
sequestred, as the Possessions in the Hands
of Ecclesiastical Corporations may. 2 Mod.
257

4. An impropriate Church may by the *And in Re-*
Statute 32 H. 8. be sequestred for Pensions, *compence, by*
Proxies and Synodals. 1 Mod 259. *the same Sta-*
tute, Remedy
is given in the Spiritual Court to Lay Impropriators, for Tithes due to
them, before which there was no Remedy for either, but in the Temporal Courts. 1 Mod 260 But as to all other Matters, as I take the
Law to be, they remain as they were before this Statute, which only intended Remedies for Ordinaries in the Matter of Pensions, &c and in
lieu thereof gave Lay Impropriators Remedy for their Tithes, in the same
Courts Ecclesiastical, but neither meant or intended further.

3 *Visitable only by the Patron.*

1. The Suggestion in a Prohibition was,
that *Prince* was seised of the Rectory of
Shrewsbury, ut de Feodo & Jure, and that he
being so seised, *de Jure* ought to present a
Vicar to the said Place; but that the Bishop
of the Diocese had, of his own Accord, appointed a Parson thereunto; this Exception
was taken to it, (*viz*) he doth not say, that
he was Impropriator, but only that he was
seised of the Rectory in Fee, so it not appearing that he was Impropriator, he ought
not to present a Vicar. Justice *Dolben* replied, That in several Places in *Middlesex,*
the

the Abbot of *Weftminfter* did fend Monks to
fay Mafs, and fo the Vicarages were not
endowed; but he put in, and difplaced
whom he pleafed, that he often heard my
Lord Chief Juftice fay, That the Abbot
had as much Reafon to difplace fuch Men,
as he had his Butler, or other Servant *Cur'*,
Declare upon the Prohibition, and try the
Caufe 3 *Mod.* 295. *And as this Abbot in
this Cafe, had this Power, fo every other Head
of a religious Houfe, had the fame Authority
in the Cafe of Appropriation, and the fame
Authority and Power every Lay Impropriator
hath at this Day,* notwithftanding the *Pre-*
tence of Gibfon's Codex, *D* Watfon *and
others to the contrary* · *And the Pretence that
fome have made that fome of thefe Impropria-*
*tions not having Vicarages endowed, are void,
or, at leaft, defective, as not being conforma-*
ble to the Stat. of H 4 *and R* 2. *I take upon me to fay, from the Authority of the Books,
and to infift, that fuch Pretence is as vain
and idle as any of the Reft; for that at this
Diftance of Time, it is to be prefumed, that
what was done, was well and effectually done,*
omnia præfumuntur folemniter effe acta,
*and the Validity of any of thefe Matters may
not now be drawn in Queftion, for Reafons
too many and needlefs here to be particula-*
rized.

2 *Pemberton*, where one is made Patron,
he hath the fame Power as the Founder,
and where the Patronage defcends to the
Heir, he hath the Power of a Founder, *co
Nomine*, as Patron, for the Patronage draws
all Things with it *Num.* 464.

r 3. Lord

3. Lord Chief Juſtice *Holt*, An Eccleſiaſtical Corporation always hath a Viſitor;
and therefore you never heard of a *Mandamus* moved for an Abbot or Prior; every
private Corporation hath a Viſitor. 1 *Show.
Rep* 252

4. There was a Vicar of a Living appropriate to a Priory before the Diſſolution of
Religious Houſes, and ſuch Vicar was *Ad
nutum Prioris, &c.* Cro Jac. 517, 518

5 The King is ſupreme Patron. 1 *Ro*
476. Though the
Law of *Eng-
land* be, that
every Spiritual Perſon is viſitable by the Ordinary, yet it is to be noted,
that Donations, Impropriations, &c and even Appropriations were, even
in the Times of Popiſh Superſtition, Idolatry and Tyranny here, and
that though they were in the Hands of Eccleſiaſticks, exempt and free
from all Eccleſiaſtical Dominion, and ſo it was that *W* the Conqueror,
notwithſtanding his Obligation to the Pope, &c by his Charter, without either the Pope, or Aid of Parliament, but as ſupreme Head of the
Church of *England*, exempted the Abbey of *Battel* from the Viſitation,
and all Juriſdiction of the Ordinary, as in *Davis* 72 *b* 73 *a*, and
though it ſhould be admitted, That Ordinaries might viſit theſe Religious Bodies, *quoad* their Rules and Orders, yet could they not, without
Danger of a *Præmunire*, viſit them as to their Appropriations, and the
Caſe is ſtill much ſtronger againſt theſe Church Incroachments, and
ſham, uſurped, and falſe Juriſdictions, at this Day, as theſe Benefices
are made Lay Fees, and incorporated into the Body of the Common
Law, and again and again exempted from all Eccleſiaſtical Juriſdiction,
under no leſs Penalty than the Forfeiture of Liberty and Fortune, as
well real, as perſonal, as is clear from the Statutes of Proviſions, and
many adjudged Caſes thereupon, and eſpecially from the Statute of
Queen *Mary*, who, though ſhe actually went conſiderable Lengths towards Reſtoring the Church, or what was then ſo called, to her former
Juriſdiction, or rather, Uſurpations, yet ſhe was prevailed with by the
Advice of her Prelates and Clergy, for the Peace and Quiet of the Nation, to enact, That none ſhould moleſt or diſturb Impropriators or Lay-
Men in the Injoyment of theſe Benefices, under the Penalties aforeſaid,
and therefore if any, under our preſent happy Eſtabliſhment in Church
ſhall attempt the contrary, as I fear ſome Eccleſiaſtical Writers have, I
cannot favour it with the Queſtion, but pronounce ſuch an one, in ſuch
Undertaking, to out-go the Papiſts themſelves in Church Tort   I know
Arguments have been attempted, (for none, or Force, can be really
produced) for theſe Church Invaſions from the Payment of Proxies, &c

from the Defects in appropriating, &c from the Ordinary's Swearing in, &c. Church-wardens, and licensing Ministers to these Livings, &c yet these Objections are, I say, meer Appearances and Shadows, and to the first of them, it is a sufficient Answer, to say, That the Crown it self pays Proxies, for such of these Benefices as remain in their Hands, and yet that was never any Argument for Episcopal Jurisdiction over them, and I crave Leave to insist that there's no Difference to be taken in this particular, of Exemption from the Bishop's Authority, between the Crown and the meanest Subject in of an impropriate Living. The true Reason wherefore these Livings pay these Matters, is, not as a Consideration for their Trouble, &c in Visiting, as I have heard idly contended, or rather pretended, but as they were reserved to Ordinaries, and, I conceive, they were, at first, a Consideration for ordinary Consent to the Appropriation, for it is observable the Bishop was to consent thereto, and the King for his Royal Assent had a Fine, and these be cause they both, King and Ordinary, lost the Benefit of Lapse by the Appropriation, there being, by such Means, a perpetual Parson provided, and so no Lapse, in such Case could incur As to Church-wardens, it has been expresly determined, that their Swearing them in, &c in the Ecclesiastical Courts, is no Argument against perpetual Lay Incumbents of these Livings, and as to what the Canons direct in this Matter, they bind not the Laity, so require no Consideration ; but what the Ordinary does, in this Point, he does meerly as a ministerial Officer appointed, I might say, commanded, to this Duty, by the Superior Temporal Laws, and not as an Ecclesiastical Judge as some have fondly dream'd, as to Bi shops Licences, in these Cases, I look upon them as nude and vain, for that these Ministers (as in every other Case where they come not in by Presentation, &c are, *ad nutum* the Lay Rector ; for Admission, Insti tution, and Induction, are nothing without Presentation, and Mr Justice *Dolben* says, as hath been mentioned, the Abbot of *Westminster* placed and displaced such at his Pleasure ; and if this be so, how idle must it be, to lay a Stress upon a Bishop's Licence to a Man to Day, who may be removed to morrow, without assigning any Cause for such Removal, as hath been often resolved ? And here much more vain would it be, should a meer Diocesan, Suffragan, or other inferior Ordinary, presume to licence a Person to such a Benefice, where he must needs know he has no Jurisdiction, and also is absolutely certain, from the Clerk's Prior Retainer, he is then at the Time of this his further Licence in Posses sion of a Licence from another Bishop, and that when it shall be con sidered that every Bishop's Licence is of Force, not only over the whole Kingdom, but thro' all these his Majesty's Dominions, but still more ab surd it must needs be, to say no worse, if a meer Diocesan shall presume to licence a Man, and that, to his Knowledge too, in Possession of a Li cense from that Provincial, to whom this Diocesan owes canonical Obe dience, as well as civil Deference, and Regard Another Matter I shall presume to submit to Consideration is, what Conclusion might be made

upon

upon him, should at any Time an Ordinary be found, by Acts or undue Insinuations, either sole, or in Combination with others, entering into Contrivances, and prevailing with any poor, pusillanimous, dastardly, Clerk, in such Case, to submit to do the qualificatory Acts before him, only necessary in presentable Cases, (I do not say this that I apprehend it ever will, but that it never may be the Case) thus to act, I conceive would not only be a wicked Part, if done with Intent to prejudice or maim a Lay Rector's Right, but would also be weak and unbecoming the Sacred Character to attack a Right, which the Law hath so well fortified, especially, when it shall be considered, that such Act, or rather mean, and low Concession of an unthinking, or ungrateful, and designing Clerk, could be of no Avail to the tortious End proposed; as the same could neither bind, nor prejudice his Lay Rector, as it would be against common Sense and Honesty, as well as the Rules of known Law, that the Patron should be prejudiced by such confederate Act, cloathed with such injurious and fraudulent Circumstances. It is certain the Bishop cannot disappropriate, and it is quite as certain the Clerk cannot, and it is as certain as either, or both the former, that both together cannot, nothing but the deliberate Act of the Party himself can prejudice his Right; indeed it must be allowed, these Acts being bare-faced, and done in Defiance of the Law, may draw near to some of the Statutes which have been mentioned; but I cannot, at present, see any other Consequences from them. As to the remaining Objection of these Livings, or some of them, being defective, or wanting something which was necessary, to the perfecting of them, or that there is a Want of Proof, &c. it is to be considered, that after such a Length of Time, *omnia præsumuntur*, &c. There are almost innumerable Instances of adjudged Cases to this Point, but though the Defects do not arise from Length of Time, or Want of Proof, but that the same are as plain and manifest, as can possibly be imagined, as that the Royal Assent was wanting, or a Condition annexed thereto, which was never performed, or that a Vicarage was not thereout sufficiently indowed, or that the Founder had not Authority to grant, as being but Tenant in Tail, &c. yet as these Livings were given to the Crown by Statute, and so came down to the Patentees, none of these Matters may now be examined, &c. I have heard another Objection from a Dignitary of our Church, from whom I might justly have expected more Knowledge in these Matters, that it lies upon the Patron to prove the Exemption, which I conceive to be a very great Mistake, as that would be, to require what in many, if not most, Cases, would be impossible, as Proof may be wanting at such a Distance of Time, and yet the Matter compleat, and I take Liberty to affirm, that if it has never been presentative, nor the Clerk come in by Episcopal Means, it can never be subject to his Visitation; he never had the Charge or Cure of Souls, &c. and therefore never had any Thing to visit. But then suppose, as I have heard it put by the Dignitary aforesaid, who has Ecclesiastical Jurisdiction, if the Clerk of an Impropriation

be

be an Heretick, Schifmatick, immoral, &c who muft vifit? I anfwer he Lay Rector. But fuppofe he neglect? Why then the King, on Infor- mation' in his Chancery, before the Lord High Chancellor, will either compel him to correct fuch Errors, or do it for him I crave Room for a few Words more, which is to obferve, that where any Officer or his Official has, or may clandeftinely, and without the Privity of the Im- propriator, or by other undue Means prefumed to vifit any of thefe, or attempted Methods for drawing them under their Jurifdiction, that no fuch, noi any other Act, or Acts of theirs, fhall not, nor cannot, bring, what in its own Nature is exempt, within their Jurifdiction, fuppofing any of them iniquitous and weak enough to infift on the Juftice, or Be- nefit, of fuch an Act, for that they are not to be benefited of their own Acts, efpecially when tortious; for that it was without the Patron's Af- fent, for that no Act of the Ordinary can difappropriate; for that a Man fhall not be prejudiced by the Act of a third Perfon, for that fuch Patron cannot be oufted of Poffeffion, being perpetual Incumbent, and for that all Ecclefiafticks, of what Denomination foever, are exprefly for- bid to interrupt the Poffeffions of fuch, under the Pains of the Statutes of Provifions To conclude this Matter, and clofe this Digreffion, I take Liberty to declare, I conceive it next to impoffible any Ordinary or Official fhould miftake or find any Difficulty in diftinguifhing the Cafes where he may and ought, and where he neither may, nor ought, to vifit, &c. if he will take this Rule with him, that where the Clerk comes in through him in his judicial Capacity, as by a rightful Admiffion, Inftitution, and Induction; or by fuch Collation, Inftallation, &c. he has a Right to vifit; for that the Clerk received rightfully a Charge from him; but if he came in by Admiffion, &c without Prefentation, or by the Appointment or Nomination of a Layman, &c there the Ordinary has no Jurifdiction, for the Clerk came not in by his Means, he re ceived no Charge or Power from him, fo there is no Caufe where- fore the Bifhop fhould vifit him, &c. or the Clerk owe the Ordinary any Obedience; and though it fhould be admitted, which would be unjuft to grant, that the Ordinary's Licence were neceffary to fuch Clerk; yet as he could only in fuch Cafe, be confidered as an Inftru ment in the Hands of the Law, to do this Act, and a mere minifterial Officer; he cannot vifit but at the Hazard and Expence, which has been mentioned.

XXV. Do-

XXV. *Donatives.*

1. *How favoured.*

1. *General.*

1. TILL King *John's* Time, all the Bishopricks in *England* were Donative.
2 Ro *Abr* 342.

2 Tho' it be by a Lay Hand, yet *mere
Laicus* is not capable of it; for his Function
is Spiritual *Co Lit.* 344 *a*

3 A Church Parochial may be a Donative, and exempt from all ordinary Jurifdiction. *Co Lit.* 344. *a.*

4. They pafs by the Gift of the Lay Patron. 2 Ro. *Ab* 356. 2 Keb. 556.

5. No Lapfe of a Donative. *Co. Lit.*
344 *a* *Palm.* 221. *Cro. Jac* 63 *Yelv.*
60, 61. *Mo.* 765. *Cro. Jac* 518.

6. In Cafe of a Donative, the Promotion
of the Incumbent doth not make a Ceffion.
Salk 541. *Ro Abr.* 330, 341. 1 *Inft* 144.
Show. Parl. Cafe 184.

7 Refignation muft be to the Patron,
and not to the Ordinary, and can be to no
other; though to the Patron and a Stranger
is good; for as to the Stranger, it is confidered as a void Act, but good as to the Patron, who lawfully may take it *Yelv.* 61.
Cro Jac 63. *Mo* 765. 1 *Bro. & Go.* 201.
Cro. Jac. 163.

8. On fpecial Verdict adjudged, That the
Incumbent of a Benefice donative, fhould
refign to his Patron, and that it being the

Patron's Foundation, is also of his Visitation, and Correction, and the Ordinary hath nothing to do with it. *Mo pl* 1062. *Vide* 8 *Aff* 29 and 32.

9. Donatives are not within the Statute 21 *H* 8. *c* 13. of Pluralities, not being in the King's Books, nor deemed, in Judgment of Law, as Benefices. *Vide* the Stat

10 The Patron of a Donative need not present to it, but may take the Profits himself. *Palm.* 221. 6 *H* 7. 14.

2. *Exempt from Ordinary Visitation and Jurisdiction, and only visitable by the Patron, or Donator, or Visitor appointed by him.*

1. The Ordinary hath nothing to do with a Donative, which may pass by Gift, *sans* Institution, or Induction. 8 *Aff pl* 31 *Da* 46. *b.*

2 A Parson of a Donative is not subject to Censures, as other Rectors. *Show Parl. Cases* 184

3 An Incumbent of a Benefice donative may resign to his Patron, and being of the Foundation of the Patron, is also of his Visitation and Correction; and the Ordinary has nothing to do with it *Mo* 765.

4 All Donatives of the King, and not only so, but of private Persons also, are out of the Jurisdiction of the Ordinary, and not visitable by him. See 20 *E* 3. *Fitz. Excom.* 9. 16 *E* 3 *Fitz. Brief* 660 21 *E* 3 60. 6 *H* 7 14. 5 *Co. Cawdiy's Case, fo* 15. 12 *Co* 42.

5. The

5 The Deanery of *Fernes*, a Donative by the King, being void, Queen *Eliz. anno* 20 of her Reign, gave and granted this Deanery to *Turner*, who was afterwards deprived by the Bishop of *Fernes*, for that he, *Turner*, was mere *Lay home*, & *ment* capable of such a Dignity, this Deprivation was held void, being *coram non judice*, and not voidable, as was contended on the other Side. *Da The Dean of Ferne's Cafe* See 12 *Co.* 42

6. If a Deanery is a Donative, *per* Letters Patents of the King, it is not visitable by the Bishop; and by Consequence, out of his Jurisdiction, and so any Sentence of his of Deprivation must needs be void; as being *coram non Judice*, as Judgment *de Frank-fee* in Court of antient Demesne. 11 *H* 4 17. or Judgment given in the *Marshalsea*, for a Contract made out of the Verge, &c. 19 *E.* 4 20 *E.* 4 15 and Judgment given in the Common Pleas, upon Appeal of Murder brought there 22 *E.* 4 33 such Judgments are void, the Judges not having Jurisdiction in such Causes. *Dav.* 46 *b.* 12 *Co.* 42.

7 A Benefice donative by the Patron only is a Lay Thing, and the Bishop shall not visit it, and therefore he cannot deprive, and if he meddle with it, he is in Case of a *Præmunire*· And in such Case was *Barloe*, Bishop of *Bath*, *Tempore E.* 6. and was forced to get a Pardon, for having deprived the Dean of *Wells*, which was a Donative, by Letters Patents of the King. *Bro Ab Præmunire* 21. 2 *Inst.* *Dav* 44 *a* 3 *Inst.* 122.

8. A Bishop visiting and depriving a Dean, or *other Clerk, of* a Donative of the Queen, *or other*, commits a Contempt against the Queen, for which he is punishable. *Da.* 46, 47 12 *Co.* 42.

9 *Maddox* moved for a Prohibition against the Chancellor of *Peterborough*, because he libelled in the Spiritual Court against him, for Marrying without a Licence in *Bedlesdon* Church, suggesting the Church to be a Donative, and that the Donor ought to appoint, *ex Jure*, Commissioners to visit, and that the Ordinary had nothing to do with it; and to *Twisden* Just. the Suggestion seemed good, but having another Benefice which was Presentative, would not grant the Prohibition 1 *Mod.* 22. 1 *Sid* 437 S C. *Vide Co Lit* 344 *Cro. Jac* 63. *Yerv.* 60. *Mo.* 765 *Bro & Go* 201.

10. If a Clerk preach Heresy, or otherwise offend, the Ordinary may not meddle with him, but the Patron may visit and correct, or deprive him. 13 *E* 4. *Bro. & Go* 202. *Yelv* 61, 62. *Cro Jac* 63.

11. Deprivation by the Ordinary, in the Case of a Donative, is a Contempt, for which such Ordinary ought to be punished, yet it being a Nullity, it shall not hurt the Party no more than a Judgment at Common Law, being given *coram non Judice*, shall hurt the Parties, against whom it is given; and the Reason of the Case *Vere* and *Jefferies* in *Mo.* 228. seems to be a Rule to this Point; and so in the Principal Case the Deprivation is meerly void; for that the Bishop, as Ordinary, could, by no Means, have Jurisdiction, this being a
                                                    Thing

Thing wholly out of, and exempt from his Jurifdiction, by the Law. *Da.* 46. *b.* 47. *a.*

12 The Parfon of a Donative is not bound to take a Faculty for Preaching, and if the Bifhop attempt to vifit, the King's Bench will prohibit him 1 *Mod.* 90.

13 *Hale* faid, in the Cafe of a Donative, whether there be all the Ornaments requifite for a Church, the Bifhop fhall not inquire, neither fhall he punifh for not repairing. 1 *Mod.* 90.

14. If the Bifhop vifit a Donative he is guilty of a Contempt, and if he gives Sentence of Deprivation, he incurs a *Præmunire Da.* 44. *a. Bro. Ab.* Tit. *Præmunire,* 8 *Aff pl* 29

15 A Benefice donative by the Patron only, is a Lay Matter, and the Bifhop may not vifit it, and therefore may not deprive, and if he any wife meddle with it, he is in the Cafe of a *Præmunire. Bro. Abr.* Tit. *Præmunire* 21.

16. The Vifitation of all the King's Donatives belong properly to the Lord Chancellor. *Fitz Nat. Brev* 42. *a. Dav* 46 *b.* or he may make a fpecial Commiffion. 6 *H* 4. 14 *Dy* 273.

17. Where Peculiars are in Lay Hands, they are free from all ordinary Jurifdiction, the Archbifhop, nor particular Bifhop, cannot vifit, and Inftitutions, &c. by either, would be meerly void. 3 *Lev.* 211.

Banco Regis, Mich. 1726. *Caftle* and *Richardfon.*

18 The Plaintiff was chofen Chapelwarden to a Donative, and was profecuted in the Ecclefiaftical Court, for not taking

his

his Oath of Office; whereupon he moved for a Prohibition; for that the Chapel is a Donative, and exempt of all ordinary Jurisdiction; but the Court were pleased to rule it, that though a Chaplain, or Parson of such a Donative, is not subject to Deprivation, or Suspension of the Ordinary, but the Donor is only Visitor in such Case, yet as to other Officers, they are under the same Jurisdiction of the Ordinary as other Places; for the Parson or Chaplain the Donor only puts in, not the other Officers The Judges also agreed that a Parish-Clerk might be donative.

XXVI. *Chapels.*

1. *Whether* Ecclesia, aut Capella.

1. UPON the Question, whether it were *Ecclesia, aut Capella pertinens ad matricem Ecclesiam*, the Issue was, whether it had *Baptisterium & Sepulturam*; for if it had the Administration of Sacraments, and Sepulture, it was in Law judged a Church, 2 *Inst.* 363.

2. Presentation to a Chapel made it a Church. *Palm.* 221.

2. *Are not Benefices in Judgment of Law.*

1. FREE Chapels are not within the Statute of Pluralities, not being in the King's Books, nor deemed in Law as Benefices. *Vide Stat.* 21 *H.* 8. *c.* 13.

2 Churches

2 Churches and Chapels erected and endowed by private Founders, are not at all
in the King's Books, nor deemed, in Judgment of Law, as Benefices. *Vide Stat.*
21 *H.* 8 *c.* 13

3. *By whom visitable.*

1 AS the King might anciently have
founded free Chapels, and exempted them from all ordinary Jurisdiction, so
he may, by his Letters Patent, licence any
common Person to found such a Chapel,
and to ordain that it shall be donative, and
not presentable, and that the Chaplain shall
be deprived, *&c.* by the Founder, and not
by the Ordinary, and this seems to be the
Beginning or Original of Donatives in *England,* and antiently all Bishopricks in *England* were donative by the Crown. *Peter
Gregory De Beneficiis,* saith expresly, in so
many Words *Si tamen Capellæ fundatæ per
Laicos non fuerint a Diocesano approbatæ (ut
Loquuntur) Spiritulasitæ non censentur* Beneficia, *nec ab Episcopo conferri possunt, sed sunt
sub Dispositione Fundatoris; ideo fundatores &
hæredes eorum possunt tales Capellanias donare,
sine Episcopo, cui voluerint, tanquam* Profana
Beneficia · That is, if Chapels founded by
Laymen were not approved by the Bishop,
and *spiritualized,* they were not to be
esteemed Benefices, nor could be conferred
by the Bishop, or Ordinary, but remained
at the Disposal of the Founders and their
Heirs, and they may give them to whom they
please,

pleafe, without the Ordinary, as Things un-
hallowed, or, as the Churchmen term it,
tanquam prophana or unfpiritualized, *fo that
untzl thefe* Profana Beneficia *have received
Epifcopal Benediction, (let the Intention of the
Founder be never fo pious, or the Act never fo
beneficent and good with Refpect to Religion,
or Charity,* &c.) *they are not to be efteemed*
Beneficia, *without an Addition* (as Additio
probat minoritatem) *but are in their Senfe,
to be termed, and looked upon too, as Prophana
Beneficia, fo that the Sanctity, muft neceffarily arife, in the Senfe of fome Men, not from
the pious Intention of the Founder, there is no
religious Weight in that, that all comes from
the pious Father, who breaths Bleffings; but
where he hath not fanctified, the Care is left
to the Lay Patron or Founder.*

2. The King fhall vifit his Free Chapels,
and Hofpitals. 8 *Aff.* 29. *Fitzh. Nat. Br.*
42. A

3. The King is Ordinary of a free Chapel; becaufe it is without Cure *de Animis*,
and when a Lapfe is, the King is not compellable to prefent, but the Ordinary, in
the *Interim*, hath the Cure, and he fhall
provide for it. 1 *Ro. Rep.* 464. *Tamen
quære.*

4. If the King founds a Church, an Hofpital, or Free Chapel donative, he may
exempt the fame, from ordinary Jurifdiction, and his Chancellor fhall vifit the fame,
nay, if the King found the fame, without
any fpecial Words of Exemption, the Bifhop
fhall not, but the King's Chancellor is to
vifit the fame. *Co. Lit.* 344. *a.* For the Clerk
comes

comes in, without any Inſtitution or Induction (which are the Matters which give the
Ordinary Jurifdiction). 11 *H* 4. *Rol Abr.*
356

5. The King's or his Progenitors Free
Chapels, no Ordinary ſhall viſit, but the
Lord Chancellor *Fitz. Nat Brev.* 42 A.

6 *Twiſden*, *Fitzherbert* ſaith, if a Chaplain of the King's Free Chapel keep a Concubine, the Biſhop ſhall not viſit, but the
King 1 *Mod.* 90.

7 The Lord Chancellor is Viſitor of all the
King's Free Chapels; and 2 *H* 5. doth make
him ſo of all Colleges of the King's Foundation. 1 *Mod* 84. *I take this Statute only to be
in Affirmance of the Common Law; for that
not only the King, but even every private
Founder, at Law, is natural Viſitor of his own
Charities*

8 If the Ordinary will viſit the King's
Free Chapel, the King may ſue a Prohibition to reſtrain him; for no Ordinary, but
the Lord High Chancellor, may viſit ſuch.
Fitz. N. B 42. *a.*

4. *Suits concerning them.*

1. *Where to be tried*

1. IF a Man hath a private Chapel, whereat the Vicar of *A.* is bound by himſelf,
or ſufficient Chaplain, to celebrate Divine
Service every *Sunday*, and Feſtival Day,
throughout the Year, privately for the Maſter, and his Servants, and Family, within
the

the Manor, &c. Action *sur le* Case lieth for the Master; for though Divine Service be Spiritual; yet forasmuch as by Prescription, it belongeth to a private Person, and is to be performed, for his Ease, at his Chapel, within his Manor, &c. it shall be intended to have first commenced by Grant, and therefore, for Nonfeasance of such Spiritual Act, an Action *sur le* Case lieth, and Damages shall be recovered for them 5 *Co.* 73 *a. Vide* 22 *H* 6. *fo.* 46. *similar Case*

2. *David Jones*, Vicar of *N.* was libelled against in the Spiritual Court, for that by immemorial Custom, the Vicars of *N* had, by themselves, or others, said and performed Divine Service in the Chapel of *Charebury*, for which there was such a Recompence, and that he neglected; the Defendant came for a Prohibition, and without traversing the Custom, suggested, that all Customs were triable at Common Law, and Mr *Harcourt* urged, that it was enough for a Prohibition, that a Custom appeared to charge the Vicar with a Duty, for which he was not liable at Common Law *Et per Holt* C. J A Parson may be bound to an Ecclesiastical Duty by Custom, and when he is so bound, the Spiritual Court may punish him, if he neglects that Duty The Custom might have a reasonable Commencement by Composition in the Spiritual Court, and begin by an Ecclesiastical Act, and a bare Prescription only is not a sufficient Ground for a Prohibition, unless it concern a Layman, whereas here it is an Ecclesiastical Right, an Ecclesiastical Person, and an Ecclesiastical

cal Duty, and the Prescription not denied, notwithstanding 2 *Inst.* 491 I, said Lord C J. *Holt*, never could get a Prohibition to stay a Suit in the Spiritual Court against a Parson for a Pension by Prescription. *Salk. 550. Vide* 1 *Vent* 3, 120, 265

3. Where is a private Chapel only for one and his Servants and Family, within his Manor of *D.* a private Action *sur le* Case *sur le* Prescription shall be maintainable, by the Lord, &c for in such Case he alone, and none of his Family, should have the Action, and though Divine Service be Spiritual, yet as it is by Prescription, and belongs to a private Person, and is to be celebrated for his Ease and Convenience, within his Manor, it shall be intended to have commenced at first by Grant, and therefore, for Nonfeasance of this Spiritual Duty, an Action upon the Case lieth, and Damages shall be recovered therefore; and with this accords the Case of the Prior of *Woobourne*, *anno* 22 H 6 *fo* 46 but when the Chapel is not private to him and his Family, but publick and common to all his Tenants (which may be many) of his Manor, no Action lieth, for in such Case, did an Action lie, then every Tenant, as well as the Lord, might have his Action upon the Case, and so infinite Actions be brought for one and the same Default. *Et boni judicis est lites dirimere, & expedit Reipublicæ, ut sit finis Litium, propter communem omnium utilitatem*, and yet they shall not be without Remedy in such Cases, for that they may sue for such Default in Court Christian, as is *Litt l b* 2.

Yet, as I con-
ceive, in the
latter of these
Cases, name-
ly, where the Chapel is a publick and common one for the Lord and
his Tenants. Relief may be properly fought and had in Equity, without going into the Ecclesiastical Courts, both as the Courts of Equity
have a concurrent Jurisdiction with the Courts Christian, and as also by
the Rule, it is good Cause to give Equity Jurisdiction, for that thereby
Multiplicity of Suits are prevented; and in the present Case probably the
Court Christian may reject the Prescription, &c and then there must
be Resort to the Courts of *Westminster-Hall* for a Prohibition, or the
Bishop's Sentence may be erroneous, and then the Party must march still
at a great Expence further by Appeal to the Provincial, and even he
possibly may pronounce a like erroneous Sentence; but be that as it
will, even he is not the Dernier Resort; but then the Matter for Justice
must be carried over to the King; all which tedious and expensive
Courses and their Consequences are saved, by allowing the Equity Ju
risdiction I contend for in such Cases, as in the Case of a Copyholder.
Cro Jac 368. 1 *Rol* 108. and *Mo* 842.

cap. Frankalmoigne, 30. *b. Vide* 27 *H* 8. 27 *a*.
5 *Co. William*'s Case, *fo*. 72, 73. 22 *H*. 6.
fo. 46. *Sid*. 34, 35.

4

AN

A N

A P P E N D I X.

Of the Remedies.

The Introduction.

I Conceive it not improper to conclude this Labour with fome Mention of the feveral Writs fpoken of in the Profecution of it, and as the Prohibition, and Præmunire, the Confultation, and Attachment, and fo much of the Learning thereupon, as I thought neceffary to my propofed End, hath been dealt of before pretty fully, I apprehend, it would be needlefs to fay any thing further of them; and therefore I fhall proceed briefly to the other Procefs; and firft,

I. *To whom Writs to be directed.*

IF one recover againſt a Biſhop, he may pray a Writ to the ſame Biſhop, or to his Vicar General, if he be out of the Realm, or to the Metropolitan. *F. N B* 38 Q.

II. *The Writ* De cautione admittend'.

THE Writ *De cautione admittend'* ought not to iſſue, till an Affidavit be filed; that the Biſhop refuſed to admit of Caution. 1 *Vern.* 119.

III. Aſſiza utrum, ſive Juris utrum.

1. ASSIZA *utrum, ſive Juris utrum,* is the higheſt Writ that a Parſon, or Vicar, can have, for Recovery of the Glebe, *&c.* in Right of his Church. *Co Lit* 159

2 The Reaſon why theſe original Writs, *Aſſiza utrum,* or *Juris utrum,* are called by the ſpecial Names of Aſſize more than other original Writs is ; becauſe that by theſe Writs it is commanded to the Sheriff, *quod ſummoneat* Twelve, which is, as much as to ſay, to ſummon a Jury, and becauſe by theſe Writs a Jury is to be ſummoned and returned, the Law calls them Aſſizes, *ab effectu.* Co Litt. 159. a. b.

K k 2　　　　IV. *Writs*

IV. *Writs of Right, of Advowson,* Darreine Prefentment, *and of* Quare impedit.

1. *The Difference, and where to be brought, &c.*

1 **O**F Advowfon of Churches there are but three original Writs. 1. A Writ of Right, and the other two are of Poffef-fion, 1. *Darreigne Prefentment.* 2. *Quare impedit.* Stat. 13 E. 1 c. 5 Vide *Keble's Readings fur cest Statute in Gray's Inn Hall, anno* 1638. `

2 A *Quare impedit* muft be brought in the County where the Church is. *Fitz. Abr Quare non admifit,* 1.

V. *The* Ne admittas.

1. *What.*

A *Ne admittas* is a Writ which lieth for the Plaintiff in a *Quare impedit,* or *Darreigne Prefentment,* and it fuppofeth the Bifhop will admit the Defendant's Clerk, pending the Suit; and therefore this Writ is directed to the Bifhop, and it ought to be fued in fix Months after Avoidance, for after the fix Months elapfed, he may not have this Writ, but of the King, *Nullum tempus occurrit Regi;* therefore he is not tied up to the fix Months. *Fitz N B.* 37 F And the Defendant may fue this Writ as well

well as the Plaintiff; but this Writ doth not lie, unless a Plea be pending in the King's Court, by *Quare impedit*, or *Darreigne Presentment.* Fitz. N. B 37. H.

2. *From whence issuable.*

IT may be granted out of the Chancery directed to the Bishop, That he do not admit, *&c* before that the King be certified in Chancery, that a Plea of *Quare impedit*, or *Darreigne Presentment*, is pendant in the Common Pleas, and if, in Truth, there be no such Plea pending, then the Party grieved may require the Chief Justice, to certify the King in his Chancery, that no Plea is pending, that the Party may have a Writ for the Bishop to proceed. *Fitz N B.* 37. H.

3. *What to be done thereupon, and of the* Quare non admisit.

1 WHEN one sues a *Quare impedit* against another, and after, pending the Suit, he sues a *Ne admittas* to the Bishop, *&c* and then they accord or agree in the Common Bank to present by Turns, in such Case, he may have a special Writ, out of Chancery, to the Bishop, to admit him, who ought by this Accord and Agreement, to present to the first Turn, but first the King is to send a *Certiorari*, to the Justices of the Common Bank, to certify him in his Chancery of this Accord, and upon such Certificate the King is to send his writ to

the Bishop to admit such Clerk, as by the Accord ought to have the first Presentment and Turn, and the Form of the Writ is in the *Register*, and in *Fitz N B.* 39 E F

2. If one recover an Advowson, and hath a Writ to the Bishop to admit his Clerk, and he will not admit him, then the Party may sue an *Alias* and *Pluries*, or Attachment, *&c.* or a Writ out of the Chancery, or Common Pleas, at his Election, *de Quare non admisit*, as well in Term-time, as in Vacation, but it is better in Term to sue in the Common Pleas, and in his Writ he ought to rehearse the Recovery. *Fitz. N. B.* 47. C. *Vide Fitz. N B. fo.* 48. Tit *Qu. incumbravit.*

VI. *The Writ* De clerico admittendo.

THIS is a Writ directed to the Bishop, for the admitting a Clerk to a Benefice, upon a *Ne admittas*, tried for the Party who procured the Writ. *Register, fo.* 31.

VII. *The* Quare non admisit.

1. *Where it lieth, and to whom.*

1 THIS Writ must be brought where the Refusal was *Bro. Abr Quare non admisit,* 3

2. If one recover his Presentation against the Bishop, he may have a Writ to the same Bishop, or to the Metropolitan, to admit his Clerk.

Clerk ; fo if a Man recover againſt another. *Fitz N. B.* 38. B. C.

2. *What a good Plea in.*

IT is a good Plea in *Quare non admiſit*, to ſay, That the Church is litigious. *Fitz. Abr. Quare non admiſit,* 10, 12.

3. *Contempts in.*

1. *How puniſhed.*

FOR all Contempts againſt any Court of Record, by Command of the King, by his Writ under his Great Seal, the Offender ſhall be fined, and impriſoned ; as in *Quare non admiſit, Quare incumbravit, &c* Attachment *ſur* Prohibition. 8 *Co.* 60. *a.*

VIII. Quare incumbravit.

1. *Where it lieth.*

1. SANS Judgment a *Quare incumbravit* does not lie. *Fitz. Abr. Quare incumbravit,* 1.

2. A *Quare incumbravit* lieth not, unleſs a *Non admittas* be directed to the Biſhop, pending the Writ. *Fitz. Abr. Quare incumbravit,* 3, 5.

3. *Quare incumbravit* lieth, where the Biſhop incumbers *infra tempus femeſtre,* though no Action be obtained before of the ſame Church. *Fitz. Abr Quare incumbravit,* 6.

4. It

4. It was adjudged *per Cur',* That one might have a *Quare incumbravit* without taking any Notice in his Writ or Count of any Recovery. *Fitz. Abr Quare incumbravit,* 7

5. If one recover againſt a Biſhop, by *Quare impedit,* or Aſſize of *Darreigne Preſentment,* if the Biſhop's Clerk be in, he who recovered hath his Election to have a *Quare non admiſit,* or *Quare incumbravit, &c.* Fitz. Abr. Quare incumbravit, 7 Vide antea *Quare non admiſit.*

2. *Where to be brought.*

A *Quare incumbravit* is to be brought where the Church is. *Fitz Abr. Quare non admiſit,* 1.

IX. *The Writ* De vi laica removend'.

1 THIS Writ lieth where any Debate is between two Parſons, or Proviſors for a Church, and one of them enters into the Church with great Power of Laymen, and holds the other out with Force and Arms, in which Caſe this Writ lieth for him ſo holden out, directed to the Sheriff, that he remove the Power which is within the Church: And the Sheriff ſhall be commanded, that if he find any Men there withſtanding, that he take the Power of his County, if need be, and arreſt the Bodies before the King at a certain Day, to anſwer the Contempt.

tempt. And this Writ is returnable, and
shall not be granted before the Bishop of
the Place where such Church is, hath certified in the Chancery such Resisting and
Force. *Law Terms, sub hoc Tit.* It is said,
that this Writ is granted, not only upon
such Certificate of the Bishop into the
Chancery, that there is such a Force in his
Diocese, but also upon a Surmise made
thereof by the Incumbent himself, without
such Certificate of the Bishop, and there is
a several Form for either Case. *Blount's
Law Dict* and *Cowel's Interp sub hoc Tit.*
Vide *Secular Clergy, Where ousted, The Remedy.*

2 The Writ, *De vi laica removenda,* lies,
as well upon a Surmise made by the Incumbent, or he who is grieved, *&c* without
any Certificate made of it in Chancery by
the Bishop, as upon a Certificate made of
it in Chancery by the Bishop *Fitz. Nat.
Br.* 54 D

3 For the Form of the Writ, see *Fitz.
Nat Br* 54 E F. 55. A. B

4 If the King collate to a Prebend of
any Bishop by Title devolved upon him,
and the Bishop make Resistance, then the
Writ shall be directed to the Sheriff, and
shall be, *prout Fitz Nat. Brev.* 54. E. F.

5. This Writ, *De vi laica removenda,*
may be made returnable, or not returnable,
at the Pleasure of him who sues it out, and
may be returnable in the Common Pleas, as
well as in the King's Bench *Fitz Nat Brev.*
54. G.

6 By

6. By this Writ the Sheriff ought not to remove the Incumbent in Possession of the Church, whether such Possession be rightful, or not, but only to remove the Force, and to suffer the Incumbent to injoy his Possession; and if the Sheriff either hath, or will, remove the Incumbent in Possession, the Incumbent, so in Possession, shall have a Writ directed to the Sheriff, commanding him, that he do not remove him, &c if he hath done it, that, without Delay, he make Amends; and if he do it not, the Party may have an *Alias* and *Pluries*, and Attachment against such Sheriff. *Fitz. Nat. Brev.* 44 H.

X. *The* Duplex querela.

VIDE *Ecclesiastical Courts subordinate, In Cases where,* &c. *and The Matter Presentation.*

The End of VOL. II.

An ANALYTICAL

TABLE

OF THE

CONTENTS.

The Introduction.

of the CONTENTS.

I

of the CONTENTS.

An Analytical TABLE

of the CONTENTS.

An Analytical TABLE

III. *Ec-*

of the CONTENTS.

An Analytical TABLE

B. *Their*

L l 3

An Analytical TABLE

2 *Their*

of the CONTENTS.

L l 4

An Analytical TABLE

of the CONTENTS.

An Analytical TABLE

IV. *The Ecclesiastical Courts subordinate and subject to the Controul of the Superior Temporal Courts.* 320

A. *Where the Jurisdiction of these Courts come in Question, or any Law is to be expounded concerning them.*
322
B. *Where the Ecclesiastical Courts are irregular in their Proceedings, or act oppressively, or injuriously, or either want or exceed their Jurisdiction.* 320

C. *Where*

of the CONTENTS.

β. 4.

2

of the CONTENTS.

An Analytical T A B L E

2

of the CONTENTS.

An Analytical TABLE

1. *Suing*

of the CONTENTS.

2. *For*

An Analytical TABLE

of the CONTENTS.

V. *The Ecclesiastical Courts are also subordinate and subject to the Controul of the Superior Temporal Courts in many Cases where both the Matter and the Person, or one of them, either are of Ecclesiastical Sort, or are so pretended by Ecclesiasticks to be,* I

Mm 3 A. *The*

An Analytical TABLE

of the CONTENTS.

M m 4   1. *Before*

An Analytical TABLE

of the CONTENTS.

of the CONTENTS.

7. *How*

3. *The*

of the CONTENTS.

9. *Where*

I   XXIV. *Blas-*

of the CONTENTS.

An Analytical TABLE

I

of the CONTENTS.

An Analytical TABLE

of the CONTENTS.

An Analytical TABLE

               2. There

of the CONTENTS.

The Contents of the Appendix. 497

N n 4   II *The*

An Analytical TABLE, &c.

N. B. The Writs of Prohibition, the *Præ-*
munire and *Mandamus,* are particularly and
feverally treated of in their proper Places in
the Work; fo are not again mentioned in the
Appendix, as the fame would be unneceffary.
An

An Alphabetical
TABLE
OF THE
Principal Matters.

A.

Administrator and Administration.

Where

A Table of the Principal Matters.

Appropriation and Impropriation.

How favoured.

Not to be questioned after such Length of Time. They are not within the Statute of Pluralities. They are Lay Fees, and neither presentative nor Spiritual Functions. It is not void by the Clerk's being made a Bishop, but tenable with any other Presentment, and may be prescribed for. 475

No Usurpation can be of these Livings. 461. *For the Parson though Lay is perpetual*

Though they are defective the Presumption is for them. 461, *&c.*

They are so far favoured, that all Suits concerning them are to be in the Temporal Courts. 468, 469, *&c. Save in Cases of Tithes and Proxies, where, at Election, they may sue or be sued either in the Temporal or Spiritual Courts, and that by Statute only, for at Law it was not so.* 468, 471

These Livings are so favoured as to be clearly exempted from all Episcopal and Ecclesiastical Jurisdiction whatsoever, *save as aforesaid.* 472, *&c.* The Kings of *England* always exercised this Power of exempting

B.

𝕭𝖆𝖕𝖙𝖎𝖘𝖒.

A Table of the Principal Matters.

The

A Table of the Principal Matters.

A Table of the Principal Matters.

A Table of the Principal Matters.

O o 2 Whether

A Table of the Principal Matters.

They

Matters

A Table of the Principal Matters.

Not

A Table of the Principal Matters.

E.

Eccleſiaſtical Encroachments.

Eccleſiaſtical Judges and Officers.

A Table of the Principal Matters.

Church-

A Table of the Principal Matters.

Eccle-

They

A Table of the Principal Matters.

Ecclefiaftical Perfons.

A Table of the Principal Matters.

A Table of the Principal Matters.

Their

A Table of the Principal Matters.

I   Scan-

VOL II. P p 𝕴𝖓𝖘𝖙𝖆𝖑-

2   *In*

A Table of the Principal Matters.

Mortuaries.

O

Oblations, Offerings.

Obventions.

P.

Parents and Children.

Their Relation.

CHildren are *de sanguine Patris & Matris, sed Pater & Mater non sunt de sanguine puerorum* And by *Isidore, Pater & Mater & Puer sunt una caro*, and therefore no Degree is between them, otherwise it is between Brothers and Sisters, and Half Blood is no Impediment, as to Administration of Goods, *&c.*

Parishes. Vide Church and Church-Livings.

General.

2   Parish

A Table of the Principal Matters.

A Table of the Principal Matters.

Prohibition.

Proxies, Procurations, Synodals.

R.

Railing.

Rules.

A Table of the Principal Matters.

S.

𝕾𝖈𝖆𝖓𝖉𝖆𝖑, 𝕾𝖑𝖆𝖓𝖉𝖊𝖗, &c.

P p 4 *Where*

A Table of the Principal Matters.

T. Tem-

A Table of the Principal Matters.

T.

Temporal Courts.

Their Office.

ARE to keep all Inferior, (*and particularly the Ecclesiastical Courts*) within their due Bounds, and to prevent their
Encroachments on other Jurisdictions,
whether Supreme or Inferior; and that
though such Temporal Courts so prohi-
biting cannot determine the Matter in
Question.   *Page* 390, *&c.*

Testamentary Matters.

Wills and Testaments.

General.

Persons

&c.

A Table of the Principal Matters.

The

A Table of the Principal Matters.

A Table of the Principal Matters.

What

A Table of the Principal Matters.

Hho

A Table of the Principal Matters.

MVSEVM
BRITANNICVM

F I N I S.

See the end of the Book for N. 1[?]

Lightning Source UK Ltd.
Milton Keynes UK
UKHW022248240720
367133UK00003B/95

9 781385 595473